Creating Sustainability Within Our Midst

Creating Sustainability Within Our Midst

Challenges for the 21st Century

Fourth Biennial Conference at Pace University
June 23 – 27, 2007

Edited by Robert L. Chapman

PACE UNIVERSITY PRESS · NEW YORK

© 2008 Pace University Press
41 Park Row, Rm. 1510
New York, NY 10038

Typeset in Times New Roman by Ana Aragón Tello.
Cover photo "A Lakeside Sunrise in Benton County, Oregon" by Ron Nichols, 2002.
Photo courtesy of USDA Natural Resources Conservation Service.

ISBN 0-944473-91-1

Conference Committee

ROBERT CHAPMAN	Pace Institute for Environmental and Regional Studies, Pace University
MELISSA EVERETT	Sustainable Hudson Valley
JOHN GOWDY	Rensselaer Polytechnic Institute
GUS KARAM	Pace University
MARSHA KOPAN	USSEE Secretariat
GLENN-MARIE LANGE	Earth Institute, Columbia University
MICHAEL LEVANDOWSKY	Pace University
KARIN LIMBURG	SUNY College of Environmental Science and Forestry
VALERIE LUZADIS	SUNY College of Environmental Science and Forestry
JAMES PITTMAN	Prescott College
RICHARD SCHLESINGER	Pace University
ISABEL DE LA TORRE	Earth Economics

Table of Contents

Contributors

Ruchi Badola is Professor and Head of the Department of Ecodevelopment Planning and Participatory Management at the Wildlife Institute of India.

Brent Bleys is a doctoral candidate in the Department for Mathematics, Operational Research, Statistics and Information Systems for Management at Vrije Universiteit Brussel, Belgium.

Jing Chen is Assistant Professor of Finance in the School of Business at the University of Northern British Columbia, Canada.

Janet Clark is Senior Associate Director of the Toxics Use Reduction Institute at the University of Massachusetts Lowell. She is also a member of the Lowell Center for Sustainable Production.

Dana L. Coelho is Presidential Management Fellow at the United States Forest Service, Pacific Northwest Research Station.

Michael Daley is Assistant Professor of Economics in the Department of Business and Communications at the University of New England.

Joshua Frank is Assistant Professor of Economics at SUNY Cortland.

Syed Ainul Hussian is Professor in the Department of Landscape Level Planning and Management at the Wildlife Institute of India.

Frederic B. Jennings, Jr. is an economic consultant at EconoLogistics and founder of the Center for Ecological Economic and Ethical Education.

Carlos A. López is a doctoral candidate in Ecological Economics at the Rensselaer Polytechnic Institute.

Jean E. Maier is a graduate of the Master of Arts program, Action for a Viable Future, in the Hutchins School of Liberal Studies at Sonoma State University.

Joanne E. Mantell is Research Scientist in the HIV Center for Clinical and Behavioral Studies at the New York State Psychiatric Institute.

Peter H. May is Executive Secretary of the Brazilian Agroforestry Network and Chairman of the Department of Development, Agriculture and Society at the Federal Rural University of Rio de Janeiro, Brazil.

Natalie McGrath is a postdoctoral fellow in the Institute for Sustainability and Technology Policy at Murdoch University, Australia.

Peter Newman is Professor and Director of the Institute for Sustainability and Technology Policy at Murdoch University, Australia. He is also Chair of the Western Australian Sustainability Roundtable.

Richard L. Ottinger is Dean Emeritus of the Pace Law School and Co-director of the Center for Environmental Legal Studies at Pace University.

Trista M. Patterson is an ecological economist at the United States Forest Service, Pacific Northwest Research Station.

Robert B. Richardson is Assistant Professor in the Department of Community, Agriculture, Recreation, and Resource Studies at Michigan State University.

Theo Sandfort is Research Scientist and Training Director of the HIV Center for Clinical and Behavioral Studies at the New York State Psychiatric Institute.

Meike Spitzner is Scientific Coordination in Gender-Research and Consulting for Research Group II: Energy, Transport and Climate Policy at the Wuppertal Institute for Climate, Environment and Energy, Germany.

Mary M. Timney is Professor in the Department of Public Administration at Pace University.

Isidore A. Udoh is a postdoctoral fellow in the HIV Center for Clinical and Behavioral Studies at the New York State Psychiatric Institute and Columbia University.

Carl Wilson is Chief Biologist in the Lobster Research, Monitoring, and Assessment Program at the Maine Department of Marine Resources.

James Wilson is Professor in Marine Sciences and Resource Economics at the University of Maine. He is also Director of the Marine Policy program.

Liying Yan is a graduate student in the School of Marine Sciences at the University of Maine.

Foreword

The fourth biennial conference of the U.S. regional division of the Society for Ecological Economics (USSEE) was held in June 2007 at Pace University in downtown Manhattan. Just a few blocks away from the New York Stock Exchange and brokerages of the world's monetary wealth, USSEE conference delegates examined, analyzed, and debated a broad array of issues that are not the typical fare of an economics conference.

Ecological economics, "the science of sustainability," is a broad field of inquiry characterized by two hallmarks: one, that the Biosphere is a finite place and we, *Homo sapiens*, depend on finite resources for our existence; and two, that real-world problems are complex, nonlinear, and therefore require transdisciplinary approaches to solve them. "Transdisciplinarity" indicates that researchers must operate not only within their own specialties, and not only collaborate across fields, but must develop new discourses, ideas, and sometimes data structures and analyses that go even beyond the synergisms of interdisciplinarity. This is not to say that narrower approaches are not evident within ecological economics; but transdisciplinarity appears to be a common theme.

The field of ecological economics is young, having been founded in the 1980s. However, concepts developed within this field have already had broad impacts: for example, the average person on the street is now aware of their "carbon footprint" and many understand that "natural capital" is as valid a concept as "economic capital." Likewise, the need to understand, assess, and appreciate "ecosystem services" is growing rapidly, as many other scientific disciplines struggle to make their work relevant to the public.

It is an understatement to say that the world we live in is fast changing and, perhaps, our place in it increasingly fragile. Climate change, looming energy crises, human population growth, loss of open space and wilderness, loss of biodiversity, and unraveling ecosystems present new templates upon which the play of humanity will be performed in the twenty-first century. Thus, the theme of the 4th biennial USSEE conference was the question: how to create sustainability within our midst? How do we take what we know, and use it to re-invent our societies to adapt to this rapidly changing scene?

The eighteen papers published in these proceedings represent a sampling of the breadth of interests represented at USSEE '07. These range from technical analyses of welfare and uncertainty indices (Bleys, Lopez), a theoretical, thermo-dynamic analysis of ecological economics (Chen), energy economics (Ottinger), and payment schemes for ecosystem services (Patterson et al.), to such issues as governance roles of states (Timney) and how governance may emerge from adaptive behaviors of individuals (a fisheries example, Yan et al.). In their papers, Daley, Clark, and Jennings examine philosophical, dialectic, and cognitive ap-proaches to sustainability, and Frank discusses how framing the question affects environmental valuation. Maier deals with the macroscopic issues of restructuring banking, and May ponders how the emerging super-economies of China, India, Brazil, Russia, and South Africa might avoid going through the growth-with-environmental-destruction syndrome experienced by nations in earlier centuries. The final five papers are an international tour of challenges and solutions: HIV/AIDS in Nigeria (Udoh et al.); deserts and their ecosystem services (Richardson); mangroves as providers of ecosystem services in coastal India (Badola and Hussain); ecofeminism, transportation, and ecological economics in Germany (Spitzner); and regional strategies for sustainable development in Western Australia (McGrath and Newman).

Although currently a small field, ecological economics represents an important school of thought that will likely grow in size as natural capacity limits are reached, thresholds breached, and surprises occur. We must continue to foster its growth through conferences such as USSEE '07, but also by supporting education efforts within the academy as well as outside in the world of practitioners. With perseverance, we will see "ecological economics" become a household term, communities using their ecosystem goods and services sustainably, and regional, national, and global ecological-economic approaches to deal with this brave new world we find ourselves in.

Karin E. Limburg
College of Environmental Science and Forestry of the State University of New York, Syracuse
Past President, U.S. Society for Ecological Economics

Editor's Comments

When Karin Limburg first approached me to discuss collaborating with the Pace Institute for Environmental & Regional Studies (PIERS) to hold the U. S. Society for Ecological Economics (USSEE) Biennial Conference at Pace University, I did not hesitate. The missions of the two are not only compatible but also reinforce one another. Whereas USSEE's principle goal is to integrate the biophysical world with human economy, PIERS's primary focus is to incorporate normative discourse into the policy language of those institutions that directly mediate relationships between nature and culture placing particular emphasis on economics since it is acutely implicated in the current ecological crisis. And since economics and ecology cannot coexist within the discourse of neoclassical economic theory, together they must generate a language comprehensive enough to critique their own core disciplinary values by applying normative principles—the language of ethics.

Unlikely as it may seem, given the present political condition in the United States, I believe we are on the cusp of dramatic, even radical, change. Many institutions and academic disciplines are beginning to recognize serious theoretical inadequacies in their approach to the natural world. Anomalies abound. In ecology, economics, ethics and political science, singularities prevent practitioners in those disciplines from solving and even explaining problems using standard procedures that define their respective disciplines ("working rules"). Due to this relentless frustration, some are coming to realize (often reluctantly) that their models do not and cannot fit realities. Maybe it is time—long overdue—to change the rules.

Ecological economists have made a daring, paradigmatic change in rejecting the presumption of unlimited growth. In my opinion, though, they must also more emphatically reject many of the standard assumptions (working rules) of neoclassical economics: 1) self-interest as the prime motivation for human action; 2) utility and efficiency as the ultimate goals of market transaction; 3) freedom as defined through both rational choice theory and property rights. These are the assumptions most frequently targeted for criticism by heterodox economists, philosophers, and others, along with procedure issues such as cost-benefit analysis—as a measure of well-being, mathematical formalism, and methodological individualism.

There is no need to elaborate on each of these assumptions here since this audience is certainly familiar with them. The point is that the rejections I advocate above can be made only within a transdisciplinary setting that encourages ethical discourse. As Herman Daly once observed, " . . . once we admit that natural processes as well as labor and capital add value to the indestructible building blocks, then we *must* ask who has the right to appropriate nature's contribution." The "must" presents a moral imperative, while the issue of rights extends far beyond legal interpretations and policy formulation.

I would hope that when we look back on this conference, we will consider it as a vehicle for responsible environmental change and an advance in sustainable development studies. Sustainability cannot emerge from within the precincts of the current institutional structure and this group of conference participants is in the vanguard of institutional change.

Robert L. Chapman
Director, Pace Institute for Environmental & Regional Studies

1 A Simplified Index of Sustainable Economic Welfare

Brent Bleys

ABSTRACT

This paper presents the results of a case study on the Index of Sustainable Economic Welfare (ISEW) for Belgium. First, the standard methodology is used to compile the index, while afterwards some refinements to the methodology are proposed and implemented. These refinements have a significant impact on the index, as working with alternative valuation methods for important items such as natural capital depletion and long-term environmental damage results in a non-declining evolution of economic welfare over time. These findings are not in line with the threshold hypothesis, which has been put forward following other international studies on the ISEW. Next, a Simplified ISEW is proposed, selecting items using different criteria on quantitative significance (both the original and the adapted methodology are investigated). The simplified index is closely linked to the original ISEW, displaying almost an identical trend over time. This allows for monitoring sustainable economic welfare using far less data then previously needed. Finally, the SISEW is calculated for the Netherlands in order to see how readily available the data needed to compile the simplified version are. Once again the importance of underlying assumptions in the methodology of the ISEW is illustrated.

Keywords: Economic Welfare; ISEW; Simplified ISEW

1 Introduction

The Index of Sustainable Economic Welfare (ISEW) is a measure that tries to capture the overall impact of economic activity on human welfare. It integrates in its methodology both the benefits and the costs associated with economic activity. In this regard, it is very different from the Gross Domestic Product (GDP), which looks at the total size of economic activity—the total amount of final goods and services produced and consumed within a country in a given period.

An interesting way to introduce the ISEW is to think of it as consisting of two elemental categories: the uncancelled benefits and the uncancelled costs of economic activity (Lawn and Sanders,1999). The former correspond to the concept of "net psychic income" as put forward by Fisher (1906): the total services provided by final consumption goods to their ultimate consumers minus the dis-services originating from labor, pains and other discomforts. The latter can be regarded as the natural capital services (source, sink and life-support services) that are lost in obtaining the necessary through put of matter-energy to keep hu-man-made capital stock intact.

The methodology used to calculate the ISEW is summarized in Table 1. The first six categories of items relate to the uncancelled benefits account, while the last two relate to the uncancelled costs account. In practice, the ISEW is the re-sult of a lengthy series of about 20 adjustments to the personal consumption expenditures base. For a more detailed review of the methodology Cobb and Cobb (1994) or Jackson, Marks, Ralls and Stymne (1997) can be consulted.

Table 1 Main Components of the Index of Sustainable Economic Welfare

ISEW	=	+	personal consumption expenditures
		-	losses from income inequality
		+	value of domestic labour
		+	non-defensive public expenditures
		-	defensive private expenditures
		+/-	capital adjustments
		-	costs of environmental degradation
		-	depreciation of natural capital

Lawn (2003) worked out a sound theoretical foundation for the ISEW based on the Fisherian concepts of income and capital and demonstrates how each item used in the compilation of the index fits into this foundation. More recently, he placed the concepts of uncancelled benefits and uncancelled costs into a larger linear throughput model of the socio-economic process based on a coevolution-ary worldview (Lawn, 2006).

Following the effort of Daly and Cobb (1989), who worked out the meth-odology for the ISEW and compiled it for the United States (1950–1986), the ISEW was calculated in many countries. In each country, minor adaptations were made to the original methodology in order to overcome problems with data availability or to pay attention to country-specific issues. The Genuine Progress Indicator (GPI), a more recent derivative of the ISEW that adds a number of new items to the methodology, has already been compiled in the United States and in Australia.

A common finding among the series of international studies is the growing divergence between GDP per capita and ISEW per capita, especially during the 1980s and 1990s. In many countries this divergence can be explained by increasing income inequalities, rising costs of resource depletion and escalat-ing long-term environmental costs. During the 1980s and 1990s economic wel-fare, as measured by the ISEW, levels off or starts to decline in most countries for which the index was calculated. Max-Neef (1995) finds in these results a confirmation of his threshold hypothesis: "for every society there seems to be a period in which economic growth (as conventionally measured) brings about an improvement in the quality of life, but only up to a point—the threshold point —beyond which, if there is more economic growth, quality-of-life may begin to deteriorate."

Over the years, the Index of Sustainable Economic Welfare has attracted some criticism, most of which has been dealt with by proponents of the index. The criticism can be divided into two categories: methodological issues on the one hand and practical issues on the other. Methodological issues shed doubt on the value of the entire exercise (e.g. high amount of subjectivity that enters the methodology and the inability of any index to measure both welfare and sustainability at the same time), while practical issues are concerned with (the valuation of) specific items within the methodology of the ISEW or with data quality or availability. Concerns that minor adjustments to these valuation methods would have a significant impact on the index and the conclusions drawn from the ISEW studies, were expressed by many authors (Neumayer, 1999). Neumayer (2000) even argues that the threshold hypothesis, as defined by Max-Neef, fails to materialize and that the growing gap between per capita ISEW and per capita GDP "might be an artifact of highly contestable methodological assumptions."

2　The ISEW for Belgium

We will now look into the results of the ISEW case study on Belgium. I have compiled the Index of Sustainable Economic Welfare for Belgium using two different methodologies. First, I employed the methodology outlined by Jackson et al. (1997) as closely as possible. Afterwards, the impact of working with an updated methodology (Bleys, 2007b), based on insights from critical reviews of the index and more recent work on monetary valuation methods, was investigated.

2.1 Original Methodology

Building on the different international ISEW studies that have been undertaken over the years, a methodology for the calculation of an Index of Sustainable Economic Welfare for Belgium was worked out. This methodology was afterwards operationalised and the ISEW was calculated for the period 1970–2004, as gathering earlier data on most items proved very difficult. A detailed review of the ISEW methodology, the data used and the assumptions made within the Belgian study can be found in Bleys (2006).

Since some of the items within the ISEW framework are valued using incomplete data or following outdated valuation methods, improvements can still be made to the index. Nevertheless, I consider this effort to be a valuable first step towards the development of a better welfare measure.

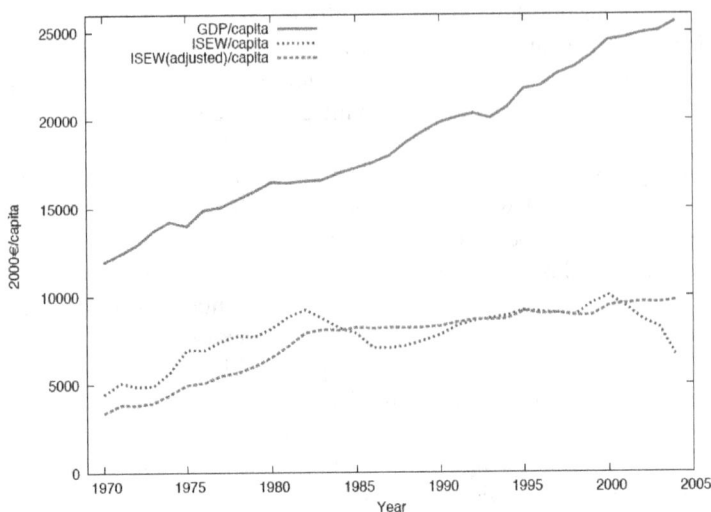

Figure 1 ISEW, ISEW(adjusted) and GDP per capita for Belgium

The results of the Belgian ISEW analysis are shown in Figure 1, where per capita GDP is plotted against the updated per capita ISEW. Both indexes are expressed in constant prices (2000 €/capita). Although average annual growth rates vary over the period under consideration, GDP/capita shows an almost continuous increase. In fact, only in 1975, 1981 and 1993, Belgium's GDP/capita fell. Looking at the ISEW/capita, we find a different pattern: two relatively long periods of steady increases are ended by shorter periods of sharp decreases, causing ISEW/capita to increase by only 48% over the period 1970–2004 (compared to an increase in GDP/capita of about 114%).

Looking at Table 2, which presents the average annual growth rates of ISEW/capita and GDP/capita for the different decades that constitute the period studied, the above findings are confirmed. ISEW/capita rises steadily through the 1970s at an average annual growth rate of 6.29%, before leveling off completely

Table 2 Growth Rates of per capita ISEW, ISEW (adjusted) and GDP

Period	ISEW/capita	ISEW(adj)/capita	GDP/capita
1970–1980	6.29%	6.78%	3.28%
1980–1990	-0.44%	2.47%	1.88%
1990–2000	2.51%	1.28%	2.12%
2000–2004	-10.01%	0,80%	1.06%

in the 1980s. The average growth rate of -0.44% per annum recorded during this decade actually masks a decline in sustainable economic welfare during the mid 1980s and an almost full recovery in the later years. The per capita ISEW continues to rise during the 1990s to peak in the year 2000 at €10,012/capita. Over the four following years, the index collapses at an impressive rate of over 10% per year.

It would be interesting to explore which items constitute the driving forces behind the two periods of decline. The sustainable economic welfare recession of the mid 1980s is largely caused by a decrease in net capital growth, which drops from €11,704 million to €-2,751 million between 1983 and 1987. Other driving factors include the rising costs of ozone layer depletion (due to a rapid increase in the amount of CFCs released into the atmosphere) and the relatively high increase in costs associated with the depletion of natural resources (non-renewable energy use increased by 15% over a period of 4 years). The second period of recession (early 2000s) is driven by a marked decrease in Belgium's net international investment position, which falls from its 2000 record high of €154,455 million to €90,475 million in 2004. A decline in net capital growth also adds to the further decline of ISEW/capita in 2004.[1]

2.2 Adjusted Methodology

The methodology of the ISEW has not changed much since the introduction of the index in 1989. Although a structural rethinking of the index is needed to deal with the criticism outlined above and with some of the outdated valuation methods within the ISEW framework, the focus in recent years has been on the compilation of the index in more countries and on are branding of the index in order to gain a broader acceptance among policy makers.

The ISEW goes far in being consistent with the Fisherian income and capital concept, yet a few problems remain. First, two items within the methodology of the ISEW should be omitted as they are hard to comply with the theoretical foundation of the index: the 'net capital growth' item and the 'changes in the net international investment position' item. Next, some valuation methods need to be updated. In Bleys (2007b), I have worked out new valuation methods for four items: natural capital depletion, the costs associated with both long term environmental damage and ozone layer depletion and the treatment of public expenditures.

The impact of the proposed adjustments on the Belgian ISEW is illustrated in Figure 1. Looking at the ISEW(adjusted)/capita line, we notice that Belgium's per capita level of sustainable economic welfare has risen over almost the entire period covered by the case study. There is, however, an interesting turning point in the data around 1982, when the growth rate of the level of sustainable economic welfare drops significantly. This can also be found in Table 2, where the annual average growth rates in ISEW per capita are given per decade: average

---

1 All monetary values in this paragraph are expressed in constant 2000 prices.

growth rates fall from 6.78% in the 1970s to 0.80% for the last four years in the case study (2000–2004).

Three items are responsible for the sudden drop in the growth rate of ISEW (adjusted)/capita: consumption expenditures, welfare losses from income inequality and costs associated with long-term environmental damages. The average growth rate of both private and public consumption expenditures has dropped after 1982, while the costs of climate change and ozone layer depletion have risen faster and faster through out the entire study period. The most important factor however, is income inequality. For Belgium, income inequalities dropped between 1973 and 1982, while afterwards inequalities started to rise again. The monetary welfare losses related to inequalities in income reflect these trends.

2.3 Comparison

When we compare the results of both analyses presented above, different conclusions regarding Max-Neef's threshold hypothesis can be drawn. In the initial case study a growing divergence between GDP/capita and ISEW/capita is noticeable, yet the recent period of decline of the latter index (early 2000s) is too short to draw any solid conclusions with regard to the threshold hypothesis as formulated by Max-Neef (1995). Whether the 2000 maximum of ISEW/capita is indeed Belgium's threshold point remains to be verified in the future. When the adjustments to the methodology of the index as proposed in Bleys (2007b) are made, per capita economic welfare increases steadily over the entire study period. The differences in outcomes illustrate the importance of underlying assumptions in the methodology of the ISEW.

3   A Simplified Index of Sustainable Economic Welfare

This section introduces the Simplified Index of Sustainable Economic Welfare (SISEW), which is in fact a simplified version of the ISEW in that it is comprised of fewer items. First, the procedure of selecting items based on a quantitative significance criterion is looked into. Next, the results of the Belgian SISEW are compared with the ones obtained by the original ISEW case study. Finally, the implications of working with a SISEW are discussed.

3.1 Item Selection

One of the most important problems in the actual compilation of the Index of Sustainable Economic Welfare is gathering the amount of data needed in the process. On average, an ISEW study consists of 20 items, some of which are indexes themselves. For the Belgian case study, 23 data sets were needed in order to arrive at the final ISEW results. For GPI studies, the amount of data needed is even larger, as the index adds a number of new items to the methodology: the value of volunteer work and the costs of crime, family breakdown, unemployment, underemployment and overwork (or the loss of leisure time).

Another recurring problem with the ISEW stems from the monetary valuation methods used to aggregate all items within its methodology. There is a lack of country-specific valuation methods, forcing researchers working on the index to take over methods used in other countries. And even when country-specific valuation methods are available, they often cannot be compared with methods from other studies as different approaches are used. As a result, there is little consistency among international studies in the methodology used to compile the ISEW.

One way to work around the problems outlined above is to omit from the ISEW methodology those items that have a low quantitative significance compared to the most others. This will not only reduce the amount of data needed, but it will also give an indication about which items require further research and debate to arrive at internationally agreed upon valuation methods.

The 'costs of noise pollution' item is a good illustration of the above-mentioned problems with the index. In the ISEW study for the United Kingdom (Jackson et al., 1997), a 1993 point estimate for traffic noise (£2.3 billion in 1990 prices) is spread over the study period using a constant escalation factor of 0.5% per year. For Belgium, however, such a point estimate is not available. As a result, the costs of noise pollution were calculated by multiplying a marginal costs of noise (generated by road traffic) estimate of €0.0003 per vehicle kilometer (Transport and Mobility Leuven, 2002) by the total number of vehicle kilometers travelled each year. In both studies, however, the importance of the 'costs of noise pollution' item is very low: for the UK, the item accounts for 1.2% of the total of all negative items, while for Belgium, the item accounts for only 0.2%. From a practical point of view, it might be useful to omit the item. Yet, we will have to keep in mind that the eventual omission of any item is based on historical observations, so that what looks insignificant now, might not be insignificant in the future.

Let us now look at how items are selected in the different versions of the Simplified Index of Sustainable Economic Welfare. The ISEW case study for Belgium (Bleys, 2006) is taken as a starting point for determining the quantitative significance of the different items in the ISEW methodology. The average percentage of each item to the total of positive or negative items within the index was calculated, and based on these percentages, three versions of the SISEW are defined. SISEW1 includes all items that represent more than 1% of these totals, SISEW2 includes those that represent more than 3% and SISEW those that represent more than 5%. Table 3 provides an overview of the different items that each of these SISEW versions are comprised of.

3.2 ASISEW for Belgium

If the SISEW is to be a good approximation of the ISEW, both indexes will have to convey the same message. As ISEW studies result in index numbers,

Table 3 Components of the different versions of the Simplified Index of Sustainable Economic Welfare

Item	Impact	SISEW1[a]	SISEW2	SISEW3	Rationale
Personal Consumption Expenditures	+	x	x	x	Personal Consumption Expenditures
Losses from Income Inequality	-	x	x	x	Welfare Effects of Income Inequality
Value of Household Work	+	x	x	x	Domestic Labour
Public Expenditures on Health & Education	+	x	x	x	Non-Defensive Public Expenditures
Private Expenditures on Health & Education	-	x			Defensive Private Expenditures
Costs of Commuting	-	x	x		Defensive Private Expenditures
Costs of Water Pollution	-	x			Environmental Degradation (Direct)
Costs of Air Pollution	-	x	x	x	Environmental Degradation (Direct)
Depletion of Non-Renewable Resources	-	x	x	x	Natural Capital Depletion
Costs of Climate Change	-	x	x	x	LT Environmental Degradation
Costs of Ozone Depletion	-	x	x	x	LT Environmental Degradation
Net Capital Growth	+/-	x	x	x	Capital Adjustment
Change in Net International Position	+/-	x	x		Capital Adjustment
		> 1%	> 3%	> 5%	

[a]Five ISEW items are not included in SISEW1: costs of personal pollution control, car accidents and noise pollution, adjustments for consumer durables and loss of farmlands

their value lies fully in the trend over time of the index. Bearing this in mind, two different conclusions stand out from Figure 2.

On the one hand, both SISEW1/capita and SISEW2/capita display a trend over time that is almost exactly identical to the one for ISEW/capita. There is, however, a difference in absolute terms, as both simplified versions of the ISEW result in per capita sustainable economic welfare levels that are higher

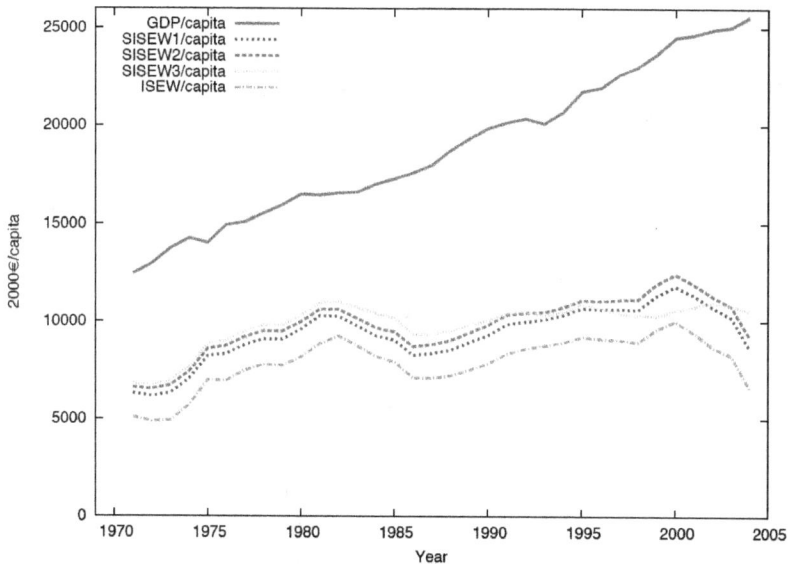

Figure 2 SISEW1, SISEW2 and SISEW3 for Belgium

than the one picked up by the original ISEW. As all omitted items are 'cost' items (see Table 3), the observed discrepancy in absolute terms can be easily explained.

On the other hand, SISEW3/capita shows a different trend over time than ISEW/capita, especially by the end of the study period. Of all SISEW versions, SISEW3/capita omits most items, as its criterion of quantitative significance is the strictest. As a result, the 'changes in the net international investment position' item is omitted from SISEW3 and it is this omission that leads to the differences in the trend over time between SISEW3/capita and ISEW/capita. The 'changes in the net international investment position' item has a high level of variation and it has had an increasing and negative impact on the course of ISEW/capita. By omitting this item, SISEW3/capita does not indicate a decline in the level of sustainable economic welfare over the last years of the study period.

A similar exercise could be done starting from the updated methodology of the index put forward in section 2.2. Here, all versions of the per capita simplified ISEW(adjusted) display a trend over time that is similar to the one for ISEW(adjusted)/capita.

3.3 Implications

Reducing the number of items in the methodology of the Index of Sustainable Economic Welfare allows for an easier compilation of the index. At the same time, the outcome of the ISEW exercise is almost unaffected, except for changes in absolute terms. Yet, as the trend over time offers the only valid ground for drawing conclusions with regard to (changes in) the level of sustainable economic welfare, the message that the simplified ISEW study conveys will be the same.

As working with a simplified version of the ISEW renders the compilation of the index easier, more studies at a national level can be undertaken. Perhaps there even is a possibility of calculating SISEW/capita for a large group of countries using a standardized set of valuation methods.

For now, I have calculated the Simplified Index of Sustainable Economic Welfare for the Netherlands to see whether the proposed simplifications would effectively allow for an easier compilation in practice.

4   Case Study for the Netherlands

A SISEW case study is conducted for the Netherlands, both using the original methodology as described in Jackson et al. (1997) and the updated one put forward by Bleys (2007b). A full review of the case study is given in Bleys (2007a).

4.1 Original Methodology

The results of the Dutch SISEW analysis are shown in Figure 3, where per capita GDP is plotted against per capita SISEW. Three versions of the SISEW are presented, each one with a different set of selected items (as explained in the previous section). SISEW1 is comprised of all 13 items presented in Table 3, while SISEW3 is made up of only 9 items (defensive private expenditures on health and education, costs of commuting, costs of water pollution and changes in the net international investment position are dropped).

A number of interesting conclusions can be drawn from this graph. First, we notice that, for all three versions of the Simplified Index of Sustainable Economic Welfare, the 2004 level of economic welfare per capita is almost the same as the 1971 level and this while GDP/capita shows a continuous increase over the same period. Next, looking at the trend over time of the different SISEWs, it is possible to split the study period into two shorter time frames: a period of decline in economic welfare up to 1987 when SISEW/capita reaches its period low, and one of rising economic welfare levels afterwards. A third and more obvious conclusion is that all three SISEW versions display more or less the same trend over time (with the one exception being SISEW3 in the period 1995–2000, when the Netherlands witnessed a dramatic decrease in its net international investment position).

These findings are confirmed in Table 4, that presents both the evolution of all indexes to their relative 1971 figures and their average annual growth rates for 5-year intervals. All SISEW indexes fall steadily throughout the 1970s and 1980s, before bouncing back in the 1990s and the early 2000s.

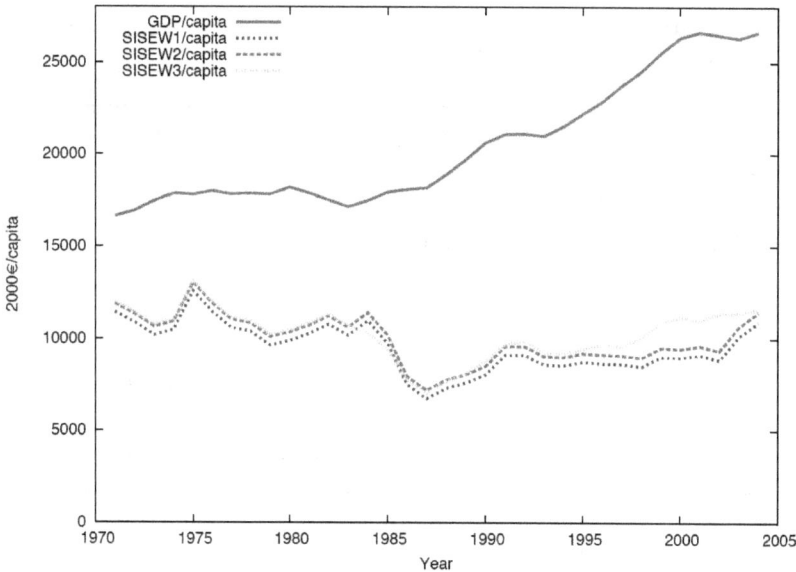

Figure 3 The Simplified Index of Sustainable Economic Welfare for the Netherlands

Note that the differences in annual average growth rates between SISEW1 and SISEW2 on the one hand and SISEW3 on the other are fully attributable to the 'changes in net international investment position' item that is excluded in the latter. Looking at GDP/capita, we find a different pattern: although average annual growth rates vary over the different periods under consideration, GDP/capita shows an almost continuous increase.

Two items can be singled out as the most important factors explaining the observed discrepancy in the trend over time in sustainable economic welfare between the periods 1971–1987 and 1987–2004. First, the costs of long-term environmental damage have risen sharply during the first period, while they more or less stabilized over the second. Emissions of ozone depletion substances increased rapidly in the 1970s and 1980s, but soon after the ratification of the Montreal Protocol, they were reduced to almost zero soon . Emissions of carbon dioxides peaked in 1980 at a level that was only reached again in the late 1990s. Second, net capital growth fell significantly between 1975 and 1987, after which it recovered, partly due to the fact that the labor force in the Netherlands grew at a slower rate in the 1990s than in the two previous decades.

Other important items in the study are welfare losses from income inequalities and the costs associated with natural capital depletion. A decrease in income inequalities in the Netherlands between 1971 and 1983 was completely annulled by an increase in the later years of the study period: overall the Atkinson Index of income inequality rose from 0.079 in 1971 to 0.102 in 2004. Except for the years after the second oil crisis, non-renewable energy use increased

Table 4 Trends in (top) and Average Annual Growth Rates of (bottom) per capita Indexes

	SISEW1	SISEW2	SISEW3	GDP
1971	100.0	100.0	100.0	100.0
1975	95.2	95.3	95.4	101.8
1980	86.3	87.0	87.2	109.4
1985	85.1	85.6	78.5	107.9
1990	70.2	71.4	73.2	124.0
1995	76.3	77.3	78.6	133.5
2000	78.4	79.4	92.9	158.3
2004	95.2	96.2	96.5	160.1

	SISEW1	SISEW2	SISEW3	GDP
1971–1975	-1.2	-1.2	-1.2	0.4
1975–1980	-1.9	-1.8	-1.8	1.5
1980–1985	-0.3	-0.3	-2.1	-0.3
1985–1990	-3.8	-3.6	-1.4	2.8
1990–1995	1.7	1.6	1.4	1.5
1995–2000	0.5	0.5	3.4	3.5
2000–2004	5.0	4.9	1.0	0.3

throughout the entire period studied in the Dutch case study. The costs associated to this rise have gained importance in ISEW (from just over 30% in 1971 to 45% in 2004), yet this gain is mostly due to the escalation factor that is used in the estimates to reflect increases in replacement costs associated with a higher non-renewable energy use. It should be noted here that this escalation factor has attracted a lot of criticism over the years (Dietz and Neumayer, 2006).

The preliminary findings of the SISEW study for the Netherlands are clearly not in line with Max-Neef's threshold hypothesis, which states that, for every developed country, economic growth will contribute to economic welfare only up to a certain point—the threshold point—after which further economic growth will have a negative impact on economic welfare.

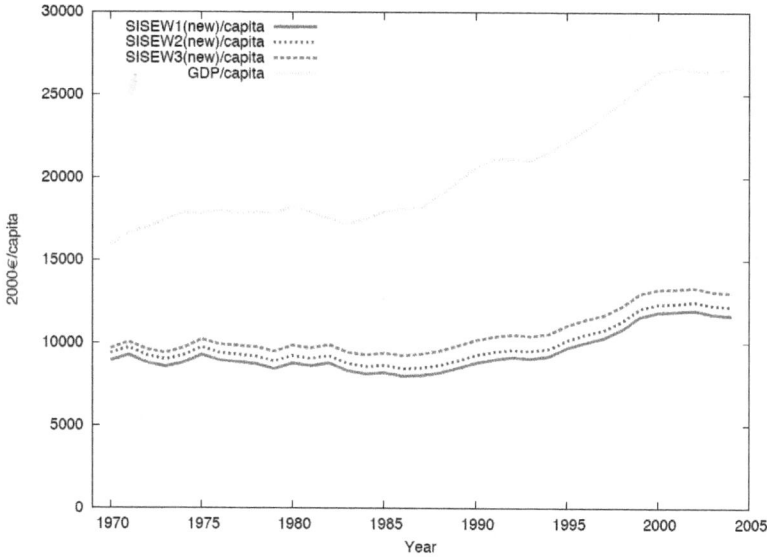

Figure 4 SISEWs with Adjusted Methodology

4.2 Adjusted Methodology

In this section, the impact of the adjustments made to the original methodology as proposed in Bleys (2007b) on the Dutch SISEW case study is looked into. Figure 4 illustrates the overall effect of all adjustments on the three versions of the SISEW. The SISEW(new) indexes show a different trend over time than the SISEW indexes presented in the previous section. Some interesting conclusions emerge. First, we notice an overall increase in sustainable economic welfare levels over the period 1971–2004. Second, whereas per capita economic welfare more or less stayed at a constant level in the 1970s and 1980s, the Netherlands have witnessed a sharp increase in the 1990s. In the early 2000s, a new period of stagnation appears to be setting in. Third, all three versions of the SISEW display the same trend over time. SISEW1(new)/capita is plotted against the original SISEW1/capita index in Figure 5 in order to illustrate the different trends over time of both indexes.

Leaving out both the 'net capital growth' item and the 'changes in the net international investment position' item, results in an index which shows a similar trend over time than the original SISEW1/capita, yet has a smoother course than the latter (as the two omitted items have data sets with high levels of variation).

The new valuation method for natural capital depletion has the most striking impact on the adjusted index. As the costs of replacing a barrel of oil equivalent of non-renewable energy are kept constant over time instead of using an escalation factor of 3% per year, the use of non-renewables before 1988—the year for

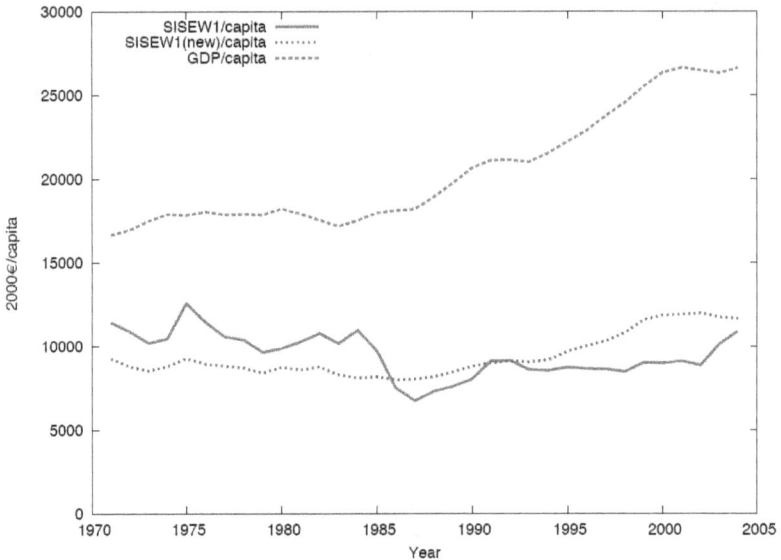

Figure 5 SISEW1/capita—Old versus New

which the replacement cost was estimated by Cobb and Cobb (1994)—is valued higher, while the opposite is true for the years after 1988.

The other proposed adjustments to the valuation methods used in the SISEW methodology have less marked impacts, as they shift the baseline index upwards or downwards. The new valuation method for the long-term environmental damage caused by climate change results in higher estimates of the associated costs, as linking the original 1990 marginal social cost estimate (Jackson et al., 1997) to actual carbon dioxide concentrations leads to higher MSC estimates in the later years of the case study.

Accounting for more types of public consumption expenditures evidently results in an upward shift of the per capita SISEW. The new stock-based valuation method for ozone layer depletion has the same effect, as it allows for an outward flow of ozone depleting substances from the atmosphere, where previously all emissions were accumulated endlessly.

Basically there are three items explaining the rise of sustainable economic welfare levels in the 1990s. First, private expenditures on consumption increased at a rate that was much higher in the 1990s than it was in the 1970s and 1980s. This increase in growth rate is closely linked to the higher GDP growth rate in the 1990s (see Figure 4). Second, the monetary estimates of the value of domestic services increased in the 1990s, mainly as a result of an increase in the relative wages earned by cleaning personnel. Third, the growth rate of the costs of long-term environmental damage dropped significantly in the 1990s: the costs associated with ozone layer depletion actually decreased, while the growth rate of the costs of climate change dropped from 5.5% in the 1970s and 1980s to 3.8% in the 1990s.

5   Conclusion

This paper reviews the ISEW case study on Belgium. The results of the analysis are presented for both the standard methodology as used in many international studies as well as for an adjusted methodology that has been put forward as a reaction to different criticisms that the ISEW has attracted. Afterwards, the case study is taken as a starting point for the development of a simplified version of the Index of Sustainable Economic Welfare (ISEW), which omits items from the original methodology that only have a minor impact on the final results. Finally, the SISEW is compiled for the Netherlands to see how readily available the necessary data are in practice. The conclusions that can be drawn from this paper are twofold.

First, the importance of the underlying assumptions within the methodology of the index is underlined once again. By properly separating capital stocks and flows of services, an adjusted methodology for the Index of Sustainable Economic Welfare was developed, which omits the 'net capital growth' and the 'changes in the net international investment position' items and incorporates several updated valuation methods for items such as the costs of long-term environmental damage and natural capital depletion. Using this adjusted methodology leads to very different conclusions with regard to the trend over time of sustainable economic welfare levels, both for Belgium as for the Netherlands. It is therefore extremely important that a widely accepted list of items and a more robust set of valuation methods are established in the near future, in order to add to the validity of the ISEW as a proper measure of economic welfare. Yet, as the development of such a set might take some time, for now, ISEW studies should clearly stress all assumptions made within the framework of the index and warn against interpreting the results too literally.

Second, by reducing the number of items in its methodology, the Simplified Index for Sustainable Economic Welfare (SISEW) allows for an easier compilation of the index. At the same time, the outcome of the ISEW exercise is almost unaffected, except for changes in absolute terms. Yet, as the trend over time offers the only valid ground for drawing conclusions with regard to (changes in) the level of sustainable economic welfare, the message that the SISEW study conveys will be the same. The case study on the Netherlands has proven that gathering the data necessary for the compilation of the SISEW is quite straightforward, at least for developed countries. However, compiling a set of country-specific valuation methods is far more complicated.

References

Bleys, B. (2006). The Index of Sustainable Economic Welfare for Belgium: First Attempt and Preliminary Results, MOSI Working Paper, number 27, Vrije Universiteit Brussel, Brussel, Belgium.

Bleys, B. (2007a). *A Simplified Index of Sustainable Economic Welfare for the Netherlands, 1971–2004,* (to be published).

Bleys, B. (2007b). *The Index of Sustainable Economic Welfare: Proposed Adjustments to the Methodology,* (to be published).

Cobb, C. and Cobb, J. (1994). *The Green National Product: A Proposed Index of Sustainable Economic Welfare,* University Press of America, Lanham, MD.

Daly, H. and Cobb, J. J. (1989). *For the Common Good. Redirecting the Economy toward Community, the Environment and a Sustainable Future,* Beacon Press, Boston, MA.

Dietz, S. and Neumayer, E. (2006). Some Constructive Criticisms of the Index of Sustainable Economic Welfare, in P. Lawn (ed.), *Sustainable Development Indicators in Ecological Economics*, Edward Elgar, Cheltenham, UK, pp. 117–135.

Fisher, I. (1906). *The Nature of Capital and Income,* Kelley, NewYork, NY.

Jackson, T., Marks, N., Ralls, J. and Stymne, S. (1997). *Sustainable Ecomonic Welfare in the UK, 1950–1996, New Economics Foundation,* London, UK.

Lawn, P. (2003). A Theoretical Foundation to Support the Index of Sustainable Economic Welfare (ISEW), Genuine Progress Indicator (GPI), and Other Related Indexes, *Ecological Economics* 44(1): 105–118.

Lawn, P. (2006). *Sustainable Development: Concept and Indicators, in P. Lawn (ed.), Sustainable Development Indicators in Ecological Economics,* MPG Books, Bodmin, UK, pp. 13–51.

Lawn, P. and Sanders, R. (1999). Has Australia Surpassed its Optimal Macro-Economic Scale? Finding Out with the Aid of 'Benefit' and 'Cost' Accounts and a Sustainable Net Benefit Index, *Ecological Economics* 28(2): 213–229.

Max-Neef, M. (1995). Economic Growth and Quality of Life: a Threshold Hypothesis, *Ecological Economics* 15(2): 115–118.

Neumayer, E. (1999). The ISEW: Not an Index of Sustainable Economic Welfare, *Social Indicators Research* 48(1): 77–101.

Neumayer, E. (2000). On the Methodology of ISEW, GPI and Related Measures: Some Constructive Suggestions and Some Doubt on the 'Threshold' Hypothesis, *Ecological Economics* 34(3): 347–361.

Transport and Mobility Leuven (2002). *Verkeersindices: Congestie-en Milieukosten,* Transport and Mobility Leuven, Leuven, Belgium.

2 Discounting the Future at a Decreasing Rate and the Marginal Damage Costs of CO_2 Emissions

Reducing the Uncertainty

Carlos A. López

ABSTRACT

Carrying out a sensitivity analysis of the estimated marginal costs of CO_2 emissions under different constant rates of pure time preference shows that, everything else being equal, the former depends heavily on the values assumed for the latter, especially in the distant future. This well-known result has led the literature to conclude that the practice of discounting is one of the major sources of uncertainty in estimating the costs of climate change. But this might not be the case if we consider a decreasing rate of time preference instead of a constant rate. Using one of the models from the peer-reviewed literature, this paper shows that allowing for a decreasing rate of pure time preference substantially reduces the uncertainty in estimating the costs of climate change. In addition, estimated costs are consistent with those from the peer-reviewed literature for the near future (say, 100 years hence), but are larger for the very distant future. Therefore, these results reduce the uncertainty that militates against strong mitigation policies in the present.

I   Introduction

Discounting is one of the main concerns in the literature of climatic change. Since the main effects on climatic trends due to current climate policies are likely to be occurring in the distant future, the treatment we give to the streams of monetary costs and benefits becomes a central issue in our current models. Recently, Richard Tol suggested that the uncertainty in the estimation of the marginal damage cost of CO_2 emission, albeit substantial, is not as large as some people think (Tol, 2005). He founds his argument in the analysis of 103 estimates from 28 published studies. There exists, he says, two major sources of uncertainty. The first one, the equity weighting, imposes an egalitarian treatment among countries, and leads to both higher estimates and higher uncertainty. The second one, the pure rate of time preference, also proves to have an important effect on the value of the costs estimates: the lower the discount rate, the higher the costs estimates. In fact, Tol reports that a pure rate of time preference of 3% leads to a mean estimate of 16 USD/tonC, while a discount rate of 1% brings a mean estimate of 51 USD/tonC. When restricting the sample to 31 estimates from two peer-reviewed studies, Tol finds that for a time horizon of 100 years in the future, an increase in 1% in the pure rate of time preference leads to a decrease of 23 USD/tonC in the marginal cost estimate.

The overall conclusion, however, is that "for all practical purposes, climate change impacts may be very uncertain but is unlikely that the marginal damage costs of carbon dioxide emissions exceed 50 USD/tonC and are likely to be substantially smaller than that" (Tol, 2005). This assessment on the uncertainties needs to be taken with caution. Two main reasons follow. First, Tol is referring to a time horizon of only 100 years from now. Second, many of the studies of the sample use a constant positive rate or pure time preference. It is true that both practices may help to focus the analysis on the impacts happening in the near future, but it is also true that both represent an underestimation of the impacts happening in the distant future. In 1997, Geoffrey Heal published an "editorial comment" on discounting in the context of climate change. There, he says that "the key point about the environmental area is the following: it forces one to consider long time horizons. In the climate change area, a century is the minimum time horizon that makes sense. Probably it is too short" (Heal, 1997).

Looking further into the future means to look how the uncertainty on the marginal cost estimates increases. This paper simulates the model presented by Azar and Sterner (1996), which is included in Tol's sample, and shows that in 500 years from now a discount rate of time preference of 3% yields an estimate value close to 13 USD/tonC, while a 0.1% rate yields an estimate of 75 USD/tonC. The difference increases even more if one looks further: in 1000 years from now, the estimate calculated upon a 3% discount rate is still close to13 USD/tonC, while the 0.1% estimate is 140 USD/tonC. At this date, an increase in 1% of the pure rate of time preference leads to a decrease of more than 150 USD/tonC in the cost estimate. The uncertainty may be small for small time horizons, just as Tol says, but it is likely to increase and become a central issue in the economics of climate change if one is forced to consider time horizons longer that one or two centuries. It is a common place now to say that exponential discounting at a constant positive rate is not a good option to calculate present values of costs happening centuries hence. There are many calls for using instead a decreasing rate of pure time preference in the context of climate change. However, there are not too many examples in the literature of the marginal cost estimates showing the virtues of adhering to that approach.

This paper shows two main virtues of applying a decreasing rate of pure time preference. First, it reduces the uncertainty of the estimates if compared to exponential discounting. Second, while yielding similar estimates for the near future to those from exponential discounting, it provides higher estimates for the very long run, and thus helps to reduce the ambiguity in the motivation of strong abatement policies in the present. Newell and Pizer (2003) tested a similar method (a decreasing rate of pure time preference) to calculate the present value of the flow of marginal damages from Nordhaus' model (Nordhaus, 1994). They report one of the virtues from decreasing discount rates: it is a method that does not underestimate the distant future in the same extent as exponential discounting does. However, they do not report the second virtue, i.e., the reduction of the uncertainty in the estimation produced by discounting at constant rates.

Despite the emphasis of the literature on another major source of uncertainty, namely the aggregation of monetized impacts over countries, in this paper we will adhere to the strong assumption that the planet is a homogenous economic region. This procedure, however, will help to isolate the uncertainty derived solely from the discount rate. This paper is organized as follows: Section II presents the conventional wisdom of exponential discounting. The distribution of weights to values happening at different moments in time is highlighted. Section III presents a simulation of the Azar and Sterner (1996) model and replicates its results. Section IV presents arguments in favor of a decreasing rate of discount and runs a new simulation of the model. Section V concludes.

II Discounting re-visited: The conventional wisdom

The practice of discounting is a rule that assigns time-dependent weights to values occurring at different moments in time. Let $A(t)$ represent that rule, usually called "the discount factor", and let $X(t)$ be the sequence of values in time. Note that $X(t)$ can be either the net benefit obtained from some project at time t or the instantaneous utility function at time t. For simplicity in calculations, we explore the continuous case. Therefore, in the context of the model presented in the next section, $X(t)$ represents the increase in marginal damage occurring at instant t. The aggregation of the weighted values into an overall index of present-discounted values is habitually done by computing

$$\int_0^\infty A(t)X(t)dt \qquad (1)$$

One of the methods commonly used by economists to discount future values is to define an exponential discount factor. Formally, $A(t) = e^{-\rho t}$ where $\rho \geq 0$ is a constant discount rate. A numerical illustration will help to explore the basic rationale of constant discounting. Assume that $X(t)$ is an instantaneous utility function and that $A(t)$ is an exponential discount factor. For the sake of the argument, assume that utility $X(t)$ is constant and equal to some number (say, 100 "utils") and that it can be discounted at different rates, say 0%, 5% and 10%. From Figure 1, it is clear that when the discount rate is positive, the exponential discount factor assigns time-declining weights to the constant utility values over time. In addition, the weights decline faster the larger is the discount rate. In this example, in year 50 the constant utility stream of 100 accounts

Discount Factor

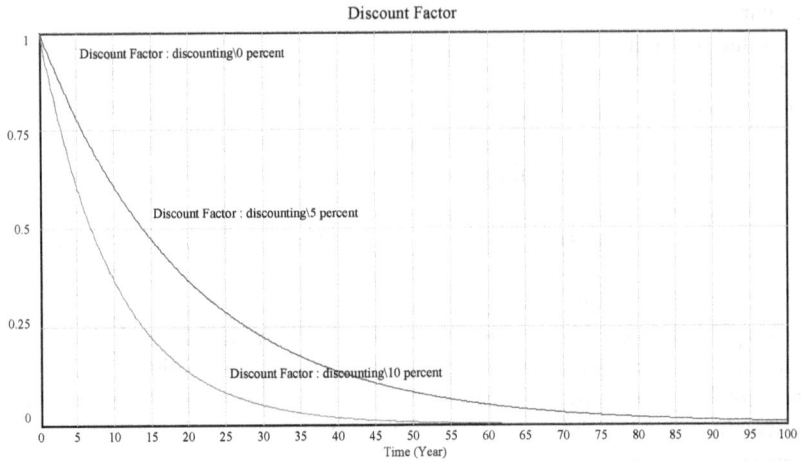

Figure 1 Distribution of weights in time under different values of constant discount
rates

for 8.2085 at a discount rate of 5%, and only for 0.6737 at the discount rate of
10%. It is also clear that a zero discount rate assigns an equal weight to the utility stream: in year 50, as well as in year 100, utility accounts for 100.

Even in this basic setting, we can observe the major implication of the discounting practice: the overall aggregated present value happens to be very sensitive to the election of the discount rate (see Figure 2). Discounting at a zero
discount rate allows for an always increasing "present value" index in which
the contribution from instantaneous utility to the infinite sum of any moment t
is just as equal as its contribution in any other moment t'. In this case, the integral (5) does not converge. In contrast, discounting at positive rates yields a
drastic difference on the convergence value of the sum. In this example, starting
at year zero, discounting at a rate of 5% makes expression (5) to converge to the
value of 2106 only by year 179 while discounting at 10% makes (5) to converge
to the value of 1106 by year 83. Instantaneous utility beyond those dates will
contribute with negligible amounts to the respective present values.

Some basic lessons can be learned from this example. First, we note that positive discount rates imply time-decreasing weighting of instantaneous values.
The larger the discount rate, the greater the velocity at which the discount factor declines. In addition, a zero discount rate assigns a constant weighting to instantaneous values. Secondly, in the case for a zero discount rate, the integral in
(1) does not converge to any particular value. The reason for this is that every
moment t contributes to the sum as well as any other moment t'. This is not the
case when using positive discount rates: The larger the discount rate the lesser
and the sooner the convergence value is observed. These results are of importance when the concern for intergenerational equity is taken into the analysis.
When dealing with constant instantaneous utility, the use of positive discount

Present Value

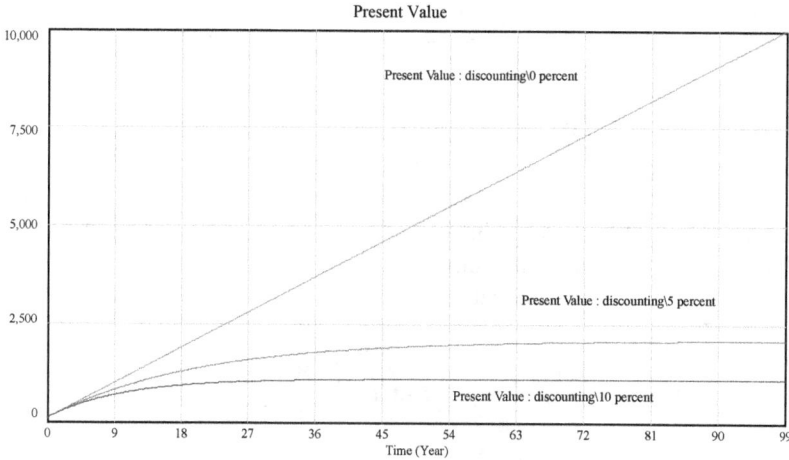

Figure 2 Aggregation of present values of a constant stream under different constant
discount rates

rate is criticized from ethical considerations and the use of a zero discount rate
is suggested. However, in scenarios in which utility is not constant due to a non-
constant path of consumption, then the choice for "the right" discount rate becomes a more complex issue.

Economists often claim that discounting the future at a zero discount rate
may be unjustified in scenarios in which per capita income is growing. In such
cases, the egalitarian treatment given to all generations implied by this practice
can be associated with a "Robin Hood activity stood on his head", to use the
words of Baumol (1968). In his view, this practice "takes from the poor to give
to the rich" (quoted in Philibert, 2003). Gollier (2002) presents a similar argument: "With a sure positive growth of the economy, we do not want to benefit
overmuch future generations who will enjoy a larger GNP per capita. Under decreasing marginal utility of consumption, one more unit of consumption in the
future is less valuable than one more unit of consumption today."

Since the egalitarian treatment of all generations may lead to sacrifices in the
present to ensure additional benefits for the future and richer generations, many
economists would say in the end what Schelling says: "Depreciating the consumption of high-income future makes sense" (Schelling 1995). To better illustrate these arguments we have to introduce the concept of the "social discount
rate". As it is commonly known, the social rate of discount is the aggregation
of two main concepts: the pure rate of time preference and a measure of how
consumption growth affects the instantaneous utility. Following Perman, et al.
(2003) and Heal (1998), we define the social rate of discount as the negative of

the rate at which the value of a small increment of consumption changes as its date is delayed.[1] Consider a particular form for expression (1):

$$\int_0^\infty e^{-\rho t} U(c(t)) dt \tag{2}$$

in which $U(\cdot)$ is a strictly concave utility function and $c(t)$ is per capita consumption. The value of a small increment in consumption is, simply, $e^{-\rho t} U'(c(t))$, where $U'(c(t))$ is the marginal utility from consumption. Then, the negative of the rate of change of this magnitude is

$$r(t) = \frac{\frac{d}{dt}[e^{-\rho t} U'(c(t))]}{e^{-\rho t} U'(c(t))} = \rho + \eta(c(t)) \frac{\frac{d}{dt} c(t)}{c(t)} = \rho + \eta(c(t)) \theta(t) \tag{3}$$

where $\eta(C(t)) = -\dfrac{U''(c(t))}{U'(c(t))} c(t)$, that is, the consumption-elasticity of marginal utility. Here, the term ρ, the "pure rate of time preference", is the utility-discount rate used in (2). If $\theta(t) > 0$, then the social rate of discount will be larger than the pure rate of time preference, meaning that an additional unit of consumption today is worth more that in the future, when consumption is much more abundant. Under this view, even after assuming an egalitarian treatment of instantaneous utility (see the 0% line in Figure 1), the scenario of growing per capita consumption allows for a positive social discount rate. However, in scenarios of constant per capita consumption rates the social rate of discount is equal to the pure rate of time preference. If the latter is positive, then the ethical problems may rise again.

III A model for estimation of the marginal damage costs of CO_2 emissions: Simulation and results

This section briefly presents the Azar and Sterner (1996) model for climate change, which we will refer to as the A-S model. They define the following function to capture the marginal cost of a unit emission of CO_2:

$$MC = \int_0^T G(t) \frac{\partial C(m_h)}{\partial m_h} V(t) dt \tag{4}$$

where $G(t)$ represents the fraction of a unit of CO_2 emissions today that remains in the atmosphere at time t, $C(m_h)$ relates global costs to anthropogenic carbon

---

1   Here, since it is preferable to work with positive numbers, we follow the conventional practice of defining the social discount rate as the negative of the rate of change of discounted marginal utility. For more on this, see Heal (1997 and 1998).

levels in the atmosphere, m_h, $V(t)$ is the present value function used to discount future values and T is the time period in which the damage is assumed to remain.

The carbon cycle

In his DICE model for climate change, Nordhaus (1991 and 1993) assumes that the fraction $G(t)$ follows an exponential behavior. In the A-S model, however, it is argued that the actual process of carbon removal in the atmosphere is much more complex. It is preferable to use the model for the carbon cycle presented by Maier-Reimer and Hasselmann (1987) since it captures the atmosphere-ocean interaction. They claim that in the long future, an equilibrium between the atmosphere and the ocean will occur such that 15% of the emitted carbon remains in the atmosphere. The response function for a unit emission can be approximated by:

$$G(t) = A_0 + \sum_{j=1}^{4} A_j e^{-\frac{t}{\tau_j}} \tag{5}$$

where $A_0 + \sum_{j=1}^{4} A_j = 1$

Azar and Sterner explain that the parameters depend on the emission scenario of CO_2: "The higher the accumulated emissions, the higher the fraction of a unit emission that remains in the atmosphere; the fraction of a unit emission that remains in the atmosphere when the atmosphere-ocean equilibrium is established, is as high as 30% for an emission scenario which stabilizes atmospheric concentrations at twice the pre-industrial level" (Azar and Sterner, 1996). Figure 3 plots the atmospheric carbon retention under the MRH-model for the parameters shown in Table 1 and the carbon retention under the exponential model using parameters from Nordhaus (1993). It is easy to see that, unlike Nordhaus exponential behavior, this model implies that about 20% of 1 unit emitted today is retained in the atmosphere even after 500 hundred years. The particular values for the A's and τ's are chosen to rather correspond to stabilization at relatively low accumulated emissions (1.25 times the pre-industrial levels).

Table 1 Parameters for the Carbon cycle model

A's	τ's (years)
$A_0 = 0.131$	---
$A_1 = 0.201$	$\tau_1 = 363$
$A_2 = 0.321$	$\tau_2 = 73.6$
$A_3 = 0.249$	$\tau_3 = 17.3$
$A_4 = 0.098$	$\tau_4 = 1.9$

Source: Maier-Reimer and Hasselmann (1987), taken from Azar and Sterner (1996).

Carbon retention

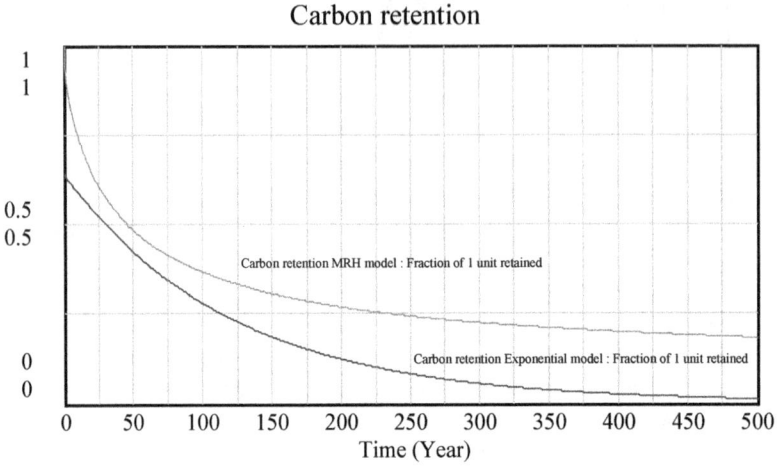

Figure 3 Atmospheric retention of CO_2: the MRH-model and Nordhaus model

The global costs function

Following the A-S model, we assume here that the damage function is given by

$$C(k, m_h, Y(t)) = k \frac{m_h}{m_p} Y(t) \qquad (6)$$

where m_h is the anthropogenic level of CO_2 in the atmosphere (160 Gton C), m_p is the pre-industrial level of CO_2 in the atmosphere (600 Gton C), k is the fraction of world income that will be lost for a CO_2-equivalent doubling (assumed to be equal to 1.25%)[2] and $Y(t)$ is the world income. The A-S model assumes that the world income follows the following logistic growth equation:

$$Y(t) = \frac{Y_\infty}{1 + \frac{(Y_\infty - Y_0)}{Y_0} e^{-\alpha_Y t}} \qquad (7)$$

where Y_∞ is the world income at "infinite time" ($8 \times Y_0$ USD per year), Y_0 is the world income at present time (2×10^{13} USD per year) and α_Y is the rate of growth of a small world income (3%). Figure 4 plots world income following equation (7).

Stabilization of world income at 16×10^{14} USD per year happens at 240 years hence. The particular values for the parameters of (7) are taken from Nordhaus's DICE model (Azar and Sterner, 1996). Equation (6) informs that carbon damage is a linear function of world income. In particular, this function implies that the

---

2   See Azar and Sterner (1996) and the debate surrounding the Stern Report for further discussion on this value.

World Income

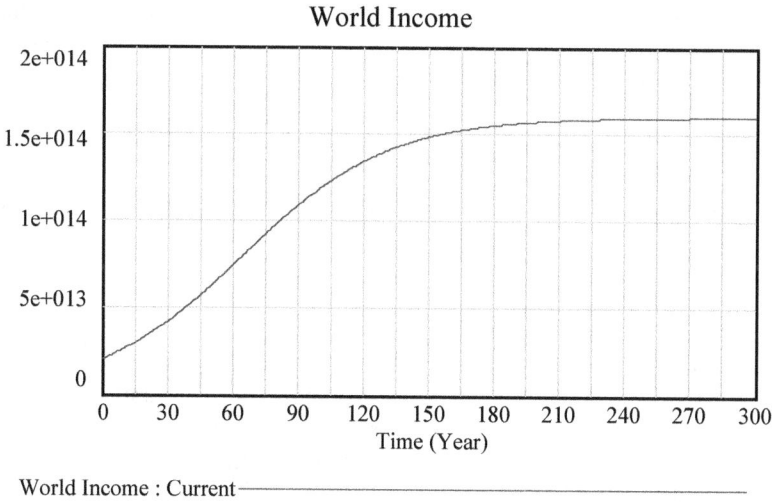

World Income : Current——————————————————————————

Figure 4 Evolution of world income under the logistic growth model

damage costs represent 0.004 dollars of every dollar of world income. Note that the A-S model assumes that this cost is not sensitive to the level on world income. If the carbon level does not change over time, the latter means that the graph of damage carbon costs *versus* time is a scaled-down version of the world income curve.

The present value function

The last element in equation (4) is the present value function, $V(t)$, used to discount the future value of marginal damage costs. As Ludwig et al.. (2005) and Weitzman (1998) explain, the relation between present value functions and discount rates is given by

$$V(t) = e^{-\int_0^t r(z)dz} \tag{8}$$

where $r(z)$ is a time-dependent discount rate.[3] Appendix A shows that if (3) defines the social discount rate, then the present value function is

$$V(t) = e^{-\rho t} \frac{U'(c(t))}{U'(c(0))} \tag{9}$$

---

3   Note that if $r(z)$ is constant, then the present value function is the discount factor $A(t)$ defined in (5), and its rate of change is the pure rate of time preference.

Now consider the special case in which the consumption-elasticity of marginal utility is equal to one. This leads us to assume $U(C(t)) = \ln[c(t)]$, which implies that equation (9) becomes

$$V(t) = e^{-\rho t}\frac{c(0)}{c(t)}\tag{9'}$$

Since $c(0)$ and $c(t)$ are per capita values, we can re-write expression (9') as

$$V(t) = e^{-\rho t}\frac{P(t)}{P(0)}\frac{C(0)}{C(t)}\tag{10}$$

where $P(t)$ is the world population at time t and $C(t)$ is the aggregated consumption at time t. We assume now that $C(t)=Y(t)$, that is, the consumption variable is equal to the world income. Following the A-S model, we finally assume that world population follows a logistic growth path. Formally, the population level at time t is determined by

$$P(t) = \frac{P_\infty}{1 + \dfrac{P_\infty - P_0}{P_0}e^{-\alpha_p t}}\tag{11}$$

where P_∞ is the stabilization population level (10.6 billion people) occuring at 300 years hence, P_0 is the present level of population (5.7 billion people) and α_p is the growth rate for small populations (2%). Again, the particular values for the parameters of (11) are taken from Nordhaus's DICE model.[4]

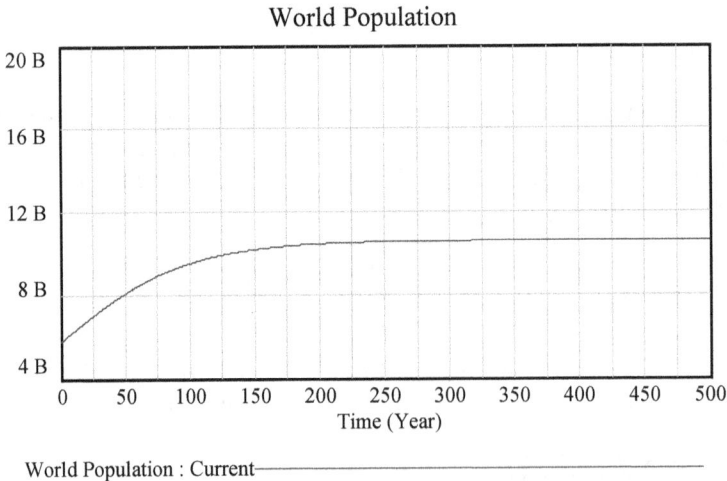

World Population

World Population : Current——————————————————

Figure 5 Evolution of world's population under the logistic growth model

---

4   The population level in 2006 is more than 6 billion people. However, to isolate the effect of the tests of next section, we keep the population level at 5.7 billion people.

Simulation of A-S model and results

The estimation of the marginal damage costs of carbon emissions is now straightforward. First, take the partial derivative of equation (6) with respect to the anthropogenic level of carbon concentration in the atmosphere:

$$\frac{\partial C(k, m_h, Y(t))}{\partial m_h} = \frac{k}{m_p} Y(t) \tag{6'}$$

Second, recall that $C(t) = Y(t)$. Finally, substitute equations (6'), (10) and (5) in equation (4) to obtain:

$$MC = \frac{k}{m_p} \frac{C(0)}{P(0)} \int_0^T e^{-\rho t} P(t) \left[A_0 + \sum_{j=1}^4 A_j e^{-\frac{t}{\tau_j}} \right] dt \tag{12}$$

Figure 6 shows the marginal damage costs calculated from (12) for a continuum of time horizons using the same discount rates reported in the A-S paper. We can observe the same pattern identified from Figure 2: The greater the discount rate the lesser and sooner the convergence of the integral in (12).

Starting at year zero and using a discount rate of 3%, we observe convergence of the marginal damage costs estimates by year 400 hence around the value of 12.8923 USD/ton. At the discount rate of 1%, convergence is observed at the value of 32.65 USD/ton only by year 870 in the future. Lower discount rates imply that the integral of (12) is still growing significantly (approximately at 5 cents per year) by year 1000, as it is observable. The following table compares the results reported in the A-S paper with the ones observed in this simulation. When not a perfect match, the simulation results are very close to those presented in the A-S paper.

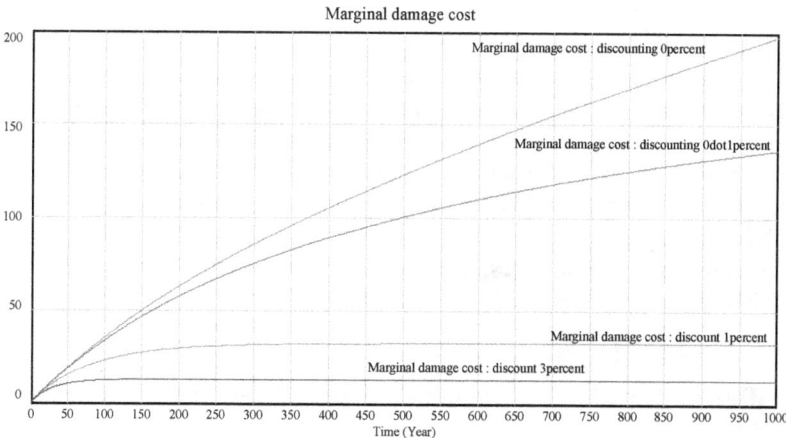

Figure 6 Estimates of the marginal damage costs of CO_2 emissions at different rates of constant pure rates of time preference

Table 2 Accuracy of simulation: The marginal cost of CO_2 emissions*

	Pure rate of time preference			
	0% per year	0.1% per year	1% per year	3% per year
Marginal cost of CO_2 emissions (A-S paper)	85–200	75–140	32–33	13–13
Marginal cost of CO_2 emissions (this study)	85.57–197.37	75.24–136.36	31.7–32.65	12.89–12.89

* The lower value is calculated using a time horizon of 300 years. The upper value is calculated using a time horizon of 1000 years.

It is convenient to summarize the main factors and processes that the A-S model captures. As Azar and Sterner properly explain, this model accepts the conventional estimates of the economic damage caused by increasing the CO_2 levels in the atmosphere. It is important to have in mind that these estimates do not take into account the risk of catastrophic events. Instead, the model presented here focuses on the next two issues: The process of retention of CO_2 in the atmosphere and the method for discounting future costs. Concerning the first issue, the A-S model represents a departure from the DICE model in the sense that it does not assume an exponential function for the retention process. This framework uses the model presented by Maier-Reimer and Hasselmann (1987) (see equation 5) because, in the opinion of the authors, it gives a more consistent treatment in the very long run (see Figure 3).

Concerning the second issue, Azar and Sterner argue that their method for discounting in fact represents a more ethically sound approach to the treatment for future costs. In what it seems to be the second important departure from the DICE model, the discount approach used in their framework relies in the concept of the social discount rate. In the previous section we explained that this rate is the aggregation of two things: the pure rate of time preference and a parametrical treatment (that depends on the degree of inequality aversion) of economic growth. The dynamic behavior of world income represented in Figure 4 suggests that the present value function of future costs actually decreases with time. They conclude that this discount method increases the aggregate cost of global warming very considerably. In fact, in Figure 6 it is visible that when the model uses low discount rates, the estimates of the marginal damage cost are still increasing in the very long run.

IV Discounting at a decreasing rate: Rationale, simulation and results

In this section, we study a different approach for the pure rate of time preference. Three main reasons are provided. The first one, the distribution of income over time, follows from the assumptions of the A-S model inherited from the DICE model. The logistic model for the behavior of world income yields a period of increasing income and then a period in which income is stabilized. The parameters used in the DICE model imply that income will be growing until it reaches a level that is bigger than actual world income by a factor of 8. Under these assumptions, generations of people living until 200 years from now will observe and enjoy consumption growth, while generations of people living beyond that date will observe income stabilization and relatively constant consumption paths. While the use of a positive (social) rate of discount may be justified for the treatment of the utility of people living from now to year 2200, it may be unethical for the period that starts at that date. In other words, the use of a constant positive value for the pure rate of time preference may not be the best practice for this scenario. Instead, a decreasing rate of time preference may be preferable.

The second reason: we aggregate the arguments provided by Gollier (2002) and Weitzman (1998 and 2001). Gollier investigates the relationship between the socially efficient discount rate and the time horizon if economic growth is exogenously determined and follows a random walk. The main motivation is "the difficulty in using the standard cost-benefit analysis with a constant discount rate for public investment projects whose costs and benefits are generated over a long period of time, as is the case for projects related to mitigating global warming, or for the management of nuclear wastes. Discounting far distant costs at the same rate as for the shorter term is equivalent to ignoring these long-term effects. Using discount rates that are decreasing with the time horizon would reduce the exponential effect of discounting." (Gollier, 2002). It is true that in the model presented in previous sections we are not assuming that income is following a random walk. The main argument that Gollier presents, however, is useful enough to motivate the use of a decreasing rate of time preference.

Weitzman gives similar points of view. In his 1998 paper, he says that "few are the economists who have not sensed in their heart of hearts that something is amiss about treating a distant future event as just another term to be discounted at the same constant exponential rate gotten from extrapolating past rates of return on capital. Indeed, there is experimental evidence that people generally discount the future at declining rates of interest. Responding to this kind of ambivalence have been various proposals to reconcile 'normal' discount rates for the near future and 'low' discount rates to the far future." Additionally, in his statistical analysis of 2001 of the opinions of over 2000 economists, Weitzman concludes that "the very widespread of professional opinion on discount rates means that society should be using effective discount rates that decline from a mean value of, say, around 4 percent per annum for the immediate future to around zero for the far-distant future. Furthermore, the decline in effective social discount rates is sufficiently pronounced and comes on line early enough, to warrant inclusion of this sliding-scale feature in any serious benefit-cost analysis of long-term environmental projects, like activities to mitigate the effects of global climate change" (Weitzman, 2001).

The third reason leads us directly to the discount method presented in this section. In the late nineties, Chichilnisky (1997) and Heal (1997 and 1998) highlighted the existence of empirical evidence on how people seem to treat the future.[5] "The period-to-period rate of discount is inversely related to the distance in the future. The experimental evidence shows the rate of discount between period t and $t+1$ decreases with t. Interestingly, studies of human responses to sound summarized in the Weber-Fechner law, indicate similar responses to changes in sound intensity." (Chichilnisky, 1997). The human perception of the "futurity" of any event, says the argument from these authors, declines as the event is delayed into the future. And while it is true that the experimental evidence of people behaving in that way does not mean that such findings are necessarily of normative or prescriptive value; it is also true that this approach, based on the Weber-Fechner law, provides a simple method of discounting that gathers many of the reasons exposed above, and that it is susceptible of incorporation into the model of previous sections.[6]

Geoffrey Heal (1997, 1998) and Graciela Chichilnisky (1997) suggest the use of the following discount factor:

$$A(t) = e^{\beta \ln(t)} \tag{13}$$

where β is a negative constant. Following an analogous procedure of that from previous sections, we define the social rate of discount to be the negative of the rate of change of the discounted value of marginal utility. Formally,

$$r(t) = -\frac{\frac{d}{dt}[t^\beta U'(C(t))]}{t^\beta U'(C(t))} = -\frac{\beta}{t} + \eta(C(t))\theta(C(t)) \tag{14}$$

where the first term is the decreasing pure rate of time preference and the second term is exactly the same as in equation (3). Appendix B proves that if (14) stands for the social discount rate, then the present value function is

$$V(t) = t^\beta \frac{U'(c(t))}{U'(c(1))} \tag{15}$$

Recall that $\beta < 0$. Figure 7 depicts the different weighting implied by this discount procedure. Comparison with Figure 3 shows the dramatic difference with the conventional exponential discount factor.

Analogous considerations to those in the preceding section concerning the particular form of the utility function lead us to write

---

5   The evidence reported includes the following literature: Lowenstein and Thaler (1989); Cropper, Aydede and Portney (1994) and Lowenstein and Elster (1992).

6   These authors do provide normative value to these experimental findings. See Heal (1998).

$$V(t) = t^\beta \frac{P(t)}{P(1)} \frac{C(1)}{C(t)} \tag{16}$$

Substitution of equations (6'), (16) and (5) into equation (4) leads us to the new model for estimating the marginal damage cost:

$$MC = \frac{k}{m_p} \frac{C(1)}{P(1)} \int_1^T t^\beta P(t) \left[A_0 + \sum_{j=1}^4 A_j e^{-\frac{t}{\tau_j}} \right] dt \tag{17}$$

The following simulation assumes four different values for the constant β. The main criterion for the election of those values is consistency with the previous simulation in the early years. Thus, when $\beta=-0.03$, $\beta=-0.01$, $\beta=-0.001$ and $\beta=0$ we have that the initial pure rate of time preference is 3%, 1%, 0.1% and 0%, respectively. Figure 8 shows the marginal damage costs from (17) for a continuum of time horizons using these different values of β.

First, notice that the estimates of marginal damage cost are less sensitive to the selection of those values. Additionally, the convergence behavior is dramatically different: for any of the values of β, the integral of (17) does not seem to converge to any particular number. In fact, at year 2000 hence, the marginal damage cost is increasing year to year in some value between 0.098 and 0.123 USD/tonC, depending on the value of β. This is clearly visible in Figure 7: By year 2000, the slope of the MC curve is practically equal in the four cases. Second, in comparison with the exponential discount factor case, the MC estimates fall in a shorter interval when a decreasing pure rate of time preference is used. The following table compares estimates in these two different cases for different values of the discount rate.

Decreasing Discount Factor

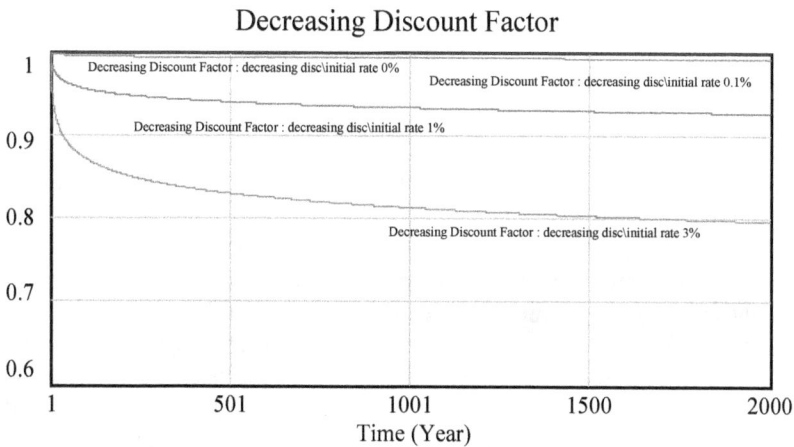

Figure 7 Distribution of weights in time under different values of decreasing discount rates

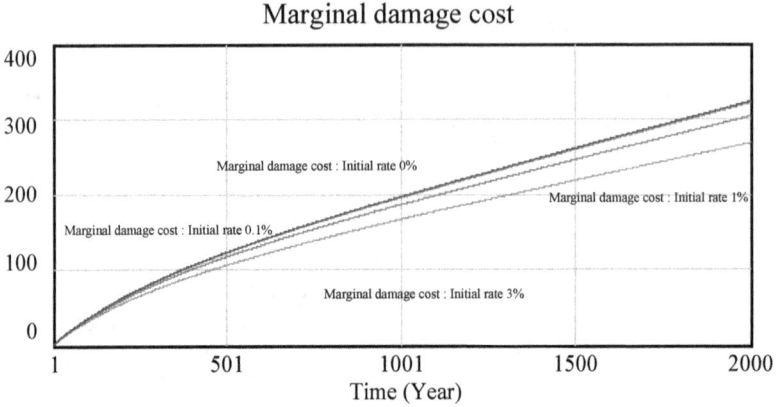

Figure 8 Estimates of the marginal damage costs of CO_2 emissions at different rates of decreasing pure rates of time preference

Table 3 The marginal cost of CO_2 emissions: different discount procedures*

	Pure rate of time preference				
	0	0.1%	1%	3%	Interval
Constant rate	85.57-197.37	75.24-136.36	31.7-32.65	12.89-12.89	72.68-184.48
Decreasing rate (Initial value)	85.07-196.84	84.69-195.77	81.31-186.20	74.31-166.64	10.76-30.2

* The lower value in each box is calculated using a time horizon of 300 years. The upper value is calculated using a time horizon of 1000 years.

The values reported in the last column of the table are the difference between the higher and the lower values for each time horizon among the different discount rates. The decreasing rate of pure time preference reduces substantially the uncertainty produced by the practice of discounting the future. Note also that the convergence of integrals of equations (12) and (17) is observable looking at the different values reported in both rows. Consider the case of a 3% discount rate: the difference between the MC estimates for year 300 and year 1000 is null if the estimation assumes constancy of that rate. In contrast, in the case in which a decreasing rate is used, we can see that the integral in equation (17) does not converge to any particular value in any of the cases studied. The second row of the table shows that the MC estimates are growing even when the initial discount rate is 3%. This phenomenon is also observable comparing Figure 8 and Figure 6.

V   Conclusions

The literature on the economics of climate change identifies the discounting practice as being one of the major sources of uncertainty in the estimation of the marginal costs of CO_2 emissions. After analyzing 103 estimates from 28 published studies, however, Richard Tol concluded that, albeit substantial, the uncertainty was not as large as some people think. It is unlikely, Tol says, that the marginal damage costs of greenhouse emissions exceed 50 USD/tonC. This is true when considering relatively short time horizons (say, 100 years from now). Yet 100 years from now is the minimum time horizon "that makes sense" in the context of climate change, and probably "it is too short", to say it with the words of Geoffrey Heal. The sensitivity analysis developed in this paper shows that looking further into the future means to observe how the uncertainty increases consistently. For instance, in 500 years from now, a discount rate of time preference of 3% yields an estimate close to 13 USD/tonC, while a 0.1% rate yields an estimate of 75 USD/tonC. The difference increases even more if one looks further: in 1000 years from now, the estimate calculated upon a 3% discount rate is still close to 13 USD/tonC, while the 0.1% estimate is 140 USD/tonC. At this date, an increase in 1% of the pure rate of time preference leads to a decrease of more than 150 USD/tonC in the cost estimate.

This striking behavior leads us to conclude that the uncertainty is relatively small in the near future, just as Tol says, but also that it increases substantially in the very long run, which is precisely the term at which we are forced to look in the context of global warming. This behavior is heavily driven by the rationale of exponential discounting at constant positive rates of pure time preference. As this paper shows, the present value of marginal damage costs converges sooner and at lesser numbers the larger the discount rate. This is why economists often claim that the conventional discount practice underestimates in great extent values happening in the very distant future. This is why economists are suggesting the use of alternative discount approaches, such as a decreasing rate of pure time preference.

Based on some of the arguments in the literature, this paper simulated a climate change model from the peer-reviewed literature and applied to it an alternative discount approach. A sensitivity analysis at different initial values of the discount rate shows an interesting behavior: First, at relatively small periods of time (say, one century hence), the estimates are similar to those from some models in the literature. However, unlike them, the estimates are still increasing if one looks further into the future. This paper showed that using a decreasing rate precludes the present value of the marginal costs to converge even at time horizons as larger as 2000 years hence. This behavior was already noticed in the application of a similar approach to the Nordhaus' model (Newell and Pizer, 2003).

The combination of two main factors may explain this behavior. In one hand, the model simulated here is not assuming an exponential behavior for the carbon retention on the atmosphere, as the Nordhaus' DICE model does (Nordhaus 2003). Instead, by using the Maier-Reimer and Hasselmann (1987) model for carbon cycle, which is claimed to represent better the atmosphere-ocean inter-action, we can see, for example, that about 18% of every unit of carbon emitted today will remain in the atmosphere even 5 centuries hence. On the other, the distribution of weights assigned to values happening in the distant future as-sociated to a decreasing rate of discount is dramatically different from the one associated to a constant discount rate. Under the method used here, over 80% of the actual values happening at 5 centuries from now are collected into the present value index under a decreasing rate starting at 3%, while only 0.67% of those values are collected at a constant rate of 3%.

Second, the uncertainty related to the discount practice is substantially re-duced. This paper showed that, assuming everything else is certain, using con-stant rates from 0% to 3%, the uncertainty interval for a time horizon of 300 years is close to 72 USD/tonC. Not surprisingly, the interval increases to 184 USD/tonC for a time horizon of 1000 from now. In contrast, the uncertainty interval is substantially reduced when using decreasing rates starting at values less than 3%. For a time horizon of 300 years, the range is only 10 USD/tonC; for a time horizon of 1000 it increases only to 30 USD/tonC. Two main virtues may arise from this study. The higher estimates for the distant future, and the lesser sensi-bility to ethical parameters, may help to reduce ambiguity in the promotion of mitigation policies in the present. Finally, the reduction of the sensibility of the marginal costs estimates to ethical parameter permits researchers focus more in others sources of uncertainty, like the aggregation of impacts among countries, a better understanding of the carbon cycle, or a better model for global damage costs due to a doubling in the CO_2 concentration in the atmosphere.

References

Azar, Christian and Thomas Sterner (1996). "Discounting and distributional conside-rations in the context of global warming," *Ecological Economics* 19, 169–184.

Baumol, William (1968). "On the Social Rate of Discount," *American Economic Review* 58 (4), 788–802.

Chichilnisky, Graciela (1997). "What is Sustainable Development?" *Land Economics* 73, 467–491.

Gollier, Christian (2002). "Time Horizon and the Discount Rate," *Journal of Economic Theory* 107, 463–473.

Heal, Geoffrey (1997). "Discounting and climate change. An editorial comment," *Climatic Change* 37, 335–343.

Heal, Geoffrey (1998). *Valuing the Future: Economic Theory and Sustainability.* Columbia University Press, New York.

Ludwig, Donald, William Brock and Stephen Carpenter (2005). "Uncertainty in Dis-count Models and Environmental Accounting," *Ecology and Society* 10(2).

Maier-Reimer, E. and Hasselmann, K. (1987). "Transport and Storage of CO_2 in the Ocean—An inorganic ocean-circulation carbon cycle model," *Climate Dynamics* 2, 63–90.

Newell, Richard and William Pizer (2003). "Discounting the distant future: how much do uncertain rates increase valuations?" *Journal of Environmental Economics and Management* 46, 52–77.

Nordhaus, William (1991). "To slow or not to slow: The economics of the greenhouse effect," *The Economic Journal* 101, 920–937.

Nordhaus, William (1993). "Rolling the DICE: an optimal transition path for controlling greenhouse gasses," *Resource and Energy Economics* 15, 27–50.

Nordhaus, William (1994). *Managing the Global Commons.* MIT Press, Cambridge.

Perman, Roger, Yue Ma, James McGilvray and Michael Common (2003). *Natural Resources and Environmental Economics.* Pearson Higher Education, United States.

Philibert, Cedric (2003). "Discounting the Future," Internet Encyclopaedia of Ecological Economics, International Society for Ecological Economics.

Schelling, Thomas (1995). "Intergenerational Discounting," *Energy Policy* 23, 395–401.

Tol, Richard (2005). "The marginal damage costs of carbon dioxide emissions: an assessment on the uncertainties," *Energy Policy* 33, 2064–2074.

Weitzman, Martin (1998). "Why the Far-Distant Future Should Be Discounted at Its Lowest Possible Rate," *Journal of Environmental Economics and Management* 36, 201–208.

Weitzman, Martin (2001). "Gamma Discounting," *The American Economic Review* 91, 260–271.

Appendix A

If $r(t) = \rho + \eta(C(t))\theta(t)$ is the social discount rate, where

$$\eta(C(t)) = -\frac{U''(C(t))}{U'(C(t))}C(t) \text{ and } \theta(t) = \frac{\frac{d}{dt}C(t)}{C(t)}, \text{ then the present}$$

value function is $V(t) = e^{-\rho t}\dfrac{U'(C(t))}{U'(C(0))}.$

Proof: First, integrate $r(t)$ from time zero to time t:

$$\int_0^t [\rho + \eta(C(t))\theta(t)]dt = \rho t - \int_0^t \frac{1}{U'(C(t))}dU'(C(t)) = \rho t - \ln\left[\frac{U'(C(t))}{U'(C(0))}\right]$$

Now, from the definition of present value function it follows directly that:

$$V(t) = e^{-\rho t + \ln\left[\frac{U'(C(t))}{U'(C(0))}\right]} = e^{-\rho t}\frac{U'(C(t))}{U'(C(0))}$$

Appendix B

If $r(t) = -\dfrac{\beta}{t} + \eta(C(t))\theta(t)$ is the social discount rate, where

$\eta(C(t)) = -\dfrac{U''(C(t))}{U'(C(t))}C(t)$ and $\theta(t) = \dfrac{\dfrac{d}{dt}C(t)}{C(t)}$, then the present

value function is $V(t) = t^{\beta}\dfrac{U'(C(t))}{U'(C(0))}$.

Proof: First, integrate $r(t)$ from time one to time t:

$$\int_{1}^{t}\left[-\frac{\beta}{t} + \eta(C(t))\theta(t)\right]dt = -\ln(t^{\beta}) - \int_{1}^{t}\frac{1}{U'(C(t))}dU'(C(t)) = -\ln(t^{\beta}) - \ln\left[\frac{U'(C(t))}{U'(C(1))}\right]$$

Now, from the definition of present value function it follows directly that:

$$V(t) = e^{\ln(t^{\beta}) + \ln\left[\frac{U'(C(t))}{U'(C(1))}\right]} = t^{\beta}\frac{U'(C(t))}{U'(C(1))}$$

3 Economics of Sustainable Energy Efficiency and Renewable Energy

Richard L. Ottinger

I will start my presentation with a brief summary of the principle points I will be making, followed by an elaboration of some of the most salient points.

Today, most selection and pricing of energy resources is relegated to the marketplace. This is so even in jurisdictions where energy resources, pricing and supply have not been privatized and remain largely a function either owned or regulated by governments.

Getting the prices right is critical to successful promotion of energy efficiency and renewable energy in market-dominated economies. Key factors include

1. **Subsidies:** eliminating existing and proposed multi-billion dollar direct and tax subsidies to coal, oil, natural gas and nuclear resources that distort the market in their favor and against efficiency and renewable energy investments;

2. **Lobbying Reform:** eliminating or at least controlling the lobbying contributions to the executive and legislature that underlie the granting of such subsidies and frequently lead to lax enforcement of enacted laws and regulations;

3. **Externalities:** including the externality costs to society from the environmental and health damages related to the mining, processing and combustion of fossil and nuclear fuels, through pollution taxes or regulatory requirements. These should include in the cost of petroleum fuels the military costs of maintaining their security of supply and the value of the risks of fuel insecurity and inadequacy of supply;

4. **Carbon Pricing:** with respect to pollutants contributing to global warming, establishing a market price for carbon and other greenhouse gas emissions either through a tax on such pollutants or through a cap and trade program, thus promoting efficiency and renewable energy investments in the marketplace because they involve negligible greenhouse gas emissions;

5. **Life Cycle Costing:** requiring that energy resource acquisition decisions be made on the basis of life-cycle costs since comparison on a first cost basis ignores the economic benefits of costless fuels over the life of efficiency and renewable resources;

6. **Decoupling:** decoupling of profits from sales in utility compensation to eliminate economic penalties for saving energy through efficiency measures; .and

7. **Utility Regulation:** in the case of electric and gas utilities, requiring access of renewable resources to the grid on a reasonable cost basis, instituting net metering, eliminating utility requirements for excessive costs for back-up power, eliminating unreasonable availability requirements for intermittent resources such as wind and solar energy, and crediting the high value of peak hour availability of solar energy.

The failure to consider these factors significantly distorts the cost comparison between efficiency and renewables on the one hand, and fossil and nuclear fuels on the other hand, and gives the latter a price advantage. Alone, government subsidization of fossil and nuclear fuels is a huge and widespread phenomenon, on the order of US$250 billion per year globally.[1] These failures call for removal of fossil and nuclear subsidies and justify intervention in energy markets in favor of efficiency and renewable resrouces where they persist.[2]

Other factors contributing to the price difference include the fact that fossil fuel infrastructure already exists, and was largely built with public funds,[3] whereas plants and infrastructure for renewables must be built now, and (in privatized energy sectors) at private cost. While there are no fuel costs for renewable and efficiency resources, start-up costs for renewables tend to be high.[4] The prices of equipment needed to construct renewable energy plants may also be increased by import duties.[5] Research and development funding for energy, which might help to reduce the cost of renewable technology, is largely spent on fossil fuels and nuclear technology.[6]

Furthermore, transaction costs in establishing a renewable energy production facility are often high compared to fossil fuel plants due to a lack of familiarity with their technology, siting, resource assessment, planning and financing needs on the part of developers, financial institutions and relevant regulatory authorities.[7]

Legal and regulatory barriers

Regulations and standards governing the power sector were designed for fossil fuels, and often discriminate against renewable fuels whether deliberately

1   *World Energy Assessment: Overview 2004 Update*, above note 6 at 72. See also discussion of subsidies in *Transitioning to a Renewable Energy Future* above note 14 at 44–45.

2   *National Policy Instruments: Policy Lessons for the Advancement and Diffusion of Renewable Energy Technologies Around the World*, above note at 3.

3   *National Policy Instruments: Policy Lessons for the Advancement and Diffusion of Renewable Energy Technologies Around the World*, above note at 22.

4   *Renewable Energy Policies and Barriers*, above at 4; *National Policy Instruments: Policy Lessons for the Advancement and Diffusion of Renewable Energy Technologies Around the World* above note at 1.

5   See for example the high import tariffs sought to be imposed on solar power equipment for a project in Bolivia, discussed in E7 (now E8) Renewable Energy Technology Diffusion (2003) at 19; report available at http://www.e8.org/upload/File/e7_Renewable_Energy_Technology_Diffusion_Final_Report.pdf (visited 12 April 2007).

6   *Changing Climates: The Role of Renewable Energy in a Carbon-Constrained World*, above note 2 at 14. *World Energy Assessment: Overview 2004 Update*, above note 6 at 72, notes that in 2000 only approximately 8% of the total of industrialized countries' energy research and development funding was spent on renewable energy research and development. IEA provides a similar figure for the period 1987–2002, in *Renewable Energy: Market and Policy Trends in IEA Countries* (2004) at 53, available at http://www.iea.org/Textbase/publications/free_new_Desc.asp?PUBS_ID=1263 (visited 12 April 2007).

7   *Renewable Energy Policies and Barriers*, above note at 5.

or not.[8] This is the case, to varying degrees, regardless of whether a country's power sector has been opened to competition. The sector tends to favor large enterprises running large, centralized power plants (the most cost-efficient types of fossil fuel plants).[9] However, many types of renewable energy do not fit this model well.

To start with, in privatized markets there may be no provisions allowing independent power producers to sell their power onto the grid, a crucial first step. Rules and charges for connecting to the grid may be unnecessarily difficult and expensive, particularly for intermittent energy sources such as wind and solar power (even though solar resources are often available at times of peak power needs).

For example, utilities may impose unreasonable interconnection requirements, such as excessive standby rates, high transmission access rates[10] and fixed unavoidable charges (which lengthen the payback period to intermittent resource providers), as well as intermittent-generator exit fees to compensate for stranded costs that are usually fictitious. Dispatchers often require commitments of availability and impose penalties for failure to comply that are unreasonable for intermittent resources. Government agencies may have excessively burdensome approval requirements for interconnection of intermittent resources. Small power generators may be required to obtain expensive liability insurance[11] or performance or payment guarantees,[12] out of proportion to the operator's size and increasing its transaction costs.

Dispatchers, utilities and government procurement regulations also fail to credit intermittent resources with the benefits provided, such as peak-load reduction, value added reseller support to prevent power surges, emissions reductions, fuel diversity and risk avoidance.

In addition, renewable power installations may have problems in obtaining siting and development approvals, due to lack of familiarity with such installations on the part of officials, financial institutions and authorities, complicated planning approvals and creating public misgivings.[13]

Other market distortions

Renewable energy projects often are perceived to have higher levels of failure risks (as compared to fossil fuel installations), making obtaining financing

8   *National Policy Instruments: Policy Lessons for the Advancement and Diffusion of Renewable Energy Technologies Around the World,* above note at 1.

9   J Pershing notes that this bias may be the result of implicit subsidies, in *Removing Subsidies: Leveling the Playing Field for Renewable Energy Technologies* (Thematic Background Paper, Bonn 2004) at 3 available at http://www.renewables2004.de/de/cd/default.asp (visited 12 April 2007).

10   *Renewable Energy Policies and Barriers,* above note at 5.

11   *Renewable Energy Policies and Barriers,* above note at 5.

12   *Does Electricity Market Regulation Contribute to Energy Sustainability?,* above note 13 at 227.

13   *Renewable Energy Policies and Barriers,* above note at 5. *Renewable Energy Technology Diffusion,* above note 5 at 8, also notes this issue.

more difficult or more expensive, particularly in developing countries.[14] The much greater costs of the risks of insecurity and inadequacy of supply are not usually taken into account at all.

There also is a lack of knowledge of and personnel trained in financing mechanisms to support renewable energy projects. However, the situation may be improving in this regard, as investors have become more comfortable with renewable energy projects over the last few years.[15]

Large, well-financed sales teams encourage traditional energy sources, and decision-makers may have a common financial stake in these sources. Perhaps as a result, many government, commercial and industrial officers prefer known fossil resources to newer renewable resources.[16] Banking and other financing officials may also share this preference. In contrast, renewable energy providers have few promotional resources, and few personnel are trained in renewable energy site assessment, equipment installation, operation and maintenance, making renewable eresource projects more difficult to sell, establish and maintain.[17]

On a different issue, project initiators and managers providing renewable energy programs for rural communities often fail to understand the energy and related social needs of those communities, and fail to adapt projects to meet these needs. If projects do not meet their intended local needs, renewable energy applications can be impeded for decades.

Indirect Measures: More Accurate Pricing of Fossil Fuels

A. Removing fossil-fuel subsidies

Removing subsidies for the production and use of fossil fuels can be very effective in reducing the price differential between renewables and fossil fuels, one of the most significant barriers to the greater use of renewable energy. Fossil fuel subsidies damage the environment both by encouraging increased use of fossil fuels and by discouraging the use of clean alternatives by making them less economically competitive.[18]

Governments usually grant fossil fuel subsidies under the pretext of protecting domestic jobs, promoting use of domestic resources, and protecting the poor from high energy prices. But in most developing countries, the poor receive virtually no benefit from the subsidies, and most benefits flow to corporations

---

14   See for example *Renewable Energy Technology Diffusion,* above note 5, at 8, 10, 11.

15   See *Renewables: Global Status Report 2006 Update,* above note 1 at 15.

16   *Renewable Energy Policies and Barriers,* above note at 6, use the phrase "lack of utility acceptance" [of renewable energy] to describe the "historical biases and prejudices on the part of traditional electric power utilities".

17   *Renewable Energy Policies and Barriers,* above note at 6. See also *Renewable Energy Technology Diffusion,* above note 5 at 12, 20.

18   *Reforming Energy Subsidies,* above at 9, 14.

and the wealthy.[19] It would be more efficient and far less costly to subsidize the energy needs of the poor directly than to subsidize fuels for all users.

Removing subsidies is not only a cost-free measure, but, by definition, it is a certain revenue-enhancing one. Revenues saved can be used to promote renewable energy alternatives. The problem in removing subsidies is political—recipients of subsidies lobby governments extensively against subsidy removal.[20]

The political difficulties of eliminating subsidies and the transition problems for local economies in fossil-producing countries cannot be minimized. Nevertheless, several diverse countries have reduced or eliminated fossil-fuel subsidies successfully, usually in slow increments and together with "safety nets" for those most affected.[21] Though difficult, it is possible—and essential.

B. Including externality costs: CO2 emission limits and trading schemes

No accurate assessment can be made of the comparative costs of clean energy without considering the substantial externality costs of fossil fuels. Therefore, as with removing subsidies, including externality costs into the price of fossil fuels (for example by setting emission limits, introducing an emissions trading scheme, or imposing a pollution tax) can promote efficiency and renewable energy by reducing the price barrier.[22]

C. Including externality costs: pollution taxes

Taxing pollutants or polluting fuels is an alternative method to make polluters pay the costs of the damage to society from their pollution. Such taxes raise the price of emissions-intensive goods and lower profits for fossil-fuel use, thus allowing market forces to encourage adoption of renewable resources. The money raised from the taxes can also be used to directly promote renewable resources.

Pollution taxes (including carbon emission taxes) have been imposed in Brazil, Denmark, Finland, Italy, Latvia/Lithuania, Sweden and the United Kingdom (which funds its Renewable Purchase Obligation subsidies with electricity taxes). The European Commission just has recommended that Europe adopt a common carbon **tax.**[23] Pollution taxes are politically difficult because inevitably they affect some energy-intensive industries and jobs. In a number of countries that have legislated such taxes, major industries have been exempted to avoid competitively disadvantaging domestic production. However, the competitive

19   *Reforming Energy Subsidies,* above note at 14.

20   *Reforming Energy Subsidies,* above note at pp. 23-24, 29.

21   *Removing Subsidies: Leveling the Playing Field for Renewable Energy Technologies,* above note 9 at 20.

22   *Transitioning to a Renewable Energy Future,* above note 14 at 45.

23   Horizon Solutions, *Special Report Global Climate Change: Economic and Market Mechanisms* available at http://www.solutions-site.org/special_reports/sr_global_climate_change_4.htm (visited 13 April 2007)

effects of pollution taxes may be able to be ameliorated in other ways, for example with reductions in other taxes.

Indirect Measures: Energy Market Reform and Regulation

A. Reforming energy market to introduce competition

In the last few decades there has been a general trend to reform national energy markets to introduce competition. This has had mixed results in terms of promotion of renewable energy, as restructuring will not further environmental and social goals unless specific regulations are introduced to safeguard them.[24] Some consider that restructuring has had significant negative effects on the environment.[25]

However, if environmental goals are considered at the outset, restructuring can be of benefit. When national energy markets are privatized, performance-based regulation tends to replace rate-of-return regulation for energy distribution companies. Performance-based regulation can encourage energy distribution companies to provide electricity efficiently and to promote the use of renewable energy, by rewarding performance measured against specific benchmarks.[26]

Some energy commissions have placed a price cap on utility charges, giving the utilities an incentive to keep costs low. However, a revenue cap is far superior because a price cap provides strong incentives for utilities to increase sales, thus discouraging efficiency and renewable investments.

B. Other energy market measures

Net metering laws are popular among many U.S. states and effectively provide for self-generated power, backed up by electricity distribution grid. When consumption exceeds the amount of power generated by the customer, power is sourced from the electricity distribution grid and the meter runs forward. When self-generation exceeds consumption, the meter runs backward. Customers are only liable for the amount of electricity used.[27]

---

24   P A Bradford, *Environmental Lessons From Electricity Restructuring* at 410 and R Lyster, *The Implications of Electricity Restructuring for a Sustainable Energy Framework: What's Law Got to do With it?* at 436, both in *The Law of Energy for Sustainable Development*, above note J Christensen notes that most national energy sector restructurings have not in fact paid much attention to environmental issues, above note at 13.

25   *The Implications of Electricity Restructuring*, above note 107 at 415.

26   *Regulatory Assistance Project, Performance-Based Regulation for Distribution Utilities 2* (2000), available at http://www.raponline.org/Pubs/General/DiscoPBR.pdf (visited 13 April 2007)

27   *Renewable Energy Gains Momentum: Global Markets and Policies in the Spotlight*, above note 75 at 35

Improving energy efficiency can also make renewable energy more attractive: as the demand for energy is reduced, the higher costs of renewable energy are more manageable.[28]

Other Measures Indirectly Affecting Renewable Energy

A. Rationalizing investment and import restrictions

Many developing countries impose high duties on equipment imports, including equipment required for renewable energy. If renewable energy use is to be promoted, these duties must be eliminated or reduced, as must many restrictions on investment of foreign capital.[29] Import duties on wind turbines have been successfully waived in Pakistan.[30]

B. Improving legal framework to encourage investment

In many developing countries, legal institutions are not sufficiently developed, or not strong enough or well enough resourced, to support environmental policies and give investors confidence that agreed projects will be able to be completed.[31] In these cases enacting direct renewable energy laws will not be of much assistance, and governments will first need to lay the groundwork by ensuring the legal system is respected and enforced, and contains the appropriate mechanisms to encourage innovation and investment.[32] This may include corporations law, intellectual property law,[33] laws on the movement of capital and information, and anti-corruption laws. To help support micro-finance, a separate legal framework such as a micro-credit regulatory commission may be useful.[34]

---

28   *National Policy Instruments: Policy Lessons for the Advancement and Diffusion of Renewable Energy Technologies Around the World,* above note at 24.

29   For example see *National Policy Instruments: Policy Lessons for the Advancement and Diffusion of Renewable Energy Technologies Around the World,* above note at 19.

30   *Renewables: Global Status Report 2006 Update,* above note 1 at 9.

31   See inter alia I Tellam, *Energy: From Economic Input to Human Right,* 2 (December 2004, Volume 1) at 7, available at http://www.energycommunity.org/2.pdf (visited 13 April 2007)

32   See for example *Energy Development and Utilization in Africa,* above note at 359, 369; *Renewable Energy Technology Diffusion,* above note 5 at 6, 28.

33   See on the importance of IP laws Deploying Climate-friendly Technologies through Collaboration with Developing Countries, above note 67 at 32.

34   S Khan, Micro-credit Needs a Legal Framework, Financial Express, May 2006, available at http://www.financialexpress-bd.com/index3.asp?cnd=5/7/2006&section_id=5&newsid=23705&spcl=no (visited 13 April 2007). The importance of an "enabling framework" is also mentioned by Soluz Inc president in *Power to the People: Plugging Developing Nations into Renewable Energy,* above note 68.

4 Framing Bias or Social Constructionism?

How Does Framing Affect Environmental Valuation?

Joshua Frank

ABSTRACT

Relatively little attention has been given in economics to a social constructionist perspective compared to the extensive attention it has received in other social sciences. A general social constructionist approach to economic market value is outlined here. A distinction is made between a superficial view of a social construction (such as the rules and customs of an exchange) and a deeper view of social constructions as shaping our reality at a subtle and pervasive level.

The focus here is also firmly on the application of a social constructionist perspective to economic markets and its real implications for market decisions and transactions rather than "theorizing about theorizing". In particular, environmental value is used as an example of applying a social constructionist perspective. The impact of this perspective on both environmental valuation and environmental decision-making (given valuations) is analyzed.

Introduction

The comedian-magician team of Penn and Teller have a show on the Showtime pay television network called "Bullshit!" in which they debunk pieces of popular wisdom they deem questionable. In one particular piece they challenge assumptions regarding consumer food preferences by taking us behind the scenes to show us the creation of amusingly low quality dinner combinations (such as poorly-prepared TV dinner items) that they serve with much ado in an ostensibly expensive and very high quality restaurant. Those customers who are not in on the gag (and who are chosen for their alleged gourmet tastes) almost universally judge the food to be of very high restaurant quality. Before informed of its true origins, the diners claim to have received very high utility from the food. One could argue that this is a case of psychological bias. But did they actually receive low utility and were deceived by the context in estimating their utility? Or are people's prejudices of certain types of prepared food unjustified and the

dishes actually are capable of providing high utility? A more satisfying explanation is that the utility of that meal is highly dependent on social context and
cannot be said to exist in a meaningful way absent of its context. More broadly,
while a specific amount of utility may be received from consumption of a good
or service, it is not meaningful to talk of the utility received as an amount
independent of a social context. The utility received is not a given, rather it is
socially constructed. Furthermore, the ad hoc and post hoc estimation of that
utility (one step removed from the actual utility received) also are dependent on
social context, even when the utility is assumed to be fixed.

Utility is not nearly as accessible as economic theory typically assumes.
Even after the fact, we have a great deal of difficulty accurately assessing the
utility we received from consuming a product or service. How much utility did
we get from that last hamburger? Or that big screen television? Can we really
meaningfully compare the two even after consumption, i.e. how may hamburg-
ers are equivalent in satisfaction provided to a big screen television? If we do,
those comparisons depend a great deal on how that consumption experienced
is framed for us.

Psychological vs. Sociological "Frames"

Those economists that are familiar with framing affects most likely know it
from behavioral economics, and in particular the work of (Tversky & Kahneman, 1981), which in turn takes the concept from psychological theory. With
psychological framing, contextual information can affect affect economic decisions by distorting assessments of alternatives or preferences. For example, if
the results of an experimental medical treatment are "framed" in terms of the
number of people expected to be "saved", this results in different preference
than when that same treatment is framed in terms of the number of people expected to die, even when the results are arithmetically the same. Assessments
of probability are also sensitive to the manner in which a scenario is "framed".
These frames can also be important for environmental valuation. For example,
providing information regarding species or wilderness areas can impact how
they are valued in a contingent valuation survey. Providing visual images of
the areas or species at risk also has been shown to impact valuation on surveys
(Anderson, 2003). Furthermore, placing several other willingness to pay questions on a survey before an environmental contingent valuation question can
also alter the results of that question.

But this psychological concept of framing is a cognitive process, which re-
moves framing from its social context. Furthermore, most discussions of psychological framing treat it as a distorting force, causing deviation of choice
from an objective truth. Thus it implicitly assumes the presence of an underlying "objective" reality.

However, there is also a sociological concept of a frame. These frames are
the social constructions that are the backdrop for all of our perceptions and

choices. Frames, from a social constructionist perspective, are socially defined boundaries that define what we perceive and how we perceive it. Also, and importantly, they define what we *exclude* from our perceptions. We learn ways of perceiving, thinking and being in the world from society around us. We then internalize these social constructions, often treating them as if they are objective truth. The language we learn also plays an important role in framing and defining our world. These frames are grounded in a view of the world that is taken for granted (Berger & Luckman, 1966). At times we may be able to focus on questioning these assumptions about our world. However, in order to function day to day in society, we must suspend our disbelief and take our socially constructed world for granted as reality. From this perspective, we always perceive through frames. The socially constructed concept of a frame also rejects the notion of variance from the objectively optimal decision. If there even is any such thing as an objective optimum, it is too inaccessible to be meaningful. The concept of a socially constructed frame is both deeper and richer than the cognitive/behavioral concept most economists are familiar with.

The concept of "deep" social constructionism

Economists have some understanding of the importance "social constructions", but only at a superficial level. Most economists would probably recognize, for example, that a nexus of trade such as the NASDAQ stock exchange, a set of rules for labor-firm market interaction such as the resume submission/interview process, and social institutions such as our legal system concerning the disposition of property are all vital to economic functioning and are all "social constructions". While these socially constructed institutions and their implications for economic functioning are important, mainstream contemporary economic theory has almost completely neglected a deeper sense of how our world is socially constructed.

What will be called here "deep" social constructionism is epitomized by the case presented in Berger and Luckmann's book *The Social Construction of Reality* (1966). According to the authors, the entire reality of our world that we often take for granted as objective truth is socially constructed. Even what we think of as our "raw" perceptions are really interpretations. Even when looking at simple object for example, at a wooden door, we normally perceive it as a "door" or "wood" and may make further interpretations in our initial perceptions regarding quality, function, etc. rather than perceiving it as the pure sensory pattern of textures, shape, and color that it is. "Deep" social construction is defined here as those social interactions and building blocks that define our world at the very basic level. This is quite different than the "superficial" social constructions that make up the surface-level social institutions which generally economists acknowledge as important to economic functioning. Other disciplines, including both social sciences (such as sociology and history) and

Deep and Absolute Dimensions of Social Constructionism

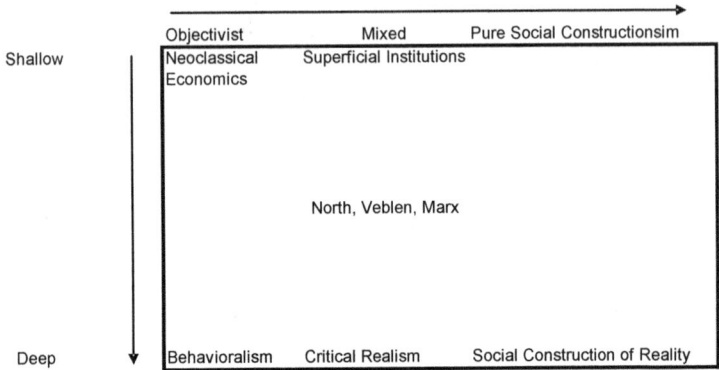

	Objectivist	Mixed	Pure Social Constructionsim
Shallow	Neoclassical Economics	Superficial Institutions	
		North, Veblen, Marx	
Deep	Behavioralism	Critical Realism	Social Construction of Reality

Figure 1

humanities (such as literature) have devoted much attention to how our reality is socially defined. This concept has the potential to be equally important to economics, and has important implications in particular for how we value and make decisions regarding the environment.

In other social sciences, there is ongoing debate regarding how much of our reality is objective and how much is purely subjective. The purpose here is not to make any claim that the world is "purely" subjective and that there is no objective reality. Rather, the argument being made is that the world is "deeply" socially constructed, meaning that socially defined frames affect our perspectives and our decision-making at the most basic level and in a pervasive manner, though they may not absolutely define our world. Figure 1, differentiates depth and absolutism into two dimensions, and showing the location of some schools of thought in these dimensions. One school of thought shown in the figure is critical realism. Critical realism draws its origins from Bhaskar (1987) and has been expanded into economics by others such as Lawson (1998) and does address the deep layers of social constructions that define our reality. It seeks to stake a middle ground between viewing our world as completely subjective and the naïve view of a completely objective reality. Some theorists outside of the neoclassical school, particularly institutionalists, have acknowledged the deeply socially constructed nature of economic value and economic decisions, but the extent of this has varied.

Argument for a "Social Construction of Economic Value"

A consumer is considering purchasing a big screen plasma television for approximately $1500. What causes them to decide whether or not to purchase this good? A traditional economic perspective assumes the consumer compares the expected utility obtained from that purchase to all other possible options.

But even ignoring all of the information shortfalls regarding malfunction rates, future technology options, unexpected expenses that may require that money, etc., at the most basic level, such a relatively simple utility comparison likely is not done and cannot be done. Can the consumer truly accurately assess, for example, the utility they will get from consuming one $1.50 hamburger a day for the next three years to the utility of the improved viewing experience of the new television? Behavioral economics can make some claim to accounting for bias that may occur in comparing these options, for example, through improper discounting. However the concept of "bias" central to this more traditional behavioral perspective strongly implies a perturbation from some objective value. While psychology-based behavioral economics considers cognitive limits and errors in judgment, it typically relies on a concept of underlying objectivity and a "right" answer for the consumer (though they may not always reach this right answer). However, a "social construction of economic value" perspective assumes that there may be no useful answer to this question.

The concept of social dependency in consumption is not new. Veblen's uses the term conspicuous consumption to describe economic choices that depend on what consumption implies regarding our social class. But this is only one of many dimensions of social dependency. The utility we receive from consuming a good privately and detached from any social class connotations also depends on a socially constructed frame. And our interpretation of that utility (ad hoc and post hoc) also depends on a socially constructed frame.

Some economists may concede that this could be true for utility which is a internal, subjective experience. However, many economists would argue that firm decisions are more objectively grounded. It is argued here that this is not the case. While some economic valuations might be completely socially constructed, for other economic valuation questions there may be an objective underlying truth. However, even when they do exist, these true values may be inaccessible even to experts because of our inability to separate ourselves from our socially defined reality. Experts are arguably just as subjective in their view of risk as laypeople. Regardless of the expertise of the judger, truths do not exist independent of people and their social context, and bias, irrational action, and narrow interest group behavior affect the judgment of experts (Otway & Thomas, 1982; Plough & Krimsky, 1987). Scientific facts are not really facts at all, but rather, are inseparable from the course of scientific inquiry which creates them (Lynch, 1985). This social constructionist perspective need not be absolute to be deep and pervasive enough to largely define our economic choices.

One assumption neoclassical economists sometimes make is that even if some firms have distorted perspectives, competition will week out any "irrational" decision-making (for example in Alchian, 1950; and Friedman, 1953). But this of course assumes that there is an objectively "optimal" decision in every situation. Furthermore, natural selection does not exclusively favor the organizational perspectives that fit best with the external environment. Each organization has its own set of beliefs or "myths", and their fit with the institutional environment has survival value in itself. These myths may be taken for granted as legitimate and can have value to help an organization survive, aside from any impact they have on work outcomes (Meyer & Rowan, 1991). Furthermore, the concept of an optimal decision takes for granted that firms are in the business of making decisions, while a social constructionist perspective not only challenges which decisions will be made, but whether an organization even makes decisions at all. The entire concept of "decision-making" may be an inaccurate representation of what managers do. Actors in organizations who believe they are making decisions may actually be acting according to institutional behavioral scripts. Their thinking is being guided by mental schemas which are dependent on their social environment (DiMaggio, 1997; Powell & Dimaggio, 1991). After managers and firms take actions based on institutional scripts or standard operating procedures, they then reinterpret their actions in terms of decision-making. This is done after the fact in order to rationalize their actions (Laroche, 1995).

Implications for the environment

Those seeking to influence public opinion and policy are aware of the impact of socially-constructed frames on valuation of the environment. For example, it is no accident that those arguing for or against drilling in Alaska's ANWAR describe the benefits in different ways. The amount of oil potentially available in this wildlife refuge has been at times put in the context of the number of days of oil use that it would meet all of the United State's consumption, or that it would provide "enough oil to eliminate imports from" some specific, possibly unstable, foreign country, or taking into account the likely retrieval rate, it would provide X% of our oil needs for Z years. These and other ways of presenting the potential level of oil of drilling in ANWAR give quite different impressions of the benefits. Advocates are equally careful when publicly framing ANWAR's environmental costs. Another recent example of framing debate on environmental issues is the changing terminology regarding the rising average temperature of the Earth. "Climate change" is being used by many rather than "global warming" based on the conclusion that "global warming" may create a pleasant and benign impression that is inconsistent with the potential catastrophic consequences of rapidly rising temperatures across the planet.

In general, the implications of a social constructionist approach to the environment can be split into two broad categories: (1) its impact on the valuation of the utility of the environment compared to its alternatives and (2) evaluating risks and optimal decisions given the utilities of outcomes. More generally, this is the distinction between means and ends. It is argued that both economic ends (i.e. the utility received from a good or service), and economic means to ends (i.e. the decisions of economic actors considered to be optimal given the utilities of outcomes) are deeply (though perhaps not absolutely) socially constructed.

An example of a question addressing the economic "ends" for a consumer would be: "how much utility did I get from walking in the woods?" (or eating a hamburger, or any other consumption activity. Clearly, as previously discussed, social context is relevant to the answer. For a firm, a question regarding economic ends might be "is our current rate of return 'good'"? While the rate of return itself might be considered objective (though this is debatable as well), the evaluation of that rate of return depends on socially-defined frames.

For a consumer, questions about means to an end might concern risks, such as what is the health risk of purchasing a home in an area with air or groundwater pollutants. They might also concern decisions where information is scarce or costly, such as whether it is worthwhile to install solar panels in a home or take energy conservation measures. These and virtually every other decision consumers make regarding how to reach their utility goals depend on the socially-defined frames within which they make their decisions. Firms are also highly influenced by social frames in their means to reaching predefined goals (such as a given profit level). Firms must evaluate the risk that the potential side-affects of their production process will result in harm that leads to liability for the firm. Energy firms must evaluate the future availability of fossil fuel supply sources and the future constraints that may have to work under due to international politics and public action caused by climate change concerns. A variety of firm decisions that are key to environmental outcomes will depend on socially constructed frames and their influence on decision-makers.

Social Construction of Environmental Valuation

There are any number of social factors that will affect how the environment is valued. Two will be the focus of the discussion here. The first is the role of the media and claims-makers on environmental valuation. The second is the role of social cues.

Before discussing how these valuations may be influenced by socially-defined frames, it is important to recognize that the scope and depth of what a social constructionist perspective to economics may imply goes far beyond what is discussed here. Such a perspective implies that our world view is socially-defined in ways we often take for granted. Perhaps we cannot even recognize many of these assumptions. The analysis here starts by looking at how social constructs determine environmental valuation. This implicitly assumes that monetary valuation of the environment is possible and appropriate. This method of weighing environmental costs and benefits against the production of other goods and services should not necessarily be taken for granted. However, others have raised the point previously regarding whether this type of valuation is possible (for example, Vatn & Bromley, 1994 among others argue against monetary valuation of environmental resources). Therefore, the discussion here will start with the presumption that monetary valuation of the environment is possible and even desirable and proceed to the question of what a social constructionist perspective can tell us about how these valuations are made.

Role of "Claims-makers" and the media in environmental valuation

In constructing social problems such as environmental debates, sociology emphasizes the role of "claims-making activities". Often these claims-makers are advocates on both sides of a public policy debate who seek to frame the issue from a perspective favorable to their cause. However, firms seeking to sell their goods and services are also "claims-makers". They are seeking to influence public perceptions and public choices to increase the number of people purchasing their products. In fact, if money, manpower, and other resources are used to measure the power of claims-makers, then for-profit firms have far more influence on the public than non-profit advocates and government employees.

When economists try to place an economic value on the environment, they typically do so using dollars or other currency as a unit measure. However, economists also recognize that currency is a medium of exchange and those units of measure are only meaningful relative to the goods and services that they can purchase. Therefore, environmental valuation is actually occurring relative to alternative goods and services that can be purchased in economic markets. The valuation of the environment is a relative measure. If the value on average of non-environmental goods and services produced by firms increases, then the relative value (in real terms) of the environment declines.

Valuations of the environment in monetary terms are made in two general contexts. Either economists force a comparison (for example through the use of contingent valuation surveys), or those comparisons are made implicitly by economic agents (for example by choosing pay for a home with access to certain environmental amenities or lack of environmental "bads" like pollution, or by choosing to pay to travel to and use an environmental resource). In either case, the agent compares the environmental goods to the general bundle of goods and services which are exchanged for money in the market to ascertain an appropriate price. Since these other goods and services are exchange for money in the market, they almost universally provide some economic agent with a monetary benefit. In other words, they each have an advocate or a "claims-maker". The messages from these claims-makers for non-environmental goods and services bombard us constantly through advertising and other marketing efforts.

While neoclassical economists may debate the role of advertising in "informing" consumers versus changing their preferences, the general perspective of other social sciences is clear. Media messages have influence and the activities of claims-makers socially construct our reality in important ways. Firms seek to maximize the market value of what they produce and devote a significant portion of their budget to delivering messages that socially construct consumer values in a favorable manner.

There are a number of pro-environmental "claims-makers". These groups do work to promote the environment. However, these groups do not have the benefit of receiving a market price for environmental goods and services that they can reinvest in marketing their product. Instead, these groups generally function within the non-profit sector. While the efforts made by these organizations should not be minimized, the resources they have available to them is very small relative to the resources devoted to promoting goods and services sold by for-profit firms. In fact, all of the resources devoted to influencing public perceptions about the environment combined by all pro-environmental claims-makers are dwarfed by the marketing resources of even a single very large corporation such as McDonalds, Exxon, or WalMart. This is true whether one looks at money, human resources, media output, or some other measure of resources or output.

The fact of the matter is that for valuation purposes, all alternative uses of money are the "competition" for defining environmental value, and that through the normal functioning of free markets, virtually all of these alternatives have powerful and dedicated advocates. While there are some dedicated advocates for the environment, their resources are very small relative to the alternatives. The resources devoted to environmental advocacy are also very small relative to even a conservative valuation of the goods and services provided by the environment. Therefore, if valuation for goods and services is in large part socially constructed through the claims-making activities of economic agents, then the environment will be relatively undervalued. This undervaluation occurs because the environment lacks a comparably funded claims-maker to similarly aid in the construction of value.

Role of Social Cues in Environmental Valuation

An important premise of the social construction of value is that assessing utility received and arriving at a value for goods and services is far more complex than neoclassical economic theory suggests. This is especially true when the goods and services themselves are inherently complex as is the case with the environment. When faced with complexity in valuing goods and services, economic agents will rely in to a large extent on the social cues they receive. One of the most powerful social cues we receive regarding how things should be valued is price itself. This is part of what led to high perceived utility in the anecdotal experiment by Penn and Teller referred to in the introduction. Regardless of whether the experimental subject or the "plant" in the dining couple was paying the bill, the experience was made to replicate an upscale restaurant dining experience, and the implied price that was socially communicated by the setting no doubt had much to do with the fact that the subjects estimated that they received a high utility from the food product.

Two known economic concepts are related to the impact of market price as a signal of value, but neither captures the phenomenon completely. One is Veblen's (1899) concept of conspicuous consumption, where price leads goods to be valued higher based on their use as social signals. In this case price itself can cause increased value to consumers. This is one important type of social signal produced by price, and it can have environmental implications because environmental goods (except for extravagant vacations to exotic environments) tend not to lend themselves to conspicuous consumption. This might decrease their valuation relative to alternatives that do lend themselves to conspicuous consumption. However, conspicuous consumption does not fully capture the signaling importance of price. With conspicuous consumption, social status is the driver of higher valuations for high-priced goods. But what about the Penn and Teller scenario? The cause of the increase in utility was probably not motivated by social status considerations. It was simply an implied quality signal provided by the price. Of course, social status does play some role in that somebody who wants to be thought of as having a discerning palate may not want to give an assessment of food that makes them appear ignorant of the subtleties of fine cuisine. But it is likely that even if the subjects were assessing food anonymously and dining alone, they would still be influenced by the signals produced by price and restaurant ambience into rating the quality of the food itself higher than they otherwise would. This influence is about the signal that *price gives directly to the consumer* rather than about the signal *price makes from the consumer to others in their social circle.*

The other related economic phenomenon is "anchoring" (Tversky & Kahneman, 1974). Anchoring occurs when economic agents cling to an initial value and do not adjust enough in altering that value. To use an environmental valuation example, take a contingent valuation survey asked one group of people whether they are willing to pay $5 to preserve a wilderness area and then followed this up with an open-ended question asking just what is the most that respondent would pay. A second group of respondents is asked whether they are willing to pay $200 to preserve a wilderness area and then given the same open-ended follow-up question. According to the anchoring concept, the first group of consumers would end up with a lower average willingness to pay in the follow-up question than the second group of respondents, since the first number arbitrarily provided to them will affect their final answer. Market prices as "anchors" are an important way that they can affect final value. However, though this distinction is subtle, the anchoring concept is cognitive, and fails to take into account the social nature of the signal. Early experiments in anchoring studied the impact on decisions of random numbers that varied from person to person such as the last four digits of a social security number or a home phone number. In the experiments, the subject contemplates (on their own) these personal numbers, and then formulates a response in relation to these numbers. Prices, on the other hand, have the added trait of being a social consensus, and therefore may be more powerful than a random cognitive anchor. The judgments of others have been shown to be very influential in altering the estimations of experimental subjects. For example, Sherif (1937) showed that estimates of how much a light moved in a dark room converged toward a group norm, even when the norm was false. When people are making choices under uncertain circumstances, it may make sense to reduce the errors in their own estimates, by "hedging" using the estimates of others. For consumers facing complex and uncertain valuations of goods and services, market prices can be a useful social signal indicating the value others place on those consumption options.

Price then provides an important signal in three different ways relevant to environmental valuation. First, it provides a social status signal from the consumer to others in the Veblenian sense. Second, it provide a cognitive (non-social) anchor for value. And third, it provides a social signal for how others value a good or service. Aside from any social status considerations, this creates a norm for individuals in their own valuations.

Environmental goods tend to often be provided for free or at low cost. On the other hand, other goods and services are typically provided at a higher, profit-maximizing price for the producer. Therefore, a powerful price signal is sent regarding environmental goods. This signal plays an important role in socially constructing the value of the environment, both in terms of how utility is converted into a monetary valuation, and in how utility itself is conceived. Goods provided for free, such as many environmental goods and services, will have their perceived value reduced as a result of their price (or lack of a price) in the market. These include environmental amenities such as clean air, clean water, a walk in the woods, wildlife, a stable climate, etc.

The Social Construction of Environmental Decision-making

Social frames define not only the values we give to the environment, but how economic agents make decisions given the environmental valuations they perceive. Even when the monetary value of the environment in a specific period is taken as given, environmental decisions still involve weighing complex issues such as time discounting, equity, and intrinsic value, and risk. Social constructions effect how (and whether) we discount flows of money, benefits, and costs in the future. They affect how we value equity issues and how we treat intrinsic value, such as the existence value of animals, species, and ecosystems.

Even firms that make decisions with "objective" criteria such as maximizing profit are subject to social construction in their decision-making. The decision-making analytic tools themselves such as discounted net present value, payback period, cost-benefit analysis, and others may appear objective, but their use is socially prescribed and socially defined. Furthermore, there are a number of factors that can be added optionally into such models, factors that must be roughly estimated, and factors that must be included qualitatively outside of a model—how all of these are treated is subject to social construction.

One aspect of the social construction of decision-making that may be especially relevant for environmental issues is the social construction of risk. Frank & Carlisle-Frank (2007) discusses how the discipline of economics fails to consider the socially-constructed nature of risk estimation by firms, and concludes that their data and interviews with firms regarding insurance risk and dog breed are more consistent with a sociological perspective of risk analysis than an economic perspective. Sociologists increasingly view risk as socially constructed rather than something which can be objectively measured (Tierney, 1999). Risk is thought of as embedded in a social structure (Stallings, 1990). Risk does not exist independently from the human observation of risk and its social construction. Perceptions of risk depend on social representations. These social representations define our way of viewing the world and the events that take place (Kirby, 1990). From a pure social constructionist perspective, scientific facts are not really facts at all, but rather, are inseparable from the course of scientific inquiry which creates them (Lynch, 1985). The conceptualization of risk assessment as a purely rational activity which is capable of finding objective truth is at odds with this perspective (Wynne, 1982). Though statisticians may believe they can objectively assess risk, social change continually modifies societal and individual vulnerability levels (Tierney, 1999). Risk levels are continually in flux, and using historical data to assess risk does not necessarily lead to an unbiased or accurate assessment of risk.

Risk assessment is key to the actions of economic agents regarding a number of environmental issues. The risk of catastrophic consequences to climate change is one example. Risks of major global negative economic consequences due to passing peak oil production is another looming risk that arguably has been not given adequate attention. There are of course numerous environmental pollutants that cause risk of negative health consequences. Other risks include breakdown of ecological systems due to human action, hazards from genetically modified foods, nuclear technology, nanoengineered particles, and numerous other technological advancements. Most of the decisions that firms and consumers make involving the environment include the assessment of risks and the likelihood of uncertain consequences.

One important way risk is socially constructed is through social cues that help us in determining how seriously to take certain risks. While experts hired by firms may have more information than laypeople in assessing risk, they still rely on social cues from people within their firm, experts at other firms, as well as from society in general. One of the most important social cues is just what risks people treat as if they are worthy of attention. The social construction of risk can lead to self-reinforcing societal denial. If people or firms treat a risk as minor or insignificant, this sends out a message to society influencing the risk perceptions of others. Lack of concern breeds lack of concern, even when scientific evidence suggests otherwise.

The mass media also plays an important role in influencing risk assessments and is arguably one of the most important forces in its social construction (Short, 1984). In its coverage of risk factors in society, successful narratives in the media tend to create links between events organizing them into patterns, and these patterns often propose or imply a causal explanation (Stallings, 1990). Media coverage of risk naturally has biases, such as focusing on certain stories with particularly strong narrative potential, even when many other examples of a problem exist (Nichols, 1997). Media news presentation is not just an attempt to get out facts, but is shaped by assumptions of the news presenters about narrative, storytelling, and human interest (Schudson, 1989). News media's impact results not only from outright statements, but also from its role in selection and application of the cultural lenses (Binder, 1993). It is not only the risk factors presented by the media that influence us, but also the fact that certain risks are *absent* from coverage that socially constructs our perceptions (Stallings, 1990; Gusfield, 1981).

While global climate change has received some increased media attention recently, the attention it receives now is far short of its global significance if the more dire estimates of its potential damage are to be believed. Furthermore, other risks that are more imminent, such as oil production peaking and falling far short of demand have received almost no attention. The relative lack of attention to these and other risks related to the environment and natural resources occurs in the media, in firms, and in discourse by the public at large. The lack of attention to these matters sends a clear message that others are not concerned about them. It sends a message suggesting the social consensus is that these risks should not be taken too seriously. This sense of a social consensus may in fact be false, but it nevertheless acts to influence the risk perceptions of people in general.

Conclusion

The case for the social construction of economic value and in particular the social construction of environmental valuation and decision-making was examined here. While the analysis attempted to be specific enough to show the practical value of such a perspective, the discussion necessarily remained fairly general. There is still much to potentially be gained from examining specific economic issues in more detail, utilizing a perspective that examines what messages are transmitted by the media, claims-makers, and society at large that drive economic choices in various situations. Pursuing this type of research will help us understand how environmental valuations and choices are socially constructed and what this means for business as well as public policy decisions.

An argument is made here for economic thinking that emphasizes a deep social construction of economic value in order to fully understand real decisions in the real economy. However, such a perspective does not necessarily require a new "school of thought". It can be accommodated through an expansion of what is called "behavioral economics". There appears to be a trend in behavioral economics toward favoring those ways of thinking that give an illusion of scientific rigor through overemphasis on mathematics and on scientific reductionism, similar to the historic trend in mainstream economic thinking. If behavioral economics were broadened to include social dimensions of behavior as well as its current emphasis on individual cognition, and if it chooses to embrace concepts that are difficult to quantitatively measure or that challenge objectivity, it could lend more insight into the way economic decisions are actually made.

The discussion here focused primarily on problems with environmental valuation and environmental decision-making caused by the way environmental issues are socially framed. However, a perspective that includes how these decisions are socially constructed suggests solutions as well as problems. Social and media influence can be very powerful to change beliefs and outcomes in either direction. Public opinion on important issues can reach a "tipping point" and start to change rapidly once people see similar concerns in those around them. While socially constructed decisions will vary from those that originate from the model of the rational economic actor with stable preferences, the socially constructed decisions need not be worse or more problematic. In some ways, social frames can lead to more socially optimal decisions, with choices that are more cooperative and altruistic than those of *homo economicus*.

References

Alchian A. (1950). Uncertainty, Evolution, and Economic Theory. *Journal of Political Economy* 58, 211–222

Anderson, D. A., (2003). A Picture is worth $10 million: Adult Object Permanence and the Neglected Power of Sight. United State Society for Ecological Economics Annual Meeting, May, Saratoga Springs, New York.

Bhaskar, R. (1987). *Scientific Realism and Human Emancipation*, London: Verso.

Binder, A. (1993). Constructing Racial Rhetoric: Media Depictions of Harm in Heavy Metal and Rap Music. *American Sociological Review,* 58(6), 753–767.

Berger, P. L. & Luckmann, T. (1966). *The Social Construction of Reality.* Garden City, NY: Doubleday.

DiMaggio, P. (1997). Culture and Cognition. *Annual Review of Sociology*, 23, 263–287.

Frank, J. & Carlisle-Frank, P. (2007). Discrimination Based on Breed of Domesticated Dogs among Insurance Companies: Economic vs. Interdisciplinary Explanations. *Journal of Social and Ecological Boundaries, forthcoming.*

Friedman, M., (1953). *The Methodology of Positive Economics. In Essays in Positive Economics.* Chicago: University of Chicago Press.

Gusfield, J. R. (1981). *The Culture of Public Problems: Drinking-Driving and the Symbolic Order.* Chicago: University of Chicago Press.

Kirby, A. (1990). *Nothing to Fear: Risks and Hazards in American Society*, Tucson, AZ: University of Arizona Press.

Laroche, H. (1995). From Decision to Action in Organizations: Decision-Making as a Social Representation. *Organizational Science,* 6, 662–675.

Lawson, T. (1998). *Economics and Reality.* London: Routledge.

Lynch, M. (1985). *Art and Artifact in Laboratory Science: A Study of Shop Work and Shop Talk in a Research Laboratory.* London: Routledge and Kegan Paul.

Meyer, J. W. & Rowan, B. (1991). Institutionalized Organizations: Formal Structure as Myth and Ceremony. *The New Institutionalism in Organizational Analysis,* Powell, W. & DiMaggio, P. (eds.), Chicago: University of Chicago Press.

Misra, J., Moller, S., & Karides, M. (2003). Envisioning Dependency: Changing Media Depictions of Welfare in the 20th Century. *Social Problems,* 50(4), 482–504.

Nelson, R., Winter, S. (1982). *An Evolutionary Theory of Economic Change.* Cambridge: Harvard University Press.

Nichols, L. T. (1997). Social Problems as Landmark Narratives: Bank of Boston, Mass Media and "Money Laundering". *Social Problems*, 44(3), 324–341.

Otway, H. & Thomas. K. (1982). Reflections on risk perception and policy. *Risk Analysis,* 2, 69–82.

Plough, A. & Krimsky, S. (1987). The emergence of risk communication studies: Social and political context. *Science, Technology, & Human Values,* 12, 4–10.

Powell, W. & DiMaggio, P. (1991). *The New Institutionalism in Organizational Analysis,* Chicago: University of Chicago Press.

Schudson, M. (1989). The sociology of news production. *Media, Culture, and Society,* 11, 263–282.

Sherif, M. (1937). An experimental approach to the study of attitudes. *Sociometry,* 1, 90–98.

Short, J. F. (1984). The social fabric of risk: toward the social transformation of risk analysis. *American Sociological Review,* 49, 711–725.

Stallings, R. A. (1990). Media Discourse and the Social Construction of Risk. *Social Problems,* 37(1), 80–95.

Tierney, K. J. (1999). Toward a Critical Sociology of Risk. *Sociological Forum,* 14(2), 215-242.

Tversky, A. & Kahnemen, D. (1974). Judgment under Uncertainty: Heuristics and Biases. *Science,* 185, 1124–1131.

Tversky, A. & Kahnemen, D. (1981). The Framing of Decisions and the Psycho-logy of Choice. *Science,* 211, 453–458.

Vatn, A. & Bromley, D. W. (1994). Choices without Prices without Apologies. *Journal of Environmental Economics and Management,* 26, 129–148.

Veblen, T. (1899, reprinted 1994) *The Theory of the Leisure Class,* New York: Penguin Books.

Wynne, B. (1982). Institutional mythologies and dual societies in the manage-ment of risk. In *The Risk Analysis Controversy: An Institutional Perspec-tive,* Kunreather, H. C. & Ley, E. V. (eds.), New York: Springer-Verlag, 127–143.

5 Missing Feedback in Payments for Ecosystem Services

A Systems Perspective

Trista M. Patterson and Dana L. Coelho

ABSTRACT

A general systems analysis of current approaches to payments for ecosystem services reveals a weakness, a missing feedback that ought to be in place pushing the system toward its goal of balancing human needs with the adaptive capacity of ecosystems. In situations of rising demand for ecosystem services, among limited means for producing them, the likelihood that payment systems effectively shift, but do not preclude ecosystem service losses is high. We propose that explicit price or information signals to ecosystem services consumers would create the necessary feedback, thereby "closing the loop", and increasing the likelihood that efforts to stem declines in ecosystem services will succeed. To date, attention for this feedback loop has been more casual, than concerted. As a result, PES systems have perhaps left unharnessed the full range of opportunities to reduce the growing deficit between rates of ecosystem service supply and the rate that society utilizes (and in many cases, impacts) them. The importance of the construction and conceptualization of these feedback loops, among the various tools at hand for adaptive responses to the challenges of sustainable development, are discussed.

Keywords: ecosystem services, complex systems, feedback, consumption, supply and demand

Introduction

In November 1990, at a café in the central square of Siena, Italy, the theme of the upcoming ISEE conference in Stockholm in 1992 was discussed. The working title of the conference "Maintaining Natural Capital" did not really capture the essence of the issues to be raised. In an intense discussion Herman Daly suddenly proclaimed "Let's use 'Investing in Natural Capital' instead" (Jansson et al.., 1994). The shift from maintaining (in essence preserving the stock of capital) to investing marked recognition of renewable natural capital as a dynamic entity that needs to be understood and actively managed. The shift gave credit to the fact that it is not sufficient to assume that if we only live on the rent of the natural capital stock it will be conserved. Instead we will have to find ways to value and manage the capacity of natural capital to generate and sustain the rent, actively adapt to the dynamic nature of complex systems and learn to live with uncertainty and surprise (Costanza et al., 1993; Levin, 1999; Carpenter et al., 2001; Limburg et al., 2002).

Ekins et al. (2003, p. 160)

In the "Critical Natural Capital" special issue in *Ecological Economics*, Ekins et al. (2003) recounted a particularly inspiring moment in ecological economics history, which occurred during a formative period for ecosystem service documentation, awareness-raising, and research. It recalled a shift from *maintaining* natural capital, to *investing in* natural capital, and underscored the need for management of complex natural systems to produce the ecosystem services future generations would need to survive.

The effect of language choice has been important, both in the success of some trajectories of ecosystem service research, and in the conceptual bounds that it places on lines of inquiry. *Investing, capital, value,* and *rent* are all terms deeply resonant with American and other capitalist societies. However, *investment in* natural capital emphasizes supply or holding capacity and the flows into the stock of natural capital, whereas *maintaining* natural capital (as in a stock to be maintained) would attract attention to both inflows and outflows. Herman Daly's work has long called attention to living within the biophysical capacity of the planet, a goal which must be met both by moderating (investing in) the supply of natural capital, as well as the demands placed on it (Daly, 1974, 1996; Daly and Farley, 2004). Yet the body of work produced by ecological economists since 1990 has more often focused on the supply, rather than the demand side of the ecological economics equation. There are exceptions of course, most notably the ecological footprint (Rees, 1992; Wackernagel and Rees, 1996, 1997) and the collective work of Inge Røpke (e.g., Reisch and Røpke, 2004).

There is no question that it is important to invest in the stocks of natural capital for all the reasons Ekins et al. (2003) lay out. However, we argue that it is equally and perhaps more important, given the trajectories of current society, to investigate, experiment with, and socially invest in curbing demands on natural capital systems. This paper adopts a systems perspective to call attention the absence of demand-side information in current approaches to payments for ecosystem services and identifies opportunities for corrective intervention.

Method

As established by Jay W. Forrester at MIT in the 1950's, systems theory was originally developed for military application (e.g., guidance systems). The concept was applied early on to urban dynamics (Forrester, 1969) and world dynamics

(Forrester, 1971), revealing new and often counter-intuitive implications of policy decisions over time. Systems theory has since found resonance within many fields, from business management (Senge, 2006), to macroeconomics (Witt, 1997; Liu, in press), to fisheries biology (Collie and Walters, 1987), and underlies the concept of adaptive management (Walters and Holling, 1990).

At its simplest level, a "system" is characterized by at least one stock (an accumulation of matter, energy, information, etc.) and at least one flow into or out of that stock. An open system is one where outflows respond to but do not influence inflows. A closed system is one where outflows both respond to and influence inflows allowing for learning and adaptation via information feedbacks (Figure 1).

The feedback loop is a defining structure of complex adaptive systems and the logic underlying systems theory. Feedback loops drive the non-linear behavior seen in many natural and social systems (e.g., predator-prey population cycles, neo-classical economic laws of supply and demand). Positive feedback loops reinforce flows into or out of a system, pushing it away from equilibrium, while negative feedback loops regulate flows, bringing a system closer to a desired state or equilibrium. To "close the loop" requires a stock (state of the system), information about that stock (perceived state), and a decision rule (goal) affecting the flow into and out of the stock.

Systems analysis is a field of inquiry seeking to understand and increase the efficiency and effectiveness of any number of social, ecological, industrial, organizational, and other systems by taking a "systems approach" and therefore explicitly exploring feedback loops. By understanding how a system is functioning (identifying its stocks and flows) one can catch a glimpse of leverage points at which change can be targeted to increase performance (Meadows, 1999).

A general systems analysis of current approaches to payments for ecosystem services (PES) reveals a weakness. Current programs are set up as open systems, within which there is not sufficient information to create a feedback loop that addresses the discrepancy between the perceived state of the system and the

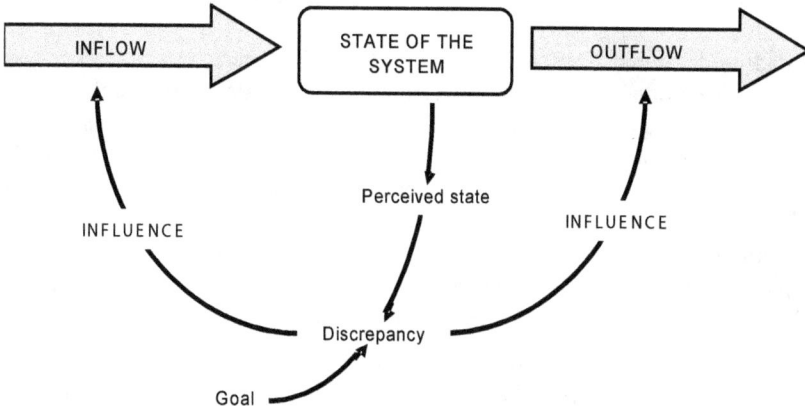

Figure 1 Basic system diagram (based on Meadows, 1999)

stated goal or desired outcome. The next section will apply the systems perspective described above to PES approaches. We explore the stated goals, structure of payer-payee relationships, and targeting methods. We conclude with a conceptual solution as well as directions for future research.

The Problem

Ecosystem services declines are well documented and the drivers of this decline—population growth, affluence, technology, land use change, etc.—widely explored (MEA, 2005; Rees, 2006; Ehrlich, 2008; Ehrlich and Daily, 1992; and many others). The declines are symptomatic of a reduced planetary ability of natural systems to adapt and regenerate, and translate to a reduced biological capacity to support human life on Earth. Concerns for the rapid rates of decline have lead to calls for quantification, assessment, monitoring, and investment in critical natural capital (e.g., De Groot, 2003). Natural capital represents an extension of the concept of 'land' as a factor of production, has both nonrenewable and renewable dimensions, and includes generation of ecosystem services and other life-supporting functions (De Groot, 1992; Costanza and Daly, 1992; Ekins, 1992). Critical natural capital has been defined as that part of the natural environment that performs important and irreplaceable functions (see special issue in *Ecological Economics*, Ekins et al., 2003).

Payments for ecosystem services (PES) have recently been brought forward as a market-based response to declines in ecosystem services, largely through spurring investment in natural capital, especially in the biodiversity rich tropics. There are four general characteristics of a PES transaction (Wunder, 2005):

1. Voluntary;

2. Well-defined service;

3. Well-defined buyer(s) and seller(s); and

4. Contingent on actual service provision (subject to monitoring, verification).

Broadly considered, PES schemes attribute market characteristics to ecosystem service production. The most specific of these translate ecosystem services (e.g., carbon sequestration) into something that can be traded, such as carbon credits. Some interpretations of ecosystem services are more general and don't enter markets in a tradable sense, for example conservation easements which are strictly place-based.

Further, there are three criteria commonly considered for targeting PES systems to maximize economic efficiency and conservation effectiveness (Pagiola, 2008; Wünscher et al., 2008; Wendland et al., forthcoming):

1.   Level of service provision (benefits);

2.   Risk of land conversion and therefore service loss (vulnerability); and

3.   Landowner participation cost (foregone income, transaction costs, etc.).

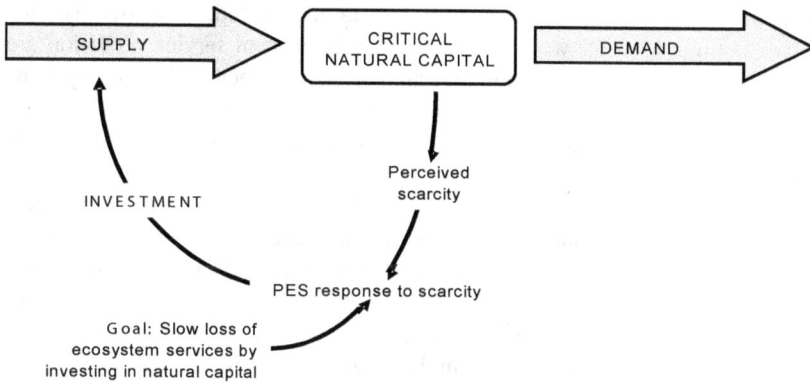

Figure 2 PES as an open system, supply-side focused intervention

The stated or implied (often it is not directly stated) goal of PES schemes is to slow the loss of ecosystem services, by investing in and improving the supply of ecosystem services. We argue that, from a systems perspective, this is necessary, but not sufficient as a goal because it does not reflect a desired system *state*, leaving the system "open" and devoid of necessary feedback (Figure 2). Imagine that your doctor told you she was going to help you bleed to death more slowly by carefully infusing more blood. Would you feel optimistic about your overall, long term health? If a second treatment option were offered that would not only slow the bleeding, but stop it and provide you with information on how to avoid injury in the future would you feel more secure and empowered to change your behavior, even if it were more expensive?

The implicit goal, too often unstated or understated, of sustainable development is "the maintenance of ecological functionality within the context of economic and social wants and needs" (Straton, 2006, p. 409). It is towards this goal that PES programs, individually and collectively, and along with the entire suite of conservation, restoration, and sustainable development mechanisms ought to strive. PES systems currently focus almost exclusively on slowing the loss-rate by constructing mechanisms for service providers to receive payment for supplying valuable ecosystem services. As supply-side interventions, PES (and other approaches not addressed here) are currently missing the opportunity to also engage and impact consumer demand for ecosystem services.

The Solution

Among the principal drivers of ecosystem services declines are population and consumption (Ehrlich and Holdren, 1971; Ehrlich and Ehrlich, 1990; MEA 2005). In situations of rising demand (population growth and increasing affluence) for ecosystem services, among limited means for producing them, the likelihood that payment systems effectively shift, but do not preclude ecosystem service losses is high. In other words, if declines in ecosystem service provision are symptomatic of the loss of productive and adaptive capacity within ecosystems (including those that are "protected" from conversion), then current PES investment solutions are necessary but not sufficient to solving the more fundamental problem.

If, however, mechanisms can be developed that provide accurate, current, digestible information about the state of critical natural capital (to individuals, governments, etc.) behaviors and regulations can react, can adapt, and push the system in the right direction. It is important that these mechanisms include the full suite of available social actions, not only from the supply side but also demand side in order to maintain critical natural capital and maximize net social benefit.

We propose that where possible, payments for ecosystem service schemes should be modified to create an explicit price or information signal to ecosystem services consumers of the scarcity of critical natural capital, creating the missing feedback and thereby "closing the loop" (Figure 3). PES schemes structured around a more direct link between service producers and end consumers via higher prices for and more complete information regarding the source and impact of consumable natural resources provide the opportunity not only to secure supply (by compensating landowners/managers) but to also inform and reduce demand.

The price needs only to be high enough to pass information to the consumer about the impacts of their behavior on the stock of critical natural capital. This may be accompanied by additional, non-monetary information relevant to strengthening the link and the power of the regulating feedback loop.

There are various degrees of this feedback loop functioning in current PES programs. The feedback loop can be said to be functioning depending on the degree to which the payment or accompanying information succeeds in moderating consumer behavior (in conjunction with other options such as addressing supply).

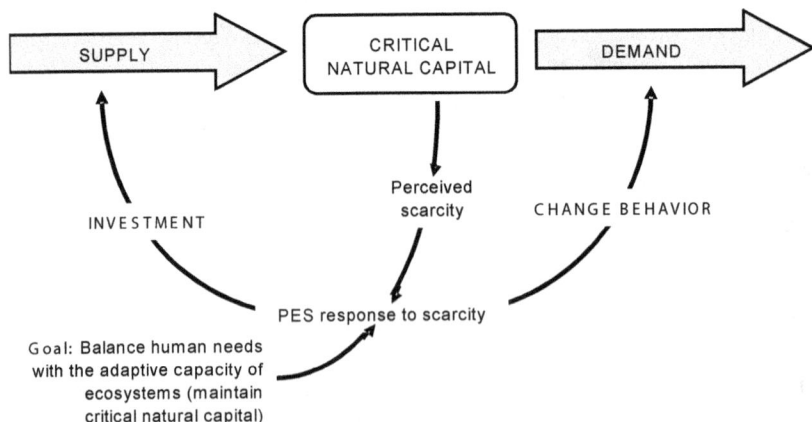

Figure 3 PES as a closed system, supply- and demand-side interventions

One example would be a successful bottle return program, wherein consumers are charged the full cost of the bottle upfront but reimbursed the waste disposal fee when they make the effort to recycle. Consumer behavior is directed towards recycling in an effort to reduce demand for the waste assimilation services of nature.

The right-side feedback loop is not functioning when neither payment nor information feeds back to the consumer, thereby missing an opportunity to address ecosystem service scarcity by reducing demand. One example of a payment system not functioning is when a conservation organization pays a forest landowner not to convert land to a strip mall, while the demand for strip malls is such that development occurs elsewhere (also known as leakage). Here the ultimate driver of development, consumer demand, is unaffected by the conservation action. A similar situation exists within the voluntary carbon market. While some consumers choose to pay to offset their carbon footprint many others opt not to, either because of a lack of or dismissal of available information. A mandatory carbon tax, on the other hand, would eliminate the free-rider problem; higher prices reflecting more of the true costs of consumption would be passed onto consumers. Ideally, this would positively influence demand-side pressure on the ecosystem service of climate-regulation, whereas a supply-side approach would be to (philanthropically or otherwise) incentivize carbon sequestration.

Closing the Loop: A Costa Rican Application

Costa Rica's national PES program is among one of the first and most widely known PES systems (Russo and Candela, 2006; Chomitz et al., 1999; FONAFIFO, 2005). Some have concluded that the simple, flat payment structures would be more effective if payments were targeted towards areas of high value, high vulnerability, and low cost (Sanchez-Azofeifa et al., 2007; Hartshorn et al., 2005). We would posit a second critique that because the program was designed to maintain and increase the *supply* of ecosystem services and because payments were largely funded through grants and a fuel tax (not directly related to the services themselves) the opportunity was lost to connect to both supply and demand.

Current lines of research have focused on how effective the Costa Rica PES program has been in addressing in-country and global declines in ecosystem services. Some have suggested that declines in deforestation may have resulted, even in absence of the PES systems (Sanchez-Azofeifa et al., 2007; Hartshorn et al., 2005). The rapid establishment of tourism may have acted as additional incentive to retain forest, but as an industry with high net impacts to natural capital (Gössling and Hall, 2008), may ultimately create additional ecosystem service pressure, rather than reduce it. We draw attention to this issue because, at the broadest scale, incentivizing the supply of ecosystem services from forested areas while at the same time increasing the demands on those areas is an example of the open system problem we believe PES systems can, with consideration, better address in the near future.

We also see existing PES programs serving as positive examples to be built upon. For example, the FONAFIFO PES program includes a nominal water tariff. In 2005 this fee was increased and committed to within-watershed conservation via payments to upstream landowners. Charged to holders of water use permits and passed onto commercial and household consumers, the fee represents a shift from voluntary agreements to compulsory payments (Pagiola, 2008). Two things about this approach are notable: first, it is helping to raise baseline household awareness of what ecosystem services are (clean drinking water), where they come from (forested areas), and how they are enriched (through conservation and restoration). This information is contributing to a positive (reinforcing) feedback loop on the supply side by connecting forest conservation with an increasingly popular image of 'green' Costa Rica being used to market other environmental services to outsiders, for example through tourism ventures. Second, it is creating a direct price signal that, along with the information passed onto the consumer, may reduce demand. Due to the small monetary value of the fee, it could not yet be said to be regulating demand (creating a negative or balancing feedback loop), but does create a placeholder in which such a feedback can develop over time.

Conclusions and Future Research

Payments for ecosystem services policies, programs, and research have demonstrated numerous benefits. Yet there are also weaknesses, namely an inability to deal with the modern penchant for consumption bordering on *affluenza* (De Graaf et al., 2001) and an accompanying reticence to examine and auto-regulate consumption decisions. This paper has explored, from a systems perspective, the consequences of a (to date) fairly narrow focus in constructing payment for ecosystem service schemes. We argue that this has emphasized investment in the supply of natural capital without concomitant attention to maintenance of natural capital from the demand side.

Ours is only a conceptual solution to the problem, namely the use of price and information signals within PES schemes as carriers of information on the scarcity of critical natural capital back to its consumers. However, we see potential to be explored with more concerted and specific research and examples. Obviously creating such a closed loop PES system that directly engages both producers and consumers is difficult, or else we would be doing it already. Crafting such a system requires data sources and collection frameworks that are at present unavailable or underdeveloped (Beier et al., 2008). Efforts to quantify and spatially link production and consumption of ecosystem services such as fish, timber, recreation, carbon sequestration, water provision, waste assimilation, etc. should be encouraged. Non-consumptive uses of ecosystems are frequently impacted by consumptive uses. Therefore we also stress the importance of directing thought, consideration, and research toward the considerable challenge of how to create the same informational feedback (signal) for non-marketable ecosystem services (e.g., biodiversity existence value, cultural values). Additional areas of inquiry may be how to bundle these services with other, marketable services (e.g., water, carbon), or account for dynamic economic transitions (such as the transition from agrarian to tourism industries in the Costa Rica example, above).

Our point is not to argue that the capitalist system is ultimately capable of correcting declines in ecosystem services and sustaining critical natural capital, even if payments for ecosystem services are more directly connected to consumer demand. This will require much broader, more comprehensive reform. Left particularly unaddressed (both in this paper and by the capitalist system more fundamentally) are the unmet needs of equity and distribution. Similar challenges exist for applying market based solutions to ecosystem service deficits, and further documentation is needed to confirm whether PES has corrective potential in this area (Wunder, 2008).

Implementation of a more direct and closed system broadly seeking the goal of balancing human needs with the adaptive capacity of ecosystems also demands an accompanying shift in thinking about personal and collective responsibility for stewardship of the planet, and extensive research and emphasis in the areas of behavioral change and quality of life. Consumption is closely tied to current measures of wellbeing (e.g., GDP) and, by extension, reducing consumption is still widely viewed as causing suffering or reducing wellbeing (Redefining Progress, 1995; Cummins et al., 2003), it often incites argument over the distributional impact of conservation and sustainable development policies (e.g., "green" tax reform, see Metcalf, 1998; Turner et al., 1998), and stimulates concerns that efforts to curb deficits in ecosystem services will result in further exploitation by others (e.g., Jevon's paradox as described by Wackernagel and Rees, 1997). These fundamental and sensitive issues need further exploration from multiple perspectives and scientific fields. Ultimately, the demand side of ecosystem services is fertile, largely uncharted territory for transdisciplinary investigation in the field of ecological economics.

Acknowledgments

The authors gratefully acknowledge the editor and reviewers of these proceedings for their time, energy, and clear and insightful suggestions.

References

Beier, C., Patterson, T., Chapin, F. S., 2008. Ecosystem services and emergent vulnerability in managed ecosystems: a geospatial decision-support tool. *Ecosystems*.

Carpenter, S. R., Walker, B., Anderies, J. M., Abel, N., 2001. From metaphor to measurement: resilience of what to what. *Ecosystems* 4, 765–781.

Chomitz, K. M., Brenes, E., Costantino, L., 1999. Financing environmental services:

the Costa Rican experience and its implications. *The Science of the Total Environment* 240, 157–169.

Collie, J. S., Walters, C. J., 1987. Alternative recruitment models of Adams River sockeye salmon (*Oncorhynchus nerka*). *Canadian Journal of Fisheries and Aquatic Sciences* 44, 1551-1561.

Costanza, R., Daly, H. E., 1992. Natural capital and sustainable development. *Conservation Biology* 6, 37–46.

Costanza, R., Waigner, L., Folke, C., Maeler, K. G., 1993. Modeling complex ecological economic systems: towards an evolutionary dynamic understanding of people and nature. *BioScience* 43, 545–555.

Cummins, R. A., Eckersley, R., Pallant, J., Van Vugt, J., Misajon, R., 2003. Developing a national index of subjective wellbeing: the Australian Unity Wellbeing Index. *Social Indicators Research* 64, 159–190.

Daily, G. G., Ehrlich, P. R., 1992. Population, sustainability, and Earth's carrying capacity. *BioScience* 42(10), 761–771.

Daly, H. E., 1974. The economics of the steady state. *The American Economic Review* 64(2), 15–21.

Daly, H. E., 1996. *Beyond Growth.* Beacon Press, Boston, MA.

Daly, H. E. and Farley, J., 2004. *Ecological Economics: Principles and Applications.* Island Press, Washington, DC.

De Graaf, J., Wann, D., Naylor, T. H., 2001. *Affluenza: The All-Consuming Epidemic.* Berrett-Koehler Publishers, San Francisco, CA.

De Groot, R., 1992. Functions of Nature. Wolters-Noordhoff, Groningen, Netherlands.

De Groot, R., Van der Perk, J., Chiesura A., van Vliet, A., 2003. Importance and threat as determining factors for criticality of natural capital. *Ecological Economics* 44, 187–204.

Ehrlich, P. R., 2008. Key issues for attention from ecological Economists. *Environment and Development Economics* 13, 1-20.

Ehrlich, P. R., Ehrlich, A. H., 1990. *The Population Explosion.* Simon & Schuster, New York, NY.

Ehrlich, P. R., Holdren, J., 1971. Impact of population growth. Science 171, 1212–1217.

Ekins, P., 1992. A four-capital model of wealth creation. In: P. Ekins, M. Max-Neef (Editors), Real-Life Economics: Understanding Wealth Creation. Routledge, London/New York, pp. 147–155.

Ekins, P., Folke, C. E., De Groot, R., 2003. Identifying critical natural capital. *Ecological Economics* 44 (2-3), 159–163.

FONAFIFO (Fondo Nacional de Financiamiento Forestal), 2005. FONAFIFO: Más de una década de acción. FONAFIFO, San José, Costa Rica. (in Spanish)

Forrester, J. W., 1969. *Urban Dynamics.* Productivity Press, Portland, OR.

Forrester, J. W., 1971. *World Dynamics.* Productivity Press, Portland, OR.

Gössling, S., Hall, M. C., 2008. *Tourism and Global Environmental Change: Ecological, Economic, Social and Political Interrelationships.* Routledge, New York, 344 pp.

Hartshorn, G., Ferraro, P., Spergel, B., Sills, E., 2005. *Evaluation of the World Bank—GEF Ecomarkets Project in Costa Rica.* North Carolina State University, Durham, NC.

Jansson, A.M., Hammer, M., Folke, C., Costanza, R., 1994. *Investing in Natural Capital: The Ecological Economics Approach to Sustainability.* Island Press, Washington, DC.

Levin, S., 1999. *Fragile Dominion: Complexity and the Commons.* Perseus Books, Reading, MA.

Limburg, K. E., O'Neill, R. V., Costanza, R., Farber, S., 2002. Complex systems and valuation. *Ecological Economics* 41 (3), 409–420.

Liu, Z., Koerwerc, J., Nemotod, J., Imurae, H., In press. Physical energy cost serves as the "invisible hand" governing economic valuation: Direct evidence from biogeochemical data and the U.S. metal market. *Ecological Economics.*

MEA (Millennium Ecosystem Assessment), 2005. Ecosystems and Human Well-being: Current State and Trends. Island Press, Washington, DC.

Meadows, D., 1999. Leverage Points: Places to Intervene in a System. The Sustainability Institute. Hartland, VT.

Metcalf, Gilbert E., 1998. A distributional analysis of an environmental tax shift. NBER Working Paper No. W6546. Available at SSRN: http://ssrn.com/abstract=160691.

Pagiola, S., 2008. Payments for environmental services in Costa Rica. *Ecological Economics* 65, 712–724.

Redefining Progress, 1995. Gross production vs genuine progress. Excerpt from the Genuine Progress Indicator: Summary of Data and Methodology. Redefining Progress, San Francisco, CA.

Rees, W., 1992. Ecological footprints and appropriated carrying capacity: what urban economies leaves out. *Environment and Urbanization* 4, 121–130.

Rees, W., 2006. Globalization, trade and migration: undermining sustainability. *Ecological Economics* 59, 220–225.

Reisch, L. A., I. Røpke (Editors), 2004. *The Ecological Economics of Consumption.* Edward Elgar, Cheltenham, UK.

Russo, R.O., Candela, G., 2006. Payment of environmental services in Costa Rica: evaluating impact and possibilities. Tierra Tropical 2 (1), 1–13.

Sanchez-Azofeifa, G. A., Pfaff, A., Robalino, J. A., Boomhower, J. P., 2007. Costa Rica's payment for environmental services program: intention, implementation, and impact. *Conservation Biology* 20 (10), 1523–1739.

Senge, P. M., 2006. *The Fifth Discipline: The Art & Practice of the Learning Organization.* Doubleday. New York, NY.

Straton, A., 2006. A complex systems approach to the value of ecological resources. *Ecological Economics* 56, 402–411.

Turner, R.K., Salmons, R., Powell, J., Craighill, A., 1998. Green taxes, waste management and political economy. *Journal of Environmental Management* 53 (2), 121–136.

Wackernagel, M., Rees, W., 1996. Our Ecological Footprint: Reducing Human Impact on the Earth. New Society Publishers. Gabriola Island, BC.

Wackernagel, M., Rees, W., 1997. Perceptual and structural barriers to investing in natural capital: economics from an ecological footprint perspective. *Ecological Economics* 20, 3–24.

Walters, C.J., Holling, C.S., 1990. Large-scale management experiments and learning by doing. *Ecology* 71 (6), 2060–2068.

Wendland, K.J., Honzák, M., Portela, R., Vitale, B., Rubinoff, S., Randrianarisoa, J., Forthcoming. Targeting and implementing payments for ecosystem services: opportunities for bundling biodiversity conservation with carbon and water services in Madagascar. *Ecological Economics.*

Witt, U., 1997. Self-organization and economics what is new?. Structural Change and Economic Dynamics 8, 489–507.

Wunder, S., 2005. Payments for Environmental Services: Some Nuts and Bolts. CIFOR Occasional Paper No. 42. Jakarta, Indonesia.

Wunder, S., 2008. Payments for environmental services and the poor: concepts and preliminary evidence. *Environment and Development Economics* 13, 279–297.

Wünscher, T., Engel, S., Wunder, S., 2008. Spatial targeting of payments for environmental services: a tool for boosting conservation benefits. *Ecological Economics* 65 (4), 822–833.

6 The Role of the States in Sustainable Development Policy

New Laboratories of Democracy

Mary M. Timney

ABSTRACT

In the absence of policy action at the national level, US states and local governments have taken the lead in crafting sustainable development policy. This paper
reviews the activity of states and local governments to meet the requirements of
the Kyoto Protocol and to "go green," in general. This is not the first time that
states have taken over a policy area. During the 1980s states also developed energy policies while the Reagan Administration turned to the market alone. I argue
that the states' lead in this policy area will force the President and Congress to
draft meaningful energy and sustainable development policies.

In 1932, Justice Louis D. Brandeis described the states as "laboratories of democracy" that could experiment with public policy without risking consequences
at the national level in his dissent to *New State Ice Co. v Liebmann* (Greve 2001).
The metaphor has been widely interpreted to describe the tension between the
states and federal government in the policy process.

The critical need for the US to develop policies for sustainable development
has often focused on the national level of government. The Bush Administration has refused to consider such policies, including implementing the Kyoto
Protocol, arguing that they would inhibit economic growth in the country. In the
absence of action at the Federal level, states and local governments all over the
US have moved ahead to devise individual and significant approaches to sustainability. Looking at the websites of most major cities in this country reveals
a plethora of policies, incentives, goals, and programs to reduce greenhouse
gases and achieve sustainability within decades.

States have always acted to further the interest of their citizens, especially in
the absence of Federal policy. During the 1980s, when the Reagan Administration turned energy policy over to the market, several states worked to develop
their own comprehensive energy policies. This happened largely because they
had learned during the 1970s energy crises that they could be held hostage by
skyrocketing market prices and limited supply of energy.

Market-based policies—such as, electricity deregulation, for example—have several built-in flaws that can lead to conflicts with other policies at the state and local levels of government. Foremost among these is the fact that market-based policies lead inevitably to increased energy consumption which puts upward pressure on prices and demand for new energy production that may further damage the environment. As a result, the goal of sustainable energy policy recedes and citizens are faced with ever-rising costs for heating, cooling, and lighting their homes and businesses.

This paper looks at energy management policies that state and local governments have developed to achieve the multiple goals associated with energy policy that states have consistently had for over thirty years—adequate supplies, affordable prices, and environment protection. It examines the conflicts between public interests and market interests and identifies some of the consequences of delegating energy policy totally to the market. Several examples of innovative energy policies developed by state and local governments are identified as ways that sub-national governments can protect the interests of their citizens and move toward a sustainable energy future.

Finally, I argue that the state level may be the most appropriate place for sustainability policy because of the moderating effect that occurs in the development of national policy.

Introduction: A Brief History of State Energy Policy[1]

Prior to the energy crises of the 1970s, neither states nor the federal government had specific energy policies. The states were responsible for regulating investor-owned public utilities which generated and delivered electricity and delivered natural gas to customers within each state. Federal energy policy, as it had been since the 1910s, was focused primarily on ensuring adequate supplies of oil and natural gas and protecting the interests of domestic oil companies through favorable tax policies. In the mid-1950s, the US government, through the Atomic Energy Commission, promoted and subsidized the development of the nuclear power industry.[2]

In the 1970s, the nation was jolted out of complacency by two oil price shocks, the result of market manipulation by Middle Eastern producers and the Organization of Petroleum Exporting Countries (OPEC), including Arab countries, Nigeria and Venezuela. In 1973, an embargo by the nation of Iran created severe shortages in the U.S. and caused the price of gasoline to double overnight (from 35 to 70 cents per gallon). Five years later, OPEC established production quotas that caused the price to double again. The price of all other energy sources, including electricity, also rose dramatically and the country became painfully aware of how

---

1   Much of the following discussion is taken from my book Power for the People: Protecting States' Energy Policy Interests in an Era of Deregulation, published by M.E. Sharpe in 2004.

2   Coal, which is abundant in the U.S., is the only energy source that has not enjoyed government subsidies.

much energy was being wasted through inefficient automobile design and cheap building construction.

The impact in the states was felt differently. The costs of winter heating were felt most strongly in northern states, while southern states experienced higher bills for air conditioning. States that were energy producers, such as Oklahoma and Texas and Alaska at the end of the decade, reaped huge tax benefits when price controls were lifted by the federal government. It became clear that the country needed an overarching energy policy to better manage energy resources, identify current and potential energy sources, and protect the country's strategic interests from foreign energy powers.

Congress enacted two laws that encouraged states to develop energy policies. The Energy Policy and Conservation Act of 1975 required states to establish energy offices to promote energy conservation and to reduce energy consumption throughout the state by five percent below the expected level of use without conservation. The Energy Conservation and Production Act of 1976 provided grants to states to implement energy conservation programs in government-owned buildings, low-income housing, schools and hospitals.

Energy conservation was a major focus of energy policies during the Carter Administration, which established the Department of Energy (DOE). By the end of the decade, there was a broad consensus across the country in support of energy efficiency and conservation. Kash and Rycroft asserted that "conservation had provided more new energy to the nation than any other source" (1984: 238).

When Ronald Reagan became president in 1981, federal energy policy shifted from demand side management (conservation) to market-driven supply development. The DOE under Reagan was stripped of the energy efficiency programs and tax incentives that Carter had developed. The focus of the department was redirected to nuclear weapons development as part of the buildup of defense capability during the Cold War.[3] Reagan had pledged to dismantle the DOE when he was running in 1980. While he didn't have the political support to do that, the shift in emphasis accomplished the same effect. The price of oil on the world market collapsed in the early 1980s[4] and the administration argued that the market would provide new energy resources when they were needed. Government programs were not necessary so the federal government allowed energy policy to lapse.

States did not, however. Having learned the hard way what can happen when energy prices spike, most states continued to support their energy offices throughout the 1980s. A major court decision in the early 1980s held that oil companies had overcharged customers during the 1970s and ordered the major companies to refund millions of dollars to the states. The money had to be used

---

3   By this time, the nuclear power industry was at a standstill, following the near meltdown of the Three Mile Island plant outside Harrisburg, Pennsylvania, in 1979.

4   Ironically, the conservation programs of the 1970s played a major role in creating a glut of oil on the world market which led to the collapse of OPEC oil prices.

for energy programs and many states chose to use the funds to keep their energy offices running and to provide energy assistance to low-income residents.

In a study of seventeen states in the early 1990s, I found that a majority had developed their own energy policies and that they were beginning to develop programs to combat global warming. The study showed that states have three primary interests in energy policy: adequate supplies of energy for all users and for economic development; reasonable prices for all users; and environmental protection in energy production and use. A follow-up study of state websites in 2001 found that states continue to hold these interests. In the aftermath of the electricity crisis in 2001, the state of California stepped in immediately to protect those interests. Several other states did as well and the growth of state electricity deregulation came to an abrupt halt.

Conservation remains a primary objective of state energy offices. In California, demand side management programs over the ten years preceding deregulation had reduced demand by fifteen percent below what it would otherwise have been while the population was rapidly growing. The 1992 Energy Policy Act (EPACT) required utilities to develop demand side management programs where it could be demonstrated that investments in conservation would be as profitable as investments in additional generation (Timney, p. 54). In the 1970s, a mantra of the Federal Energy Agency (which preceded the DOE) was "A barrel of oil saved is worth more than a new barrel."[5]

Electricity Deregulation in the States

Electricity deregulation, also known as restructuring, was made possible by two separate pieces of Federal legislation. The Public Utilities Regulatory Policies Act of 1978 (PURPA) opened up the transmission grid to so-called qualifying facilities that produced electricity independently of the utility companies, generally through co-generation or small renewable generators. The utilities were required to connect these facilities to the grid and to purchase their power. This effectively set the precedent of requiring the utilities to carry electrons generated by some other entity and formed the base for future deregulation.

The Energy Policy Act of 1992, enacted during George H.W. Bush's presidency, created a class of exempt wholesale generators (EWGs) that could generate and sell electric power at wholesale without being subject to regulatory restrictions. This section of the law was drafted by President Bush's good friend, Enron CEO Kenneth Lay of Houston, Texas. It was this law that made state electricity deregulation possible. Utilities were required to purchase electricity generated from outside suppliers under PURPA and EWGs were authorized to act as traders to broker the sales of excess electricity from one state to another. Computer technology made it possible to track supply and demand throughout

---

5   Contrast this with Vice President Cheney's comment that conservation can make you feel virtuous but is not a sound basis for an energy policy.

the transmission grids. Large users would be able to purchase electricity from the lowest bidder and the end of the regulated monopoly seemed to be at hand.

Between 1995 and 2003, twenty-four states enacted some form of restructuring legislation.[6] After the debacle in California in 2001, however, a number of states put their plans on hold so that only nineteen states had completed deregulation and no new state has enacted such a policy since 2003. Today only 16 states have full deregulation and some of them are looking at re-regulating because of high prices.

Until recently, George W. Bush promoted energy development as the primary focus of national energy policy, unlike his father who supported a balanced approach to national energy policy that had efficiency and conservation at its base. The weak energy policy adopted in 2005 had some support for efficiency and renewable energy but is much stronger in promoting development, subsidizing energy companies, and drilling in the Arctic National Wildlife Refuge and other environmentally-sensitive areas. So far, Congress has not approved drilling in Alaska, but its proponents keep trying. Another factor in the mix today is the growing reality of global warming, which is due in large part to burning of fossil fuels for energy production. Since the 2006 elections which established the Democratic majority in Congress, efforts to enact national energy and sustainability legislation have more support, even in the White House. Given the politics in Washington and the Democrats' precarious majority, however, there is no guarantee that significant sustainability legislation will actually be enacted.

States Take the Lead

While the policymakers in Washington dither over energy policy, states have once again begun to develop their own energy policies and programs. Moreover, cities all over the country, working with their state governments, have also devised energy management programs. States and cities are more aware of the impacts of rising energy prices on their residents, businesses, and government budgets. Every time energy prices go up, the cost of running government buildings, schools, hospitals, etc. rises, necessitating cuts elsewhere in the budget or revenue enhancements (tax increases) of some kind. Thus, it is in the interests of the states to reduce their own energy costs and by extension to assist their residents in reducing theirs.

States also can envision the effects that global warming may have on their area, depending on where they are located and the type of economy they have. The impacts of global warming are becoming more visible each year. The melting of the polar icecaps has reached significant levels so that low-lying areas will begin to see higher tides and reduced shoreline. The severity of the hurricanes of 2005 presaged the destruction that global climate change may bring. Although

---

6 Deregulation is often referred to as restructuring since the industry itself has to be restructured in order for the market to work effectively.

Hurricane Katrina's devastation has not been attributed to global warming, environmental damage from development of the Louisiana wetlands was a factor.

States are developing energy policies probably as an outgrowth of the 1992 EPACT. The law required all states to establish energy offices so that there are fifty offices in this country devoted to energy efficiency and management. This has legitimated energy policy as a state function. States also took the lessons from the California energy crisis as a warning, whether or not they had deregulated electricity. The lesson is the same today as it was twenty years ago—states have to protect their interests against outside forces, whether natural or economic and perhaps especially in the absence of federal policy leadership.

Lessons from Electricity Deregulation

Most states deregulated electricity because they were promised that choice of provider would lead to lower prices—simple economics. The reality is that the real beneficiaries of deregulation are the large users—factories, hotels and shopping malls, for example—who are able to negotiate directly with suppliers. Most residential consumers either do not get much of a choice or have not seen any reduction in prices. The largest part of the price of electricity is in transmission and delivery and these segments of the market are still regulated. For those of us who have chosen a supplier different from the regulated utility, savings are very hard to see and billing has become far more complex In any case, savings are probably in the range of pennies per month, not a significant amount.

What deregulation does, however, is take away the state's ability to require utilities to promote demand side management. Companies are now in competition to sell as many electrons as they can and no company has the incentive to promote conservation, which would amount to telling their customers to buy less of their product. That's the only way the market can work, after all. So, one important lesson of deregulation is that state governments have to develop programs and incentives to encourage energy efficiency and conservation.

A second lesson is that the market cannot protect public interests--that's not its function. Those state interests in energy policy that have remained stable over more than thirty years are (1) having a sufficient supply of energy for all current users and for economic development, (2) at a price that all users can afford, (3) delivered in such a way that environmental damage is minimized. States have to continue to take a strong role in planning and management of energy resources, especially states that have deregulated. This means ensuring that there will be sufficient capacity available to meet peak demand periods either in the state or through contracts with other suppliers. One of the reasons that the supply fell so much in California, during the winter when demand for electricity falls far below the peak, was the fact that the companies took several generators off-line for maintenance at the same time. The regulated utilities had always staggered maintenance so that supply would remain sufficient. The independent companies that bought those facilities were not required to consult with each other and the resulting shortfall of in-state electricity generation caused the prices to rise and sporadic brownouts to occur.

A third lesson is that you can't depend on the federal government to help you out. The Federal Energy Regulatory Commission contributed to the crisis in California by refusing to place a price cap on wholesale electricity in January. This sent a signal to the market that the federal government was unwilling to place any curbs on runaway prices. When the cap was finally imposed in May, the market settled down immediately, but by then one of the country's largest utilities had already declared bankruptcy. The current position of the federal government on global warming, despite the growing body of evidence of its occurrence and the conclusions of a majority of the world's scientists, again sends the market a message to continue business as usual. Any solid policies for mitigation of global warming will have to come from the states at this point.

For all these reasons, states have incentives to develop their own energy and sustainability policies and to work with their cities to improve energy management and sustainable development. States and cities are also taking the lead in developing policies to reduce greenhouse gases and ameliorate somewhat the advance of global warming.

State and Municipal Energy Policies

An Internet search of energy policy activities in the states and cities turns up a wealth of examples across the U.S. Here is a sampling of these policies and programs to illustrate the wealth of energy programs in the states, both "red" and "blue."[7]

Renewable Portfolio Standards (RPS)

Eighteen states have adopted renewable portfolio standards that mandate that a percentage of electricity within the state will be generated from renewable sources. States have set goals for renewable generation as high as 25% by 2020 (Renewable Energy Policy Project). Cities are also promoting renewables. Voters in Columbia, Missouri, approved a proposal to adopt a local renewables portfolio standard in November 2004. The city is required to generate or purchase electricity generated from eligible renewable energy sources at escalating levels, beginning at 2% in 2007 and achieving 15% by December 31, 2022 (Database of State Incentives for Renewable Energy).

The State of Nevada's RPS is being used to accelerate the market for distributed Photovoltaic (Solar) Systems. The program provides double renewable credits

---

7 Energy policy is neither a Republican nor Democrat thing. Republicans like Theodore Roosevelt were the first conservationists; Richard Nixon established many environmental agencies in Washington; George H. W. Bush had a much better understanding of energy policy than Bill Clinton did, despite the presence of Al Gore in his administration.

that can be sold or traded to retailers of electricity to drive down the net cost of the systems to participants. In 2004, the Washoe Tribe was the first participant in the Solar Energy Systems Program. The state's goal is to create a demand for PV systems and "create a 'market pull' that will in turn create new, skilled jobs" and the development of a solar energy industry in Nevada (Public Utilities Commission of Nevada).

Another Indian tribe, the Rosebud Lakota Sioux Reservation in South Dakota has developed a utility scale wind generation project. The reservation lies in the great prairie where winds of 18 mph are typical on a summer day. The tribe has constructed twenty turbines that generate enough electricity to produce revenues of $600,000 per year (www.stopglobalwarming.org).

Green Building Initiatives

States and municipalities are promoting the construction of green buildings, which "use resources more efficiently and effectively and provide healthier environments for working, learning and living" (New York State Department of Environmental Conservation). The state provides technical assistance and tax incentives to encourage green building. The Freedom Tower proposed for the World Trade Center site incorporates many green building elements.

Other State Initiatives

The Apollo Alliance summarizes other programs that states have developed that exceed federal proposals. Minnesota, for example, will require twenty percent renewable fuel (ethanol) for vehicles by 2012. Several states have adopted stronger standards or faster phase-in schedules for appliance efficiency standards. Twenty-four states have dedicated funding streams for clean energy or efficiency programs that do not have to rely on year-to-year budget appropriations (Apollo Alliance).

Municipal Initiatives

Cities across the country are embracing renewable energy and sustainable development. New York City Mayor Michael Bloomberg has developed PlaNYC with programs to reduce the city's carbon footprint significantly by 2030. The plan is visionary and includes controversial policies, such as congestion pricing to reduce traffic congestion in Manhattan.

Two other cities are featured here, Madison, Wisconsin, and Portland, Oregon. The Mayor of Madison established an Energy Task Force to promote green building standards and develop a long-term energy generation and distribution plan for the city. The city also has a Sustainable Design and Energy Committee whose mission is to work to implement the recommendations in "Building a Green Capital City: A Blueprint to Madison's Sustainable Design and Energy Future." The committee's website states that it will focus on "sustainable community development, energy conservation, renewable energy, green building, and greening city operations." (City of Madison, WI).

The City of Portland has established an Office of Sustainable Development whose mission is "to provide leadership and contribute practical solutions to ensure a prosperous community where people and nature thrive, now and in the future" (City of Portland). Through the efforts of this office, Portland and Multnomah County have reduced greenhouse gas emissions to 1990 levels, the requirement of the Kyoto Protocol. The office promotes and works to retain and recruit "green" business. It offers a variety of programs for energy management, toxics reduction, recycling, green building and promotion of sustainable technologies and practices.

Over 300 U.S. cities have pledged to adopt the Kyoto Protocol goals, despite the Bush Administration's refusal to comply with the treaty because of fears of economic dislocation. Many other cities have established programs to promote sustainable development and energy management.

Lessons from Electricity Deregulation

Electricity deregulation produced some positive benefits for state and local policy. In California, the deregulation policy exempted municipally-owned electricity companies from restructuring. As a result, three cities that had municipal utility districts (MUDs) for electricity—Alameda, Los Angeles, and Sacramento—were spared the price-gouging and brownouts that affected the rest of the state. Several municipalities and MUDs began investigating the possibility of developing generating capacity in the aftermath. Sacramento MUD (SMUD) is an interesting case of the potential for citizen-owned utilities. Earlier in the decade, the citizens of Sacramento voted to decommission the nuclear power plant owned by SMUD and pay higher bills for a period to amortize the investment. As owners, the citizens were able to dictate to the utility their choices for generating fuel in a more forceful and direct way than the larger market might have allowed.

In states that still have active deregulation, the policy can be designed to empower municipalities to become large energy users and to negotiate electricity prices for their residents. The primary beneficiaries of electricity deregulation everywhere are the large users, generally industries, commercial users, hotels, shopping malls, etc. They are able to negotiate with providers anywhere long-term contracts locking in low prices. The State of Ohio law enables cities to be designated "purchasing aggregates," giving them the market power of a large user. In this model, all the residents of the city are mandated to be part of the aggregate in exchange for guaranteed lowest electricity price. Thus, residents no longer have choice of provider, but they are buying their electricity at a lower price, which was the main goal of electricity deregulation.

Even in California, where deregulation has been suspended since 2001, large users can still negotiate directly with suppliers. The City of Hayward, in 2002, considered the possibility of becoming the energy broker for the electricity to be generated by a proposed new plant to be located in the city. The plant has never been built since the company, Calpine, had to declare bankruptcy; however, the concept of cities as brokers is viable and could serve as a proxy for a municipally-owned utility.

The New State Laboratories

Justice Louis Brandeis argued that states can be laboratories for programs and policies without risk to the rest of the country. Boeckelman finds that states can influence federal policy adoption, depending on the issue and the strength of the policy area. Welfare reform originated in the states and is arguably one of the most effective federal policies of the past twenty years.

At the same time, state level policy design may be superior for establishing far-reaching policies that can significantly advance sustainable development. When the federal government takes over a policy area, states may find that their own policies have been weakened. In the 1970s, the state of Pennsylvania's law on surface mining became the model for the national law. As a result, the Federal government assumed primacy of surface mining regulation and Pennsylvania was left with a weakened ability to enforce its own policies. The Clean Air Act established minimum national standards for air pollutants. States, in theory, can set more stringent standards, but it is politically difficult to do so. Given the reality of national politics, it may be preferable to keep sustainability policy at the state level where more innovative and far-reaching policies can be developed. The laboratories of democracy are working effectively today to design and promote exciting policies that can lead the United States into a sustainable future.

References

Apollo Alliance. "State Blueprint for Clean Energy & Good Jobs." http://www.apolloalliance.org.
Boeckelman, Keith, 1992. "The Influence of States on Federal Policy Adoptions," *Policy Studies Journal*, Vol. 20, Issue 3, pp. 365–375.
City of Madison, WI. Mayor's Energy Task Force. January 11, 2005. http://www.ci.madison.wi.us/mayor/energy/index.html. Accessed March 6, 2006.
City of Portland, OR. Office of Sustainable Development. http://www.sustainableportland.org/. Accessed March 6, 2006.
Database of State Incentives for Renewable Energy. http://www.dsireusa.org. Accessed March 6, 2006.
Greve, Michael S. (2001). Laboratories of Democracy: Anatomy of a Metaphor. Federalist Outlook. AEI Online (Washington). http://www.aei.org/publications/pubID.12743/pub_detail.asp.
Kash, Don E. and Robert W. Rycroft. 1984. *U.S. Energy Policy: Crisis and Complacency.* Norman, OK: University of Oklahoma Press.

New York State Department of Environmental Conservation. New York State Green Building Initiative. http://www.dec.state.ny.us/website/ppu/grnbldg/index.html. Accessed March 26, 2006.

Public Utilities Commission of Nevada. April 28, 2004. "Washoe Tribe to be First Solar Demonstration Program Participant." http://www.puc.state.ny.us.

Stop Global Warming. July 13, 2005. "8th Stop on the March!" http://www.stopglobalwarming.org/march/. Accessed July 15, 2005.

Timney, Mary M. 2004. Power for the People: Protecting States' Energy Policy Interests in an Era of Deregulation. Armonk, NY: M. E. Sharpe.

7 The Precursors of Governance in the Maine Lobster Fishery

Liying Yan, Carl Wilson, and James Wilson

ABSTRACT

The purpose of the model is to understand how social structure emerges from individual competition in a complex natural and human environment. The model simulates Maine lobster fishery, a social-ecological complex adaptive system. In the model, fishers interact with one another and their environment, and continuously learn how to fish and adapt in a patchy bio-physical environment. Fishers do not have knowledge of the resource distribution and they only have imperfect knowledge of other fishers' performance. The evolution of fishers' fishing strategies and the patchy, changing and poorly known social-ecological environment are the central factors that lead to the general patterns of competition/cooperation and the generation of social structure. When fishers in the model are allowed to cut other fishers' traps, territoriality emerges, which makes governance feasible.

Introduction

We describe an agent-based model in which the rules governing the actions of individual agents evolve.[1]
The context of the model is the Maine lobster fishery. The lobster fishery is interesting because:

1. Technological, biological and social circumstances have led to self-organized governance at a very local level.

2. There is a sense of stewardship, a sense that self-interest is consistent with conservation,

3.   Effective enforcement, and

4. Reasonably effective conservation.

5. This local governance is the 'lowest' level of a multi-scale governance arrangement—local, state, and federal.

6. Similar institutions did not emerge from the activities of the same people working in other fisheries using different technology.

1   This paper is based on the presentation that was given at USSEE conference in 2007 and draws heavily on a paper we published recently (Wilson et al., 2007). This document explains in greater detail the mechanics of the classifier system (Holland, 1976).

The broad question the model addresses is the circumstances that lead to the emergence of social structure. The model starts at a very micro level by modeling the decision process of the individual fisher, specifically, the trap placement decision:

- When a fisher hauls a trap, how does he/she decide where to put it next?
- How does he/she interact with other fishers and the environment?
- How does this lead to the emergence of social structure?

We assume fishers are:

- Boundedly rational, that is, in possession of only some of the information relevant to their environment and only imperfectly able to analyze and act upon that information,
- Profit maximizers (trying to catch as many lobsters as they can),
- Working in a patchy, changing resource and
- Engaged in strategic interactions with other competing fishers.
- Fishers are able to observe and exchange information with other fishers; however,
- New information is costly to fishers in the sense that time they spend to acquire that information is time they do not have the time to acquire other information.

In this kind of environment successful competition requires continuous learning and adaptation. We model two kinds of competition:

- Scramble competition in which fishers race to find the lobsters first, and
- Interference competition in which fishers directly interfere with the ability of other fishers to compete—trap cutting.

Both kinds of competition play out in a multi-scale bio-physical environment. In this environment there are three spatial scales (Figure 1)—a global scale that is a 70 x 70 grid; an intermediate scale with 24 irregular ecological zones, and a very local scale that is the 3x3 neighborhood (around each trap). There are also three temporal scales: an annual scale with an indefinite number of years, a seasonal scale in which water temperature changes affect lobster metabolism (and catchability at different depths) and a daily scale, 240 days per year.

The bio-physical environment is patchy and changing. Each point on the map (Figure 2) records different depths, bottom types and the current population of lobsters (in that cell). This is a relatively regular environment except for lobster catchability, distribution and density, which change daily in response to fishing, seasonally in response to temperature and annually due to new recruitment.

This bio-physical environment serves as a background for an agent-based simulation in which individual agents compete and cooperate with one another to find lobster. In this kind of environment successful competition requires continuous learning and adaptation. Consequently, the most important aspect of the agent-based classifier system (Holland, 1976) model is the fact that the decision rules of the individual agents evolve.

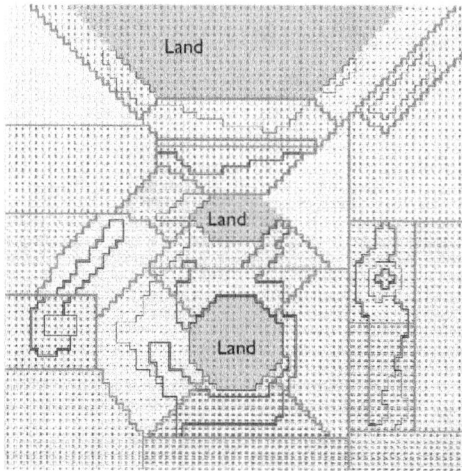

Figure 1 Spatial scale of the model. The whole map is a 70 x 70 grid, and 24 ecological zones are divided by lines.

A decision rule is defined as a unique combination of environmental conditions and a specific action; i.e., "if these environmental conditions, then this action". The list of all the rules held by an agent can be thought of as the agents' memory. Rules can be general or specific to the circumstances. For example, at any particular moment in the fall of the year a fisher might be faced with a fairly general rule that says simply: "If it is fall, fish in deeper water." Alternatively, in that same situation a fisher might find a much more specific rule also applies. For example: "If it is fall, the bottom type is sand, water is shallow and my catch rate is low, then move to deeper water with a rocky bottom." The general form of a rule is shown in Figure 3. Associated with each condition is an action

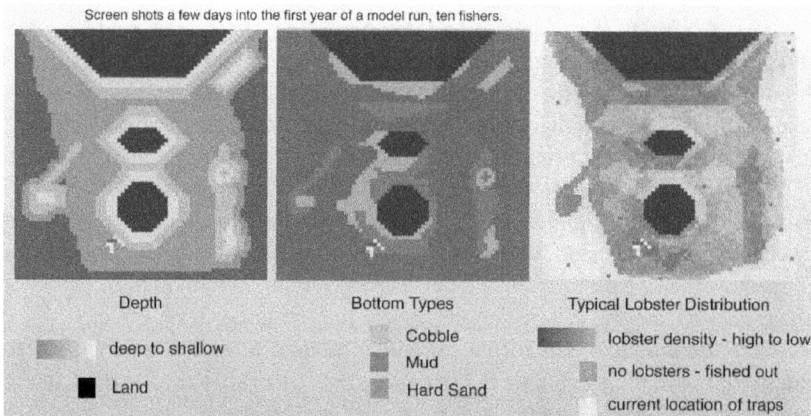

Figure 2 Maps of the bio-physical environment (Screen shots are in year 10, with 10 fishers and 20 traps.)

Rule Base in LCS

condition	:	action	:	strength
#0##	:	01	:	43
#011	:	00	:	32
1011	:	11	:	14
011#	:	01	:	27
0111	:	11	:	18
1#01	:	10	:	24
		. . .		

Figure 3 A generalized rule structure

and a strength which indicates how well the rule has worked in the past. At any moment a fisher might find several rules ranging from very specific to very general apply to the circumstances or conditions he is experiencing. Each rule is a binary string (xx digits in length) with the inclusion of the # character. # is used to indicate "doesn't matter". In other words, a general rule might be a digital string with many # signs. A more specific rule might have very few # signs. Effective adaptation might require very few rules in a simple environment. A complex environment, such as outlined here, requires numerous rules for effective adaptation; we use up to 1,200 per fisher.

In the course of the model run rules are 'tested' and remembered by how well they perform and assigned a strength that reflects their performance. A strong rule is one that has performed well in the past in a particular set of circumstances. A rule only applies to a particular set of circumstances.

Learning through Experience

In the model learning takes place through the experience of the fisher. Fishers acquire experience by continually testing old and inventing new decision rules. (Rules can be thought of as hypotheses.) Productive rules are retained; unproductive rules are discarded. The testing process is diagrammed in Figure 4. The logic is straightforward. The fisher observes the environment, recalls rules used in similar circumstances, chooses a rule that has worked well in these circumstances in the past, applies the rule to the environment and then watches to see how the rule performed. If it performed well its strength in his memory is changed accordingly; if it performed poorly its strength is diminished.

When the model begins fishers are given random rules. Not many of these rules will prove to be valuable but over time new rules are added to the fisher's rule base. New rules are generated in four different ways.

Biophysical and Human Environment

1. Agent senses environment

4. Agent acts and changes the environment

5. Gets feedback about the performance of the rule

2. Recalls rules used in similar circumstances

3. Chooses a rule that performed well in the past

New Rules

Classifiers: Current set of rules (memory)

3b. Strength of rule used just previously is changed

6. Changes rule strength appropriately

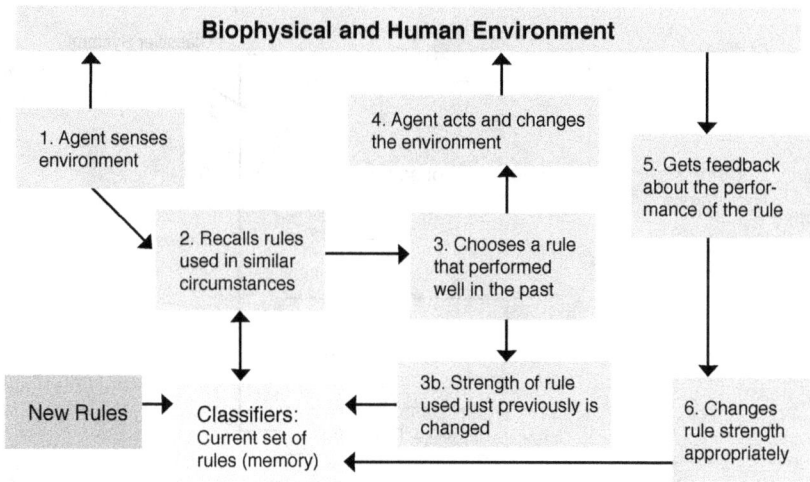

Figure 4 Schematic of zeorth classifier system (ZCS) (Wilson, 1994)

1. **Covering:** When no existing rules apply to current circumstances a new, fairly general rule (many # signs) with those particular circumstances is invented (Wilson, 1994).

2. **Imitation:** When fishers imitate the actions of other fishers they acquire knowledge and translate it into a new rule.

3. **Cross-over:** Occasionally, two existing and closely related rules are 'mated' to produce a new related rule (Holland 1975).

4. **Mutation:** Periodically, not frequently, a slight change in an existing rule is created by 'flipping' one of the bits in the rule string (Holland 1975).

On the first day of the first year of the simulation, a fisher who has random rules does not know how to fish. After the fisher hauls a trap, he/she senses the environment, and sends the information to the classifier system to make decision. For instance, "it is summer, where shall I put the trap?" A bunch of rules match the circumstance, e.g. "if it is summer, go to shallow water," "if it is summer, go to deep water," "if it is summer, stay where you are," etc, and all of them have the same strength, 0, because they have never been tested. The fisher has no preference, and randomly picks one, e.g. "go to deep water." But with this rule, the fisher does not catch any lobster, which deteriorates the strength of the rule. Next time when the fisher meets a similar circumstance, he picks other rules, say "go to shallow water," which turns out to be a good one, and is strengthened by the good feedback. The rule will be chosen again and again later, which makes it stronger and stronger. The fisher eventually forgets to go to deep water in summer (the rule is discarded by the classifier system), and learned that lobsters are easily caught in shallow water in summer. At the meantime, fishers invent and test new rules and learn from others.

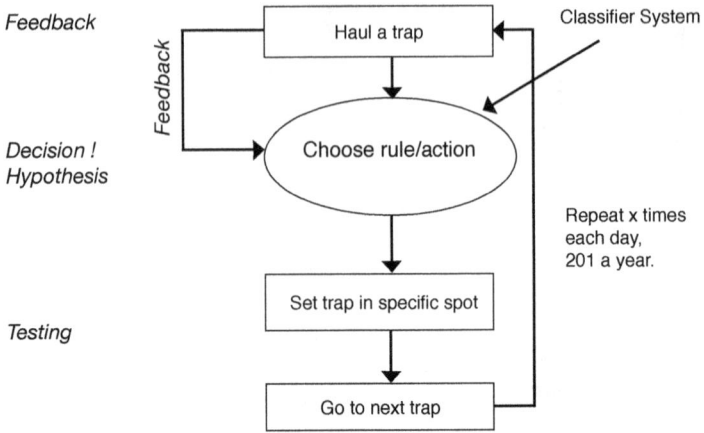

Figure 5 The architecture of the model with only scramble competition

For each fisher this process of rule choice and evolution is embedded in a process described in Figure 5. The fisher hauls a trap; observes the circumstances at that moment, sets the trap in a new or the same location according to the rule chosen and then goes on to haul the next trap. The fisher repeats this process for x traps each day for 240 days. The model computes this process simultaneously for x fishers (usually 30). Each action of each fisher changes the local environment and as time progresses temperatures and lobster catchability and location change. So what the fisher learns at one point in time at one place is not likely to be of value at other times and places; hence the need for a large number of rules.

At the end of each year, profits are counted, a decision to enter or exit is made and new lobsters are recruited to the fishery. This process can be repeated indefinitely but in the model we usually limit each run to 50 years.

Hierarchical decision making

The complexity of this environment generates a very large search space. Approximately 14 trillion rules would be needed to completely describe it. A non-hierarchical search in this kind of changing, complex environment is generally not computable. We simplify the problem by creating a three stage hierarchical decision process, as illustrated in Figure 6.

For each decision fishers first decide upon a broad strategy, i.e., whether to explore a new area, move to the location of their best performing trap, stay at the current location or move to the location of someone else's trap (imitation). This decision making process radically reduces the number of possibilities a fisher

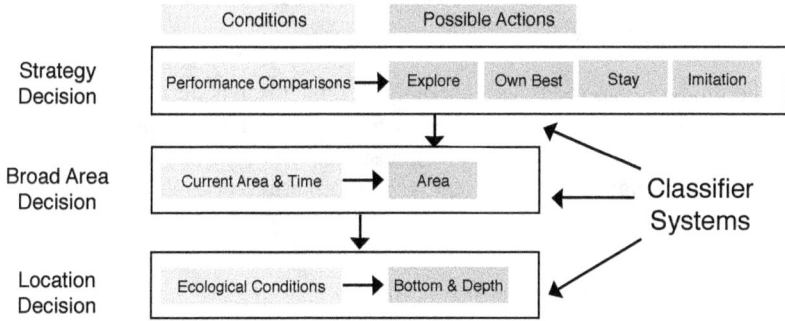

Figure 6 The architecture of the hierarchical classifier systems

has to consider at any point, generally fewer than about 3,000 (as opposed to 14 trillion), and makes the model computable. Table 1 lists the environmental circumstances, the translation of those circumstances into the condition part of a rule and the actions that might take place in scramble competition.

Table 1 Environmental information, conditions evaluated, and actions available to fishers in scramble competition

Environmental Information	*Conditions Evaluated*	*Possible Actions*
Global Information	**For Choice of Strategy (CS#1)**	**Actions for CS#1**
• Season	• Current catch vs Own best	• Stay at current location
• "Coffee house" / Public information about global catch rate	• Own best vs Other's best	• Go to own current best
	• Current catch vs Other's best	• Imitate other best fisher
• Change in global catch rate . . .	• Change in current catch	• Go to an historically productive area—explore
	• Change in global catch . . .	
Broad Area Information		
• Current area (1 of 24 broad locations)	**For Choice of Broad Area (CS#2)**	**Actions for CS#2**
• Orientation of area (compass direction from land)	• Season	• Go to a new area (1 of 24)
• Stemming (travel) cost to farthest trap	• Current location	
• Historical catch in each area . . .		
Local Information		
• Bottom type of current trap	**For Choice of a Particular Location (CS#3)**	**Actions for CS#3**
• Depth of current trap	• Current time	• Same depth and bottom type as current
• Catch rate of current trap	• Current depth	
• Catch rate of other own traps	• Current bottom type	• Different depth and bottom type
• Frequency of encounter with each other fisher		
• Imperfect knowledge of other fisher's catch (depends on frequency of encounters) . . .		

Patterns of Scramble Competition

If the model is run so that only scramble competition is permitted (i.e., fishers are not allowed to cut one another's traps), there are four robust patterns that emerge; all are a function of patchiness and communication among fishers. They are individual search pattern, group formation, diversity of behavior and collective efficiency.

1 Individual search

Individuals evolve search rules intended to maximize their returns to fishing. The short term search pattern is generally when fishers find a good spot they stay there for several days until the catch rate drops at that spot. After a while—one to several days—according to the partial information about others' performance and the catch rates of his other traps, it becomes apparent that some other location is a better place to be, and then he jumps to a new location. This pattern is a function of the patchiness of the environment and cost of information. With a uniform environment no pattern emerges. Because catch rates on the whole map are same, randomly placing traps would be the best and only strategy.

2 Group formation

Information obtained from others improves the outcome from individual search. In the model, fishers' information about others' catch rates is partial and a function of the frequency of the encounters of two fishers. The more frequently encounters take place, the more reliable the information and the more likely is imitation. The positive feedback arising from imitation leads to persistent groups. Hence, within groups the cost of information decreases and outside of groups the cost increases.

3 Diversity of behavior

If everybody fishes within a group and imitates all the time the scope of information for the group as a whole declines due to the lack of exploration. In order to get more information about the lobster distribution and obtain as high a catch rate as possible in the complex environment, fishers learn that both fishing in and out of the group is advantageous. When the collective benefit decreases in the group, fishers start to fish autonomously, and get more benefit by exploring, and vice versa. The collective result leads to the fourth pattern described below, a more diverse, efficient fleet.

4 Collective efficiency

The combination of individual search, group formation and diversity (i.e., both group and autonomous action) leads to collective efficiency, i.e., traps are allocated

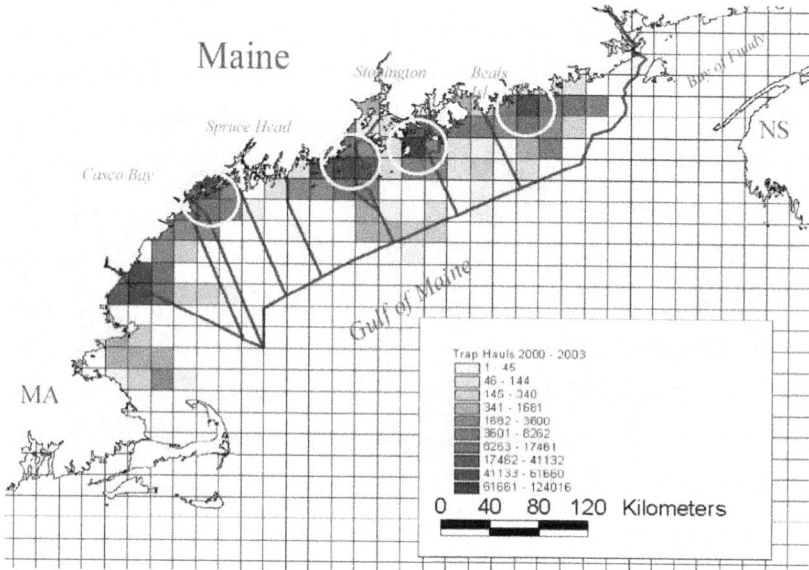

Figure 7 Trap distribution map of Gulf of Maine

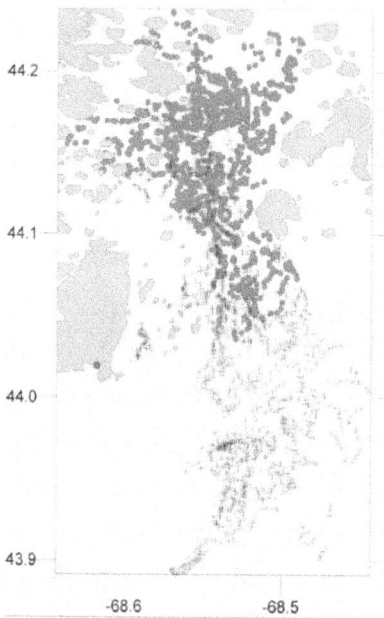

Figure 8 Trap distribution map of Jericho Bay, near Stonington. Dark grey represents the location of trap hauls in July and light grey November. The data set shown here includes 12 fishers' 18,000 trap hauls from June 2002 to Feb. 2003.

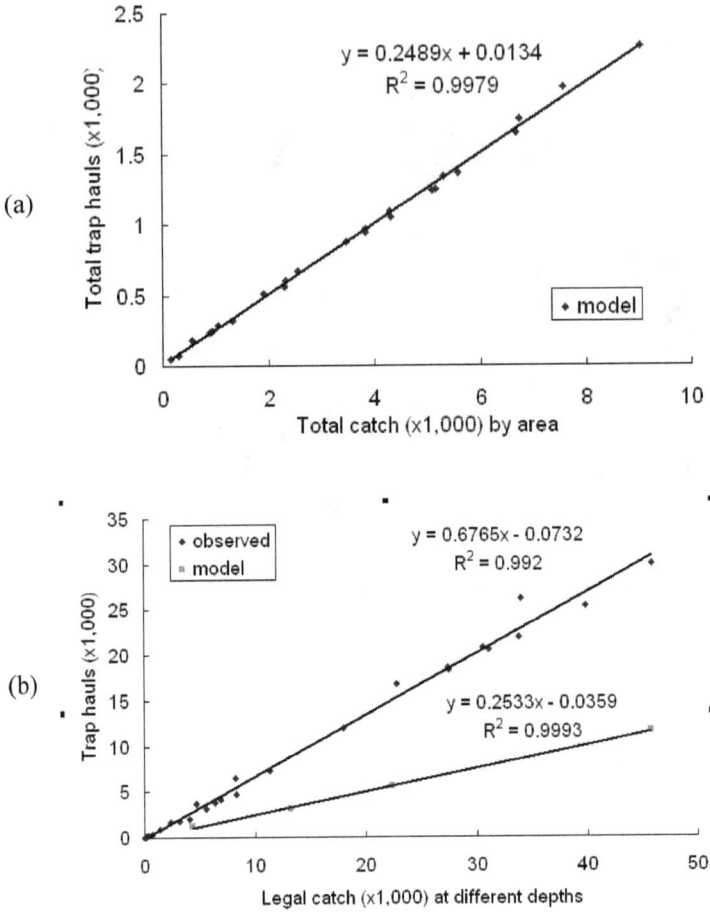

Figure 9 The efficient allocation of fishing effort. (a) shows the way traps are allocated by depth in both the real fishery and the model fishery. In both cases, the number of traps allocated to a depth is in almost strict proportion to the catch available at those depths. The different slopes for each line reflect the different densities of lobster relative to traps in the model and the real fishery. (b) shows the same allocation efficiency by ecological area in the model only. Data from the model are catch rate and trap hauls in year 50.

in proportion to the changing availability of lobster. This is a clear pattern that emerges from the model. Also, we studied a large data set from the real fishery, and found the same pattern. Figure 7 shows the large scale of the trap distribution in the gulf of Maine, and Figure 8 is a finer-scale view of Jericho Bay.

Figure 9 shows the data of the efficient allocation of fishing effort both from the real fishery and the model.

Territoriality

With only scramble competition, fishers fish like roving bandits, i.e., they fish all over the map. The last pattern, territoriality, arises from interference competition—trap cutting. In order to reduce competition, fishers can directly interfere with the competitive ability of other fishers by cutting their traps; it is as if retailers could burn one another's stores. The benefits and costs of cutting are different with neighbors (same group) and non-neighbors (another group). Cutting neighbors' traps is unfavorable due to high retaliation costs resulting from high frequency of encounters. When fishing with neighbors and cutting nonneighbors' traps, neighbors can be expected to act in a way that is consistent with the fisher's own actions, thereby reinforcing his/her actions; when fishing with nonneighbors and cutting nonneighbors' traps, nonneighbors will act in a way that counters the fisher's actions, thereby nullifying his/her actions.

Another classifier system was designed for fishers to make trap cutting decisions. Fishers are from two different harbors, A and B. Figure 10 illustrates how trap cutting module (circled by a large oval) fits into the whole model and two forms of feedback (circled by two small ovals) from trap cutting. When fishers place traps in a new spot, two fishers in the same ecological area, randomly picked and paired by the model, make a decision about whether to cut or ignore the other's trap according to the calculation of benefit and cost, which is the direct feedback that goes to the trap cutting classifier system. After taking actions,

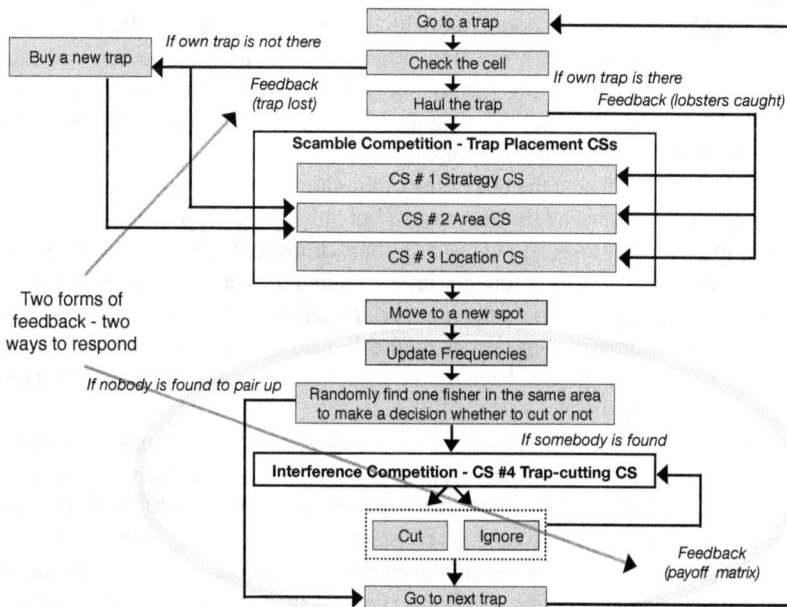

Figure 10 The architecture of the model with both trap placement classifier systems and trap cutting classifier system, and two forms of feedback to CS.

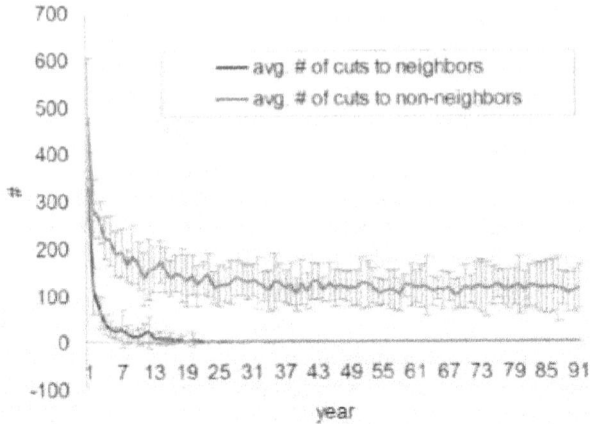

Figure 11 Trap cutting of neighbors and nonneighbors.

fishers go to haul their next trap. If the trap is cut, they will buy a new trap and put it into a new place, and at the meantime, the cost of losing a trap is the second form of feedback that is sent to the trap placement classifier system and teaches fishers that traps are more likely to be cut in the current area.

With interference competition, the fifth pattern, territoriality, emerges. Because traps are expensive, worth several days fishing, fishers learn to not cut their neighbors' traps, i.e. cooperate with neighbors, because retaliation cannot be avoided. Also they learn in some areas traps are likely to be cut, and thus they retreat and avoid fishing with nonneighbors, which results in segregation. Finally, they do learn to cut nonneighbors' traps, i.e., compete with nonneighbors, when they do encounter them.

Figure 11 shows that at the beginning of the simulation, fishers cut others' traps randomly, about half of all the encounters, but quickly they learn to not cut neighbors' trap and the number of cuts to neighbors drops to 0. The number of cuts to nonneighbors drops quickly too, but later it maintains in a constant level. That is because fishers segregate, i.e., the number of encounters between neighbors and nonneighbors decreases (Figure 12). Figure 12 also shows that fishers do learn to compete with nonneighbors, because the percentage of cuts per nonneighbor encounters increases.

Figure 13 shows the percent of all visits by fishers from a particular group (Harbor A in the model) in each ecological zone. Without interference competition, fishers fish all over the map. After fishers learn where to place their traps, the pattern of trap allocation remains constant. With trap cutting, it shows the segregation pattern. The 24 ecological zones quickly separate into three categories, one dominated by fishers from Harbor A (lines on the top of the figure), one dominated by fisher from Harbor B (lines at the bottom of the figure), and contested areas (lines in the middle) that are visited by both groups. Trap cutting usually happens in contested areas.

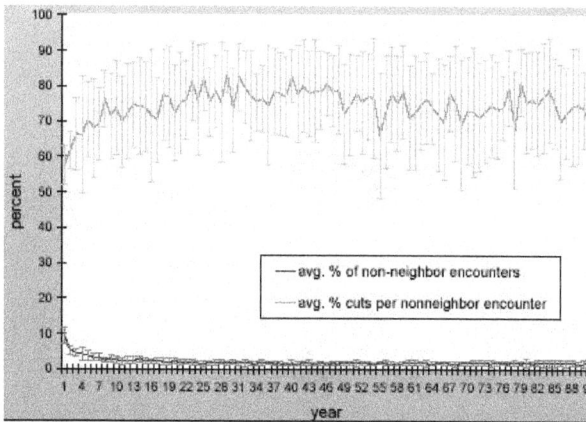

Figure 12 Percent of nonneighbor encounters and percent of cuts per nonneighbor encounter

Figure 14 is a visual description of Figure 13. It shows the territories after 100 years. White means 100% of visits are from Harbor A, and black means 0%. Without trap cutting, all 24 ecological areas are grey, which means fishers fish all over the map. With trap cutting, the pattern is dramatically different. Most zones are either black or white. Only several zones are grey, and they are contested zones in which most trap cutting happens.

Conclusions

A patchy, changing environment makes knowledge of the resource valuable, provides a strong incentive for individual search, for the formation of groups and for diverse fishing strategies. The collective result is efficient exploitation of resources; but there are no boundaries, just roving bandits and no ability to exclude. The possibility of trap cutting causes a radical change in spatial location of fishing and the formation of territories.

The social result is the formation of self-organizing, persistent groups, whose members communicate frequently, operate within well defined boundaries, and depend upon each others' restraint for their economic well being.

These are circumstances that facilitate (but do not assure) successful collective action.

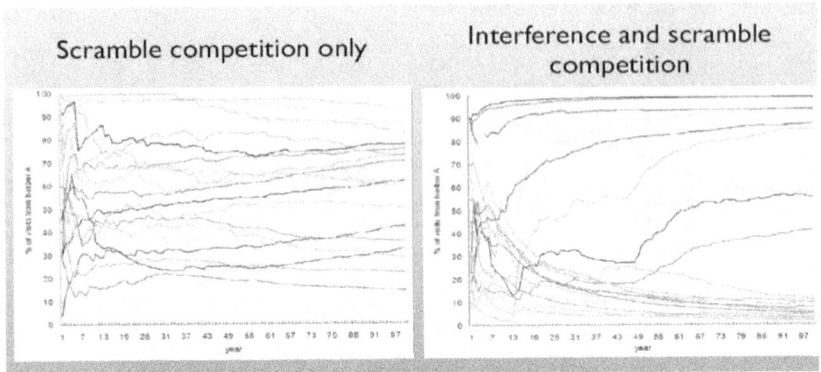

Figure 13 Evolution of territory with and without trap cutting. Each series in the figures
records the percent of fishing by fishers from Harbor A in one of 24 ecological
areas.

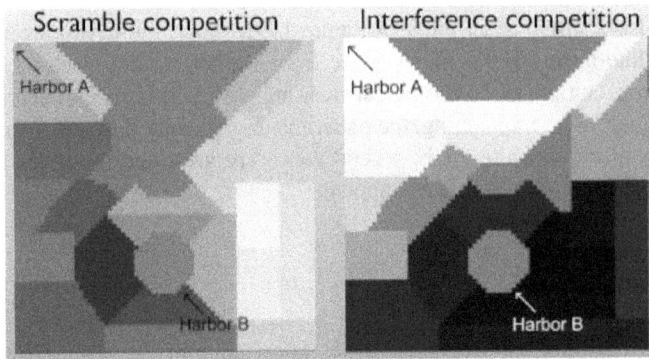

Figure 14 Area fished with and without interference competition. Percent of fishing in
24 ecological areas by fishers from Harbor A—black =100%; white = 0%

References

Holland, J. H. (1975). *Adaptation in Natural and Artificial Systems*. Ann Arbor,
MI: University of Michigan Press.

Holland, J. H. (1976). Adaptation. In R. Rosen and F. M. Snell, *Progress in
Theoretical Biology*, Vol. 4. New York: Plenum. 263–293.

Wilson, J., Yan, L., and Wilson, C. (2007). The precursors of governance in the
Maine lobster fishery. Proceedings of the National Academy of Sciences
USA 104:15212-15217.

Wilson, S. W. (1994). ZCS: A zeroth level classifier system. *Evolutionary Computation (2)*:1–18.

8   Ecological Economics

An Analytical Thermodynamic Theory

Jing Chen

Abstract

More and more researchers in ecological economics have recognized that the
biophysical approach provides a better foundation to understand human society and its long term evolution than mainstream economic theory. However,
ecological economics textbooks are still written from the mainstream economics perspective. This is largely due to a lack of analytical theory in ecological
economics. One would expect that an analytical theory based on sound physical
foundation would provide a clearer understanding of our daily activities than
mainstream economics, whose foundation has been challenged by more and
more researchers. This is indeed the case. In this paper, we present a newly
developed analytical thermodynamic theory of ecological economics and show
how it provides much more realistic and intuitive understanding of economic,
social and biological phenomena than mainstream economic theory. This theory
turns the insights from ecological economics into an analytical model that can
be applied to day to day business activities. It will help transform ecological economics from a niche subject into the theoretical foundation of social sciences.

Keywords: ecological economics, analytical thermodynamic theory, cost structure, return

1   Introduction

More and more researchers in ecological economics have recognized that the
biophysical approach provides better foundation to understand human society
and its long term evolution than mainstream economic theory. However, ecological economics textbooks are still written from the perspective of mainstream
economics (Stern, 2007). This is largely due to a lack of analytical theory in
ecological economics. One would expect that an analytical theory based on a
sound physical foundation would provide a clearer understanding of our daily
activities than mainstream economics, whose foundation has been challenged
by more and more researchers. This is indeed the case. A newly developed
analytical thermodynamic theory of ecological economics provides much more

realistic and intuitive understanding of economic, social and biological phenomena than mainstream economic theory (Chen, 2005). In this paper, we will present a more detailed discussion of the production theory, which forms one part of the analytical theory, and show how the new production theory provides a simple and systematic understanding business investment problems we encounter frequently.

Because of the fundamental link between thermodynamics and life, many attempts have been made to develop analytical theories based on the principle of thermodynamics and apply them to living systems and human society. These include Lorenz' chaos theory and Prigorgine's far from equilibrium thermodynamic theory. Lorenz, a meteorologist, simplified weather equations, which are thermodynamic equations, into ordinary differential equations. He found chaos properties from these equations. Prigorgine developed the theory from some chemical reactions. The theories of Lorenz and Prigorgine greatly influenced the thinking in biology and social sciences. However, they do not model life process or social activities directly. Chaos theory and Prigorgine's theory, while providing good insights to the research in biological and social sciences, are mostly analogies. Many of the recent works on the application of physics to economics are summarized in Farmer et al. (2005). These works apply the techniques from research in physics to economics and do not directly model economic activities as physical processes.

Since uncertainty is an integral part of life processes, the advancement of stochastic calculus is essential for the development of an analytical thermodynamic theory of life and human society. In the past several decades, some fundamental works in the area of stochastic calculus were undertaken by people with very diverse backgrounds. Three works are particularly relevant to the development of our theory. The first is Ito's Lemma, which provides a rule to find the differential of a function of stochastic variable. Ito's Lemma was obtained in 1940s. But its importance was not recognized until its wide spread application in financial economics several decades later. Ito was awarded Gauss Prize in 2006, sixty years after his theory was initially developed.

The second tool is Feynman-Kac formula, which maps a stochastic process into a deterministic thermodynamic equation. Richard Feynman (1948) attempted to simplify calculation in quantum mechanics by transforming problems in stochastic processes into problems in deterministic processes. The new mathematical technique enabled him to perform many computations in quantum mechanics which were very difficult in the past. With this he established the theory of quantum electrodynamics. The breakthrough in physics is often generated by the breakthrough in new mathematical methods, which enables us to describe the subtler parts of the nature. An important motivation in Feynman's research was his seek for universality. "The question that then arose was what Dirac had meant by the phrase 'analogous to,' and Feynman determined to find out whether or not it would be possible to substitute the phrase 'equal to.'" (Feynman and Hibbs, 1965, p. viii) Feynman, together with Tomonaga and Schwinger, was awarded Nobel Prize in physics for this work in 1965. Despite its highly technical nature, Feynman-Kac formula is a very general result and has proved to be extremely useful in many different fields. In particular, Feynman-Kac formula has been widely used in the research in finance recently. It was even suggested that "Feynman could be claimed as the father of financial economics" (Dixit and Pindyck, 1994, p. 123).

The third is Black-Scholes (1973) option pricing theory, which provides an analytical formula of observable variables to price a financial instrument whose payoff depends on a stochastic process. This is a landmark contribution in social sciences. It shows that a complex economic problem can be effectively modeled by a stochastic process, a simple and deterministic analytical theory about it can be developed and much information about it can be obtained through such an analytical theory. Fischer Black, one of the co-developers of the Black-Scholes theory, was a legendary figure in finance.

Fischer never took a course in either economics or finance, so he never learned the way you were supposed to do things. But that lack of training proved to be an advantage, ... since the traditional methods in those fields were better at producing academic careers than new knowledge. Fischer's intellectual formation was instead in physics and mathematics, and his success in finance came from applying the methods of astrophysics. Lacking the ability to run controlled experiments on the stars, the astrophysist relies on careful observation and then imagination to find the simplicity underlying apparent complexity. In Fischer's hands, the same habits of research turned out to be effective for producing new knowledge in finance. (Mehrling, 2005, p. 6)

Black-Scholes option theory provides the earliest inspiration in developing an analytical thermodynamic theory of life and human society. More detailed discussion about its history can be found in Chen (2005). In the following, we will briefly discuss the basic ideas of this theory.

There are two fundamental properties about life. First, living organisms need to extract resources from the environment to compensate for the continuous loss of resources required to maintain various functions of life. Second, for an organism to be viable, the total cost of extracting resources has to be less than the amount of resources extracted (Odum, 1971 and Hall et al, 1986). The second property could be understood as natural selection rephrased from the resource perspective. The purpose of our work is to derive a self-contained mathematical theory of production from these two fundamental properties about life.

From the physics perspective, resources can be regarded as low entropy sources (Georgescu-Roegen, 1971). The entropy law states that systems tend toward higher entropy states spontaneously. Living systems, as non-equilibrium systems, need to extract low entropy from the environment to compensate for their continuous dissipation. It can be represented mathematically by lognormal processes, which contain a growth term and a dissipation term. From the entropy law, the thermodynamic dissipation of an organic or economic system is spontaneous. The extraction of low entropy from the environment, however, depends on specific biological or institutional structures that incur fixed or maintenance costs. Additional variable cost is required for resource extraction.

Higher fixed cost systems generally have lower variable costs. Fixed cost is largely determined by genetic structure of an organism or design of a project. Variable cost is a function of environment. From the Feynman-Kac formula, a result widely used in science literature and increasingly used in finance literature, we derive the thermodynamic equation that variable cost of a production system should satisfy. An organism survives if the amount of resources it extracts is higher than the total cost. Similarly, a business survives if its revenue is higher than the total cost of production. We set the initial condition of the equation so that total cost is equal to the amount of resource extracted or revenue generated. Then we solve the thermodynamic equation to derive an analytic formula that explicitly represents the relation among fixed costs, variable costs, uncertainty of the environment, discount rate and the duration of a production system, which is the core concern in most economic decisions.

It is often suggested that economic theories, for analytical ease and tractability, sacrifice their relevance to reality (Hall, et al, 2001). This new theory shows that an economic theory based on the firm foundation of reality is actually analytically easier and more tractable. In this paper, we show that the analytical representation of various factors in production processes enables us to directly compute and analyze the returns of different production systems under various kinds of environment in a simple and systematic way. The results are highly consistent with the empirical evidences obtained from the vast amount of literature in economics and ecology. Furthermore, the theory, by putting major factors of production into a single mathematical model, provides precise insights about the tradeoffs and constraints of various business or evolutionary strategies that are often lost in intuitive thinking. For example, in the business literature, some emphasize training of employee, others emphasize cost cutting. But employee training is costly. The tradeoff between better training and lower cost is often not explicitly discussed in the same literature. Our theory provides specific suggestion whether more training or cost cutting is more profitable under different kinds of circumstances.

Mainstream economists pay little attention to the biophysical foundation of human society because they believe special qualities of human beings will make physical constraints less relevant. A biophysical approach puts the physical constraint of human society at the center of its analysis. The validity of a physical theory is best manifested by the existence of a corresponding mathematical theory that is derived from the most fundamental properties of life and is consistent with a wide range of patterns observed in both economics and ecology. After all, all physical laws are represented by mathematical formulas. The computability of the mathematical theory will transform biological science, which include social science as a special case, into an integral part of physics.

Simplicity and universality are the hallmarks of this theory. All the results in the paper have been taught at undergraduate classes and the students embrace the ideas enthusiastically. Since all the results are calculated from simple analytical formulas, they can be reproduced and applied easily by researchers and students. An Excel file containing all the calculation and graphs in this paper can be obtained from the author.

This paper is structured as follows. Section 2 presents the derivation of the analytical thermodynamic theory. Section 3 presents some detailed results from this theory. Section 4 compares the analytical thermodynamic theory with the neoclassical economic theory. Section 5 concludes.

2 An analytical thermodynamic theory of production

The theory described in this section, which is adapted from Chen (2005), can be applied to both biological and economic systems. For simplicity of exposition, we will use the language of economics. But the extension to biological system is straight forward and is consistent with the ideas put forth by Odum, (1971) and Hall et al, (1986).

A basic property in economic activities is uncertainty. While a business may face many different kinds of uncertainty, most of the uncertainties are reflected in the price uncertainty of the product. Suppose S represents unit price of a commodity, r, the expected rate of change of price and σ, the rate of uncertainty. Then the process of S can be represented by the lognormal process where

$$\frac{dS}{S} = rdt + \sigma dz \tag{1}$$

$dz = \varepsilon \sqrt{dt}$, $\varepsilon \in N(0,1)$ is a random variable with standard Gaussian distribution.

The production of the commodity involves fixed cost and variable cost. In general, production factors that last for a long term, such as capital equipment, are considered as fixed cost while production factors that last for a short term, such as raw materials, are considered variable costs. If employees are on long term contracts, they may be better classified as fixed costs, although in many cases, they are classified as variable costs. Firms can adjust their level of fixed and variable costs to achieve high level of return on their investment. Intuitively, in a large and stable market, firms will invest heavily on fixed cost to reduce variable cost, thus achieving higher level of economy of scale. In a small or volatile market, firms will invest less on fixed cost to maintain high level of flexibility. In the following, we will derive a formal mathematical theory that focuses on this issue.

In natural science, there is a long tradition of studying stochastic processes with deterministic partial differential equations. For example, heat is a random movement of molecules. But the heat process is often studied by heat equation, a type of partial differential equations. In studying quantum electrodynamics, Richard Feynman (1948) developed a general method to study probability wave function with partial differential equations. Kac (1951) provided a more systematic exposition of this method, which was later known as Feynman-Kac formula, whose use is very common in natural sciences (Kac, 1985). Recently, Feynman-

Kac formula has been widely used in the research in finance. What I want to do is to apply Feynman-Kac formula to derive variable cost in production as a function of other parameters.

Let K represents fixed cost and C represents variable cost, which is a function of S, the value of the commodity. If the discount rate of a firm is r, from the Feynman-Kac formula (Øksendal, 1998, p. 135), the variable cost, C, as a function of S, satisfies the following equation

$$\frac{\partial C}{\partial t} = rS\frac{\partial C}{\partial S} + \frac{1}{2}\sigma^2 S^2 \frac{\partial^2 C}{\partial S^2} - rC \tag{2}$$

with the initial condition

$$C(S,0) = f(S) \tag{3}$$

To determine *f(S)*, we perform a thought experiment about a project with a duration that is infinitesimally small. When the duration of a project is sufficiently small, it has only enough time to produce one unit of product. In this situation, if the fixed cost is lower than the value of the product, the variable cost should be the difference between the value of the product and the fixed cost to avoid arbitrage opportunity. If the fixed cost is higher than the value of the product, there should be no extra variable cost needed for this product. Mathematically, the initial condition for the variable cost is the following:

$$C(S,0) = \max(S - K, 0) \tag{4}$$

where S is the value of the commodity and K is the fixed cost of a project. When the duration of a project is T, solving equation (2) with the initial condition (4) yields the following solution

$$C = SN(d_1) - Ke^{-rT}N(d_2) \tag{5}$$

where $d_1 = \dfrac{\ln(S/K) + (r + \sigma^2/2)T}{\sigma\sqrt{T}}$

$d_2 = \dfrac{\ln(S/K) + (r - \sigma^2/2)T}{\sigma\sqrt{T}} = d_1 - \sigma\sqrt{T}$

The function *N(x)* is the cumulative probability distribution function for a standardized normal random variable. Formula (5) takes the same form as the well-known Black-Scholes (1973) formula for European call options.

Formula (5) provides an analytical formula of variable cost as a function of fixed cost, uncertainty, duration of project and discount rate of a firm. A new theory is ultimately justified by its implications. We will look at the properties and implications of this theory. First, when fixed costs, K, are higher, variable costs,

C, are lower. Second, for the same amount of fixed cost, when the duration of a project, T, is longer, variable cost is higher. Third, when uncertainty, σ, increases, variable cost increases. Fourth, when fixed cost approaches zero, variable cost will approach to the value of the product. Fifth, when the value of a product approaches zero, variable cost will approach zero as well. All these properties are consistent with our intuitive understanding of production processes.

Suppose the volume of output during the project life is Q, which is bound by production capacity or market size. We assume the present value of the product to be S and variable cost to be C during the project life. Then the total present value of the product and the total cost of production are

$$SQ \text{ and } CQ + K \tag{6}$$

respectively. The return of this project can be represented by

$$\ln\left(\frac{SQ}{CQ+K}\right) \tag{7}$$

and the net present value of the project is

$$QS - (QC + K) + Q(S - C) - K \tag{8}$$

Unlike a conceptual framework, this mathematical theory enables us to make quantitative calculation of returns of different projects under different kinds of environments. We will provide a systematic analysis in the next section.

3   Systematic analysis of the performance of a project

The profit or return of a project is determined by fixed cost, variable cost and total output during the life of the project. Variable cost is a function of fixed cost, uncertainty, duration of the project, and discount rate. Since how much to invest or commit at the beginning of the project is the most important decision to make, we will first discuss how fixed cost is related to uncertainty, duration of the project, discount rate and total output in determining the performance of the project. Then we will discuss how other factors are related to each other.

Fixed cost and uncertainty

Calculating variable costs from (5), we find that, as fixed costs are increased, variable costs decrease rapidly in a low market uncertainty environment and change very little in a high market uncertainty environment. Put it in another way, high fixed cost systems are very sensitive to the change of market uncertainty level while low fixed cost systems are not. This is illustrated in Figure 1.

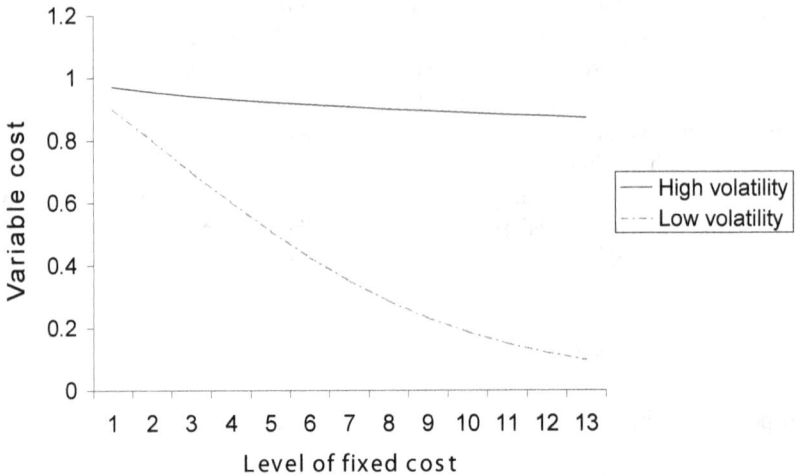

Figure 1 Fixed cost and uncertainty: In a low uncertainty environment, variable cost
drops sharply as fixed costs are increased. In a high uncertainty environment,
variable costs change little with the level of fixed cost.

The above calculation indicates that higher fixed investment is more effective in
a low uncertainty environment and lower fixed cost investment is more flexible
in high uncertainty environment. This explains mature industries, such as household supplies, are dominated by large companies such as P&G while innovative
industries, such as IT, are pioneered by small and new firms. Microsoft, Apple,
CISCO, Yahoo, Google and countless other innovative businesses are started by
one or two individuals and not by established firms. Despite the financial and
technical clout of large firms, small firms account for a disproportionately high
share of innovative activity (Acs and Audretsch, 1990).

Similarly, in scientific research, mature areas are generally dominated by top
researchers from elite schools, while scientific revolutions are often initiated by
newcomers or outsiders (Kuhn, 1996).

Fixed cost and duration of the project

We study how the level of duration of projects affects rate of return. If duration
of a project is too short, we may not be able to recoup the fixed cost invested in
the project. If the duration of a project is too long, the variable cost, or maintenance cost may become too high. This is a natural tradeoff between duration
and maintenance cost. With the mathematical theory, we can make quantitative
calculations. To be specific, we will compare the profit level of one project with
that of two projects with duration half long while keeping other parameters
identical. We also assume the annual output of two types of projects are the same

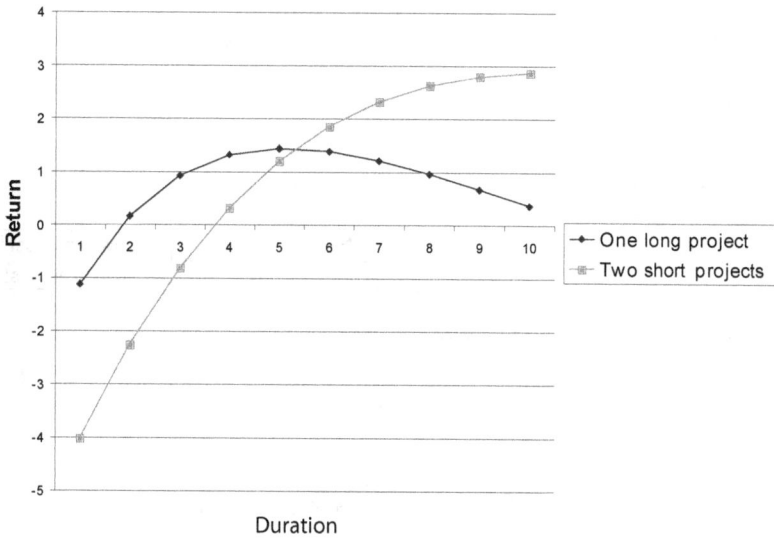

Figure 2 Fixed cost and duration of the project

We find that when duration is short, the profit level of one long project is higher than two short projects. When duration is long, the profit level of one project is lower than two short projects. This is consistent with intuition. The detailed calculation is illustrated in Figure 2. It explains why individual life does not go on forever. Instead, it is more efficient for animals to produce offspring. This also determines most businesses fail in the end (Ormerod, 2005). Calculation also shows that when the level of fixed cost increases, the length of duration for a project to be of positive return also increases. This suggests that large animals and large projects, which have higher fixed cost, often have longer life. There is an empirical regularity that animals of larger sizes generally live longer (Whitfield, 2006).

Fixed cost and discount rate

We discuss how the level of fixed cost affects the preference for discount rates. Assume there are two production systems, one with fixed cost of 10 and the other with fixed cost of 5. Other parameters with the production systems are the same. Unit value of the product is 1, duration of the projects are 10 years and the level of uncertainty is 60% per annum. We calculate how variable costs change with different discount rates. When discount rates are decreased, variable costs of high fixed cost systems decreases faster than variable costs of low fixed cost systems. (Figure 3) This indicates that high fixed cost systems have more incentives to maintain low discount rates or lending rates. It helps us understand why prevailing lending rates are different at different areas or times.

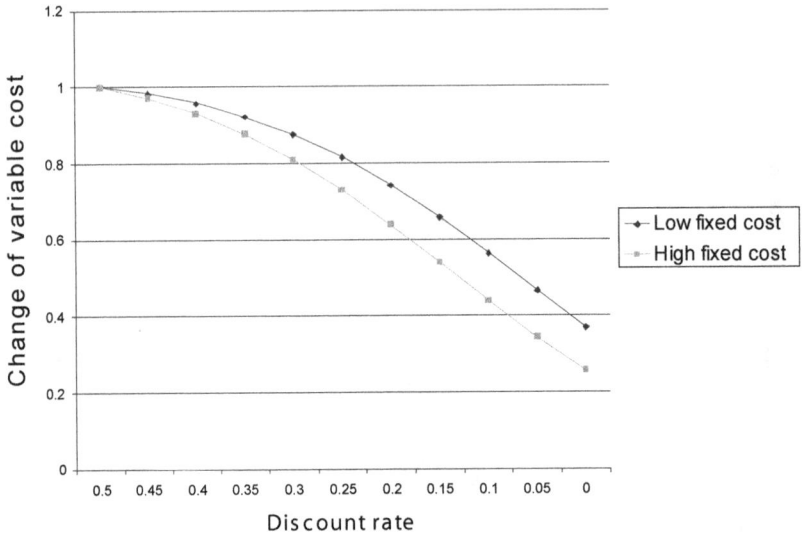

Figure 3 Fixed cost and discount rate

In medieval societies or in less developed countries, lending rates were very high and in modern economy, lending rates charged by regular financial institutions are generally very low. To maintain low level of lending rates, it takes a lot of credit and legal agencies to inform and enforce, which is very costly. As modern societies are of high fixed cost, they are willing to put up the high cost of credit and legal agencies because efficiency gain from lower lending rate is higher in high fixed cost systems.

While this result about fixed cost, discount rate and variable cost seems to be new, the human mind understands it instinctly. In the field of human psychology, there is an empirical regularity called the "magnitude effect" (small outcomes are discounted more than large ones). Most studies that vary outcome size have found that large outcomes are discounted at a lower rate than small ones (Ainselle and Haendel 1983; Benzion, Rapoport, and Yagil 1989; Green, Fristoe, and Myerson 1994; . . .). In Thaler's (1981) study, for example, respondents were, on average, indifferent between $15 immediately and $60 in a year, $250 immediately and $350 in a year, and $3,000 immediately and $4,000 in a year, implying discount rates of 139%, 34% and 29%, respectively (Frederick, Loewenstein and O'Donoghue, 2004). This shows that human mind intuitively understands the relation between discount rate and variable cost at different level of assets.

Fixed cost and the volume of output or market size

We discuss the returns of investment on projects of different fixed costs with respect to the volume of output or market size. Figure 4 is the graphic representation

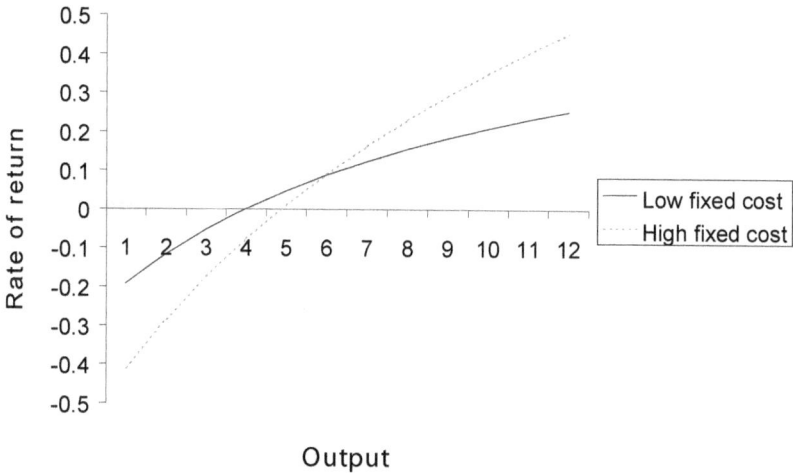

Figure 4 Fixed cost and the volume of output: For a large fixed cost investment, the breakeven market size is higher and the return curve is steeper. The opposite is true for a small fixed cost investment.

of (7) for different levels of fixed costs. In general, higher fixed cost projects need higher output volume to breakeven. At the same time, higher fixed cost projects, which have lower variable costs in production, earn higher rates of return in large markets.

From the above discussion the level of fixed investment in a project depends on the expectation of the level of uncertainty of production technology and the size of the market. When the outlook is stable and market size is large, projects with high fixed investment earn higher rates of return. When the outlook is uncertain or market size is small, projects with low fixed cost breakeven easier.

In ecological system, the market size can be understood as the size of resource base. When resource is abundant, an ecological system can support large, complex organisms (Colinvaux, 1978). Physicists and biologists are often puzzled by the apparent tendency for biological systems to form complex structures, which seems to contradict the second law of thermodynamics (Schneider and Sagan, 2005). However, once we realize that systems of higher fixed cost are more competitive in the resource rich and stable environments, this evolutionary pattern becomes easy to understand.

Uncertainty and duration

When uncertainty is high, intuition suggests that duration of a project should be kept short. We compare the profit level of one project with that of two projects with duration half long at different levels of uncertainty. When uncertainty is low, projects with long duration are more profitable. When uncertainty is high,

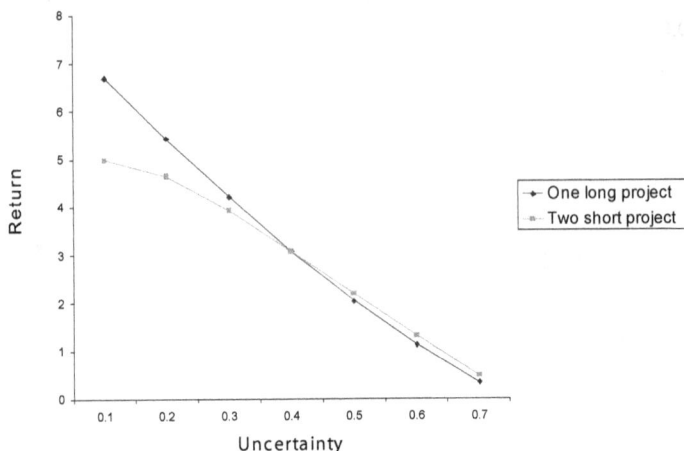

Figure 5 Uncertainty and duration

projects with short duration are more profitable. It is illustrated in Figure 5. It should be noted that the patterns emerged from computation are more complex in this case. The profit differentials between one long project and two short projects are not always monotonic with respect to the increase of uncertainty. The advantage of a mathematical theory is that we can make detailed and precise investigation.

The above calculation suggests that in a highly uncertain environment, project duration should be kept short. This is indeed what software engineers have proposed (Beck and Andres, 2002). Instead of working from the beginning to the end according to a detailed plan, as is the norm in engineering projects, new software developments, which are often of highly uncertain in their features and functions, should consist of many mini projects with short duration so they can be revised frequently.

Uncertainty and discount rate

Variable cost is an increasing function of discount rate. When uncertainty is low, variable cost is much lower with low level of discount rate. When uncertainty is high, variable costs are not sensitive to discount rate. Therefore, only in stable environment, reducing discount rate is important.

4   A Comparison with Neoclassical Economic Theory

Since its birth, the foundation or "assumptions" of neoclassical economic theory has been criticized for its lack of relevance to reality. To this, Friedman replied:

In so far as a theory can be said to have "assumptions" at all, and in so far as their "realism" can be judged independently of the validity of predictions, the relation between the significance of a theory and the "realism" of its "assumptions" is almost the opposite of that suggested by the view under criticism. Truly important and significant hypotheses will be found to have "assumptions" that are wildly inaccurate descriptive representations of reality, and in general, the more signifi-cant the theory, the more unrealistic the assumptions (in this sense). The reason is simple. A hypothesis is important if it "explains" much by little, that is, if it abstracts the common and crucial elements from the mass of complex and detailed circumstances surrounding the phenomena to be explained and permits valid pre-dictions on the basis of them alone. To be important, therefore, a hypothesis must be descriptively false in its assumptions; it takes account of, and accounts for, none of the many other attendant circumstances, since its very success shows them to be irrelevant for the phenomena to be explained. (Friedman, 1953, p. 16)

He further challenged:

As we have seen, criticism of this type is largely beside the point unless supple-mented by evidence that a hypothesis in one or another of these respects from the theory being criticized yield better predictions for as wide a range of phenomena. (Friedman, 1953, p. 31)

Chen (2005) offered very detailed discussion on how the new theory, which is based on more realistic assumptions, does "yield better predictions for as wide a range of phenomena". The following is adapted from Chen (2005), which com-pares the new production theory briefly with neoclassical economic theory.

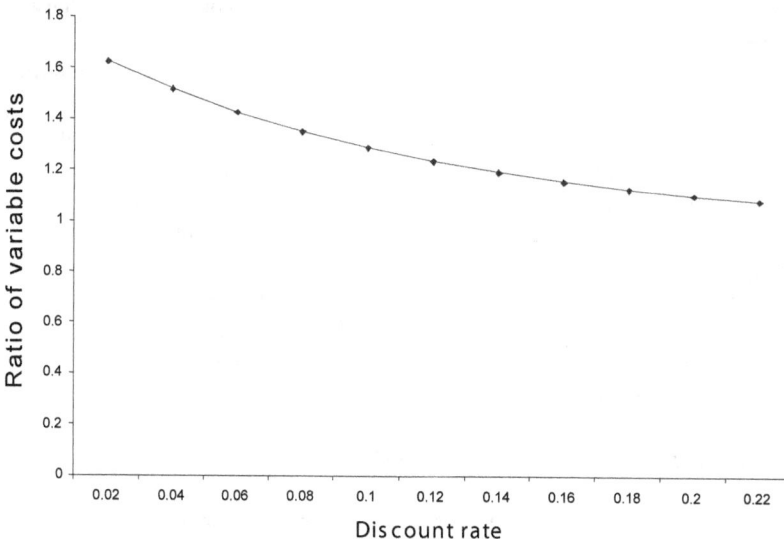

Figure 6 Uncertainty and discount rate

Consistency with physical and biological theories

Neoclassical economics was founded around 1870 by Jevons, Walras and others, who believed that economics should be built on a sound physical foundation. Since the dominant platform of physics in Jevons and Walras' time was Newtonian mechanics, it was natural for them to adopt this platform. However, theories derived from rational mechanics often do not offer good explanation to economic behaviors. Gradually, explicit identification with physics disappears while analogies between physics and economics are frequently mentioned. The following quote from Samuelson's Nobel lecture is quite representative:

> There is really nothing more pathetic than to have an economist or a retired engineer try to force analogies between the concepts of economics. How many dreary papers have I had to referee in which the author is looking for something that corresponds to entropy or to one or another form of energy.

In the very next paragraph, however, Samuelson found some analogy himself.

> However, if you look upon the monopolistic firm hiring ninety-nine inputs as an example of a maximum system, you can connect up its structural relations with those that prevail for an entropy-maximizing thermodynamic system. Pressure and volume, and for that matter absolute temperature and entropy, have to each other the same conjugate or dualistic relation that the wage rate has to labor or the land rent has to acres of land.

Mirowski observed, "The key to the comprehension of Samulson's meteoric rise in the economics profession was his knack for evoking all the outward trapping and ornament of science without ever coming to grips with the actual content or implications of physical theory for his neoclassical economics" (Mirowski, 1989, p. 383).

Life systems are non-equilibrium thermodynamic systems. The current dominant economic theory is general equilibrium theorem. Social system is a special case of living systems. When a theory about a special case is inconsistent with general foundation, either the general foundation or the special theory is wrong. So far, economists have not challenged the validity of the non-equilibrium thermodynamic theory of life systems. This theory shows that an analytical theory of economics can be directly derived from basic physical and biological laws. By this, it establishes social sciences as an integral part of physical and biological sciences.

A comparison with production functions

Production functions, such as Cobb-Douglas production function, form the fundamental blocks in general equilibrium production theory. Cobb-Douglas function takes the form $Y = AL^\alpha K^\beta$ where Y, L and K denote output, labor (variable cost) and capital (fixed cost) respectively. Solow had made following comment about the production function:

> I have never thought of the macroeconomic production function as a rigorously justifiable concept. In my mind it is either an illuminating parable, or else a mere device for handling data, to be used so long as it gives good empirical results, and to be discarded as soon as it doesn't, or as something better comes along. (Solow, 1966, p. 1259)

By contrast, the analytical production theory developed here is derived rigorously from the fundamental property of life systems. It gives simple and clear results of returns to investment under different market conditions. The form and parameters of Cobb-Douglas function are given without rigorous justification. *A*, the coefficient in Cobb-Douglas function, "has been called, among other things, 'technical change', 'total factor productivity', 'the residual' and 'the measure of our ignorance'" (Blaug, 1980, p. 465).

Since production functions are widely used in economic literature in constructing economic models, even a small improvement on this topic should have a big impact in understanding economics.

Optimality vs. tradeoff

Optimization theory holds the central position in neoclassical economics. Paul Samuelson's Nobel Lecture is titled *Maximum Principles in Analytical Economics*. Alchian (1950) and Friedman (1953) tried to reconcile the maximization principle with evolutionary theory. Friedman stated:

> Confidence in the maximization-of-return hypothesis is justified by evidence of a very different character. . . . unless the behavior of businessmen in some way or other approximated behavior consistent with the maximization of returns, it seems unlikely that they would remain in business for long. Let the apparent immediate determinant of business behavior be anything at all—habitual reaction, random chance, or whatnot. Whenever this determinant happens to lead to behavior consistent with rational and maximization of returns, the business will prosper and acquire resources with which to expand; whenever it does not, the business tend to lose resources and can be kept in existence only with addition of resources from outside. The process of "natural selection" thus helps to validate the hypothesis—or rather, given natural selection, acceptance of the hypothesis can be based largely on the judgment that it summarized appropriately the conditions for survival. (Friedman, 1953, p. 22)

We will use an example of project investment to illustrate the problem of Friedman's argument. Assume the relevant parameters are unit value of the product to be one million, discount rate to be 4%, diffusion to be 40%, duration of the project, to be thirty years and market size to be 150 over the project life. It can be calculated from Formula (7) that a project with a fixed cost of 25 million dollar will have the highest rate of return. However, if any parameter changes, the optimal value of fixed cost investment will change as well. For example, if diffusion increases to 60%, the optimal value of fixed investment will become 11 million. Since fixed cost is spent or committed at the beginning of the project while other parameters may change over the course of project life, it is impossible to determine optimality in advance. Furthermore, higher fixed cost systems, which are often the winners of earlier market competition, suffer more from the increase of uncertainty. This means that long term survival is not necessarily consistent with short term optimization.

Earlier, we have shown that systems with higher fixed costs earn higher rates of return in large markets and stable environments than those with lower fixed costs. These systems may appear superior. However, the performance of high fixed cost systems deteriorates in high volatile environments. From this production theory, the main theme of economic and biological evolution is the tradeoff between competitiveness of high fixed cost systems in a stable environment and flexibility of low fixed cost systems in a volatile environment. Biologists haven't found a universally applicable measure of fitness (Stearns, 1992, p. 33). Our theory shows that there does not exist such a measure. For the same reason, there will not exist a universally applicable measure of optimality.

Is marginal cost equal to marginal revenue?

Traditional economic theory suggests that companies will keep increasing the output until the marginal cost of the product is equal to its marginal revenue (Friedman, 1953, p. 16). Empirical evidences show that companies generally charge a substantial price mark up on their products. This analytical theory offers a simple and clear understanding about price markup. For example, if a software is targeted to sophisticated users, its interface can be simple, which reduce development cost and its sales effort can be small, which reduce variable cost. If the software developer considers increasing the market size by targeting general users, the interface of the software needs to be very intuitive with many help facilities, which increase development cost and its sales effort and after sales service can be substantial for less sophisticated users, which increase variable cost. Since the increase of market size often involve both the increase of variable cost and fixed cost, most projects are designed that the marginal cost to be much lower than the product value to maximize potential profit.

To keep increasing the output until its marginal cost equal to marginal revenue often means that the company may have to enter difficult areas, which will have repercussion on its earlier units. For example, when employees in a WalMart store in Quebec decided to unionize, WalMart closed down that store although that store would remain profitable. To keep a unionized store open will affect the margin of other stores, whose staff will attempt to unionize as well. From Formula (7), the rate of return not only depends on the market size, but also depends on other factors. If the increase of market size will increase the diffusion rate as well, companies have to consider the total effect on long term profitability.

5 Concluding remarks

Hall and others summarized the current state of mind among many researchers in ecological economics:

> Existing "economic" models cannot effectively represent a total economy, because none has a biophysical basis; some attempts to produce such a model have been made, . . . We must conclude, however, that a truly useful and acceptable model that includes the biophysical basis of the economy is probably still far in the future. . . . We challenge new generation of economists and natural scientists to think from this perspective. (p. 671, Hall et al, 2001)

One of the purposes of this paper is to inform that a truly useful model that includes the biophysical basis of the economy has already been developed. The model turns the insights from ecological economics into an analytical theory that can be applied to day to day business activities. Since the theory was first circulated in 2000, it has been applied to many different areas. Works about this theory have generated large number of downloads on websites such as SSRN (Social Science Research Network). Several very positive reviews, such as Polimeni and Polimeni (2007), about this theory have appeared since. Some students have already benefited from the intuitive and unifying approach of this analytical theory. Presentations of this theory in many conferences have generated exciting reactions. It is now a challenge for the community of economists and natural scientists to openly acknowledge the existence of such a theory and discuss it in public. The process will help transform ecological economics from a niche subject into the theoretical foundation of social sciences.

References

Acs, Z., and Audretsch D. 1990. *Innovation and Small Firms*. Cambridge: MIT Press.

Beck, K., and Andres, C. 2002. *Extreme Programming Explained: Embrace Change, 2nd Edition*. Addison-Wesley.

Black, F., and Scholes, M. 1973. The Pricing of Options and Corporate Liabilities. *Journal of Political Economy*, 81: 637–659.

Blaug, M. 1980. *Economic theory in retrospect*. New York: Cambridge UP.

Chen, J. 2005. *The physical foundation of economics: An analytical thermodynamic theory*. Hackensack, NJ: World Scientific.

Colinvaux, P. 1978. *Why big fierce animals are rare: an ecologist's perspective*. Princeton: Princeton University.

Dixit, A., and Pindyck, R. 1994. *Investment under uncertainty.* Princeton: Princeton University Press.

Farmer, J. D., Shubik, M., and Smith, E. 2005. Is Economics the Next Physical Science? *Physics Today*, Vol. 58, No. 9: 37–42.

Feynman, R. 1948. Space-time approach to non-relativistic quantum mechanics. *Review of Modern Physics*, Vol. 20, p. 367-387.

Feynman, R., and Hibbs, A. 1965. *Quantum mechanics and path integrals.* McGraw-Hill.

Frederick, S., Loewenstein, G., and O'Donoghue, T. 2004. Time discounting and time preference: A critical review. In *Advances in Behavioral Economics*, edited by Camerer, C., Lowenstein, G., and Rabin, M. Princeton: Princeton University Press.

Friedman, M. 1953. *Essays in positive economics.* Chicago: The University of Chicago Press.

Georgescu-Roegen, N. 1971. *The entropy law and the economic process.* Cambridge: Harvard University Press.

Hall, C., Cutler J. C., and Robert K. 1986. *Energy and Resource Quality: The Ecology of the Economic Process.* John Wiley & Sons.

Hall, C., Lindenberger, D., Kummel, R., Kroeger, T., and Eichhorn, W. 2001. The need to reintegrate the natural sciences with economics. *BioScience*, 63: 663–673.

Kac, M. 1951. On some connections between probability theory and differential and integral equations. In *Proceedings of the second Berkeley symposium on probability and statistics*, ed. by J. Neyman. Berkeley: University of California, 189–215.

Kac, M. 1985. *Enigmas of Chance: An Autobiography.* New York: Harper and Row.

Kuhn, T. 1996. *The structure of scientific revolutions*, 3rd edition. Chicago: University of Chicago Press.

Mehrling, P. 2005. *Fischer Black and the Revolutionary Idea of Finance.* Wiley.

Mirowski, P. 1989. *More heat than light, Economics as social physics: Physics as nature's economics.* Cambridge: Cambridge University Press.

Odum, H. T. 1971. *Environment, Power and Society.* New York: John Wiley

Øksendal, B. 1998. *Stochastic differential equations: an introduction with applications, 5th Edition.* New York: Springer.

Ormerod, P. 2005. *Why most things fail, Evolution, extinction and economics.* London: Faber and Faber.

Polimeni, R. I., and Polimeni, J. M. 2007. Book review of the physical foundation of economics, *Ecological Economics*, Vol. 62, No. 1 p. 195-196.

Schneider E. D., and Sagan, D., 2005. *Into the cool: energy flow, thermodynamics, and life.* Chicago: University of Chicago Press.

Stern, D. 2007. Book review of Ecological Economics: An Introduction. *Ecological Economics*. In press.

Stearns, S. 1992. *The evolution of life histories.* Oxford: Oxford University Press.

Whitfield, J. 2006. *In the Beat of a Heart: Life, Energy, and the Unity of Nature.* Joseph Henry Press.

9 Pluralism and Ecological Economics

Michael Daley

ABSTRACT

This article provides philosophical support for the pluralist approach pursued by the ecological economic research program. To this end, I highlight the work of philosopher Stephen C. Pepper. Using the root metaphor method, Pepper offers a meta-theoretical system comprised of four world hypotheses, each with a unique theory of truth. Pepper's pluralistic framework could be of use to the ecological economic research program in articulating its theoretical and methodological contribution as a distinct philosophical alternative to the positivist approach underlying neoclassical economics. The structural categories defining the contextualist world hypothesis have an affinity with the theoretical approach, methodological orientation, and policy-oriented focus of ecological economics. The contextualist world hypothesis reveals a well-developed model for explaining the process of problem solving in a complex setting.

Keywords: Ecological Economics; Pluralism; Economic Methodology; Stephen C. Pepper.

Introduction

Since its birth, ecological economics has addressed methodology in a unified fashion. Practitioners embrace the idea that interdisciplinary inquiry should accept a variety of methodologies. Patterson's (2006) suggests that tolerance for pluralism stems from a foundational and 'high impact' article entitled "The Case for Methodological Pluralism" (Norgaard, 1989). Norgaard argues that diverse methodological traditions support economic and ecological thinking. Costanza and King (1999) reaffirm Norgaard's position: "[due to] the complexity of the problems, there is no one mutually agreed upon 'right' approach, model or paradigm" (1999, p. 2).

As a strategy, a pluralist attitude is laudable and useful.[1] Diversity stands on ethical grounds as a worthy value. Metaphorically, diversity also fuels evolutionary selection. Since theories offer insight into slices of reality, pluralism is a pragmatic response to understanding complex problems. A pluralist strategy is pragmatic in dealing incommensurable methodological vantage points.

---

1   McLennan (2002) offers a contrary view in an article entitled "Quandaries in meta-theory: against pluralism." in journal *Economy and Society*.

Given that economic methodology is in flux with the emergence of post-positivist approaches (e.g., see Backhouse, 1994; Caldwell, 1990[c1982]; Salanti and Screpanti, 1997; and Hands, 2001), tolerance seems appropriate and an in-house debate over methodology untimely and uneconomic. Given limited research resources and an abundance of ecological economic problems, a pluralistic approach prevents misallocating resources within the research program. Finally, different methodologies may promote interest and growth in ecological economics. Costanza (1996) offers quantitative support documenting the growth of interest in the journal *Ecological Economics*. Patterson (2006) and Ma and Stern (2006) provide further evidence that the impact of ecological economics continues to grow.

Growing interest may correlate with a policy of inclusion across disciplines. Yet, a more powerful driver is likely the overlap between observable world events—accelerating global warming, deforestation, threatened species, collapsed fisheries, etc.—and the discipline's pre-analytical vision of a binding biophysical constraint. Guided by an unyielding focus on the scale of human activity, ecological economics is a viable alternative to the market-oriented approach. If this assessment is correct, prescriptive assertions of methodological pluralism will eventually require elaboration and defense. However, despite initial success all is not well within the research program, and the impetus for methodological reflection appears more pressing than appreciated. In a frank assessment of the status of ecological economics in Australia, Patterson writes:

> Ecological economics has struggled to gain a permanent institutional foothold in Australia and New Zealand universities and research organizations [and] largely remains an 'un-institutionalized' and a 'marginalized' activity in Australasia, which represents a significant challenge for future development (2006, p. 327).

Patterson observes that retaining a critical mass of expertise within certain localities remains a problem. Also, he observes a hint of identity crisis regarding the state of Australian ecological economics. This causes uncertainty about how to relate to neoclassical economics. Patterson continues:

> One open question that now arises is 'what is the future of ecological economics in [Australia and New Zealand] in respect to neoclassical economics? Should ecological economics seek to join forces with neoclassical resource and environmental economics (as the [Ecological Economic Programme] at Australia National University has done) or should it seek to continue to go at it alone? Maybe, now that ecological economics has raised awareness amongst neoclassical economists, its role is now redundant (2006, p. 328)?

I don't believe that ecological economics is redundant nor do I advocate integration into neoclassical economics. Yet, as Patterson's work suggests, absent a clear identity and in an environment of scarce resources, institutional demands could lead to that outcome.

In this paper, I discuss a pluralist philosophical approach to methodology and suggest that ecological economics elaborate an explicit philosophical perspective to distinguish its identity and solidify its autonomy. I discuss the need to for a vision of pluralism and present the meta-philosophy of Stephen C. Pepper developed in *World Hypotheses: A Study in Evidence* (1942). After discussing Pepper's system, I outline the structural categories of the contextualist world hypothesis and suggest their affinity to aspects of ecological economics. In sum, Pepper's system sustains methodological pluralism and offers an explicit interpretation of the approach of ecological economics.

Beyond a Strategy of Methodological Pluralism

Despite rhetoric espousing tolerance, the pre-analytical vision, a prioritization of scale over efficiency, and a problem-solving/policy oriented purpose make ecological economics antithetical to neoclassical economics. In *Ecological Economics: A Workbook for Problem-based Learning*, Farley, Erickson and Daly (2005) distinguish how each research program theorizes the relationship between the natural world and the economic system. Theory turns on whether to view the economy as a subset of the natural system, or the natural system as an extension of the economy. With regard to theory, practice and policy, the former vision implies a different approach to contemporary challenges. Solving ecological problems requires reversing the order of theoretical consideration. Analysts consider the scale of activity, a just distribution of the impacts of change, and efficient resource allocation in that order (Farley, Erickson and Daly, 2005, pp. 19-25). Also, the urgency of many environmental problems links theory to action. Gowdy and Erickson paint ecological economics as a comprehensive alternative to the "flawed 'grand unification theory' of neoclassical welfare economics [even if ecological economics has not yet] coalesced into a coherent school of thought" (2005, pp. 218–219). They suggest it offers a superior alternative:

> Of all the conventional and heterodox schools of economic thought, ecological economics is the only one poised to address the problem of human survival in the coming centuries. It is a school of thought that explicitly recognizes the interconnections and interdependence of the economic, biophysical and social worlds. We offer no grand theory, but rather a flexible approach recognizing the uniqueness of specific cultures and ecosystems (2005, p. 219).

This is a direct attack on the vision, theory and methodology of the neoclassical program. Even if intolerant, it may be reasonable to argue that ecological economics is superior based on its vision, content and flexible approach. However, is it not also reasonable that proponents move beyond a tolerant attitude and defend the alternative with an explicit articulation of its philosophy?

In *Experience and Education* (1938), John Dewey confronts a similar problem faced by the educational community. The struggle centers on attempts to build and sustain progressive schools in place of traditional schools. Dewey writes:

> . . . at times of impasse and polarization, the business of the philosophy of education means the necessity of the introduction of a new order of conceptions leading to new modes of practice. It is for this reason that it is so difficult to develop a philosophy of education, the moment tradition and custom are departed from. It is for this reason that the conduct of schools, based upon a new order of conceptions, is so much more difficult than is the management of schools which walk in beaten paths. Hence, every movement in the direction of a new order of ideas and of activities directed by them calls out, sooner or later, [for] a return to what appear to be simpler and more fundamental ideas and practice of the past (1938, p. 5).

Lack of philosophical coherence is a concern for a new school of thought, especially one poised to challenge the established order. The forces of mental inertia and tradition mean the impulse to retreat to the familiar is inexorable. In regards to overcoming the traditional model, Dewey continues:

> The general philosophy of the new education may be sound, and yet the difference in abstract principles will not decide the way in which the moral and intellectual preference involved shall be worked out in practice. There is always the danger in a new movement that in rejecting the aims and methods of that which it would supplant, it may develop its principles negatively rather than positively and constructively. Then it takes its clew in practice from that which is rejected instead of from the constructive development of its own philosophy (1938, p. 20).

A fledgling movement must articulate an appropriate philosophy. In avoiding the issue, the endeavor risks defining itself in oppositional terms, thereby obscuring its identity. Lack of a constructive and self-conscious philosophy paves the way for absorption by the established order.

In the ecological economic literature, Tacconi (1998) and Luks (1998) stress the importance of a self-conscious methodology. Luks (1998) emphasizes integrating the discourse of rhetoric (e.g., metaphor analysis) into ecological economics to develop methodological issues and policy-related, communication issues. Tacconi (1998), following Norgaard (1989), captures the fact that positivist philosophy, the backbone of neoclassical economics, is constituted by a well-defined structure. Positivism includes an ontological framework comprising a 'theory of reality'; an epistemological framework comprising a 'theory of knowledge'; and a methodological framework comprising a 'theory for appraising' knowledge claims.[2] Within the discipline of economic methodology, the positivist account of science is readily assessable in orthodox affirmations and heterodox critiques of neoclassical economics (e.g., Backhouse, 1994, Caldwell, 1990[c1982], Blaug, 1992[c1980] and McCloskey, 1997[c1985]).

The complex nature and urgency of problems that ecological economists confront demand an appropriate methodological approach. Whereas neoclassical economics attempts to find universal laws and mechanisms that link market outcomes to individual economic behavior, ecological economics is a problem and policy-driven scientific endeavor that attempts explain and solve complex environmental problems at the interface of the economic and natural universe. Tacconi (1998) argues that ecological economics adheres to a different methodology than neoclassical economics. The methodology of 'post normal science' in Functawitz (1993) is a leading example. Also, Tacconi suggests that ecological economics possesses ontological and epistemological orientations. Still, the reader is left searching for a transparent philosophical account of ecological economics. Tacconi is explicit about positivist ontology, epistemology and methodology; but what philosophical adjective describes these aspects of ecological economics?

To understand its unique identity, ecological economists must be aware of and, if necessary, construct its philosophical orientation. The rest of this article focuses on the work of Stephen C. Pepper, who described a philosophical system suited to explain the philosophical orientation and pluralist leaning of ecological economics. Based on the texts and ideas of philosophers, Pepper (1942) develops a meta-analysis that defines four 'world hypotheses.' Heilbroner and Lowe doubt if 'world theories' or 'worldly philosophy' are possible under contemporary circumstances (Forstater, 2004, p. 22). Forstater suggests that 'scenarios' and 'visions' do not lend themselves to formal analytical procedures. Writing when positivism was consolidating its dominance in science, Pepper believes that world hypotheses establish a basis for methodological pluralism. Since economic methodology developed along the lines of positivist philosophy prior to McCloskey (1982), citations of Pepper in the traditional literature are non-existent. In the post positivist literature, Willie Henderson (1994) refers to Pepper in his work on 'extended metaphors.' Henderson writes:

> In philosophy, Pepper identified four that stood the test of time: formism (the root metaphor being 'similarity'), mechanism ('machine'), organicism ('the historical process') and contextualism ('the historical event'). The latter three are to

---

2　Positivist philosophy maintains the existence of immutable natural laws and mechanisms separate from those who attempt to know. As a result, the 'objective' researcher can discover these laws and mechanisms. This is the notion of dualism. Based on the assumed non-interactive positioning of subject and object, 'value free' science is possible. Furthermore, the legitimacy of knowledge claims is appraised through hypotheses that are falsified by empirical observation. Certain knowledge is the goal (Guba, 1990).

be found in most of the major schools of economics and may constitute a basis for their classification (1994: p. 354).[3]

To my knowledge, Pepper is cited only once in the economic literature. Hayes and Lynne (2004) appeal to the root metaphor method and the idea of 'structural corroboration' to support their 'ego'n'empathy hypothesis.' In the following sections, I present Pepper's metaphilosophy and focus on his explanation of contextualism. Pepper's system supports pluralism, and the contextualist world hypothesis offers a conceptual model for understanding how evidence is gathered and argument proceeds in ecological economics.

The Pluralist Metatheory of Stephen C. Pepper [4]

Stephen C. Pepper wrote in the tradition of American pragmatism.[5] Though his primary interests were in the philosophy of art, *World Hypotheses: A Study in Evidence* (1942) is a contribution in the traditional philosophy of science and metaphysics. Pepper's analysis is a response to the state of metaphysics in mid-20th century, when tolerance for pluralistic metaphysics was shattered by epistemological strictures of positivism. Pepper's metatheoretical system establishes the value of theories in philosophy in direct response to the dogmatic tenor of logical positivism. Reck writes:

> According to Pepper's metaphilosophy, metaphysics is a specific kind of belief that attempts to embrace all facts and to organize them within a coherent system. A metaphysics is, in Pepper's phrase, "a world hypothesis." A world hypothesis, moreover, is an unrestricted hypothesis, as distinct from the restricted hypothesis characteristic of the special sciences. For Pepper there is no basic difference between an empirical scientific hypothesis and an empirical world hypothesis—only a difference in scope . . . *World Hypotheses* is . . . [a]n essay on philosophical method [that] examines the source, the nature, and the grounds of metaphysics (1968, pp. 47–48).

Historian of science, Walter Weimer, claims that metatheoretical analysis started receiving institutional sanction in the philosophy of science in the 1960s (1979, p. 194). Metatheoretical analysis involves theorizing about theories. It attempts to organize a group of theories on one level from the perspective of a second level. Weimer writes:

---

3   This quote motivated me read *World Hypotheses*, which became the centerpiece of my dissertation entitled An Image of Enduring Plurality in Economic Theory: The Root-Metaphor Theory of Stephen C. Pepper.

4   Bill Harrell's web page http://www.sunyit.edu/~harrell/billyjack/Index.htm assembles articles related to Pepper's work.

5   Go to http://www.sunyit.edu/~harrell/Pepper/pep_efron.htm for Arthur Efron's biography of Pepper published in Vol. 53 & 54 of *Paunch*.

> A metatheory is a generative conceptual scheme that enables one to deal with
> any conceivable instance of phenomena falling within its domain. It is a "pro-
> ductive" or "creative" schema that provides an explanation for a perspective
> from which to view the occurrence of anything within its domain. It is a frame-
> work to which anything that can be conceived or discovered in phenomena can
> be assimilated (1979, p. 1).

Metatheories are background conceptual frameworks from which substantive theories originate and develop. Particular substantive theories are consonant with the metatheoretical framework rather than being consequences of it
(Weimer, 1979, p. 1). They serve as a common underlying structure that can
rationalize disparate surface-structure phenomena. Weimer differentiates between 'justificationist' and 'non-justificationist' orientations in tracing the evolution of Karl Popper's thought from 'dogmatic' and 'naïve' falsificationism to
'mature' falsificationism. Weimer argues that the 'mature' Popper adopts a non-
justificationist approach to knowledge claims, thereby jettisoning a monistic
model and admitting a pluralistic model of theory appraisal, or 'methodological
pluralism'.

Whereas positivism claims perceived or observed 'objects of the world' as
primary data, metatheoretical analysis develops accounts of science by analyzing the nature of the 'theoretical systems' that purport to explain phenomena in
the world. These systems are considered 'real' or 'empirical' objects that provide cognitive value. Pepper writes:

> I wish to study world hypotheses as objects existing in the world, to examine
> them empirically as a zoologist studies species of animals, a psychologist variet-
> ies of perceptions, a mathematician geometrical systems. They are rarely treated
> as objects in their own right (1942, p. 2).

Using theories as empirical data, Pepper presents a case for metaphysics that
supports a plurality of philosophical systems. He identifies logical positivism as
a valuable metaphysical system and associates it with the 'mechanistic' world
hypothesis. However, he locates mechanism among three other distinct metaphysical systems—'formism', 'contextualism' and 'organicism'—found in the
writings of philosophers.[6] In answering criticisms to his root-metaphor theory,
Pepper writes:

> The classical philosophers are the men whose writings provided the empirical
> evidence for the descriptions given in the text. What I maintain is that these

---

6   In "recovering the practice" of philosophers, Pepper anticipates McCloskey's *The Rhetoric
of Economics* (1982), which emphasizes recovering the methodological practice of economists by
studying their rhetoric or metaphors.

theories are what these writers were heading toward in their pursuit of structural corroborations (1942, p. 337).

A world hypothesis metaphysical system capable of dealing with 'all the evidence or facts' given in the world. The hallmark of a world hypothesis is its ability to have unlimited, or nearly unlimited *scope* (Pepper, 1942, p. 77).[7] Unlike theories within a discipline, a world hypothesis does not limit itself to discipline-specific evidence. In addition to scope, a world hypothesis possesses a suitable degree of *precision*; it does not generate multiple interpretations of the same data (Pepper, 1942, p. 118). Over time, a world hypothesis emerges as adequate through structural corroboration—the process by which structural categories migrate and explain evidence in different domains. A world hypothesis is not deemed adequate through data and logic; it gains adequacy based on internal 'structural corroboration', or the degree of 'scope' and 'precision' it has in handling 'all of the world's facts and evidence' (Pepper, 1942, p. 84). Also, a world hypothesis is not inadequate due to outside criticism; instead it convicts itself by interpreting evidence though limiting or imprecise structural categories. External methodological appraisal is not serious grounds for eliminating a world hypothesis.[8]

Pepper develops the 'root-metaphor theory' to explicate each world hypothesis. This theory highlights the connection of a world hypothesis to common sense experience. Each world hypothesis originates in the facts of uncriticized common sense, presumably in a pre-scientific time. A root metaphor is a focal point or mental image used to organize evidence and understand phenomena in everyday life. A theorist grapples with a morass of commonsense evidence and finds a way to explain something. The mental image that makes the explanation possible is used to structure and extend explanations in other domains.[9] If a root metaphor is fruitful and the analogy carries over, it brings more of the world's evidence into its domain. Through successful use, the structural categories get refined and the root metaphor gains cognitive value. For example, *mechanism*, whose root metaphor Pepper identifies as a 'lever', successfully identifies universal patterns and laws of the natural universe.[10]

The root metaphor theory is made operational by the 'root metaphor method.' This method permits Pepper to recreate the process of refinement that starts from the primitive experience of explaining the world from commonsense evidence. Using this method, Pepper illuminates world hypotheses by explicating their

---

7   A world hypothesis may confront anomalies causing it to attain only 'relative adequacy.' However, unlike Kuhn's (1970c[1962]) account of normal and revolutionary science, paradigm shifts do not occur due to the anomalies; world hypotheses are autonomous and enduring systems.

8   For a positivist critique of pluralism relating to *World Hypotheses* see Hoekstra (1945).

9   See Henderson (1994 & 1998) for a discussion of literary metaphor, extended metaphor, and root metaphor.

10   Capra (1982) offers examples that a worldview (i.e., world hypothesis) handles evidence in the physical, life, and human sciences. Conversely, disciplines such as biology, economics, and medicine generate accounts based on different worldviews.

structural categories. To demonstrate each world hypothesis, he describes how specific structural categories emerge from applying the root metaphor. For example, using the root metaphor 'simile,' he explains the process one employs when basing a theory on the observation that two or more things are similar. By detailing this process, he identifies the structural categories of formism (i.e., characters, particulars, participation, norms, subsistence, existents, etc.). He details the operation of a 'lever' to explicate the structural categories of mechanism (i.e., location in a field, quantifiable qualities, universal laws, etc.). He describes the idea of the 'historical event' and the 'historical process' to explicate contextualism and organicism. In this way, he reveals a distinct model of each conceptual system.

Pepper's system establishes the existence of an enduring plurality of world hypotheses. Meta-level pluralism is sustained since each world hypothesis is a historically stable model, which has attained an adequate degree of structural corroboration. A world hypothesis possesses unique structural categories capable of accounting for observed analyses across scientific disciplines. Also, each world hypothesis possesses a unique theory of truth, which establishes the idea of epistemological pluralism. Formism contains the 'correspondence' theory of truth; mechanism the 'causal adjustment' theory; contextualism the 'operational theory'; and organicism the 'coherence' theory (Pepper, 1942, pp. 180–184, 221–231, 268–279, and 308–314). These perspectives reflect a limited number of ways—a controlled plurality—to understand the world.[11] Pepper writes:

> Having done all that we can do rationally to organize the evidence on the topic in question in terms of structural corroboration, and finding as a rule that there are four equally justifiable hypotheses explaining the nature of the subject, we shall have the wisdom not to conclude that we know nothing about the topic, but on the contrary, that we have four alternative theories about it, which supply us with a great deal more information on the subject than any one of them alone could have done (1942, p. 331).

Pepper's metaphilosophical system treats world hypotheses as complements of one another. Using multiple root metaphors to organize evidence is as a pragmatic way to deal with the problem of incomplete and fallible knowledge.

Structural categories that migrate across disciplines suggest a means to inter-disciplinary discourse. Pepper's metatheoretical system offers an approach to teach economic ideas in a pluralist, post-positivist environment *and* to interface economics with the physical, life and human sciences. Discussing root metaphor and interdisciplinary curriculum, Quine writes:

> Pepper lays the foundation for the development of interdisciplinary curricula . . .
> [F]ormism, mechanism, contextualism, and organicism—are applied to such disparate

---

11   Sheila Dow (2004) discusses the importance of structured pluralism in understanding the different categories and meanings for structured and successful communication between schools of thought.

> subjects as astronomy, art, poetry, music, sculpture and drama. . . . The categories of
> each world hypothesis are precise, yet one does not have to distort them to make
> them useful in interpreting the facts of any particular discipline . . . The development
> of interdisciplinary curricula requires the use of categories and processes based on a
> metadiscipline such as Pepper's philosophy . . . A broad range of disciplines can be
> taught from the perspectives of formism, mechanism, contextualism, and organicism
> (1982, pp. 345–356).[12]

World hypotheses offer a pluralist account consistent with the methodological attitude expressed by ecological economists. Each model suggests its own epistemological, methodological, and ontological tendencies. They highlight the idea that schools of thought in economics correspond to distinct philosophical systems. In the next section, I discuss the contextualism, whose structural categories offer ecological economics a philosophical perspective into its approach.

Contextualism and Ecological Economics

Pepper's meta-analysis defines four root metaphors philosophers rely on to organize evidence. Each root metaphor generates a world hypothesis possessing unique structural categories. The long-term stability of a world hypothesis establishes its legitimacy and suggests a plurality of conceptual models that adequately explain a wide range of phenomena. The idea of unlimited scope suggests that each world hypothesis can generate interpretations in the physical, life and social sciences. Oppositely, within a discipline such as economics, different schools of thought may conform closely to the structural categories of one world hypothesis. Schools of thought have an affinity with one world hypothesis due to the nature of the conceptualized problem situation. In this section, I relate the structural categories of contextualism to aspects of ecological economics.

The 'historical event' is the best commonsense root metaphor of contextualism (Pepper, 1942, pp. 232-279). The historical event is attached to a complex web of 'life's incidences' or actions. This web of incidences constitutes the context of the event. A depiction or interpretation of an event is meaningful when portrayed with its context. In depicting an event, contextualism accepts supporting facts and evidence without reservation. Inquiry into the historical event is an effort to bring an on-going event to life, or to 're-present' it. Alternative descriptions of the root metaphor include the 'located or situated event' or the 'given problem situation. Understanding an event often occurs by means of 'acting' through it. The encroaching biophysical constraint on the economic system, as evidenced by global warming and unfolding climatic transformation, is the 'historical event' to which ecological economists direct attention.

12   Daley (2000) interprets economic theory in terms of schools of thought using world hypotheses.

As with each world hypothesis, the root metaphor generates a set of structural categories; 'change' and 'novelty' are fundamental to contextualism. Pepper writes:

> The categories [of contextualism] must be so framed as not to exclude from the world any degree of order it may be found to have, nor to deny that this order may have come out of disorder in any way you please, *so long as it does not deny the possibility of disorder or another order in nature also.* This italicized restriction is the forcible one in contextualism, and amounts to the assertion that change is categorical and not derivative in any degree at all (1942, p. 234).

Pepper sees change and novelty defining the critical nature of the ongoing epoch of human history. Such emphasis is commonplace in the ecological economics literature. Georgescu-Roegen writes: "The obvious truth is the economic system continuously changes *qualitatively*" . . . and "the most important aspect of the economic process is precisely the continuous emergence of novelty" (Georgescu-Roegen, 1979, p 321). Theorizing a "continuously coevolving system" (Farley, Erickson & Daly, p. 5) involving natural and economic phenomena appears suited to contextualism's fundamental structural categories. There is an affinity to the notion of 'emergent phenomena' characterizing the impact of human phenomena on ecological systems (Farley, Erickson, & Daly, p. 4) as well as the emergence of social institutions to deal with systemic flaws and breakdowns (e.g., Veblen 1944[c1899]).

Pepper exhibits change and novelty as subcategories of 'quality' and 'texture' by describing the act of writing the sentence: "*A period will be placed at the end of this sentence.*" (Pepper, 1942, p. 237). Quality is the sentence's intuited total meaning; texture is the words/grammatical relations making up the sentence. Quality refers to the total intuited meaning of the event; we 'see' it when we think of the Great Depression, global climate change, or the firing of the high school principal. Texture is the means by which analysis and control of an event occurs. Though analytically distinct, the quality and texture are inextricably bound and incapable of operating without the other. There is no meaning without the letters, words and phrases that constitute the sentence. There is little sense of having the letters, words and phrases if the sentence does not have meaning. Thus, the total intuited meaning of an event (its synthetic aspect) depends on the act of analyzing by decomposing it into concrete events. The contextualist approach is not reductionist. Farley, Erickson and Daley (2006) pay close attention to the proper emphasis between the analytical and synthetic aspects of the problem-solving process.

The Subcategories of Quality

Pepper describes subcategories for quality and texture to explicate the conceptual model derived from the root metaphor. The subcategories of quality include the 'spread,' the 'change,' and the degree of 'fusion' of an event. Contextualism takes the concept of time seriously using the concept of spread. Time is related to the meaning of an event as it develops through 'an ongoing action'. The meaning of an event spreads forward in time and backward in time, however, it is not reversible as in equilibrium analysis. The 'specious present' of contextualism has a past, present, and anticipated future. This contained lens (a long moment) contributes to the quality and situates the event in a particular historical moment. Contextualism carefully distinguishes between 'qualitative time' (also called duration) and 'schematic time', which is descriptive of time in mechanism.[13] Georgescu-Roegen writes: "Each novelty, however, is unique in the sense that in chronological time it occurs only once (1979, p. 321). Also, the entropy concept draws attention to qualitative change and the path dependent behavior in complex systems. The idea of explaining events in terms of culturally specific considerations relative to time and place comes to mind.

As discussed above, change contributes to the quality—or the intuited meaning—of an event. A bounded interval of 'qualitative' or 'historical' time is characterized by events past, present, and anticipated. As we pass its sequence (in schematic time), the event unfolds in a manner that defines its meaning. In contextualism, the meaning or quality of an event varies continuously as we traverse this interval of historical time. Ecological economists discuss this in terms of endogenous and complex relationships between co-evolving systems. Norgaard's (1993) highlights a system with the co-evolving processes: knowledge, values, organization, technology, and environment. Norgaard writes:

> Each of these subsystems is related to each of the others; yet each is also chang-
> ing and effecting change in the others. Deliberate innovations, chance discover-
> ies, and random changes occur in each subsystem thereby selecting on the dis-
> tribution of the qualities of components in each of the subsystems. Whether new
> components prove fit depends on the characteristics of each of the subsystems
> at the time. With each subsystem putting selective pressure on each of the other,
> they coevolve in a manner whereby each reflects the other. Thus, everything is
> coupled, yet everything is changing (1993, p. 216).

The ontological categories defining closed and open systems, which are the centerpiece of the critical realist research program, addresses this issue (Lawson, 1997, 2003). In an open system, "the boundaries of the system are semi-permeable and /or their positions are not perfectly clear and /or may change; this implies that the classification into exogenous and endogenous variables may not be fixed" (Dow, 2004, p. 283). Institutional economists use "history, politics, and culture as raw ingredients of their explanations rather than challenges to be

---

13   For a similar treatment of time see Georgescu-Roegen (1971, p. 69–72). He differentiates between instants of time and duration based on the philosophical structure detailed by Alfred North Whitehead. In the mechanistic world hypothesis time is 'schematic or linear' and describes a structured sequence related to the location of a particular in a field.

explained by economics" Norgaard (1989, p. 48). For contextualism, the nature of an event is such that change is continuous and fundamental.

'Fusion' is the third subcategory that contributes to the quality of an event. Fusion involves the idea that an event's meaning cannot be reduced to its separate details. Meaning as details (the parts) has no logical connection to that which is intuited in the whole. The blue eyes, the aquiline nose, the rounded rosy cheeks and the facial hair are not the same as the whole meaning received when one sees the face. Farley, Erickson and Daly (2006) describe ecological economic problems as "first and foremost complex, part of interconnected social and ecological systems where one "twitch" affects the next, and the next, and the next, potentially feeding back on the original twitch. In complex systems, the whole is greater that the sum of the parts" (Farley, Erickson, and Daly, 2006, p. 3). Fusion reminds us that the pre-analytical vision is perceived holistically. In a complex problem analysis can proceed in many different directions, therefore, an explicit pre-analytical vision is needed to guide the entry point of analysis and inform action based on subjective and ethical judgment.

The Subcategories of Texture

As a policy-oriented research program, the analysis and control of events constitutes an important part of ecological economics. The analysis and control of events occurs in terms of the 'texture,' which consists of the subcategories— 'strands', 'context', and 'references'. The texture of an event is determined by direct contributions (its strands) and indirect contributions (its context) from other events. However, "context, texture, and strand is itself relative to the actual qualitative structure of a given event" (Pepper, 1942, p. 248). Compare this with what Norgaard writes:

> In the coevolutionary explanation of change, . . . knowledge, technologies, and social organization merely change, rather than advance, and the 'betterness' of each is only relative to how well each fits with everything else in a coevolving whole . . . The qualities of economic and environmental systems are constantly redefining each other within the process of the coevolving whole (Norgaard, 1993, p. 218).

By way of contrast with methods of analytical or elemental analysis (reductionism), Pepper writes:

> [A strand] is a contributing detail in a texture, but it also reaches out into a context and brings some of the quality of the context into the texture. It shows that too sharp a line cannot be drawn between texture, strand, and context. It constitutes a running demonstrative criticism of the method of element analysis, and of the analytical theories. generally. For contextualism, element analysis is intrinsically distortive . . . [F]rom the standpoint of the analytical theories . . . any object or event can be analyzed completely and finally into its constituents.

> [T]hat there is an ultimate and final and complete analytical constitution of wa-
> ter [for example] is assumed. [For contextualism] there is no final or complete
> analysis of anything (1942, pp. 247–248).

This point is similar to Georgescu-Roegen's (1971, 1979) critique of the analytic method that distinguishes between arithromorphic and dialectical concepts. A contextualist analysis proceeds along many paths since the details (strands) that describe an event are numerous. This leads to a common theme in contextualism; a number of analyses can describe an event so it is necessary to have a 'point of entry' predicated on the quality of the event, which guides action geared toward solving a problem. As ecological economists realize, this requires an honest and explicit account of a pre-analytical vision because analysis serves meaningful action. Also, texture's subcategories make it possible to appreciate the power of empirical observation possessed by ecologists in studying species and habitats (Norgaard, 1989) or the anthropological approach used by Veblen (1944c1899) to canvass the cultural landscape and identify the institution of the leisure class (Daley, 2000, pp. 264-274). Analysis of an event related to action that tries to solve the problem situation. Analysis requires a practical purpose to overcome relativity.

The texture of an event is defined by its references, which relate to strands and lead to the contextualist theory of truth. References deal with the nature of the connections that link various strands throughout the context. Pepper identifies four types of references: linear, convergent, blocking, and instrumental (1942, p. 252). A linear reference moves forward and backward between two strands. It has a single origin, a direction, and a satisfaction, whereas a convergent reference involves more than one initiation and satisfaction. Blocking is a failed reference in which a strand cannot reach its satisfaction for one reason or another. Pepper writes:

> Smooth-running strands constitute the contextualist interpretation of what we
> generally mean by order. Blocking is accordingly a fact of disorder, and it inevita-
> bly involves some degree of novelty. For, concerning a strand blocked, the block-
> ing is not expected or included in the reference of the strand (1942, p. 255).

Blocking means that an action (e.g., crossing a stream on a hiking trail) is unexpectedly confounded by a conflicting action. The novelty created may be either intrusive or emergent. Intrusive novelties are explained in terms of the prior histories of the blocked strands. Emergent novelties occur when a strand is initiated or blocked without explanation by a novel event. An instrumental reference integrates the previous three references and involves volition. Specifically, it involves an action intended to overcome the presence of a blocking reference. Pepper writes:

> An instrumental action is one undertaken as a means to a desired end and as a
> result of some obstacle that intervenes between the beginning of the action and
> its end or satisfaction. Instrumental action accordingly implies a linear reference

> that has been blocked, and a secondary action which removes or circumvents the
> blocking. (1942, p. 261).

Thus, the instrumental action intervenes to mitigate a tension that involves the blocking strand preventing a terminal strand from being realized. Instrumental action propels us out of the given moment. It reaches beyond the given moment and sets the stage for yet another means/end event. In other words, there really are no ends. This is consistent with the contextualist belief in a continuously changing world characterized by novelty. In moving beyond the immediacy of the given event, we see the "evidence for a widely extended universe in which a myriad of given events are interlocked and march forward arm in arm into the future with great strides" (Pepper 1942, p. 264).

Operationalism: The Contextualist Theory of Truth

Ecological economics defines a unique content area *and* an approach to problem solving. Due to the urgency of the problem situation, the researcher is invited into the immediate process of solving problems. We see this through advocacy for the methodology of post normal science (e.g., Tacconi, 1998), which in turn suggests an epistemological orientation. In contextualism, the identification of instrumental references leads to a theory of truth, which Pepper identifies as the operational theory (1942, pp. 268–279). Operationalism involves human action and the experience of solving a problem. There is no constraint on the significance of the problem at hand; it could involve crossing a stream or confronting global warming. The problem situation is analyzed and/or worked out directly in its context. A hypothesis is constructed and operationalized with specific details about an appropriate action. The operation is true if it solves the problem and false if it fails. Pepper writes:

> The question of truth arises when a strand is blocked . . . A tentative hypothesis
> is constructed, this hypothesis being in the nature of an instrumental texture
> with definite references for action. These references are followed out, and this
> activity is the act of verifying the hypothesis. If the hypothesis is blocked, and
> accordingly the original blocked strand (the problem) is not satisfied, then the
> operation is said to be false and the whole process of analysis, construction of
> hypothesis, and verification starts over again. If, however, the following of the
> hypothesis leads to the satisfaction of the blocked strand and to the solution of
> the problem, then the operation is said to be true. (1942, p. 269).

Pepper identifies three specifications of the operational theory that characterize the development of pragmatism. Pepper writes:

> It was with a theory of truth that contextualism came to birth. The early contex-
> tualists like Peirce and James insisted that no world theory was involved in this

> conception of truth. Pragmatism . . . was, they said, simply a method. It presup-
> posed and implied nothing. It was purely empirical; purely a noting of what men
> actually did when they came to conclusions which they call true. The contempo-
> rary name for this method is called *operationalism* (1942, p. 268).

In the 'successful working' theory truth resides in action. In the 'verified hypothesis' theory truth resides in the symbolic hypothesis that guides action. Pepper claims that the verified hypothesis theory exhibits a pragmatic paradox. The theory maintains that a symbolic statement is only a tool for controlling nature. A true hypothesis gives no insight into the qualities of nature because its purpose is not to mirror nature or to integrate nature into the analysis (1942, pp. 274-275). In the 'qualitative confirmation' theory, the hypothesis reflects the qualities of nature. These perceptions about nature are incorporated into the hypothesis and realized in the act of verifying the hypothesis. Building on his example of a hunter blocked by a stream, Pepper writes:

> Suppose the hunter, on looking over the situation, should make the explicit state-
> ment: "If I take up that pole, and step on that log, and push myself off from this
> bank, I can push myself up to the other bank . . . These incipient references or
> images fill out and actualize themselves in the operations of picking up the pole
> and stepping on the log, balancing there, and placing the pole firmly against the
> bank, and so on. But these acts now are the very acts of perceptual verification of
> the hypothesis. The qualities the hunter is now experiencing are the very quali-
> ties of the event referred to as verifying the verbal statement . . . The structure
> of the verifying event is an integration of contributions coming partly from the
> operations of the hunter and partly from continuous physical textures [the envi-
> ronment] among which these operations are carried on (1942, p. 276).

The hypothesis is connected with the event that verifies it and this connection implies that the qualities of nature. Pepper concludes that the operational theory and it most sophisticated expression—the qualitative confirmation theory— gives insight into the structure of nature.

Conclusion

Ecological economics should move beyond a *strategy* of methodological plural-ism and embark on a discussion of its methodological orientation. Tolerance for a variety of methods is an appropriate attitude for the transdiscipline. However, as the program matures, this will unlikely substitute for an explicit philosophical position and may induce practitioners to define ecological economics in opposi-tion to the neoclassical economics. In the struggle for recruits, an incoherent identity makes ecological economics vulnerable to absorption by the dominant school of thought. A potential way forward is the philosophical system devel-oped in *World Hypotheses: A Study in Evidence*. Pepper's philosophy supports methodological and epistemological pluralism. Using the root metaphor method, Pepper details what a pluralist metaphilosophy looks like by developing the sets of structural categories unique to four world hypotheses. Formism, mechanism, contextualism and organicism are autonomous and adequate through possessing scope and withstanding the text of time in the history of philosophy. Pluralism is founded on the complementary nature of meta-level models and is a pragmatic response to partial and fallible knowledge.

The ability of structural categories to handle facts and evidence across disciplines in the physical, life and human sciences implies conceptual models that could foster communication across disciplines and between schools of thought. I suggest that contextualism, whose 'operational' theory of truth Pepper links to pragmatism, may offer a blueprint for understanding how practitioners organize factual evidence and structure the ecological economic approach to confronting the encroaching conflict between the economic system and the biophysical system. I offer suggestions regarding some connections between contextualism and ecological economics. The methodology of post normal science responds to the urgency of problems and reaches out to a wide peer group to successfully implement policy and engages in direct action. The complexity of co-evolving systems, mirrored in Pepper's discussion the 'web of events' giving meaning to the 'given historic event,' suggests an ontological framework requiring a pre-analytical vision. Finally, the operational theory of truth is an expression of pragmatism focusing on action in finding a successful solution of a problem. Ecological economics has a pre-analytical vision which leads to normative recommendations that policy should concentrate first on scale, next on distribution and finally on market efficiency in resolving the pressing environmental issues of our time. Just as important, research in the field is intimately connected with action as highlighted by claim to the urgency of the historical problem situation. Ecological economics is more than just the content of its subject matter. It is a powerful methodological approach with roots in the tradition of pragmatism. Contextualism offers a conceptual model for seeing how we approach these problems in research and confront them in the social sphere.

References

Backhouse, Roger E. (Ed.). (1994). *New Directions in Economic Methodology.* New York & London: Routledge.

Caldwell, Bruce J. (1990[c1982]). *Beyond Positivism: Economic Methodology in the Twentieth Century.* London: Allen & Unwin.

Caldwell, Bruce J. (1994). Two Proposals For the Recovery of Economic Practice in New Directions in Roger E. Backhouse (Ed.). *Economic Methodology.* New York & London: Routledge.

Capra, Fritjof. (1982). *The Turning Point: Science, Society, and the Rising Culture.* New York: Bantam Books.

Costanza, Robert. (1996). The Impact of Ecological Economics. *Ecological Economics, 19*: 1–2.

Costanza, Robert & King, Janis. (1999). The First Decade of Ecological Economics. *Ecological Economics 28*: 1–9.

Daley, Michael C. (2000) An Image of Enduring Plurality in Economic Theory: The Root-Metaphor Theory of Stephen C. Pepper. *Dissertation Abstract International, 61*. No. 04A p. 1545

Dewey, John. (1938). *Experience and Education*. New York: MacMillan Publishing Company.

Dow, Sheila C. (2004). Structured Pluralism. *Journal of Economic Methodology 11*(3): 275–290.

Efron, Arthur. (1980). Introduction: Pepper's Continuing Value. *Paunch, 53:* 5–53.

Farley, Joshua, Erickson, Jon D., and Daly, Herman. (2005). *Ecological Economics: A Workbook for Problem-based Learning*. Washington D.C.: Island Press.

Forstater, Mathew. (2004). Visions and Scenarios: Heilbroner's Worldly Philosophy, Lowe's Political Economics, and the Methodology of Ecological Economics. *Ecological Economics, 51:* 17–30.

Functowicz, S. O., and Ravetz, J. R. (1991). A new scientific methodology for global environmental issues. In *Ecological Economics: The Science and Management of Sustainability*, R. Costanza (Ed.). New York: Columbia University Press, 137–152.

Georgescu-Roegen, Nicholas. (1971). *The Entropy Law and the Economic Process*. Cambridge: Harvard University Press.

Georgescu-Roegen, Nicholas. (1979). Methods in Economic Science. *Journal of Economic Issues 8*(2).

Gowdy, John, and Erickson, Jon D. (2005). The Approach of Ecological Economics. *Cambridge Journal of Economics, 29*: 207–222.

Guba, E. G. (1990). The Alternative Paradigm Dialog. In *The Paradigm Dialog*, E. G. Guba (Ed.). London: Sage, 17–27.

Hands, D. W. (2001). *Reflection Without Rules: Economic Methodology and Contemporary Science Theory*. Cambridge: Cambridge University Press

Hayes, William M., and Lynne, Gary D. (2004). Towards a Centerpiece for Ecological Economics. *Ecological Economics 49*: 287–301.

Henderson, Willie. (1994). Metaphor and Economics. In *New Directions in Economic Methodology*, Roger Backhouse (Ed.). London: Routledge.

Henderson, Willie. (1998). Metaphor in Davis, John B., Hands, D. Wade & Mäki, Uskali. (Eds.). *The Handbook of Economic Methodology*. Northhampton, MA: Edward Elgar.

Hoekstra, Raymond. (1945). Pepper's World Hypotheses. *The Journal of Philosophy, 42*(4): 85–101.

Kuhn, Thomas. (1970[c1962]). *The Structure of Scientific Revolutions*. Chicago: University of Chicago Press.

Lawson, T. (1997). *Economics and Reality*. London: Routledge.

Lawson, T. (2003). *Reorienting Economics*. London: Routledge.

Luks, Fred. (1998). The rhetorics of ecological economics. *Ecological Economics, 26*(2): 139–149.

Ma, Chunbo, and Stern, David I. (2006). Environmental and ecological economics: A citation analysis. *Ecological Economics, 58*: 491–506.

McCloskey, D. N. (1997[c1985]). *The Rhetoric of Economics*. (2nd ed.). Madison: University of Wisconsin Press.

McLennan, Gregor. (2002). Quandaries in Meta-theory: Against Pluralism. *Economy and Society, 31*(3): 483–496.

Norgaard, Richard B. (1989). The Case For Methodological Pluralism. *Ecological Economics 1*: 37–57.

Norgaard, Richard B. (1993). The Coevolution of Economic and Environmental Systems and the Emergence of Unsustainability. In *Evolutionary Concepts in Contemporary Economics*, England Richard (Ed.). Ann Arbor: The University of Michigan Press.

Patterson, Murray G. (2006). Development of ecological economics in Australia and New Zealand. *Ecological Economics 56*: 312–331.

Pepper, Stephen C. (1942). *World Hypotheses: A Study in Evidence.* Berkeley: University of Southern California Press.

Quine, James. (1982). Root Metaphor and Interdisciplinary Curriculum: Designs for Teaching Literature in Secondary Schools. *The Journal of Mind and Behavior, 3*(4): 345–356.

Reck, Andrew J. 1968. Stephen C. Pepper: Philosophy of Values. In *The New American Philosophers: An Exploration of Thought Since World War II.* Baton Rouge: Louisiana State University.

Salanti, Andrea, and Screpanti, Ernesto. (Eds.). (1997). *Pluralism in Economics: New Perspectives in History and Methodology.* Brookfield, VT: Edward Elgar Publishing.

Tacconi, Luca. (1998). Scientific Methodology for Ecological Economics. *Ecological Economics, 27*: 91–105.

Veblen, Thorstein. (1944[c1899]). *The Theory of the Leisure Class: An Economic Study of Institutions.* New York: Dover.

Weimer, Walter. (1979). *Notes on the Methodology of Scientific Research.* Hillsdale, NJ: Erlbaum Associates.

10 Fostering Dialogue to Support Valuation of Sustainable Technologies

Janet Clark

ABSTRACT

The selection of greener and safer materials for production and consumption offers a context for considering the sustainability value of these materials. Such consideration of alternative materials must include technical and cost issues from an engineering and business perspective, but it can also consider health, environment, local development and other issues.

In 2006, the Toxics Use Reduction Institute (TURI) conducted an alternatives assessment on safer alternatives for five toxic chemicals: Lead, Formaldehyde, Perchloroethylene (PCE), Hexavalent chromium, and di(2-ethylhexyl)phthalate (DEHP). Associated with this study, a structured day long discussion with selected economists and other experts in innovation and technology diffusion resulted in creation of a framework to clarify situational characteristics and factors that influence the economic outcomes of adopting cleaner and safer alternatives. The intended use of the TURI Framework is dialogue among the community of stakeholders to improve work to assess the value, benefit and strategies for innovation for safer technology.

This paper maps the perspectives at play in the elements of the framework, and also the opportunities and challenges in its use. These opportunities include the flexibility to consider many kinds of sustainable technology, steps to improve economic outcomes, and the opportunity to foster and track dialogue, learning, and common values. Among the challenges are addressing complexity, respecting different perspectives, and sustaining participation.

Context

Design Tools and the TURI Project

Since 1989, the Toxics Use Reduction Institute (TURI)—and more recently and with an international perspective, the Lowell Center for Sustainable Production (LCSP)—have explored practices, improved methods, and trained engineers in industry to design for sustainability. Located at the University of Massachusetts Lowell, these two organizations are separate but linked. TURI is a state government organization that provides technology and policy research, professional

"The economic impacts of toxics use reduction in Massachusetts are explored in the 1997 program evaluation report of the Toxics Use Reduction Act (TURA) (Toxics Use Reduction Institute (TURI) 1997). This benefit-cost analysis found that economic benefits outweighed costs, even without accounting for increased revenue from capital investments in improved processes, benefits to non-TURA firms in Massachusetts from TURA program resources, or human health and ecological benefits. For the period from 1990 through 1997, the direct monetized benefits were found to be $90.5 million in 1995 dollars. The costs were found to be $76.6 million ($49.4 million in compliance costs, and $27.1 million for capital investments), so the net benefit was $13.9 million." (from TURI Five Chemicals Report, 2006)

and technical training, and an array of initiatives that support diffusion of safer technologies. It serves Massachusetts industry, government and communities. The LCSP is made up of faculty, staff and students of the university, and it works with health and environmental groups, industry, and government in and outside of Massachusetts. Through strategic engagement, the LCSP catalyzes change toward sustainable materials, production processes, and conditions of life and work.

Our approach is about "teaching to fish" rather than a prescriptive approach. No matter how you organize design work, a basic component is an "alternatives assessment" step. The data needed for such an assessment are situational, complex, evolving, and often difficult to quantify, and a science of alternatives assessment has emerged to support better green design. TURI and the LCSP have worked with other researchers in this and other countries to identify best practices and to create a useful methodology.

In Massachusetts, the TURI Planning method we have trained in industry for the last fifteen years includes a step called "Options Assessment". After diagramming a targeted unit of production, designers set improvement goals and then identify options. They must then consider and assess the hazard, performance and cost of each option. Designers then decide whether to recommend changes in production, often by adoption of a safer alternative.

In July 2005, the Commonwealth of Massachusetts requested that TURI perform an alternatives assessment for five chemicals: lead, formaldehyde, perchloroethylene (PCE), hexavalent chromium, and di(2-ethylhexyl) phthalate (DEHP). For each chemical, TURI was charged with identifying significant uses, reviewing health and environmental effects, and evaluating possible alternatives. The Institute was also directed to evaluate possible effects on Massachusetts employment and economic competitiveness associated with adoption of safer alternatives.[1]

---

1   The TURI *Five Chemicals Alternatives Assessment Study* of 2006 and associated references are available on http://www.turi.org

This project gave TURI an opportunity to refine and adapt the alternatives assessment methodology for a government perspective and budget. For each phase of the analysis, the study relied on information from experts and publicly available resources. Stakeholders, including industry representatives, government agencies, and public health, environmental and labor advocates were extensively consulted throughout the project. The study was a critical trial for the TURI Alternatives Assessment Methodology, as the project challenged researchers to select, refine and communicate the scientific and engineering data, to manage the dialogue with stakeholders, and to maintain a fair, transparent and objective process of analysis and reporting.

Part of the Institute's mandate was to assess potential effects on the employment level and the economic competitiveness of the Commonwealth associated with adopting alternative chemicals or technologies. To identify situational characteristics and factors that influence the economic outcomes of adopting cleaner and safer alternatives, we reviewed the experiences of the TURA program, and also the literature on the economics of environmental regulation and alternatives assessment. For the study, we then held a day-long discussion session with selected economists and other experts in innovation and technology diffusion. (See Attachment A for a list of participants.) The five chemical assessments as well as other specific case material yielded additional insights during this dialogue. It was revealing that most of the participants in the economic impact dialogue supported improved public health and wanted work undertaken to quantify these kinds of benefits. Other themes of the day are offered in Attachment B, and include the opportunities for solid economic benefit in environmental innovations, the significant value of bringing universities and industry together for problem-solving, the challenges of uneven outcomes and impacts on small businesses, workforce changes that dramatically impact quality of life, and the opportunities for policy and assistance options that support good economic outcomes. The result of the day was an Economic Impact Assessment Framework (see page 3 below) to guide more detailed research and dialogue concerning the economic outcomes of adopting cleaner and safer alternatives.

Adoption of safer alternatives resulted in keen stakeholder interest and tangeable findings relevant to sustainability valuations. Interestingly, some of the alternatives studied can probably be adopted without any adverse effect on Massachusetts employment. In fact, there is strong evidence that in some cases adoption of safer alternatives can produce economic benefits. In other situations, assurance of economic benefit would need more study and technology development. We also found that there are many opportunities for government to support a positive economic outcome and to mitigate some negative effects for individual firms. In some instances, targeted assistance to industry can facilitate adoption of safer alternatives that will yield employment and competitiveness benefits over time. Specific examples are offered in the following table:

Examples from the TURI Alternatives Assessment Study

No adverse economic effect	Elimination of formaldehyde dry sterilant from use in Massachusetts hair salons would produce savings and make sanitation standards at Massachusetts hair salons consistent with those in the rest of the country. Similarly, Massachusetts schools could adopt alternatives to formaldehyde-fixed dissection specimens without increasing costs.
Opportunity for market niche	Some Massachusetts firms are working to produce DEHP-free medical devices. With growing demand for such devices, firms may have opportunities for growth in this area.
Investment needed	In some cases, alternatives are more costly at this time, such as PCE vapor degreasing solvent alternatives. For many, such as alternative plasticizers for resilient flooring, firm cost conclusions cannot be reached without more information concerning the cost of processing modifications.

Valuation and Sustainability

Valuation is in part a traditional accounting exercise, with all of the challenges and solid security that accounting methods bring.

For the TURI assessment study, cost considerations specific to individual chemicals and alternatives were not evenly available, and may depend on variable energy, material, labor, production, market and other data that may change over time. In addition, the employment and competitiveness implications of adopting an alternative are tied to the policy environment. Voluntary adoption of alternatives, technical assistance programs, mandatory chemical phase-outs, or grant or loan programs designed to ease the transition to safer alternatives may all produce different market outcomes. The market itself may shift with new information, and be hard to predict. Adding to the challenge, basic policy questions of the extent and value of improved public and environmental health must be part of the valuation, and these are revealed in large part through dialogue among stakeholders on risk and value as well as through research.

Sustainability valuations are also problematic. There is a need to identify what has value, i.e., which sustainability topics are critical to consider. (See the box on the right.) Also, a way is needed to compare apples to oranges, and to give criteria and weights to things not easily quantified. Work to achieve clarity and agreement on values and truth across sectors and between individuals is plenty challenging without the complexity of full-system sustainability to address. Decision support tools that address complexity by offering structure include multiple-factor matrices, databases, and screening lists. Other tools—such as simulations and modeling—can offer vision and perspective. A good tool will support dialogue as well as a roadmap, and accurate and appropriately formatted information. Addressing safer alternatives adoption offers a focus on some of

Sustainability Impact Topics Identified by the European Union
(Bohringer and Loschel, in ISEE Nov. 2006)

Which topics should be considered in valuation efforts?
Communities, institutions and individuals may offer variations specific to
their bioregion, culture and vision.

- Economic development
- Social issues (poverty, access, aging, . . .)
- Public health
- Climate change and energy
- Production and consumption (ecoefficiency)
- Natural resources
- Transportation
- Good governance (policy coherence, participation)

these topics, such as economic development, public health, and production and
consumption. It is possible to expand the scope to consider more of the sustainability topics—if the complexity can be handled. However, a fully-engaged
dialogue can find focus and structure from a specific goal such as "material-
specific safer technology adoption", paired with a comprehensive framework.
The TURI Economic Impact Assessment Framework, (see following below)
has three stages of assessment:

> **Stage 1:** Determine the readiness of good alternatives and the agility of
> the industry and supply chain.

> **Stage 2:** Decide if the existing economic conditions favor alternatives. If
> yes, development should progress without policy and research changes. If
> no, continue the dialogue and research.

> **Stage 3:** Describe the existing barriers to alternatives adoption and also
> the existing policy context.

TURI Economic Impact Assessment Framework

This framework outlines the ways in which alternatives adoption may affect
jobs, industry, and other aspects of the economy. Please see Attachment C for
descriptions of the elements presented here.

Describe Scope of the Proposed Substitution

**Stage 1:
Technology and
Industry**

Economic impact
will depend on
readiness of
alternatives and
agility of industry

Alternatives Readiness

- Chemical use trends
- Trend drivers
- Presence of feasible alternatives
- Technical risk and reliability
- Financial viability
- EH&S impact
- Market demand and acceptance
- Availability from suppliers

Industry Agility

- Characteristics of the industry sector
- Characteristics of the supply chain
- Characteristics of the market and the competition

Stage 2: Decision

Do existing econo-
mic conditions favor
alternatives? If not,
continue.

Existing Conditions

Substitution is rewarding, cost effective, market driven, or
Barriers exist to implementing substitutions.

**Stage 3: Barriers
and Policy
Instruments**

Economic Impact
will also depend
on the nature of
existing barriers to
alternatives adop-
tion and the policy
context

Possible Barriers

- **Technical:** Alternatives not readily available
- **Informational:** Inadequate information flows between consumers, industry, researchers
- **Market:** Uncertainty about demand or lack of demand for alternatives
- **Industry:** Aspects of industry or supply chain hinder change
- **Financial:** Inadequate financial structure for financing alternatives
- **Regulatory:** Conflicting requirements or regulatory uncertainty

Industry Agility

- Characteristics of the industry sector
- Characteristics of the supply chain
- Characteristics of the market and the competition

Dialogue Planning

What would a project using the TURI Framework look like? The following sections relate TURI practices used in years of fostering dialogues about safer technology development, adoption, and policy. Lessons from the Five Chemicals Alternatives Assessment project are included as well as some suggested methods.

The description of the project scope can be very important. If a representative group of participants are engaged early in scoping and agenda-building efforts, they can add insights and also validation with their constituents and other participants who come to the dialogue later.

Participants

Who should be involved? One definition of stakeholder is "those who really count" (Freeman, R. E. 1984, *Strategic Management: A stakeholder approach*. Boston: Pitman). Participants chosen for the 2006 TURI study included experts in economics and development as they relate to industry, labor, innovation, commerce and/or environment. Wherever in the development community the dialogue is engaged, key experts, players, and concerned publics not already in the room can be identified and invited in later phases.

Goals

Our mission is toxics use reduction. This supports Massachusetts' policies that seek to advance safer neighborhoods, workplaces and households, and also increased competitiveness in our companies. Goal setting is the first opportunity to engage others, and the resulting goals should respect their mission and perspectives. Specific examples might be "safer product innovation in the decorative metal finishing sector" or "improved worker safety" or "increased capacity to bring RoHS compliant products to the European market in the electronics sector".

Goals also serve to bound the research and discussion, which is critical with the expected emergence of many good ideas throughout the series of dialogue workshops. It might be a good idea to decide how such contributions will be handled, e.g., held for later discussion or immediately spun off to a workgroup or passed along to an outside entity.

In the 2006 TURI economic impact dialogue, everyone in the room was strongly in support of public health and safety. However, participants had their own interests in the dialogue. For example, trade associations and businesses sought market advantage in the form of information about emerging technologies and regulations. Also, they sought to influence policy and regulations to ensure a "level playing field". Health and environment groups sought honest science and a cautious approach to risky materials, which they understood to be advanced through open consideration of materials assessment. Government staff sought a wise and strategic program response to environment, health and development needs. TURI has found it critical to not only acknowledge these interests in early discussions, but to check in at each dialogue meeting to ensure everyone continued to find value in the ongoing process—value which they can describe to their constituents. In this way their continued participation is better assured.

Scope, Agenda and Schedule

To build a project scope, the TURI Framework should be refined to add or eliminate elements and ask better questions for research. The agenda for the proposed project would then reflect the breadth and depth of topics to be discussed. Questions to consider include: Which elements of the framework should receive the most attention and what information should be brought to the table? What sequence seems logical, and who should be in the room? How long should be allowed for research and how long for discussion? What are the objectives of each session? How will knowledge be documented and shared?

Measuring Success

In addition to achieving the main goal, success of the Framework's application might include the following achievements:

1. Stakeholders understand and share a common goal,
2. Stakeholders find the process useful,
3. Long-term relationships are established or strengthened,
4. Sustainability impacts are situationally evaluated,
5. Strategies for success are clear, and
6. The process has built technological capacity.

If these measures of success were validated in the first meeting of the dialogue, then each meeting could briefly check in with participants. Impressions of benefit can be captured on a 1 to 10 scale, and feedback used for adjusting the content or process. When these impressions are shared, participants learn more about each other.

The following figure is generated from hypothetical responses from an industry representative. This person experienced all **Stage 1** topics as useful for building technological capacity, but the remaining topics were more mixed. A community or government representative might have different experiences, and getting better clarity yields insight and language for all to report to their constituents.

Stage 2 is a decision point. If the discovery so far is that the safer alternative is economically viable, then this piece of sustainable development can be expected to advance with existing market drivers and business innovation. This is a valuable consensus to have been reached, and the information gathered can strategically support businesses participating in the dialogue. Questions can be

Industry Stage 1

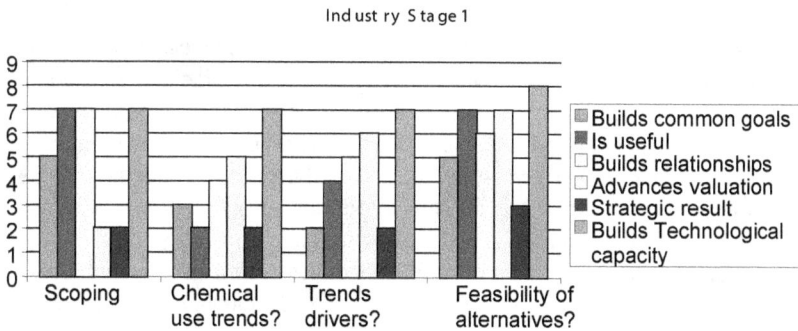

Figure 1 Hypothetical Industry Representative's Responses to Stage 1

asked to improve this value to participants in the dialogue, possibly concerning the nature of continued relationships or of reporting progress to constituents.

Stage 3 should yield a clearer understanding of barriers to adoption of safer alternatives, including:

- **Technical:** Alternatives are not readily available. Is the reason technical, reliability, cost, or risk-related, and can university or publicly-funded research be of value?

- **Informational:** There is inadequate information flow between consumers, industry, and researchers. What would be helpful: technical guidance materials for companies, clearer labeling for products, or better access to performance data from laboratories?

- **Market:** There is uncertainty about demand or lack of demand for alternatives. Would advertising, public recognition, public health announcements help?

- **Capacity:** There is a lack of necessary expertise among workers, or an industry culture resistant to change. Are needed skills and workforce volume identified? Does the structure or other aspects of the industry or supply chain hinder change?

- **Financial:** There is inadequate financial structure for financing alternatives. Are calculations available concerning environment-related investment costs and savings, or do book-keeping approaches hide the costs of using toxic chemicals? Is there a need to establish government and business accounting systems that accurately track health and environment-related costs and returns? What does not need to be quantified in order to be a valid driver? Are finance providers familiar with alternative technologies?

- **Regulatory:** There are conflicting requirements and regulatory uncertainty. If successful, stage 3 should also generate good descriptions of the regulatory context and its impacts on economically successful adoption of new technologies. Are policies (eg., technical assistance, information, incentives, market support, restrictions, tax policies, regional coordination, etc) interacting in a way that is mutually reinforcing, redundant, or conflicting?

If the dialogue has been successful, there will be elements and groundwork for a wise and engaged strategy for government policies, with clear roles for universities, and private and non-profit sectors. There will be confidence and buy-in

"In some instances, targeted assistance to industry can facilitate adoption of safer alternatives that will yield employment and competitiveness benefits over time. Government can have a role to play in facilitating adoption of alternatives that require an initial capital investment. Loan or grant programs may be particularly useful for small and medium sized enterprises. For example, California has demonstrated the viability of grant programs in facilitating the transition to safer alternatives for small dry cleaning facilities. Partnerships in research and skills development can also enhance knowledge of emerging safer technologies." (Concluding Comments of Chapter 8, page 16, of the TURI Assessment Report.)

for this emerging strategy among the participants and their constituents. Its cost and benefit can now be calculated, although it is possible the valuation will have already occurred during the dialogue and research for many of the framework elements. A successful dialogue will identify opportunities for government to support a positive economic outcome and to mitigate any negative effects for individual firms.

Building Capacity

A significant opportunity available in the use of the TURI Framework is the creation of a networked local community that can create good strategies for sustainable development. Through a process such as described in this paper, a community has now shared knowledge about a specific risk and technology, and built its skills in research and communication. An array of topics—from theory and vision to hardware and markets—have been either judged, evaluated or priced. Some roles have been established, and trust and relationships have been built. Finally, it can be hoped that the result is wise strategic action, effective handling of complexity, and individual and organizational confidence in advancing sustainability. To sustain capacity to come together in this way, the records and the final report should hold language to describe the benefits, and lessons learned and ideas for improvememnts. Such a report might involve speaking, training and coaching other leaders and communities.

Conclusions

Studies have found that environmental and safety improvements in industry can be economic good news by building efficiency, expanding markets, reducing risk and stabilizing compliance responsibilities. Additionally, the TURI "Five Chemicals Alternatives Assessment Study" identified specific safer technologies that could prove economically viable without further technology development. This contribution to sustainability is limited by the lack of confidence in the predicted economic outcomes. Establishing predictability requires attention to the complexity, the situational realities, and the perspectives at play in any particular context. The TURI Economic Impact Assessment Framework can be used to plan and manage a dialogue among diverse sectors and individuals to describe and quantify the elements that influence economic outcomes. In this way policies are created in government, industry and communities that advance sustainability and build trust.

Attachment A: List of Participants

The experts convened by TURI to discuss the economic factors to consider in determining the possible economic impacts of adoption of safer alternatives were chosen for their economic and development expertise relating to industry, labor, innovation, and environmental economics, and included:

- Stephen J. Adams, Small Business Administration
- James Goldstein, Tellus Institute
- William Lazonick, University of Massachusetts Lowell
- Teresa Lynch, Economic Development Research Group
- Edward March, University of Massachusetts Lowell
- Andre Mayer, Associated Industries of Massachusetts
- Deborah Savage, Environmental Management Accounting Research & Information Center

Three others were not able to attend the meeting but were asked for their perspectives, and their comments were incorporated into this report. These were:

- Frank Ackerman, Global Development and Environment Institute, Tufts University
- Michael Goodman, Donahue Institute, University of Massachusetts Boston
- Christopher Tilly, University of Massachusetts Lowell

Attachment B: Economic Themes that Surfaced in the TURI Dialogue

The following text is from pages 8–12 to 8–14 of the *Five Chemicals Alternatives Assessment Study,* 2006.

Protecting human health: Economic benefits of public health improvement resulting from safer alternatives may be overlooked because they are difficult to quantify, but they are very significant. The impact of a reduction in these costs was not extensively discussed by the panel, though many stated that they wanted to see this addressed.

Identifying economic opportunities: There may be economic opportunities in environmental improvement.

The Commonwealth as convener: The Commonwealth can play a useful role in facilitating industry problem-solving. There is substantial evidence supporting strategies that bring industry and universities and trade associations together, and help industry problem-solvers make the case for change.

Economic outcomes are uneven: Not all companies benefit from business opportunities created by new technology, regulations, incentives, or other conditions. Regardless of whether the overall state-level impact of a change is found to be positive, negative, or neutral, there will be economic winners and losers. For example, a trend toward capital-intensive CO_2 dry cleaning would favor larger dry cleaners, whereas a trend toward labor-intensive wet-cleaning would favor small businesses, regardless of whether the shift from perchloroethylene dry cleaning was regulatory or market driven.

Supporting small businesses: Small businesses were recognized as important to innovation, employment and entry into business ownership . They also may be disproportionately affected by environmental regulation (as well as other factors for which economies of scale are important). At the same time, if small businesses are not ready for upcoming transitions (such as international regulations like the European Union Restriction on certain Hazardous Substances Directive, "RoHS") they may lose business. If businesses in the state are ahead of these transitions and able to meet requirements or new market demands more quickly or cheaply, companies may gain business.

Maintaining a range of job types: Research and development spending, manufacturing facilities, and regulation may or may not create and maintain good jobs in the state. Research support may not directly address employment for less educated workers, although through a multiplier effect it can lead to greater demand for less skill-demanding jobs such as waitstaff or other support to professional and technical workers.

Manufacturing facilities that currently provide middle-class wages for lower-education jobs in Massachusetts today are vulnerable, and workers may benefit from advanced training to earn middle-class wages in manufacturing in Massachusetts. Business consolidation (e.g. larger dry cleaners) may cause the loss of small immigrant-owned entrepreneurial businesses.

Flexible options: Technical assistance programs are helpful in supporting positive economic outcomes from substitution, as are preferred purchasing programs, information dissemination, capital financing assistance, government assisted research, and labeling programs like Energy Star. However, voluntary options may leave behind more marginal companies and concentrate negative impacts on the economically disadvantaged.

Influence of Regulatory Policy: Regulatory action may influence the economic impact of alternatives adoption under different circumstances. Many areas of disagreement remained among panel members concerning the significance of these circumstances, which can be organized as follows from the perspective of supply chain and availability of alternatives.

Imports

In cases where Massachusetts is an importer of goods, the issue is the extent to which companies will need to cater to unique demands from the relatively small Massachusetts market in the following situations:

- If alternatives exist but are not available, the Massachusetts market alone **is likely** to be large enough to provide a market incentive for companies to improve distribution of these alternatives

- If no alternatives exist and Massachusetts is an importer of goods, the Massachusetts market alone **is unlikely** to be large enough to provide a strong market incentive for companies to develop new alternatives. There was discussion about whether California was large enough, and agreement that the European Union definitely was, as evidenced by the Restrictions on certain Hazardous Substances Directive "RoHS" and the Waste Electrical and Electronic Equipment Directive "WEEE". It was agreed that states working together, *e.g.,* New England and New York, could make a bigger market that could influence alternatives. The possibility was discussed of creating a market niche that ultimately substitutes a locally developed product for what was previously an import product, thus creating a new export industry.

Exports

In cases where Massachusetts is an exporter of goods, the issue is the competitive position of Massachusetts manufacturers in national or global markets. There is significant disagreement over whether unique Massachusetts requirements for manufacturing processes and products put Massachusetts companies at a competitive advantage or disadvantage. The different viewpoints include:

- Disadvantage: Massachusetts-specific requirements where there are existing global requirements could add expense rather than help companies meet challenges. Added costs for reducing or eliminating certain toxics that the global market does not require could reduce competitiveness. Whether Massachusetts policy appears to industry to be relatively restrictive or inviting might influence company location, expansion, or investment decisions.

- Advantage: Massachusetts requirements could help Massachusetts companies meet global challenges such as RoHS and forthcoming requirements elsewhere. Costs of regulations are often less than anticipated, and thus do not, in actuality, reduce competitiveness. There is no or little evidence to support the claim that regulatory climate is a key determinant of companies' decision-making around locating and/or investing in facilities.

Local

In service-industry cases, for example dry cleaning, auto-body, or hair salons, and certain other industries, such as cement, the market is local. Out of state purchases of the service or product are rare other than in border towns.

While there is agreement that larger markets have more influence than smaller ones, there are some disagreements on the implications of that fact for Massachusetts. Many of the reviewers agreed that an approach of collaboration with other states, such as in past efforts to reduce mercury, or ongoing efforts to reduce greenhouse gases, would help reduce costs. However there were disagreements over effects where Massachusetts sets policy ahead of other state and national initiatives, and there was some concern whether other states and countries would follow such initiatives. Whether or not other states would follow a leading state-level policy is an area of analysis for which there is extensive literature and debate but no consensus.

The role of innovation is an issue

Massachusetts currently has an innovation advantage driven by major private research universities and high technology industries such as biotech, polymers, defense, and electronics. However, the degree to which the Commonwealth has a significant influential role in developing or maintaining industrial competitive advantage is less clear.

There is evidence that Massachusetts companies could be helped to be innovative environmental leaders that use advanced technology to increase competitiveness while simultaneously meeting more stringent environmental standards. There is capacity here: the Commonwealth's existing knowledge base in both universities and companies offers unique high-tech capabilities with which to take advantage of emerging market opportunities for safer technologies. Public policy is needed to help build and maintain an advantage as, according to one expert, " . . . state subsidy is in virtually all places and at virtually all times integral to the innovation process." (Lazonick) However, it is possible that responding to market conditions rather than to government mandates is more economically attractive. State funded studies to identify emerging opportunities and ensure the high quality of the regional educational system in environmental technologies may have the best chance to increase competitiveness.

Attachment C: Explanation of the TURI Economic Framework Elements

The following text is from pages 8–7 to 8–12 of the *Five Chemicals Alternatives Assessment Study,* 2006.

Alternatives Readiness

What are chemical use trends?
Chemical use trends can be described and listed as uses, geographic locations, and impacts and quantified as volumes and substitution rates.

What is driving these trends?
There may be a number of existing drivers for substitution, including better quality or less expensive alternatives and changes in regulation or consumer preference. Detailed information may include

Costs: e.g., the cost of disposal of toxic waste, chemical prices or use taxes

Market change: e.g., export market requirements, local consumer demand, company brand image protection, or customer programs in Environmentally Preferable Purchasing

Innovation: e.g., the obsolescence of existing equipment

Regulation: e.g., the European Union WEEE and RoHS Directives

Financing/Insurance: e.g., service providers requiring risk reduction

Are there feasible alternatives?
Technical, financial, and EH&S considerations for each alternative must be researched, including market and supply.

Industry Agility

What are characteristics of the industry sector?
Characteristics to consider include size (number of employees or annual sales), ownership, the education and skill levels of workers as well as their salary ranges, some measure of innovativeness, profit margins and investment practices.

Availability of capital is part of a broader picture of facility investment in an alternative, including the timing of such a transition, the value and remaining lifetime of any existing investments, and the hurdle rate used to make investment decisions.

What are characteristics of the supply chain?
Are products containing substances of concern imported or exported, or are the products primarily local to Massachusetts? Who are suppliers and customers, and where and how large are they? Are trading partners large enough to influence the industry sector?

The location of Massachusetts in the supply chain will affect the degree and nature of Massachusetts influence on the market in a given chemical or alternative. It is also important to identify the actors that have most influence on the industry. These may include suppliers that provide information, banks that provide financing, or customers who demand a product change.

The charts below illustrate supply chain characteristics for two of the case studies as developed by one of the expert reviewers. The first chart, Figure A - 1,

Is the target chemical:	Made elsewhere, then imported into Massachusetts? (import)	In Massachusetts?	Made in Massachusetts, then exported elsewhere? (export)

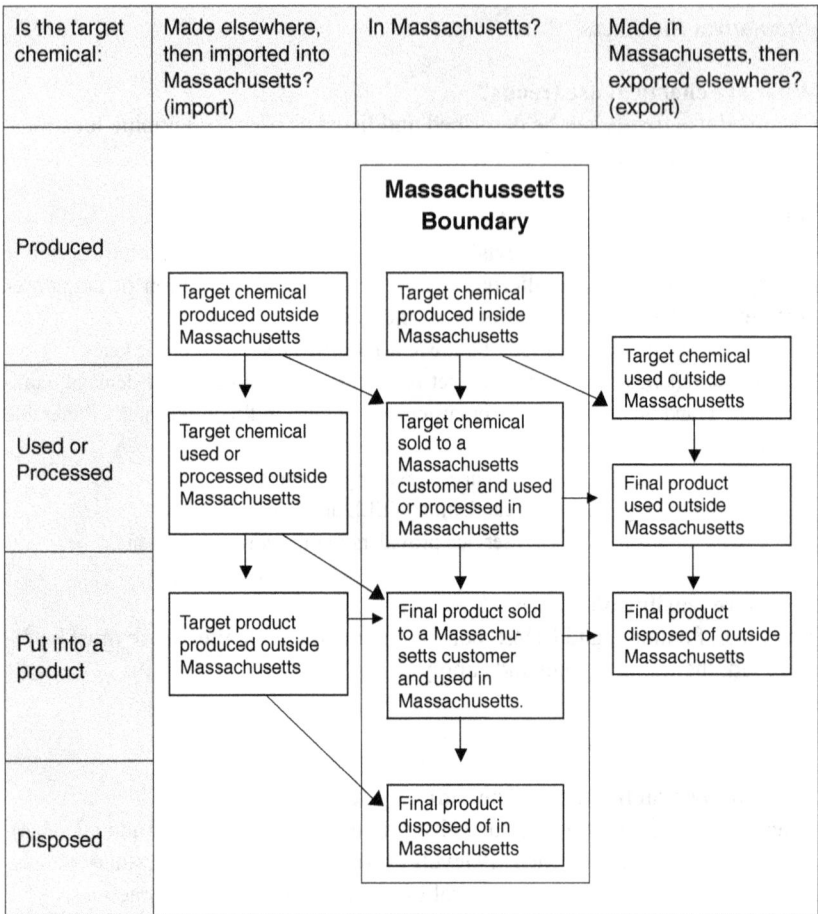

Figure A – 1 Supply Chain General Schematic

provides a general schematic to help in visualizing supply chain dynamics, and the subsequent figures provide examples.

In the case of PCE use for dry cleaning services, Figure A - 2, Massachusetts is an importer of dry cleaning machines, but dry cleaning is a local process. As an importer, Massachusetts may not have sufficient market size to drive development of non-PCE machines on its own. However, given that California regulation and technical assistance programs are already driving commercialization of alternatives, Massachusetts action could speed the process of adopting these alternatives.

In the electronics sector, Figure A-3, Massachusetts manufactures components, assembles high-tech equipment, and consumes components and equipment. In the first two cases Massachusetts is an exporter, and must respond to international market drivers in order to remain competitive. Component manufacturers must be aware of demand for lead-free components, as well as supply costs, the extent of EU demand, and location decisions.

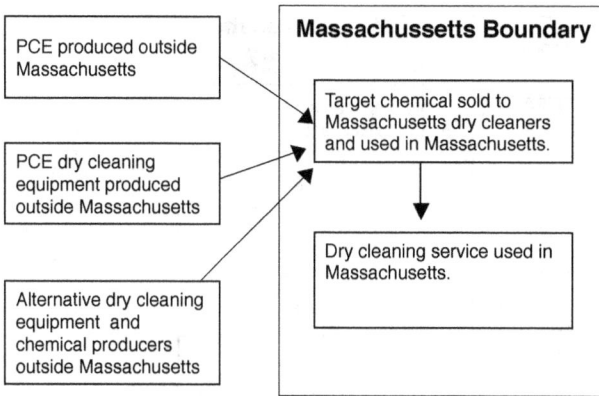

Figure A - 2 Massachusetts Perchloroethylene Drycleaners—"Local" Supply Chain
Example

What are characteristics of the market and the competition?
A shift to alternatives may raise or lower costs of producing a product or providing a service. Market characteristics will determine the extent and form of
resulting economic impacts. Factors to consider in assessing the influence of
competition and markets include the following:

- Is the market local, regional, national or international?
- What is the size of the Massachusetts market *vs.* other locations?
- Does Massachusetts compete based on location, price, and product quality?
- How much does a change in price affect demand?
- How important are non-price characteristics, such as brand image and quality?
- Are there market niches that would respond differently to changes?
- What existing regulations influence the industry?
- How frequently does the market require a new or improved product?

In some cases there may be product niches that can be capitalized for developing greener alternatives, while in other cases the market structure may prevent
charging a premium for green innovations. Market divisions may respond differently to changes. For the building materials case (formaldehyde), experts
suggest that residential, commercial, restorative, and institutional building markets have different characteristics. Green building practices are being adopted
more quickly in institutional and commercial buildings. These customers have
better access to information about alternatives than residential customers. Markets with rapid product turnover are more likely to be able to respond quickly
to changing requirements.

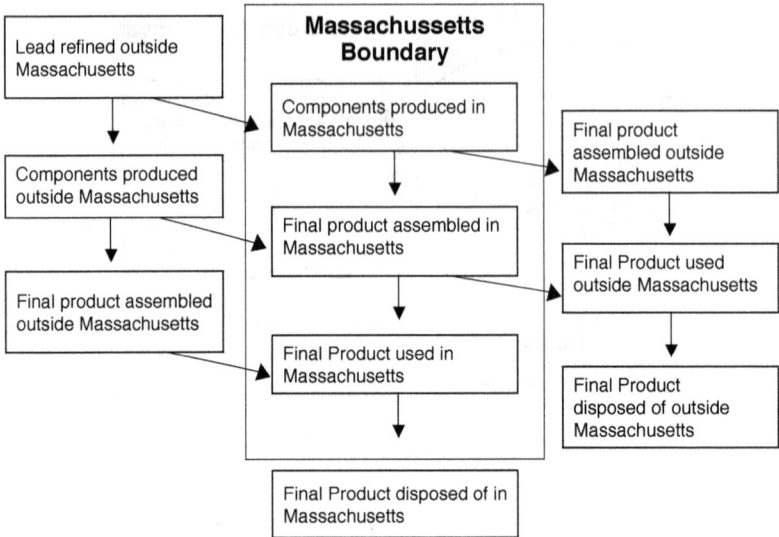

Figure A - 3 Massachusetts Lead-Free Electronics—"Export" Supply Chain Example

Factors important to a firm's ability to adapt to changes are summarized in Table A - 1.

Existing Conditions

Understanding the availability of alternatives and the agility of industry gives an indication of the existing economic conditions for alternatives adoption. In some situations substitution may already be rewarding, cost effective, market driven, and proceeding on its own. In other situations, barriers exist to implementing substitutions, and use of old alternatives continues.

Table A - 1: Industry Status and Trends Summary Table

Industry	Supply chain	Competition & Market
Size	Import/export/local	Competitive basis
Ownership	Suppliers & customers	Price elasticity
Workforce	Partner influence	Market influence
Profit margin		Market divisions
Innovation		Regulatory environment
Investment Practices		Speed of market change

Possible Barriers

The third phase of this economic assessment involves consideration of existing barriers, as well as the policies which can address these barriers and facilitate adoption of alternatives.

Technical Barriers: Alternatives not readily available
As this study demonstrates, for some chemicals and some uses alternatives are well understood and readily available. In other cases, fully-developed alternatives may be unavailable at the outset. In other instances, alternatives may be well developed from the perspective of researchers and a few leading companies, but there remain technical, reliability, cost, and risk concerns for most companies.

In cases in which alternatives are not well developed it is helpful to understand (a) the relevant time-frame for transforming costs into benefits, (b) whose interests will be served by a focus on innovation in this area, and (c) if public funds are used for research, the institutional mechanisms for ensuring that public investment results in public benefits when the innovation is successful.

Information Barriers: Inadequate information flows among consumers, industry, and researchers
Lack of information can be a barrier to change. The TURA Program has demonstrated the effectiveness of providing training and information on alternatives to businesses. Information can also be provided to consumers through labeling, product guides, advertising, and certification for contractors and products.

Market and Capacity Barriers
Uncertainty about demand or a lack of demand for alternatives can hinder a firm from moving forward into new technologies. Other industry characteristics that can hinder alternatives adoption include low profit margins or a volatile price environment, lack of necessary expertise among workers, or an industry culture resistant to change.

Financial Barriers: Inadequate financing structure
In cases in which alternatives adoption requires a significant capital investment, lack of adequate financing can be a barrier. Studies suggest that environment-related investment costs and savings are not often considered adequately in firms' investment analyses. Some approaches to book-keeping may hide the costs of using toxic chemicals, or may consider these costs in a separate department. Mayers (2005) suggests that more time be "spent re-engineering business accounting systems to accurately track environment-related costs (and returns) and determine where substantial cost-savings can truly be found." Other potential financial barriers may include lack of familiarity with alternative technologies among finance providers.

Regulatory Barriers: Conflicting requirements, regulatory uncertainty, unregulated competitors

Sometimes adoption of alternatives is delayed because it is unclear whether a regulation will hold. Some companies will delay action if they view pending future regulation as changing the playing field in an unpredictable way. Conflicting regulatory requirements may hinder industry action. For example, the use of drawer sanitizers in salons is required by regulation in Massachusetts.

Policy Instruments

The interactions among policies may be mutually reinforcing, redundant, or conflicting. Policies that influence economic impact can include:

- Technical assistance and training
- Information provided on technology and methods issues, alternatives, leading companies, products, tools, and legislation for Massachusetts companies and for consumers. Particularly helpful is advance information about trends and pending science and policy.[2]
- Incentives or financial assistance for research and development, equipment purchase, *etc.*
- Market support through Environmentally Preferred Purchasing programs in government, advertising campaigns, and volume purchasing commitments
- Tax policies
- Restrictions or requirements for use of targeted materials or products
- Coordinated actions with other states

There is a substantial body of literature about environmental policy options, including writings about market-based *vs.* traditional regulatory approaches. The policy options included here are ones that were discussed by the panel and described in the text where appropriate; it is not a comprehensive listing.

---

2   The state offers an array of informational tools as part of the Commonwealth of Massachusetts Environmentally Preferable Products Procurement Program.

11 A Cognitive View of Scale and Growth

Frederic B. Jennings, Jr.

ABSTRACT

The issue of scale is central to ecological economics, showing a limit to economic growth arising from ecosystemic constraints. But scale is often defined in physical terms, with respect to the relative size of economies and ecosystem capacities. Another way to look at scale with respect to economic growth is psychological and horizonal, based on the planning perspectives and knowledge on which all choices are made. This paper examines scale as a cognitive phenomenon, arising from the range of projections inherent in human decision. On these grounds, some major revisions in growth theory are revealed, due to the impact on interdependence—substitution and complementarity—of ordinal changes in planning horizons or 'horizon effects.' Longer horizons entail a shift in economic relations away from substitution to complementarity, making cooperation more efficient than competition. If economic growth alters the optimality of institutions in favor of cooperation—especially in a learning economy embedded in a bounded ecology—any conflict between efficiency, equity and ecological health is obviated by longer horizons. A proper regard to horizon effects and their relation to scale and growth is important for a full understanding of ecological economics.

Keywords: ecological economics, scale, complementarity, cooperation, planning horizons, horizon effects

1 Introduction

The notion of scale is central to any distinction of ecological from neoclassical economics. 'Scale' is defined as an index of "the *physical* size of the economy relative to the containing ecosystem" (Daly 2006, p. 1). Indeed, economic efficiency assumes scale and distribution are given (in terms of sustainability and fairness). Similarly, economic growth, unbounded in neoclassical theory, is seen as constrained by scale in ecological economics, where its sustainability is assessed over aeons of time. Marginal theories shall not do: a larger vision is sought.

Though "the whole focus of microeconomics is on finding the optimal scale of each micro activity of production and consumption," Daly (2006, p. 6) asks:

"Why is the central concept of *micro*economics, namely optimal scale or extent of an activity, absent from *macro*economics?" As we move from an 'empty' to a 'full' world in terms of our impact thereon, the ecological limits of further expansion transform positive features of growth into unsustainable losses. Scaling up an economy against the fixity of an ecology yields stress and danger of system collapse. Scale is central in this scenario; indeed, it determines the outcome.

With all inputs into a process scaled up proportionately, increasing or constant returns are implied. The fixed dimensions of our ecology yield a binding constraint on growth. This is why scale is central to ecological economics. Scale counts, and defines our options. Neoclassical theories of growth are like *Hamlet* without the prince.

Scale issues also raise some meaningful questions about the relation of goods and activities to each other. For example, are man-made and natural capital substitutes or complements? Substitution is emblematic in neoclassical theory: all activities suffer trade-offs solved through competitive markets. With manufactured and natural capital rivalrous, scale is not a constraint, though when they are complementary a limit on one cuts the output from both. This is another way to distinguish ecological economics from neoclassical theory.

These issues of bound vs. unconstrained growth, and of the nature of interdependence as substitution or complementarity (or negative vs. positive feedback in the language of systems) show why scale is so essential in ecological economics. But scale, when defined in these writings, is seen as a measure of *physical* output relative to ecosystem capacity. Economics, so often directed in favor of visible outcomes, seldom attends to its cognitive fount, even when dealing with ecological issues. A preoccupation with substitution dies hard, as it is so deeply embedded in our assumptions and general approach.

The argument to follow addresses scale in its cognitive aspects, seeing interdependence—substitution or complementarity in our relations—through a 'horizontal' lens. First, the notion of planning horizons is introduced and developed, then applied to scale and interdependence. The paper aims to resolve physical and psychological aspects of scale through their relevance to a horizonal theory of economic growth.

2   A Cognitive View of Scale

When scale is seen in a cognitive frame, where range and scope of analysis serve as our realm of focus here, the emphasis shifts to horizontal length, and the distinction of greater perspective from more myopic concerns. The basic conception derives from the fact that decisions are not made on known results but only among imagined projections of outcomes stemming from action. These projections have a range, a horizontal limit to understanding. Analytical scale—in this scenario—rises from planning horizons, psychologically founded on knowledge, energy and attention: indeed, the extent of foresight defines the 'bounds' of rationality in Herbert Simon's (1982–1997) sense of that term.

The introduction of planning horizons suggests a cognitive view of scale: the broader the range and scope of vision implicit in our decisions, the more encompassing are the considerations underlying each act. The fact that our world is totally interdependent plays an important role for rational boundedness here. Every act transmits effects spreading outward forever to all. Without any limit on actual consequence, it is our range of foresight that defines analytical scope: the only impacts shaping our choices are those we expect, truly or not. The role of belief in this setting is central.

The actual *ex post* planning horizon of any decision, however, is set wherever real outcomes stray from prior anticipation thereof. We can believe our horizon is long, when surprises show it is short. The emphasis here is on *true* expectation, distinct from misconceptions shown in the consequences of action. No observable data is ever acquired, however, on unexplored options, so opportunity costs are untestable in empirical terms. Every action, nevertheless, is based on imagined projections that are mostly unverifiable. The planning horizon ought to be seen in this context as an ordinal index of 'savvy' in our decisions, much like the 'move horizon' in chess.

But in a totally interdependent domain, the range of internalization of (what would otherwise be) externalities is a function of planning horizons, so horizons can also be seen as a measure of *social conscience*. Sociopathic behavior—such as by people whose planning horizon is set by the edge of their skin or their auto window (in narcissism or littering)—is thus separated from deeds at the other extreme accounting for impacts enduring forever on all life forms in our world. "Do no harm," ecologists say, against the economists' silence.

Substitution assumptions stand as the reason for the avoidance by economists of such matters. Scarcity and trade-offs are often defined as the focus of economics, and complementarities (positive feedbacks) simply are ignored. Substitution (negative feedback) confines economic consequence; spillovers shall attenuate as they radiate from a decision. Partial models suffice with externalities' status as special. Embracing complementarity, though, will lead to accepting interdependence along with horizonal theory (Jennings 2007).

All human-caused ecological losses are horizonal: in any interdependent and irreversible open domain of choice, spreading outcomes of action lasting forever are endemic. The relevant issue—with complementarity—is our range of anticipation: what is the weight of distant effects (in time or social impact) on our ongoing current decisions? Social and ecological conscience is central in any economics embracing complementarity and total interdependence; indeed, the planning horizon defines the boundary of our analysis, along with the scale of choices made. As Georgescu-Roegen (1970, p. 2) said: "no analytical boundary, no analytical process." The planning horizons in our decisions separate known from unintended effects on nature and society as they unfold through time. Planning horizons, in this sense, serve as an ordinal index of scale implicit in human choice. Shifts in planning horizons shall be called 'horizon effects.' So how will the notion of planning horizons advance our understanding of scale in economic analysis?

3   The Ecological Economics of Horizon Effects[1]

Planning horizons, in their relation to price-setting and growth, imply a case for complementarity as our primary interrelation, not substitution (as in neoclassical theory). *Ceteris paribus*, shorter horizons—as an index of rationality and the integration of interdependent human endeavors—shall lead to higher prices (slower growth) than longer horizons. An inward (outward) shift in the planning horizon engenders a rise (fall) in price and thus slower (more rapid) growth of sales for a single price-setter.[2] But this is not all of the story. Individual agents operate in a dynamic complex system moved by other people and their actions' social effects. Here resilience and adaptive flexibility are required to account for, react to and make decisions. So will the oligopoly problem—as an example of free choice in an interdependent domain—demand our attention as symbolic (and paradigmatic) of the social nature and indeterminacy of all life.[3]

But substitution and complementarity, applied to functions and welfare effects, also relate to planning horizons in their interpersonal impact. If you plan better, so can I; your horizon affects my own in a complementary manner. We

1   This subtitle was the title of my CANSEE 2003 paper (Jennings 2003).

2   This conclusion can be derived—if done properly—from Alchian's (1959) nine propositions on cost, despite the erroneous effort by Hirshleifer (1962) and its acceptance by Oi (1967) and Alchian (1968): cf. Jennings (1985, ch. 5). Formally, $M^* \equiv MR = MC$ at Q^* (the maximum profit condition), with $E^* \equiv [\varepsilon^*/(\varepsilon^*+1)]$ where $E^*>1$ because $-\infty < \varepsilon^* < -1$ [and here $\varepsilon \equiv d\ln Q/d\ln P \equiv (dQ/Q)/(dP/P)$, the elasticity of demand, which can be thought of as the percentage response of Q to a one-percent increase in P]. The whole expression can be derived very simply by substitution from the definition of MR as dR/dQ (where $R \equiv P \times Q$) with respect to Q or P, which can be written simply as $P = MR \times [\varepsilon/(\varepsilon+1)]$, yielding $\underline{P^* = M^* \times E^*}$, where the asterisk (*) denotes the level actually chosen as best by an agent. The horizonal pattern is summarized thus: $dM^*/dH < 0$ with $d^2M^*/dH^2 > 0$; $dE^*/dH < 0$ with $d^2E^*/dH^2 > 0$; so $dP^*/dH < 0$ and $d^2P^*/dH^2 > 0$. If so, then for $g \equiv d\ln Q/dt$, the growth rate of sales, $dg^*/dH > 0$ with $d^2g^*/dH^2 < 0$. Also cf. Margolis (1960).

3   On the oligopoly problem, Simon (1976, p. 140–141) remarked that:
  More than a century ago, Cournot identified a problem that has become the permanent and ineradicable scandal of economic theory. He observed that where a market is supplied by only a few producers, the notion of profit-maximization is ill-defined. The choice that would be substantively rational for each actor depends on the choices made by the other actors; none can choose without making assumptions about how others will choose. . . .
  I have referred to the theory of imperfect competition as a 'scandal' because it has been treated as such in economics . . . If perfect competition were the rule in the markets of our modern economy, and imperfect competition and oligopoly rare exceptions, the scandal might be ignored. Every family, after all, has some distant relative it would prefer to forget. But imperfect competition is not a 'distant relative', it is the characteristic form of market structure in a large part of the industries in our economy.

are role models for each other, and much of learning is imitation. *Interhorizonal complementarity* opens a link between private and social horizon effects in economics, showing a new form of interdependence seen in human behavior. The interpersonal linkage of planning horizons—contagious horizon effects— suggests that traditional interdependencies shift with horizon effects as well: longer (private and social) horizons alter the balance of interdependence in any economic context toward complementarity and away from substitution.[4]

An intuitive way to think about changes in planning horizons is that they appear on a spectrum moving from selfishness out to a global public conscience. If my horizon is short—such as in narcissistic people—then I will likely see my own needs in conflict with those of everyone else (if I take notice of others at all). Alternatively, if I have an active, viable social conscience, I place others' concerns on a par with my own in cases where they conflict (or try to resolve the discord through action). The latter reduces conflict and displaces it with a concert of interest, transforming our rivalries into allegiance to joint well-being. This is the difference of shorter from longer horizons in our relations: substitute trade-offs are redirected to complementary gains (and vice versa) with longer (or shorter) horizons.

The institutional implications of this finding are relevant to why orthodox standards have failed us so badly in ecological applications. Substitution assumptions in neoclassical theory offer the basis for a view of competition as an efficiency yardstick. But this conclusion is only true in the presence of substitute trade-offs. With complementarity, it is cooperation that is efficient. Where interests are aligned, such that we gain or lose together, resources (energy, time, money, attention) are better merged than apart: integration is sought to avoid the dangers of fragmentation. With interdependent externalities spreading outward forever from every act in nondecomposable mixtures of substitution (clashing interests) and complementarity (mutual gains), then neither rivalry nor integration is statically efficient. Instead, the proper organizational choice is contingent on planning horizons: short horizons suggest substitute trade-offs supersede common needs, while longer horizons shift our relations in favor of complementarity making cooperation efficient. The issue of scale—in a cognitive frame based on planning horizons—is central.

---

4   Continuing from note 2 above, $P_j' = P_j^* + S_l$ for any group I of firms, where S_l is the difference between the compensated (joint-profit maximizing) P_j' and the P_j^* set independently of its pecuniary impact on the other (i≠j) firms' profits. Interhorizonal complementarity means $dH_{i≠j}^*/dH_j^* > 0$. If so, then $dS_l/dH_j^* < 0$: an increase in H_j^* yields—through its contagious effects on $H_{i≠j}^*$—a shift of S_l away from substitution in favor of complementarity. For any i≠j element of S_l, namely $s_{i≠j} \equiv (Q_{i≠j}/Q_j) \times (M_{i≠j}^* - P_{i≠j}^*) \times [\varepsilon_{ij}^*/(\varepsilon_j^*+1)]$, an extension of H_j^* will likely reduce the magnitude of both $Q_{i≠j}/Q_j > 0$ (as a weighting scalar) and $|(M_{i≠j}^* - P_{i≠j}^*) < 0|$, while increasing own-elasticity (ε_j^*) and thus the negative magnitude of $|(\varepsilon_j^*+1) < 0|$, while the cross-elasticity (ε_{ij}^*) is shifted away from substitution ($\varepsilon_{ij}^* > 0$) toward complementarity ($\varepsilon_{ij}^* < 0$), so $d\varepsilon_{ij}^*/dH_j^* < 0$ as well. So regardless of the sign of S_l (as an aggregation of $s_{i≠j}$ across any group I around member j), $dS_l/dH_j^* \leq 0$: a mutual lengthening of planning horizons shifts our relations away from substitution in favor of complementarity (in virtually all economic contexts).

4   A Horizonal Look at Scale and Growth

Economists' habits of thought—derived from substitution assumptions—suggest that externalities can be ignored in favor of partial analysis. A key tenet of ecological economics is *interdependence*, that dynamic complex systems of feedback—complementarity and substitution, nondecomposably intertwined—demand a new approach where issues of scale cannot be ignored. This paper redefines scale as a cognitive phenomenon, the extent to which effects are internalized into anticipations in the process of framing a choice: scale in this sense is synonymous with the agent's planning horizons, which shift in accord with others' horizons in a contagious way. All this strengthens a case for complementarity as our most general relation, displacing substitution as supposed in neoclassical theory.

Once scale, as the planning horizon, is subsumed theoretically into ecological economics, some meaningful insights emerge. For one, with causes circular, reflexivity[5] is important: the imposition of competition on complementary settings spawns inefficiency and maladaptive failures, similar to the effects of collusion where rivalrous substitution prevails. So what form might these symptoms take? Competition—based on neoclassical substitution assumptions—sabotages social welfare in realms of common need.

Take love, for example, a non-rival good that benefits all when shared, though when treated as scarce it declines. Love is a complementary good: there is no scarcity other than what we create by withholding our love from each other. Rivalrous strategies simply undercut the output to all. Love is something given freely, and the open expression thereof enhances the growth of productive capacity and the well-being of all so touched. Thus we say "what goes around, comes around" in an attempt to encourage its spread. Love fails whenever rivalry interferes with its sharing: competition for affection decreases the total for

---

5   For a creative discussion of reflexivity, cf. Section I of Hofstadter (1985). Bertalanffy (1968), p. 45, addressed the issue thus:

> *In the world view called mechanistic . . . causality was essentially one-way . . . This scheme of isolable units acting in one-way causality has proved to be insufficient. . . . We must think in terms of systems of elements in mutual interaction.*

Rescher (1979), pp. 46–49, observed that "the network model of cognitive systematization," as distinct from "its Euclidean counterpart . . . dispenses altogether with . . . axiomatic supports" and it replaces . . .

> *. . . stratification of theses into levels of . . . <u>fundamentality</u> by a conception of <u>enmeshment</u>.*
> *. . . The network appeal is unreductive. . . . [It] shifts the perspective from unidirectional dependency to reciprocal interconnection. . . .*
> *A heavy charge can be laid against the Euclidean model on grounds of the enormous hold it has established on philosophical and scientific thought in the West. Its exclusion of circles and cycles on grounds of their violating the prohibition of Aristotelian logic against "circular" inferences and reasonings impeded the conceptualization of reciprocal causal models in science for over two thousand years.*

Also cf. Veblen's (1898) and Myrdal's (1978) concept of "cumulative causation" (which bears a close kinship to complementarity).

all.[6] Love is like learning, information, ethics, social or ecological health and trust in its system requirements. All are realms of complementary economic activity. So what is the impact of competition on complementary outputs?

Competition creates scarcity among complementary goods, while cooperation nurtures abundance. If love, learning, information, ethics, social or ecological health and trust are reciprocal goods, then neoclassical loyalties are repressing growth in these sectors. Static concepts sidestepping issues of scale ignore horizon effects, so are unable to see pathologies spawned from myopic concerns. Substitution is not the most general form of social interdependence; complementarity is. Standard theory is failing us due to its substitution assumptions.

Scale—addressed in a cognitive frame as a measure of planning horizons in choice—suggests a call for revising growth theory in numerous ways. For one, the 'problem of growth' may lie in our rivalrous systems of commerce, where reciprocality is efficient and competition is doomed to fail. Assuredly, in ecosystem management applications, sundering economic units into small competitive firms—on the belief that 'divide and conquer' is more efficient than any cohesive frame—is counterproductive in the extreme. Complementarity calls for cooperation as our efficient solution, not competition. The only question is on the importance of rival vs. reciprocal linkages in the systems on which we depend. To the extent our ambitions are complementary and not opposed, the economic case for competition is selling a poison as cure. McCloskey (1990, passim) called this "snake oil."

The case for generalized complementarity is strong in economics. First, increasing returns as a universal feature of firms' production implies that complementarity is "far more important . . . than . . . substitution" (Kaldor 1975, p. 348). Second, even discounting Kaldor's stand on falling cost, the interhorizonal complementarity of horizon effects implies a robust claim for reciprocality in nonmaterial goods. Substitution assumptions and the rivalrous systems standing thereon are ravaging all of these social linkages through a process of fragmentation damaging to their abundance. Substitution is not the dominant trait of these settings. So examining competition's effects on learning, information, ethics, social or ecological health, trust and love is sufficient.

The manifestation of failure due to competition among complements is surprisingly obvious: *short horizons* serve as symptoms of inconsistent designs unfit to their realms of application. If horizonal lengthening comes from models suited to where they are used, then inappropriate theories narrow our planning horizons as well. Learning is also a complementary good in its social effects:

6   McCloskey (1990, pp. 142–143) observed that:
    . . . There is an ethical problem in the theory and practice of economics. The problem is deeper
    than mere distaste for calculation of selfishness or greed. . . . Economics was once described
    as the science of conserving love. The notion is that love is scarce, and that consequently we
    had better try to get along without it, organizing our affairs to take advantage of the abundant
    selfishness instead. The argument is economic to the core. . . . The problem is that conserving
    on love, treating it as . . . scarce . . . may be a bad way to encourage its growth.

you are more likely to benefit from my knowledge than to be harmed. Boulding (1962, pp. 133–134) captured the complementarity of learning very well, noting that "teaching is in no sense an exchange, in which what the student gets the teacher loses." If so, then competition also *reduces* learning activity and displaces it with avoidance or entertainment of some sort. This supports a myopic culture heedless of its spreading effects on (social and animal) life into time.

With systems ill-designed to their realm, management thereof founders, with resources squandered through wasteful endeavors striving against insurmountable odds (since all the incentives are wrongly arranged). The addiction to materialistic growth among economists and consumers stands on erroneous suppositions applied where they have no place.[7] Only the "major act of demolition" demanded by Kaldor (1972, pp. 1240–1242) will lead to remediation. A horizonal economics of complementarity ought to become part of ecological economics: it incorporates scale and addresses the issue of growth in a different frame than neoclassical theory.

5   Toward an Ethical Economics

Another way of looking at scale is through an ethical lens. The range of awareness in our decisions—the planning horizon in choice—supposes a totally interdependent world where every act transmits an impact outward on everyone else forever. This in itself is a statement of complementarity in some ways, since substitution denies such spreading connections stemming from our behavior:

---

7   Some observers say our compulsive consumerism arises from a frustration of higher-order needs in Maslow's (1954, 1968) sense of that term, e.g., cf. Wachtel (1989), Kohn (1986), Scitovsky (1976) and McGregor (1960). Argyris (1960, pp. 262–263) notes that conventional organization treats its members like children; mature people in these settings show symptoms of ill health, including "frustration, failure, short time perspective and conflict." He expresses concern about the problem of organizational fragmentation on pp. 268–269: "The nature of the formal principles of organization causes the subordinates, at any given level, to experience competition, rivalry, intersubordinate hostility and to develop a focus toward the parts rather than the whole." McGregor (1960, p. 310) warned that:

> The deprivation of needs has behavioral consequences. . . . The man whose needs for safety, association, independence or status are thwarted is sick, just as surely as he who has rickets. We will be mistaken if we attribute . . . passivity, or . . . hostility, or . . . refusal to accept responsibility to . . . inherent 'human nature.' These forms of behavior are symptoms of illness—of deprivation of . . . social and egoistic needs.

McGregor (1960, p. 311) went on to explore the connection to rampant consumerism and materialism in modern society:

> . . .the fact that management has provided for these physiological and safety needs has shifted the motivational emphasis to the social and egoistic needs. Unless there are opportunities *at work* to satisfy these higher-level needs, people will be deprived; and their behavior will reflect this deprivation. . . . People *will* make insistent demands for more money under these conditions. It becomes more important than ever to buy the material goods and services which can provide limited satisfaction of the thwarted needs. Although money has only limited value in satisfying many higher-level needs, it can become the focus of interest if it is the only means available.

reactions simply attenuate in mainstream models of choice; such are bounded by negative feedbacks, settling onto equilibrium paths—static, contained, determinate, thus stable in time. The real world is more like ecology—open, unbounded and indeterminate—dynamic complex systems showing an ongoing irreversible process of adaptive, dialectic, qualitative variability. Life as structured *dis*equilibrium never reaches stability; only death brings stasis and the restoration of balance.[8]

In an interdependent domain, with all linked to everything else, substitution (negative feedback) cannot truly apply. At best, theory ought to encompass substitution and complementarity in a nondecomposable mix such as in transportation networks (Jennings 1985, 2006). Substitution assumptions show competition as efficient, whereas complementarity yields a case for cooperation instead. Once substitution is shunned, then no case for competition endures. Another approach should be introduced to address social organization and its welfare effects. Smith's (1776, p. 14) 'invisible hand' of competition is guided by self-interest untainted by any ethic, conscience or moral law: "It is not from the benevolence of the butcher, the brewer, or the baker that we expect our dinner, but from their regard to their own interest."[9] With substitution in doubt, this story will not suffice.

The planning horizon in our decisions serves as an ethical index of conscience, signifying the range of social and ecological impacts subsumed into our expectations. What is asserted is simply a fact: that planning horizons *exist* in our decisions, whether we know it or not, at least as a way of thinking about the imagined projections in choice. But planning horizons are not observable; I cannot tell you what your horizon was in any particular act, nor can I even

---

8   The notion of equilibrium—based on the second law of thermodynamics—involves *states of rest* in which no work is done. Homeostasis involves *steady states* of flowing matter and energy in a dynamic balance of forces, such that "the capacity of the organism for work, without which adaptability, and hence survival, would be impossible" is maintained at an optimal level of full, living potential. Thus, Koehler (1938, p. 61) continued, though "an equilibrium theory of organic regulation" appears acceptable, it is "entirely misleading," given the functional principles of homeostatic control based on both "the second law" and "the law of dynamic direction."

   To express the main argument against such a theory [of equilibrium] quite briefly: neither is the standard state of an organism a state of equilibrium in the common sense of the word, nor do organic processes in their totality generally tend to approach such an equilibrium.

9   Kenneth Lux (1990, pp. 87–89), in a book called *Adam Smith's Mistake*, commented thus on this statement:

   Adam Smith made a mistake. . . . Adam Smith left out just one little word—a word which has made a world of difference. And if this mistake is not corrected, then the absence of that word could threaten to unmake a world. That word is <u>only</u>. What Adam Smith ought to have said was, "It is not <u>only</u> from the benevolence . . ."; then everything would have been all right.

The word "only" appears in a previous sentence on the same point, but here is left out, treating self-interest as sufficient (without benevolence) instead of framing them both together: "Smith's sanctioning of self-interest without any qualifying or restraining force completely eliminated the moral problem in human action." Subsequent trends in economics have not reversed the misconception, nor reinstated ethics to their proper rank in the field. Also cf. Foley (2006).

calibrate mine. Another assertion is of an ordinal link between P* and H* as stated in notes 2 and 4 above. For analytical purposes, this relation is like that of P and Q underlying supply and demand curves, on which so much theory is founded. Here it is claimed that longer horizons will lead to a lower price, *ceteris paribus* for non-horizonal changes, with no exact calibration of axes in numerical units.[10] Although one's horizon cannot be observed or measured in cardinal terms, such horizon effects show up in behavior resulting from prices' impact on growth and many other relations. If planning horizons also reflect the scale or conscience in our decisions—and therewith the range of prior internalization of spillovers into projections—then they offer a useful insight to economic causality.

Consider again the notion of planning horizons as an index of conscience. Selfishness of the narrowest sort—that turns on narcissistic and totally egocentric concerns—sees other people's desires as simply irrelevant or opposed to one's own. This is the essence of substitution and the assumption of *homo economus*: self-seeking monads striving continually for some maximum personal gain *against* that of fellow agents. The overall premise is that material needs shall always conflict, though Kaldor's (1975, p. 348) case for increasing returns—suggesting complementarity is "far more important"—also implies *concerts* of interest trump opposing concerns. Horizonal theory expands this argument to nonphysical sources of value, where all emotional states should be included in this set. The process of personal growth that transforms short to longer horizons shows how ranges of vision—as they expand—tend to become more inclusive or reciprocal in their relations.

To see this, start with the most myopic and immature end of the spectrum, in which personal social concerns center exclusively on the self (though perhaps as seen by others) and then expand the planning horizon in stages. The next level of personal growth could be to care for friends or family, embracing the impact of choices on them. With this step, some potential schisms are resolved in advance, so our actions become more consonant with the aims of others, allaying conflicts and enhancing concerts of value within this group. Planning horizons, as they extend, become more responsive to others' intentions as we mature and grow while realigning efficiency with equity and ecological health (Jennings 2005).

At the other end of this spectrum (to which we all might aspire) a 'global conscience' strives to accommodate all enduring impacts on life: the concept of

---

10   Boulding (1966, pp. 22–23) addressed the need for an organizational measure of 'wits' and its value, remarking:

> The question of what is economics can be almost as troublesome as what is knowledge? . . . One longs, indeed, for a unit of knowledge, which perhaps might be called a 'wit,' analogous to the 'bit' as used in information theory; but up to now at any rate no such practical unit has emerged. . . . The bit, however, abstracts completely from the content of either information or knowledge . . . [and] for the purposes of the social system theorist we need a measure which takes account of significance. . . Up to now we seem to have no way of doing this . . .

self expands sufficiently to embrace the whole world. "Do no harm," the ecologists say. In this scenario, we would try to incorporate into our private decisions an infinite range of social effects of unbounded character and duration, subject only to rational limits and knowledge of fellows' reactions. Such a vision defines the horizonal limit at the bounds of our reason, due to inadequate understanding and to reactive feedback loops. These are the main constraints against the expansion of planning horizons (social and private) in our economy, even if social incentives were revised to fit the reality of our relations.

So what is the curative value of an expansion of planning horizons? Substitution assumptions supporting competition are ravaging ecological life across the planet, due to a self-destructive fragmentation of interpersonal effort. In a complementary universe, social cooperation is the key to efficient deployment of assets serving common needs. Strong incentives structured to reward divergent behavior at the expense of trust and ethical linkages strangle efficiency and all learning, to the extent that complementarity is our basic connection. If competition is keeping horizons short, the doctrinaire rigidities in neoclassical economics are a symptom of failure. The entire realm of growth theory also ought to be opened, to encompass scale and horizon effects.

The process of economic advance is not just technical change; it has cultural and personal levels. If indeed—as argued here—our interdependence is steeped in overwhelming complementarities, then economists' singleminded devotion to competition is part of the problem. Competition in complementary settings is doomed to fail, reducing goods for all concerned due to harmful horizon effects shrinking the scale of human decisions. Short planning horizons spawn a myopic culture indifferent to its subversion of ecological life, foreign affairs, social well-being, global peace and unborn heirs. Shortsightedness serves to endanger all we humans hold dear, rising from competition imposed outside its sphere of legitimate application.

The nature of growth engenders a shift from lower- to higher-order needs, so we evolve from materialistic constraints to wanting intangible goods in the composition of output demand.[11] Doing with less seems so much more rewarding than overconsumption (at the expense of folks starving elsewhere) that the lifestyle trumps egocentric concern with acquisitive values as a source of virtuous satisfaction. The ethics of economic growth are not irrelevant to ongoing ecological losses from myopic planning horizons (scales) embedded in our decisions. Systems in place shortening our range of vision ought to be understood as symptomatic of failures in neoclassical economics. Substitution assumptions shall not pertain to complementarities, so we ought to expect disaster out of frames so unfit to their realms of use. Simple methodological errors—elementary in the extreme, monumental in their effects—sent us into this swamp. As Georgescu-Roegen (1970, p. 9) declared at the end of his Ely lecture on production, "the history of every science, including that of economics, teaches us that the elementary is the hotbed of the errors that count most."

---

11   Cf. note 7 above.

6   Summary and Conclusions

This paper examines scale and growth in a cognitive frame, making a case for complementarity in a theory of planning horizons. The scale—in this sense—of our decisions shall lead to implications about the basic character of our relations as substitution or complementary, and to a claim that cooperation—not competition—is more efficient. The inefficiency of competition appears in the form of horizon effects, so remains invisible through a neoclassical lens. Scale or horizon effects suggest theory as a guide to action must be fit to its sphere of use. Otherwise, resources are lost to waste stemming from interpersonal conflict due to myopic concerns. Societies shift toward complementarity as horizons (scales) extend; thus social incentives should change to favor reciprocality in a cooperative frame or progress is stalled. The nature of growth entails—even demands—an adaptation of our rivalrous systems to more integration or it cannot advance. Such is the problem addressed in this paper, raising concerns stemming from a cognitive view of scale.

The argument is summarized thus. Scale is seen as the main difference between neoclassical orthodoxy and ecological economics. But scale is often defined in *physical* terms as the size of an economy in proportion to its ecology. Another representation of scale assumes a cognitive focus on the extent of vision in choice. Such an approach addresses scale as psychologically implicit in horizon effects. So recasting scale as the range of imagined projections in action invites some meaningful lessons on how our economy works.

Substitution assumptions stand in the hard core of founded doctrine (neoclassical theory), yet these suppositions are replaced here by generalized complementarity. Even ignoring Kaldor's (1972, 1975) support for increasing returns and complementarity, a horizonal theory of scale leads to the same result: that human needs are more reciprocal than they are rival in most cases. If so, we are doing it wrong, competing in every aspect of social life, for rivalry yields strife and thus shortens planning horizons. Static constructions see none of these symptoms: our rigid doctrines and ongoing conflicts are attributed to human nature and not to failures in our institutions. Social linkages are more reciprocal than opposed in economics, so organization needs to promote teamwork over rivalry. If so, then neoclassical theory—in its substitution assumptions—has led us severely astray about the efficiency of competition.

Once substitution is overcome—or joined with complementarity in a transportation network context—then new boundaries shall be needed to contain our analyses. Scale—as the range of foreseeable anticipation in our decisions—sets a horizonal limit to rationality in a concept embracing conscience, externalities, time and knowledge into a theory of planning horizons and horizon effects. Scale thus shows some meaningful implications for economic growth, that competition among complementary outputs such as in love, learning, ethics, society and ecology yields a myopic culture risking all we hold dear on this earth. The error is elementary and derives from methodological laxity: economic constructions applied beyond their proper realm appear in economic incentives subverting common goals and general well-being.

Competition—though seen as economists' standard of efficiency—yields outcomes shown to be inefficient due to horizon effects. A new ecological economics of scale and planning horizons—seen in a cognitive frame of analysis—shall lead us out of this swamp. Our current social malaise stems from myopic cultures spawned by erroneous standards incorrectly applied. The world turns—for better or worse—on the guidance of theory and its suppositions. As some wise soul once said: "Fish discover water last" (McGregor 1960, p. 317). Unexplored options stay invisible, as do all opportunity costs. Social welfare representations show a conflict between efficiency, equity and ecological health, arising from substitution assumptions. This paper asks some probing questions about this standard doctrine. Is it not time for reconstruction and a renewal of frames?

References

Alchian, Armen A. (1959). "Costs and Outputs." In *The Allocation of Economic Resources*, ed. Moses Abramovitz. Stanford University Press, Stanford, pp. 23–40.

Alchian, Armen A. (1968) "Cost." In the *International Encyclopedia of the Social Sciences, Vol. 3*. New York: Macmillan and Free Press, 404–15; reprinted as ch. 12 of his *Economic Forces at Work*. Indianapolis: Liberty Press (1977), 301–323.

Argyris, Chris. (1960). "The Impact of the Organization on the Individual." In *Organization Theory*, ed. D. S. Pugh. New York: Penguin (1971).

Bertalanffy, Ludwig von. (1968). *General System Theory: Foundations, Development, Applications*. New York: Braziller.

Boulding, Kenneth E. (1962) "Some Questions on the Measurement and Evaluation of Organization." In Harland Cleveland and Harold D. Lasswell, eds., *Ethics and Bigness: Scientific, Academic, Religious, Political, and Military*. New York: Harper and Brothers, 385–95; reprinted in Boulding's *Beyond Economics: Essays on Society, Religion and Ethics*. Ann Arbor: University of Michigan Press (1968), 131–140.

Boulding, Kenneth E. (1966). "The Economics of Knowledge and the Knowledge of Economics." *American Economic Review, Papers and Proceedings* 56(2); reprinted as ch. 1 of D. M. Lamberton, ed., *Economics of Information and Knowledge*. Middlesex, England: Penguin (1971).

Daly, Herman E. (2006). "The Concept of Scale in Ecological Economics: Its Relation to Allocation and Distribution." In the *OEEE* at http://www. ecoeco.org/publica/encyc_entries/Herman_Daly_contribution.pdf.

Foley, Duncan K. (2006). *Adam's Fallacy: A Guide to Economic Theology*. Cambridge: The Belknap Press of Harvard Univ. Press.

Georgescu-Roegen, Nicholas. (1970). "The Economics of Production." *American Economic Review, Papers and Proceedings* 60(2).

Hirshleifer, Jack. (1962). 'The Firm's Cost Function: A Successful Reconstruction?' *Journal of Business 35*(3).

Hofstadter, Douglas R. (1985). *Metamagical Themas: Questing for the Essence of Mind and Pattern.* New York: Basic Books.

Jennings, Frederic B., Jr. (1985). "Public Policy, Planning Horizons and Organizational Breakdown: A Post-Mortem on British Canals and Their Failure." Ph.D. dissertation, Stanford University.

Jennings, Frederic B., Jr. (2003). "The Ecological Economics of Horizon Effects." Presented at CANSEE 2003. Jasper Park, Canada.

Jennings, Frederic B., Jr. (2005). "How Efficiency/Equity Tradeoffs Resolve Through Horizon Effects." *Journal of Economic Issues 39*(2): 365–373.

Jennings, Frederic B., Jr. (2006). "A Horizonal Challenge to Orthodox Theory: Competition and Cooperation in Transportation Networks." In Michael Pickhardt and Jordi Sarda Pons, eds., *INFER Research Perspectives, Volume 1: Perspectives on Competition in Transportation.* Berlin: Lit Verlag.

Jennings, Frederic B., Jr. (2007). "A New Economics of Complementarity, Increasing Returns and Planning Horizons." In Wolfram Elsner and Hardy Hanappi, eds., *Varieties of Capitalism and New Institutional Deals.* Cheltenham, England: Edward Elgar.

Kaldor, Nicholas. (1972). "The Irrelevance of Equilibrium Economics." *Economic Journal 82*: 1237–1255.

Kaldor, Nicholas. (1975). "What Is Wrong With Economic Theory." *Quarterly Journal of Economics 89*(3): 347–357.

Koehler, Wolfgang. (1938). "Closed and Open Systems." Excerpted from his *The Place of Value in a World of Facts.* New York: Liveright; as reprinted in F. E. Emery, ed., *Systems Thinking.* Baltimore: Penguin (1969).

Kohn, Alfie. (1986). *No Contest: The Case Against Competition.* Boston: Houghton Mifflin.

Lux, Kenneth. (1990). *Adam Smith's Mistake: How a Moral Philosopher Invented Economics and Ended Morality.* Boston: Shambhala Publications.

Margolis, Julius. (1960). "Sequential Decision Making in the Firm." *American Economic Review, Papers and Proceedings 50*(2):526–533.

Maslow, Abraham. (1954). *Motivation and Personality.* New York: Harper and Row.

Maslow, Abraham. (1968). *Toward a Psychology of Being.* New York: Van Nostrand.

McCloskey, Donald N. (1990). *If You're So Smart: The Narrative of Economic Expertise.* Chicago: University of Chicago Press.

McGregor, Douglas. (1960). "Theory X and Theory Y." In *Organization Theory,* ed. D. S. Pugh. New York: Penguin (1971), 358–374.

Myrdal, Gunnar. (1978). "Institutional Economics." *Journal of Economic Issues 12*(4): 771–783.

Oi, Walter Y. (1967). "The Neoclassical Foundations of Progress Functions." *Economic Journal 77*: 579–594.

Rescher, Nicholas. (1979). *Cognitive Systematization: A Systems-Theoretic Approach to a Coherentist Theory of Knowledge.* Totowa, NJ: Rowman and Littlefield.

Scitovsky, Tibor. (1976) *The Joyless Economy*. Oxford: Oxford University Press.

Simon, Herbert A. (1976). 'From Substantive to Procedural Rationality.' In Spiro J. Latsis, ed., *Method and Appraisal in Economics*. Cambridge, England: Cambridge University Press.

Simon, Herbert A. (1982–1997). *Models of Bounded Rationality, Vols. 1–3*. Cambridge: MIT Press.

Smith, Adam. (1776). *An Inquiry into the Nature and Causes of the Wealth of Nations*. New York: Modern Library (1937).

Veblen, Thorstein. (1898). 'Why Is Economics Not an Evolutionary Science?' *Quarterly Journal of Economics 12*(3): 373–397; reprinted in his *The Place of Science in Modern Civilization and Other Essays*. New Brunswick, NJ: Transaction Publishers, 56–81.

Wachtel, Paul. (1989). *The Poverty of Affluence: A Psychological Portrait of the American Way of Life*. Philadelphia: New Society Publishers.

12   Banking on a Future

Finance, Exchange Rates, and the Environment

Jean E. Maier

ABSTRACT

This paper examines attempts to embed environmental ethics into financial institutions at local and international as well as public and private contexts. It also looks at the various initiatives to address global environmental problems. As growing concerns are voiced about global financial instability as well as global environmental crises, this paper considers a proposal for a new form of international money as well as an alternative concept for money to provide a valuation basis for a Currency Sustainability Standard for exchange rates.

1   Implementing Environmental Ethics Through Financial Institutions and Governance

Nearly two thirds of the services provided by nature to humankind are found to be in decline worldwide. In effect, the benefits reaped from our engineering of the planet have been achieved by running down natural capital assets . . . Unless we acknowledge the debt and prevent it from growing, we place in jeopardy the dreams of citizens everywhere to rid the world of hunger, extreme poverty, and avoidable disease—as well as increasing the risk of sudden changes to the planet's life-support systems from which even the wealthiest may not be shielded. (my emphasis)

2005 Statement of the Millennium Ecosystem Assessment Board composed of 1360 scientists and experts worldwide (cited in Speth & Haas, 2006, p. 16).

A. The Critical Nature of the Global Environmental Crisis

Environmental degradation is so widespread now that most of the global impacts are unavoidable and many are getting worse every year. James Gustave Speth and Peter Haas (2006, pp. 17–47) list and describe 10 major problems:

1.   Air Pollution and Acid Rain

2.   Ozone Depletion

3.   Global Climate Change

4.   Deforestation

5.   Land Degradation and Desertification

6.   Freshwater Degradation

7.   Marine Fisheries

8.   Toxic Pollutants

9.   Biodiversity

10. Excess Nitrogen

There is a human face to this crisis; and, in a number of the areas, the assessments are hard to imagine. Crop and forest losses in China due to air pollution and acid rain are estimated to exceed $5 billion per year. Tropical forests are disappearing at the rate of 1 acre per second. Desertification causes huge declines in food production making people vulnerable to famine, migration, and social unrest. The World Health Organization estimates that 5 million people die each year due to unsafe water sources. Seventy-five percent of ocean fisheries are overburdened, putting at risk one fifth of the world population who depend on fish as their main source of protein. An EPA review of 3000 synthetic commercial chemicals found that 40 percent had no toxicity data at all. Biodiversity losses at 1000 times the normal expected rate can have many impacts including decline in pollination of food crops. Excessive nitrogen fertilizers are wasted and washed into waterways creating dead zones devoid of aquatic life.

Many problems are interlinked and aggravated by social and economic processes. The public is enamored with technology and ignores potential negative consequences of current and emerging technologies. Global trade and industrialization aggravate this long list of global problems. Export-driven production is extremely harmful, with costly ecologically damaging ports, airports, dams and canals in addition to the environmental costs of global transport, fossil fuel use, refrigeration and packaging (Speth & Haas, 2006, pp. 17–48, 145).

B. Environmental Ethics and Financial Institutions 1970 to 2003

Efforts to address environmental issues through financial institutions (FIs) began not long after the environmental movement started in the 1970s. Non-governmental organizations and civil society organizations (NGOs and CSOs) created campaigns to address harm to indigenous groups and their lands resulting from misguided development projects initiated with World Bank or regional development bank funding.

In 1980 the U.S. Congress passed the Superfund Act (CERCLA) in response to events at Love Canal, the area of Niagara Falls built over an old chemical dump where rusting metal drums later erupted at the surface, spilling toxic liquids in backyards; subsequently birth defects increased in frequency (Beck, 1979). CERCLA not only made the commercial companies liable for the damage (some had ceased business or gone bankrupt), but in many cases extended liability to the banks funding the companies. Even banks in Europe and those involved in international development lending took notice and began doing due diligence for environmental liabilities (Barannik, 2001, p. 251; Coulson 2001, p. 300; Bouma & Jeucken, 2001, p. 24; Kearins & O'Malley, 2001, p. 354).

Through the initiative of the Sierra Club, the U.S. Congress passed the 1989 International Development and Finance Act, known as the Pelosi Amendment. This required the World Bank to do environmental assessments of any projects with possible significant environmental impacts and make them publicly available at least 120 days prior to voting; without such assessment, the U.S. Executive Director (that is, the U.S. representative) would be blocked from voting in favor of such projects (Barannik & Goodland, 2001, p. 328). As the largest contributor to the World Bank, the U.S. was alloted the largest block of votes, although not a majority. In addition, voting by tradition was based on consensus (Boas & McNeill, 2003, pp. 17–19, 100–103; World Bank, 2003, p.3). So without the U.S. vote, such projects would not go forward. Subsequently the World Bank developed a Pollution Prevention and Abatement Handbook and an environmental assessment process (World Bank, 1991, 1998). Projects were put into A, B, or C categories based on high, possible, or low risk, and detailed mitigation measures were outlined.

With the end of the Cold War when foreign aid was linked to strategic interests, and with expanding deregulation of capital flows around the world, official public funding for development projects was eclipsed by private funding with sources such as portfolio or equity investments, foreign direct investment (FDI), and project finance (Chan-Fishel, 2003; Klein & Hartford, 2005, p. 45). Figure 1 clearly shows this shift. NGOs such as Friends of the Earth (FOE) and Rainforest Action Network (RAN) noticed these trends. RAN, frustrated with stopping a logging project in one part of the world only to find a new one emerge in another distant part of the world, initiated a Global Finance Campaign seeking to intervene at a higher level in the system by stopping the funding of companies engaging in damaging projects (Firger, 2005). Within three years of an intensive campaign that included students nationwide destroying their bank credit cards, RAN negotiated an environmental policy with multinational bank Citigroup. Using standards such as those developed by the International Union for the Conservation of Nature, the bank became the first FI to ban projects that used timber from an illegal or endangered source (Rainforest Action Network, 2005, 1995–2006a, b; Multinational Monitor, 2004).

C. Evolving Standards for Financial Institutions

Seeking to broaden the movement to instill environmental ethics into the activities of financial institutions, a coalition of NGOs announced a set of guidelines for FIs called the Collevecchio Principles at the World Social Forum in January 2003 (Friends of the Earth, 2003). The declaration defined six general ethical principles: Sustainability, Do Not Harm, Responsibility, Accountability, Transparency, and Sustainable Markets and Governance.

Three months later, the World Bank announced the Equator Principles for application to private FIs. These basically extended the use of the environmental assessment standards developed by the Bank following the Pelosi Amendment. The principles tended to focus on mitigation rather than prevention, and the NGO community remains critical of their extent and implementation (Equator Principles, 2006; Global Policy Forum, 2003; Missbach, 2004).

A promising development has been the effort of NGO BankTrack to develop specific standards by which to measure multinational bank policies and their implementation. Their January 2006 report surveyed the policies of 39 international banks. The assessment framework included 13 categories, such as human rights, chemicals, fisheries and forests; each specifically outlined international standards of practice with commentary about what banks should do. For example, the Climate and Energy category listed standards like Kyoto and the Greenhouse Gas Protocol and advised banks to 1) include climate in their risk assessments, 2) require clients to include GHG (greenhouse gas) accounting and reporting, 3) require clients to meet carbon reduction targets, and 4) activate strategies to invest in energy efficiency and renewable energy projects. Banks were then graded by these standards. With the highest score achieved being D+, there was clearly room for improvement. BankTrack plans to release a new assessment that includes evaluation of policy implementation in September 2007 (BankTrack and WWF, 2006).

Standards of environmental ethics for FIs have been updated and negotiated by differing interests. Currently such standards are voluntary, which limits their effectiveness. Recently the legal community has taken notice of the Equator Principles and has considered the possibility that they could become part of customary international law or adopted legislatively (Kass & McCarroll, 2006).

D. Global Environmental Governance

Efforts at global environmental governance began in the 1970s. The 1972 United Nations Stockholm Conference on the Human Environment (UNCHE) set up the UN Environment Program (UNEP) and established an Action Plan. The World Commission on Environment and Development (WCED) in 1987 recognized that industrial countries were on an unsustainable path, but thought economic growth in a sustainable manner could resolve perceived problems. The 1992 UNCED Conference on Environment and Development, the Rio Earth Summit, sought to implement this vision with the Agenda 21 blueprint. Unfortunately it was non-binding and neglected. The last Johannesburg World Summit on Sustainable Development (WSSD) in 2002 lacked leadership; Millennium Development Goals (MDGs) were too vague, corporate partnerships were overemphasized, and talk of a "triple bottomline" diluted priorities. In their book on global environmental governance, Speth and Haas (2006, pp. 52–78, 101–105, 125–150) come to the conclusion that international laws have failed; deep and broad cultural and social changes are needed.

The United Nations University Institute for Advanced Studies in Tokyo in recent years coordinated researchers to evaluate changes in environmental governance and to offer recommendations for reform. Some of the issues raised were the need for a strong regulatory system to balance public and private interests. Furthermore, the current system of "self-regulation" by business undermines public involvement. In addition, multilateral environmental agreements (MEAs) needed to be binding on business firms as well as governments in order to be effective (Gleckman, 2004). Recommendations included creating a World Environmental Organization, adding legal clarity to the Precautionary Principle, clustering MEA secretariat sites and meetings for better coordination, creating a resolution process for disputes between the WTO and MEA provisions, and facilitating the use of the International Court of Justice Chamber of Environmental Matters (Charnovitz, 2005; Oberthur, 2005; Pauwelyn, 2005; Sampson, 2005).

Governance by the Bretton Woods institutions—the World Bank, IMF, and WTO—tends to be lacking as well. The World Bank has demonstrated a persistent lack of environmental sensitivity (see Barannik & Goodland, 2001). IMF conditionality has undermined governments and aggravated social and environmental problems. And the WTO undermines the ethics and laws of sustainability in industrialized nations. Rather than dissolve them, authors like Morten Boas and Desmond McNeill (2003) of the Centre for Development and the Environment at the University of Oslo recommend "profound" reform.

Given the limitations for resolving global environmental problems through financial institutions, environmental governance, and other initiatives like green taxes that would require public support, a better understanding of the international financial system seemed necessary as a way to consider market alternatives. This includes examining the valuation of the primary product that banks depend upon . . . money.

2 Financial and Monetary Approaches to Environmental Sustainability

A. The Global Financial System and the International Money Supply

International finance has been described as an evolving system, its major component being an international supply of money. When international rules specified that paper money be backed by gold, the system had some self-regulating features. As increasing trade and economic activity demanded an increase in the money supply, rising prices would be constrained by the rising costs of gold production needed to back the new money. But relationships in the system were changed by crises and innovation, and international rules were limited by evasion, changes in technology, and incompatible national agendas (Aliber, 2002, pp. 1–46).

B. Recent History of the Financial System

Under the Bretton Woods regime, instituted following World War II at a time when the U.S. had acquired large reserves of gold, gold was set to a price of $35 dollars per ounce. The IMF was set up to maintain fixed exchange rates based on this standard. The regime was expected to provide stability and encourage trade among nations. Various factors contributed to its downfall in the early 1970s, including rising debts of the U.S. government incurred with the Vietnam War and the War on Poverty. Devaluation of the dollar and the creation of a new IMF international money, the Special Drawing Right (SDR), failed to uphold the old system (Aliber, 2002, pp. 46–57). Before the measures could take effect, a number of countries had started to float their currencies in financial markets.

But the shift to floating rates of major currencies, which some refer to as a "nonsystem" to underscore its unreliable nature, has resulted in greater volatility and instability. One difficulty in the arrangement is that balance of payments surpluses did not require revaluation, i.e., raising the value of a currency. In addition, loosening capital flows between nations has created a "trilemma" in which independent domestic economic policies conflict with floating exchange rates and the free flow of capital. In the 1960s, banks seeking to escape regulations in the U.S. set up offshore Eurobank branches in London where clients could transfer large dollar deposits to earn higher interest rates. Eurobank deposits have gone from $1 billion in 1961 to $7000 billion in 1998; approximately 70 percent of these offshore deposits are in U.S. dollars (Aliber, 2002, pp. 47, 57–83, 124–133; Gilpin, 2001, pp. 239, 248). As other changes in the financial system have loosened capital controls, increasing amounts of dollars are in foreign lands.

In the 1970s, the international system was destabilized by petrodollars (the arrangement to sell oil in U.S. dollars) and rapid increases in the price of oil by OPEC. To deal with this, countries could either borrow dollars or devalue their currencies to acquire dollars through exports (Aliber, 2002, pp. 152–164). By the end of the decade, rising unemployment and double digit inflation undermined Keynesian approaches of government involvement in the economy and support of social welfare programs; policy shifted to cutting taxes and reducing government spending (Allen, 2001, pp. 219–220).

In the 1980s rising interest rates to deal with inflation contributed to highly valued "superdollars," which attracted foreign investors to the high rates on dollar assets (Aliber, pp. 118 –120). But these rates also undermined the U.S. mortgage and housing market, which in turn undermined the banking industry (Aliber, pp. 171–177). The high value of the dollar made U.S. exports more expensive; as exports declined the U.S. became a debtor nation and a net importer of capital (Allen, 2001, p.283).

C. Developing Country Impacts

Developing countries' place in the financial system set in motion different dynamics in response to policy changes in the U.S. and other industrialized nations. In the 1960s they welcomed debt as a way to enhance their economies through economic growth. U.S. lenders were happy to lower their risks by diversifying their loan portfolios with loans to developing countries (Aliber, 2001, p. 188).

But the petrodollar arrangement and the rapid increases in oil prices created severe deficits in the 1970s for many countries. In the Philippines, President Marcos initiated a program that encouraged "heroes of the nation" to migrate abroad to earn money to help resolve the country's balance of payments crisis. Earnings sent home, called remittances, have become a worldwide phenomenon. In 2003, remittances in the Philippines totaled $7.6 billion with a country GDP of $80.6 billion (Rupert & Solomon, 2006, pp. 87–95). As shown in Figure 1, the World Bank includes them as a sizable form of "foreign aid" (Klein & Hartford, 2005, p. 45). But rising oil prices in recent years have again burdened many poor and developing countries; higher oil costs have washed away the benefits of debt cancellation programs (Jubilee USA Network, 2006).

The 1980s added to developing country challenges. Inflation and higher interest rates caused a worldwide recession. With higher rates on their loans and less demand for their exports, loan defaults in developing countries threatened U.S. and international banks (Aliber, 2001, pp. 189–190). Labeling this a short-term financial liquidity crisis (rather than a longer term insolvency problem), Secretary of the Treasury James Baker formulated the "Washington Consensus" structural adjustment policies to address third world debt. These emphasized privatization, capital market and trade liberalization, deregulation and removal of constraints to integration into the global economy, so that economic growth could take off. Governments were expected to reduce spending, which meant cutting education, health, and social programs. IMF and World Bank loans often included such policies as conditions for approving loans. In many cases, these policies made bad situations worse, aggravating poverty and environmental damage, and increasing social conflicts (Gilpin, 2001, pp. 313–316).

D. Increasingly Frequent Crises

The international financial system has become increasingly dysfunctional with unstable exchange rates, volatile capital flows between nations, austere development policies, and the interaction of domestic policy adjustments on other countries in globalized markets. In the 1990s, Japan experienced a prolonged recession; Mexico had a severe peso crises. Towards the end of the decade, the East Asian crisis drew worldwide attention. The crisis threatened to spread and become global.

At international meetings, some participants called for a new global financial architecture. But negotiations were difficult and little was accomplished. A Financial Stability Forum was established to monitor the international financial situation (Gilpin, 2001, pp. 270, 276).

E. Financialization, Defunct Theories, and Normative Commitments

Financialization is described as "the increasing role of financial motives, financial markets, financial actors and financial institutions in the operation of the domestic and international economies" (Epstein, 2005, p. 3). A number of scholars believe that along with neoliberalism and globalization, financialization has been "very detrimental to significant numbers of people about the globe" (Epstein, p. 5). Among them, Robert Blecker (2005) notes that globalized markets have undone many of the theoretical frameworks taught in economics textbooks. Balance of payments are not automatic, exchange rates are unpredictable despite various models to forecast rates, purchasing power parity is persistently violated, and misallocation creates persistent trade imbalances. These distortions have multiple causes: capital mobility, differing monetary situations, the pursuit of absolute advantage—especially the lowest labor costs, and high import prices that cause inflation in developing countries.

He believes the solution lies with exchange rate management and context-based policies.

The field of international political economy offers a distinctive perspective to the understanding of the international financial system. Political economist Robert Gilpin (2001, pp. 12–45, 68, 150–191) notes that neoclassical economics is not just a set of theories; it embodies normative commitments. These relate to how a society chooses to use and distribute wealth; differences in normative commitments are clearly evident when comparing the U.S. market model, the Japanese corporate model, and the German "Social Market" model. In addition, the state is not a collection of rational individuals, it expresses a collective interest that is bound to citizens' loyalty, security, and prestige. He adds that the post- World War II vision that peace could be secured by the interdependence of trade ignores the unequal gains and distribution of free markets.

Gilpin (pp. 378–379, 390–397, 402) feels that better global economic governance is needed to deal with market failures and to provide for collective public goods like rule of law, financial stability, common business standards, and environmental solutions. A power mechanism is needed for international compliance; but this is unlikely anytime soon since effective international institutions have existed for only 50 years. Nation-states have stabilized sovereignty over 300 years. What will be needed is a greater base of shared beliefs and values at the global level.

F. The Global Greenback Reserve

A number of researchers have recommended the activation of IMF Special Drawing Rights as international money to bring balance back to the international financial system (Aliber, 2002; Davidson, 2005). Joseph Stiglitz (2006) has proposed an innovative alternative that he refers to as the Global Greenback Reserve System.

Stiglitz (2006) highlights a serious malfunction in the balance of payments system: "The richest country in the world, the United States, seemingly cannot

Gross unofficial flows (US$ billions)

- ■ Private, nonguaranteed debt   ■ Portfolio equity (net)
- ▒ Foreign direct investment (net)   ■ Remittances
- □ NGO grants

Gross official flows (US$ billions)

- ■ Multilateral loans and grants   ■ Export credits
- ▒ Other publicly guaranteed debt   ■ Bilateral loans and grants

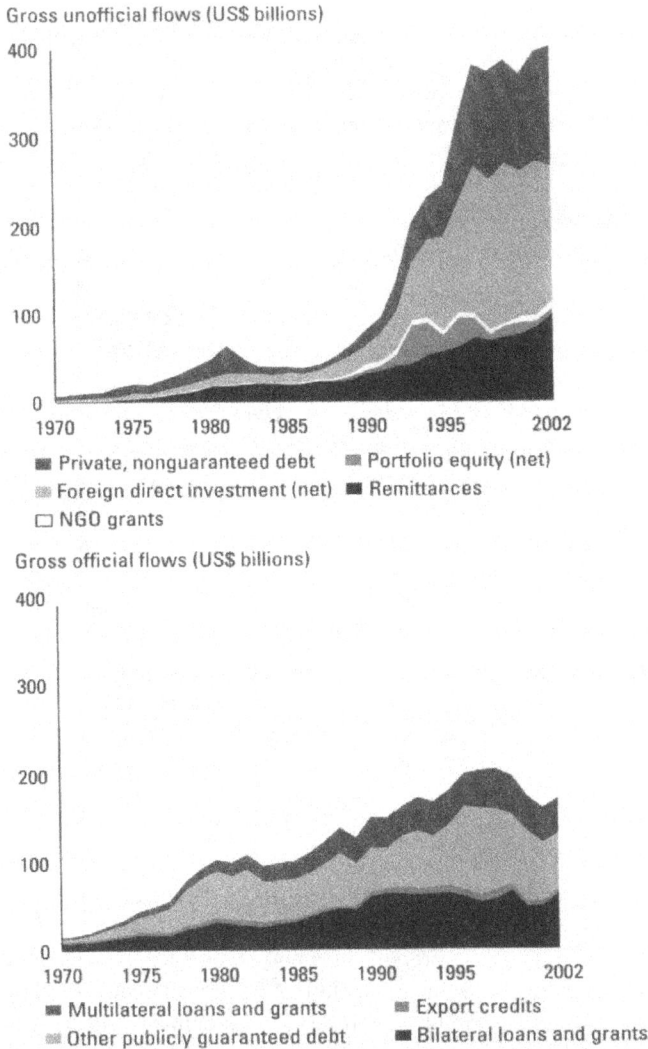

Source: World Bank, Global Development Finance database; OECD Development Assistance Committee.

Figure 1 Financial Flows of Private and Public Finance. Note major increase in private funding with a significant level of remittance funding [source Klein & Hartford, 2005, p. 45].

live within its means, borrowing $2 billion a day from poorer countries" (p. 245). There are two main causes of the problem: 1) countries buy dollars and dollar assets to devalue their currencies to deal with pressures to export, and 2) with many U.S. private loans callable at any time and with heightened concerns about international stability since the East Asian crisis, countries are increasing their holdings of official reserves. Stiglitz offers the example where a private bank loan to a developing country could charge an interest rate of 20 percent on $100 million. This country's government then buys U.S. Treasury bills paying 5 percent interest for the same amount in order to avoid financial instability should the private loan be recalled suddenly. This results in a net transfer of $15 million to the U.S., worsening the developing country's overall financial position.

In contrast to SDRs which are issued sporadically and distributed mostly to wealthy countries, global greenbacks would be issued annually and used to aid global financial stability as well as to deal with global problems such as poverty and environmental degradation. One way that Stiglitz estimated the annual issuance of greenback reserves was based on a constant ratio of reserves to global GDP; if the GDP grew at 5 percent, he estimated an annual emission of $200 billion. Greenbacks could be acquired by central banks in exchange for other official reserves by members of the system, and could be converted to dollars or euros with an exchange rate formula during a defined crises. The funds received by the system could be allocated for collective global needs like the Millennium Development Goals and/or other development projects that could have conditions attached such as preventing, reducing, or mitigating negative externalities like greenhouse gas production, nuclear proliferation, or non-compliance with MEAs.

Stiglitz's proposal seems innovative and hopeful as an alternative to strictly governance approaches and offers an economic mechanism that not only enhances financial stability but addresses global environmental problems.

G. The Currency Sustainability Standard: a New Valuation and Exchange Rate
System

One of the critical sources of instability in the financial system is the overuse of a domestic currency as international money. The current situation with vast amounts of dollars in foreign hands makes the international money system overly dependent on the value of the dollar. If petroeuros were used or if central banks started shifting to euros as reserves, the demand for euros could create high valuations for euros, which in turn could depress EU exports and EU economies. Stiglitz's Global Greenback reserve system could rebalance and stabilize the international supply of money as well as provide funds for global collective problems.

Another critical source of global instability, volatile exchange rates, still needs to be addressed. The currency sustainability standard (CSS) proposal offers a new valuation framework for currencies. It approaches money as an evolving-sociolinguistic concept. Based on a new valuation model for money, nations would compete for strongly valued currencies to import more cheaply. But valuations would be based on environmental (and social) sustainability indicators. Competition would thus not only enhance sustainability goals but also promote financial stability by pegging exchange rates to sustainability indicators and encouraging a trend toward currency value harmonization.

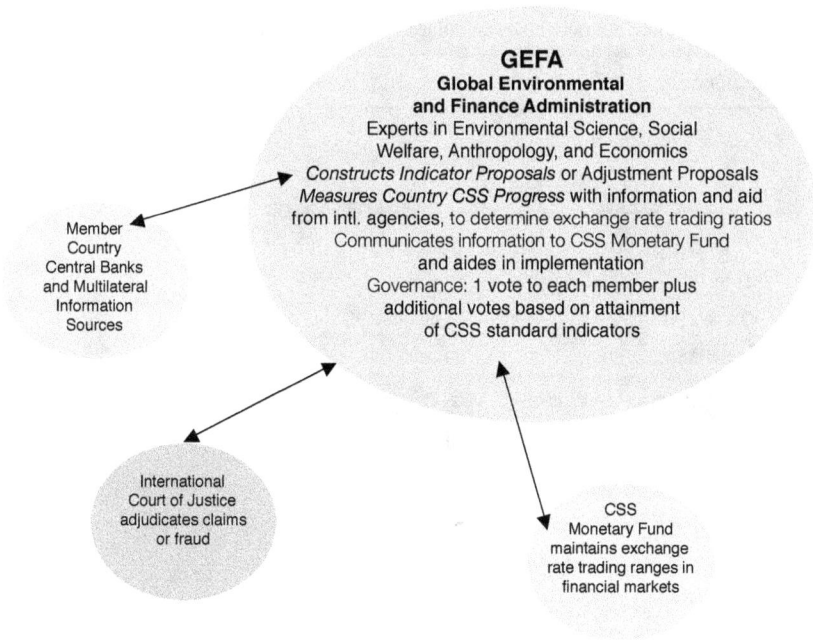

Figure 2 The Currency Sustainability Standard Process

A key part of this proposal would be the creation of acceptable sustainability indicators. These indicators would be used to measure and score countries based
on the indicator scales. Exchange trading ratios would be based on the difference between country scores.

To manage the new exchange system would require a new institutional arrangement. Rather than dismantle Bretton Woods institutions as the "Fifty Years
is Enough" movement recommends, or undertake "profound" reform as many
have called for, the proposal would recommend "re-inventing" the World Bank
and the IMF. The World Bank could be redesigned as a Global Environment
and Finance Administration (see Figure 2) composed of professionals from a
diversity of fields that would define a new culture. Social and environmental
scientists would have equal representation with economists. They would be responsible for designing the indicators and adjusting the benchmarks progressively upward to promote sustainability and address global collective needs.
They would be responsible for gathering information from international sources
to assess country performance, to assign ratings and scores, and to establish the
exchange ratios. The management structure would provide each member with
one vote plus additional votes based on each country's attainment of the CSS
indicators. The role of a CSS Monetary Fund would be to contain the exchange
ratios within the prescribed trading ratio pegs in global currency markets. The
International Court of Justice would adjudicate legal disputes.

Table 1 A Currency Sustainability Standard Scenario (continues)

I. Indicators

A. Social Sustainability Indicators:

1. Economic Equity Ratios:
Highest Paid Average (or Quintile): Lowest Paid Average (or Quintile)

1:1 to 5:1	=	100 points
5:1 to 10:1	=	50 points
10:1 to 15:1	=	25 points
Over 15:1	=	0 points

2. Export, Import of Weapons of Mass Destruction/ Weaponry

No Exchange	=	100 points
No Nuclear	=	50 points
Nuclear Exchange	=	0 points

B. Environmental Sustainability Standards

3. Greenhouse Gas Production/ Capita

Low	=	100 points
Medium	=	50 points
High	=	0 points

4. Clean Energy Investments

High	=	100 points
Medium	=	50 points
Low	=	0 points

II. Measuring Countries' Progress: Tallies of Sustainability Scores

---

	USA	Japan	North Korea	Central African Republic
1. Equity	0	50	N/A	100
2. Weapons	0	50	0	50
3. GHG	0	0	100	100
4. Clean $	50	50	0	0
TOTALS	50	150	100	250

	Russia	China	Uruguay	EU	Saudi Arabia
1. Equity	25	100	100	50	0
2. Weapons	0	0	50	50	50
3. GHG	50	0	100	0	50
4. Clean $	0	0	0	50	0
TOTALS	75	100	250	150	100

Table 1 A Currency Sustainability Standard Scenario (continued)

III. Trading Ratios*		
US: Japan = 3:1	Japan: Uruguay = 5:3	C.A.R.: Uruguay = 1:1
China: C.A.R. = 5:2	Japan: EU = 1:1	US: China = 2:1

Note: The preceeding figures are all rough estimates for the sake of explaining how a very simple model could operate. The UK and Switzerland are not included in the EU, and France is considered an outlier in terms of weapons. (Mathematically, the lowest score possible is 1).

*See commentary for further explanation.

H. CSS Heuristic Scenario

1. Indicators There are many indicators that would be appealing hypothetically on a universal basis: energy efficiency, reduction of GHG, clean energy investments, forest and biodiversity preservation, sustainable agricultural practices, toxics reduction as well as higher testing standards for synthetic substances, higher recycling and reuse rates, water quality standards, social and economic equity, nuclear containment, labor standards, and human and indigenous community rights. Economic equity is essential to support fairness and justice in human society, and it adds to environmental sustainability by tempering the excesses of the most wealthy as well as the costs of poverty—crime, terrorism, environmental destruction in the face of desperation.

For illustration purposes, the Currency Sustainability Standard scenario (see Table 1) measures economic equity by comparing the highest and lowest income quintiles of country residents. Those countries with a higher level of economic equality would receive the highest points for this indicator. Although the indicators may be uniform, they can be acccomplished in a diversity of ways depending on local or national context. In a city-state like Singapore, measures could be put into law to promote economic equity; in the U.S. educational programs or minimum/maximum wages could achieve the outcomes.

There would be some issues about how to relate equity to indigenous native communities, homemakers, or the unemployed, so alternative indicators of social welfare might need to be developed. Other indicators that have been proposed include the Gini Coefficient, MEW (Measure of Economic Welfare), or the ISEW (Index of Sustainable Economic Welfare) that is a composite that includes environmental indicators (Daly & Farley, 2004, pp. 233–236, 263).

The second CSS social indicator underscores the threat of military and violent confrontation. In a world where weapons of mass destruction, terrorism, rogue states, and states undermined by ethnic warfare are of paramount concern, an indicator to encourage nuclear and weapons containment could be critical. Nation-states would be scored based on their engagement in sales or possession of weaponry. Involvment with nuclear weapons would greatly undermine a currency's value. Weapons proliferation in general would be suppressed.

In light of recent attention on climate change, the Currency Sustainability Standard Scenario used GHG (greenhouse gas) emissions and clean energy investments to illustrate a simple way of creating incentives for changing economic behavior with monetary valuation standards. An energy per capita rating or a renewable clean energy measure could be alternatives. As noted earlier, many other environmental indicators could be included. BankTrack's evaluation scheme (2006) for multinational banks of 13 scoring areas with extensive discussion of protocols, best practices, and standards to assess compliance could be an excellent source. Yale and Columbia Universities have devised an Environmental Sustainability Index and an Environmental Performance Index. The Ecological Footprint, or the Genuine Progress Indicator (GPI) could also be considered (Global Footprint Network, 2007; Redefining Progress, 2005 & 2006; Yale and Columbia Universities, 2006; YCELP & CIESIN, 2005).

For both social and environmental indicators, a more refined gradient scale could be developed to encourage and provide incentives for countries to make smaller, marginal changes. Domestic issues such as money supply or savings and investment may need to be considered. The model presented is not intended to offer a finished possibility, but rather tries to offer a simple, teaching device for understanding the dynamics and incentives possible in the process.

2. A System of Changing Relationships Based on a country's total scores based on the indicators, the difference in values between two countries could be expressed as a ratio, e.g. in the CSS Scenario example in Table 1, the U.S. score of 50 points compares with the Japanese score of 150 points, thus 3 times the value score of the U.S. dollar would be equivalent to the value score of the Japanese yen. So the dollar/yen exchange would be 3 dollars to 1 yen. This would create new dynamics in the financial system. US exports to Japan, China and elsewhere would be less expensive and provide advantages to American producers and entrepreneurs, especially those who offer clean technologies. At the same time, producers in China and Japan would find incentives to export to countries with high currency values like Uruguay or the Central Republic of Africa.

With a CSS scenario, trade and capital flows could flow freely, but the incentives for such would be guided by sustainable outcomes as measured by the indicators. Owners of airlines, ships, and transportation systems would consider energy efficiency and greenhouse gas production in how they design vehicles or networks so that the currency of the country in which they are based would be strengthened to increase its purchasing power overseas and in international markets. A free-rider problem, that results when one company puts capital into a more efficient fleet of planes while all competing airlines would benefit from the country's stronger currency, might be dealt with through a cap and trade system. The CSS strategy would be intended for use with other complementary approaches, including green taxation. Global Greenback reserves could be used to fund the CSS Monetary Fund.

Incentives for philanthropy, foreign aid, or FDI could be based on the fact that investments in other countries that lead to measurably sustainable outcomes would result in increased valuation levels that could be divided equally between donor and recepient country. The hope would be that competition for a strong currency would reflect cooperation for all to achieve sustainable goals and outcomes that the international community formulates through the indicator standards that apply to all member countries. For example, a U.S. company could invest in a solar panel production company in India; by doing so, the U.S. company's investment would add to the dollar's value, while the calculated reduction of GHG emissions would strengthen the Indian rupee's value. The economies of both nations would benefit (the U.S. economy could acquire profits, and the Indian economy could benefit with jobs). Furthermore, the U.S. government could benefit from additional taxes, while the Indian government might save on social services to the unemployed. Public and private sectors in both countries could be aided by a stronger currency that reduces the costs of imports and adds prestige to the country. As nations strived to achieve indicators, there would be a trend towards currency harmonization, thus there could be less of a need to trade oil in one currency only.

By internationalizing sustainable standards of valuation for national currencies, money could internalize incentives for sustainable behavior and activities at all levels—individual, household, firm, and government. This would seem to have the most impact on the level of international exchanges. Although countries with high value ratios might be tempted to go on a spending import spree, they would best buy low polluting vehicles and spread their wealth amongst their citizens if they wished to maintain their currency valuations. Perhaps even for nondemocratic or corrupt governments this mechanism would encourage sustainable behavior, since a higher national currency value would be worth more not only in a Swiss bank account but also in international financial markets. For rogue states desiring nuclear weapons, the currency sustainability standard (CSS) might be another non-violent strategy that could be used as an alternative to economic sanctions or military actions. Transparency would be encouraged, since lack of data would lower sustainability scores.

3. Challenges Implementing such a system would seem to involve a number of challenges. First, it would involve designing a workable system of indicators that would be easily and clearly auditable so accountability and transparency would be assured.

The most difficult challenge would likely be political. Indicator proposals would need to offer universal appeal on an international basis so that a large number of nations would find more benefits than costs to adopting such a mechanism. In rare cases, a country handicap measure could be included for unusual situations based on disadvantages related to differing landscapes or internal dynamics.

Finally, the transaction costs of transition to such a system would need to be considered. A phase-in period may be needed. Perhaps the Global Greenback reserve system could complement the CSS mechanism and provide funding to help some countries, or it could integrate with the CSS Monetary Fund. For countries like Japan, China, Europe, and the U.S., perhaps the dynamics set in place with such a system could make trade and investment more focused on internal development that promoted sustainability, rather than a neomerchantile quest for profits around the globe. In time a more even distribution of balance of payments could result.

Ultimately the CSS system could promote both financial stability as well as social and environmental sustainability. It could internalize natural science indicators into the socioeconomic decision-making of the market, and economic growth or development could be moderated and shaped by these indicators. Maybe the dollar, euro, yen, yuan, etc. . . . could even act as vehicles for ecological and social understanding.

We could achieve a healthy local and global economy that had a better moral compass to guide it. If such an undertaking is feasible, it will call upon leadership from all countries to make the transition to a sustainable relationship with our planet before it's too late. Like the nations that came together after World War II to negotiate the UN Declaration of Human Rights, nations could come together to negotiate indicator proposals that uphold environmental principles that are universal everywhere and human justice issues that are cross-cultural.

References

Aliber, R.Z. (2002). The new international money game. (6th ed.). Chicago: The University of Chicago Press.

Allen, L. (2001). The global financial system 1750–2000. London: Reaktion Books.

BankTrack & WWF (2006, Jan. 26). Shaping the future of sustainable finance: Moving from paper promises to performance. Retrieved March 25, 2006, from http://www.wwf.org.uk/filelibrary/pdf/sustainablefinancereport.pdf http://www.banktrack.org/?show=128&visitor=1 (updated website)

Barannik, A. (2001). Providers of financial services and environmental risk management; current experience. In J. J. Bouma et al. (Eds.), Sustainable finance: The greening of finance (pp. 247–265). Sheffield, UK: Greenleaf Publishing.

Barannik, A. & Goodland, R.J.A. (1999–2000). The World Bank's environmental assessment policies: Review of institutional development. In J. J. Bouma et al. (Eds.), Sustainable banking: The greening of finance (pp. 316–346). Sheffield, UK: Greenleaf Publishing.

Beck, E. (1979, Jan.). The Love Canal tragedy. EPA Journal. Retrieved February 17, 2007, from http://www.epa.gov/history/topics/lovecanal/01.htm

Blecker, R. (2005). Financial globalization, exchange rates, and international trade. In G. Epstein (Ed.), Financialization and the world economy (pp. 183–209). Northhampton, Mass: Edward Elgar Publishing, Inc.

Boas, M. & McNeill, D. (2003). Multilateral institutions: A critical introduction. London: Pluto Press.

Bouma J. & Jeucken, M. (2001). The changing environment of banks. In J.J.Bouma et al. (Eds.), Sustainable finance: The greening of finance (pp. 24–37). Sheffield, UK: Greenleaf Publishing in association with Deloitte & Touche.

Chan-Fishel, M. (2003, Sept. 22). Project finance trends: Key players, regions, and sectors, a report prepared for Focus on Finance. Available through Google.

Charnovitz, S. (2005). A World Environment Organization. In W. Chambers & J. Green (Eds.), Reforming international environmental governance (pp. 93–123). Tokyo: United Nations University Press.

Coulson, A. (2001). Corporate environmental assessment by a bank lender: The reality. In J. J. Bouma et al. (Eds.), Sustainable finance: The greening of finance (pp. 300–311). Sheffield, UK: Greenleaf Publishing.

Daly, H. & Farley, J. (2004). Ecological economics: Principles and applications. London: Island Press.

Davidson, P. (2005). Is a declining dollar good for the U.S. economy or the global economy? Retrieved October 1, 2006, from http://econpapers.repec.org/paper/wpawuwpit/0505012.htm

Epstein, G. (Ed.). (2005). Financialization and the world economy. Northhampton, Mass: Edward Elgar Publishing, Inc.

Equator Principles. (2006, July). The "Equator Principles." Retrieved February 18, 2007, from http://www.equator-principles.com/principles.shtml

Firger, D. (2005). Dan Firger is the national Project Organizer for RAN's Global Finance Campaign. Interview June 17, 2005, and phone conversation Aug. 4, 2005.

Friends of the Earth. (2003). The World Economic Forum and the World Social Forum, 2003. Retrieved November 9, 2006, from http://www.foe.org/camps/intl/forums.html

Gilpin, R. (2001). Global political economy: Understanding the international economic order. Princeton: Princeton University Press.

Gleckman, H. (2004). Balancing TNCs, the states, and the international system in global environmental governance: A critical perspective. In N. Kanie & P. Haas (Eds.), Emerging forces in environmental governance (pp. 203–215). Tokyo: United Nations University Press.

Global Footprint Network. (2007, 5 May). Global footprint network. Retrieved May 26, 2007, from http://www.footprintnetwork.org/

Global Policy Forum. (2003, June). NGO collective analysis of the Equator Principles. Retrieved March 30, 2006, from http://www.globalpolicy.org/socecon/ffd/2003/06ngos.htm

Jubilee USA Network. (2006, July). High oil prices: Undermining debt cancellation and fueling a new crises? Time for a clean energy revolution. Policy Brief. Washington D.C.: Jubilee USA Network.

Kass, S.L. & McCarroll, J.M. (2006, 1 Sept.). Environmental law environmental law; the revised Equator Principles the revised Equator Principles; the original Equator Principles; the revised Principles; IFC policies; future implications. New York Law Review, 236 (44). p. 3. Retrieved February 2, 2007, from Factiva.

Kearins, K. & O'Malley, G. (2001). International financial institutions and the Three Gorges hydroelectric power scheme. In J. J. Bouma et al. (Eds.), Sustainable finance: The greening of finance (pp. 348–359). Sheffield, UK: Greenleaf Publishing.

Klein, M. & Hartford, T. (2005). The market for aid. Washington D.C.: International Finance Corporation.

Missbach, A. (2004, Sept.). The Equator Principles: Drawing the line for socially responsible banks? An interim review from an NGO perspective. Development: Corporate Social Responsibility Houndmills. 47(3), 78–84. Retrieved Feb. 20, 2006, from ProQuest.

Multinational Monitor Washington. (2004, Jan./Feb.). Running over Citi: Banking goliath Citigroup agrees to environmental screens for project financing in the developing world. Multinational Monitor Washington, 25 (½) 35–39. Retrieved August 1, 2005, from ProQuest database.

Oberthur, S. (2005). Clustering of multilateral environmental agreements: Potentials and limitations. In W. Chambers & J. Green (Eds.), Reforming international environmental governance (pp. 40–65). Tokyo: United Nations University Press.

Pauwelyn, J. (2005). Judicial mechanisms: Is there a need for a World Environmental Court?. In W. Chambers & J.Green (Eds.), Reforming international environmental governance (pp. 150–177). Tokyo: United Nations University Press.

RAN. (1995–2006a). Citibank 2000–2004. Retrieved November 6, 2006, from http://ran.org/what_we_do/global_finance/hist/citibank/

RAN. (1995–2006b). Finance 101. Retrieved Nov. 29, 2006, from http://ran.org/what_we_do/global_finance/finance_101_ending_destructive_investment/

Redefining Progress. (2005). Footprint of nations. Retrieved May 26, 2007, from http://www.ecologicalfootprint.org/

Redefining Progress. (2006). Sustainability indicators: Genuine Progress Indicator. Retrieved May 26, 2007, from http://www.rprogress.org/newprograms/sustIndi/gpi/index.shtml and http://www.rprogress.org/newprograms/sustIndi/gpi/gpi_reports.shtml

Rupert, M. & Solomon, M. Scott. (2006). Globalization and international political economy: The politics of alternative futures. Lanham, Maryland: Rowman & Littlefield Publishers, Inc.

Sampson, G. (2005). The World Trade Organization and global environmental governance. In W. Chambers & J. Green (Eds.), Reforming international environmental governance (pp. 124–149). Tokyo: United Nations University Press.

Speth, J.G. & Haas, P. (2006). Global environmental governance. Washington D.C.: Island Press.

Stiglitz, J. (2006). Reforming the global reserve system. Making globalization work (pp. 245–268). New York: W.W. Norton and Company.

World Bank. (1991). Environmental assessment sourcebook (Vols. I–II).World Bank Technical Papers #139 and 140. Washington D.C.: The World Bank.

World Bank & IFC (1998). Pollution prevention and abatement handbook. World Bank/IFC Publication, Washington D.C. Available online at http://www.ifc.org/ifcext/enviro.nsf/Content/PPAH

World Bank. (2003). A guide to the World Bank. Washington D.C.: The World Bank.

Yale and Columbia Universities. (2006). Environmental performance index. Retrieved May 26, 2007, from http://www.yale.edu/epi/

YCELP & CIESIN. (2005). Environmental sustainability index. Retrieved October 26, 2006, from http://sedac.ciesin.columbia.edu/es/esi/downloads.html (YCELP is the Yale Center for Environmental Law and Policy, and CIESIN is the Center for International Earth Science Information Network at Columbia University).

13 Overcoming Contradictions between Growth and Sustainability

Institutional Innovation in the BRICS

Peter H. May

ABSTRACT

The recent accelerated growth rates or efforts to emulate countries that have achieved a rapid pace of economic growth are widely acclaimed as means to uplift millions from poverty. In so doing, however, this rapid economic growth is most likely to coincide with unsustainable levels of consumption, place excessive pressure on life support systems and terrestrial sinks and foreshorten options for the future. Rather than pursuing the "Environmental Kuznets Curve" (EKC) hypothesis that higher income will bring with it the means to reduce the impacts of greater consumption, ecological economists assert that buying our way out of future scarcity with fast growth is indeed contradictory with sustainability. To better understand these contradictions and explore potential institutional innovations that may enable developing nations to better confront them (in effect, "tunneling under" the EKC), this article refers to recent experience in the BRICS countries (Brazil, Russia, India, China and South Africa). Beginning with a brief comparative summary of major development and environmental indicators, pressures on resources and society in each of the BRICS are discussed, followed by identification of institutional and policy frameworks each country has evolved to confront the challenges of growth and sustainability. The article closes with general conclusions for further research and information sharing among developing nations.

Keywords: growth, sustainability, BRICS, institutions, innovation, development policy

Introduction

The recent accelerated growth rates or efforts to emulate countries that have achieved a rapid pace of economic growth are widely acclaimed as means to uplift millions from poverty. In so doing, however, this rapid economic growth is most likely to coincide with unsustainable levels of consumption, place excessive pressure on life support systems and terrestrial sinks and foreshorten options for the future.

Rapid economic growth is widely portrayed to offer the option to "buy our way out" of developing societies' current unsustainable growth paths by quickly surpassing conditions that have caused unmitigated social and environmental impacts in other societies. In effect, technology transfer and avoidance of mistakes enable learning from those that have gone before. Such ideas are commonly found in the literature projecting tendencies along the "environmental Kuznets curve" (EKC) [1].

It is a fundamental tenet of ecological economics, however, that buying our way out of future scarcity with fast growth is in fact a recipe for disaster; such growth is intrinsically contradictory to sustainability.

The two policy options pursued by developing nations and by the BRICS countries specifically (Brazil, Russia, India, China and South Africa[1]) with regard to the growth and sustainability may be identified as: i) permit rapid growth and ensuing scarcities to signal the correct use of remaining natural resource endowments; or ii) invest heavily in education and technological innovation to decouple development from resource depletion. In contrast, the ecological economics position is that it is necessary to adopt a third option: iii) repudiate the perspective that rapid growth rates are necessary to achieve sustainability, and strive toward a stable state while pursuing equitable access to resources. This path does not, to be sure, repudiate use of market mechanisms or investment in human capital and technical innovation, but suggests the desirability of greater caution in opting for higher growth rates due to uncertain environmental consequences.

To cast this debate in a more practical light, ecological economists representing each of the five BRICS countries discuss in this paper how each country is faring in choice of development path and environmental governance in the context of demands for rapid growth as a way out of persistent poverty or stagnation. Our focus is on institutional innovations that may offer ways to surmount the contradictions that appear to make accelerated growth and sustainability incompatible, and possibly "tunnel under the EKC" [3]. Our aim is not to compare or to emulate one or the other model, but rather to let each country's growth path speak for itself while offering options for the rest.

Questions aired by the panel include:

1. How are these nations coping with the paradox between improvement in material wellbeing and exacerbation of local and global pressures on natural resources and the environment?

2. What are the distributive consequences of rapid economic growth? Are some groups profiting disproportionately at the expense of overall poverty alleviation?

3. What can the BRICS countries learn from each other as they explore alternative energy and material consumption pathways?

---

1   Although most authors [2] tend to refer to "BRIC" or "BRICs" rather than BRICS, we have preferred to include South Africa in this grouping, as a significant trading partner, consumer and producer of wealth among emerging economies.

Profile of the BRICS Countries

Comparative overview

Based on data in Table 1, the BRICS countries represent over 43% of the world's population, on 30% of its terrestrial land area, although only 13% of this land area is classified as arable. Despite their demographic importance, their economies generate only 10% of global GDP. While their per-capita incomes are only 31% of the global average, their CO_2 emissions of 2.5 t/yr per-capita, are approximately two-thirds of the global mean. These societies have become more fossil fuel dependent in consequence of their assumed development paths.

The BRICS countries are governed through a wide range of political-economic systems, from democratic capitalism to market-oriented state socialism. Some of the countries are characterized as having heterogeneous cultures, housing enormous religious, ethnic and racial diversity, while others, like Brazil and China have fairly homogeneous language and culture. Many groups (especially poor rural communities) reside in areas of extreme and highly threatened biodiversity. The BRICS share common aspirations for human development and social improvement, but invest considerably varying proportions of their savings in education, health and infrastructure, and are categorized in the lower-middle range of developing countries, with a population-weighted average HDI of 0.708.

Although for many years and for various reasons closed to global markets, all are now fairly open and share in the benefits and vagaries of globalization. Although they are competitors in some markets, there is a clear tendency towards increasing trade among one another. For example, Russia is Brazil's largest beef importer; China buys substantial raw materials from Brazil, Russia and South Africa, and exports finished products back cheaply; India sells call and accounting services to other developing nations as well as exporting these to the North.

In the following sections, the growth trajectories peculiar to each of the BRICS countries are briefly described, placing emphasis on the association of these trends with social equity and environmental quality.

Brazil

Blessed with a relatively larger resource base in relation to its population of 186 million than many of the other BRICS countries, Brazil has always thought of itself as having reserves of tremendous unexploited potential that would ensure riches for future generations and permit untrammeled profligacy by current cohorts. But this vision has been tempered by decades of slow economic growth after a "miraculous" spurt in the late 1970s under military dictatorship.

Despite redemocratization, Brazil remains one of the world's most inequitable societies, whose class structure inherited from the colonial era has left 23% below the poverty line. Investment remains limited at less than 20% of GDP, most of which comes from the private sector. Although Brazil has been running a consistently positive current account surplus, most of the budget is committed

Table 1 Comparative analysis of growth and consumption patterns in the BRICS

Indicator	Unit	Brazil	Russia	India	China	South Africa	BRICS	World	BRICS/World
Population	billion	0.184	0.144	1.08	1.296	0.046	2.75	6.365	43%
GDP	$ billion	944	763	796	2,680	256	5,439	41,290	13%
GDP growth rate (a)	2006 est. %	2.8	6.6	8.5	10.5	4.5	8.0	4.0	201%
GDP/capita	2006 est. $	5,021	5,373	737	2,068	5,565	1,976	6,329	31%
Human Development Index (2004) (a)	Index	0.792	0.797	0.611	0.768	0.653	0.708	–	
Land area	1000 sq. km.	8,459	16,381	2,973	9,327	1,214	38,354	129,663	30%
Rural population share (b)	%	16%	27%	72%	60%	43%	60%	51%	117%
Arable land (c)	% of total land area	7.0	7.3	54.4	15.4	12.1	13.0	n.a.	
Rural population density	Rural pop/ha arable land	52	32	475	554	134	201	492	41%
Fertilizer consumption	100 g/ha of arable land	1302	2777	1008	119	654	1172	136	862%
GDP/unit of energy	2000 PPP $/kg oil eqv.	6.9	1.9	5.3	4.5	3.9	4.5	4.7	96%
Energy use / capita (a)	kg petroleum equivalent	1,065	4,424	520	1,094	2,587	1,066	1,734	61%
Electricity consumption / capita (a)	kWh / yr	1,883	5,480	435	1,379	4,504	1,309	2,456	53%
Electricity generated by coal	%	2%	19%	68%	79%	93%	52%	40%	131%
CO_2 emissions / GDP	kg / 2000 PPP $ of GDP	0.2	1.4	0.5	0.6	0.8	0.7	0.5	140%
CO_2 emissions / capita (a)	tons	1.8	9.8	1.2	2.7	7.6	2.5	3.9	64%
Gross savings	% of Gross National Income	24%	32%	23%	42%	15%	27%	21%	131%

Sources: [6]; [7] (HDI); [8]. Notes: BRICS average weighted by: (a) population; (b) GDP; (c) land area. The rest are simple averages of country indices.

to national debt service and retirement benefits in excess of contributions. Investments in education and research place greater emphasis on public higher education than on basic skills and vocational training, though this is now slowly shifting. The problem seems to be not so much the lack of resources as the inability to spend wisely.

Technical optimism persists as the primary excuse for continued devastation of remaining natural resources at the agrarian frontier: increased productivity will eventually make it unnecessary to continue expanding horizontally since there is already a vast area already cleared that is underutilized. But by the time such productivity enhancements are introduced, much remaining biodiversity and associated ecosystem functions will have been destroyed, thus threatening potential productivity elsewhere (up to 40% of rainfall that falls in the agro-industrial heartland of the central savannas may be thanks to climatic stabilization by the Amazon forest).

Brazil's parastatal petroleum enterprise Petrobras, one of Latin America's largest corporations, has successfully opened part of its gas and oil exploration to external investment and is now a net exporter of fossil fuels. Part of Brazil's energy independence is due to its early commitment to renewable liquid fuels and hydropower generation. This gives it a conceivable edge in the search for alternative energy models. But emissions from frontier burning overwhelm its energy and transport emissions by three to one [4]. Indeed, new and worrying demands for expansion in land resource utilization in Brazil have arisen from the demand for biofuels themselves. The supply of a mandated 2% of Brazil's own petroleum demand by 2008 is expected to require about an additional million hectares in oilseeds [5]. If Brazil not only expands domestic agroenergy sources but exports ethanol and biodiesel, concerns arise regarding the land degrading potential of this alternative energy path.

Russian Federation

Like Brazil, the Russian Federation is also blessed with an immense landmass, much of which is sparsely populated. With a total area over 17 million km^2, Russia is the largest country in the world. Total population is about 148 million people, of which 73% reside in urban places. Population density is 9 people per sq. km. Since the Brazilian Amazon is not easily habitable, and much of Siberia is similarly inhospitable, there are some similarities in the way the two countries have occupied their respective territories. Both have only 7% of their territories in areas considered arable, though Brazil's unutilized arable potential may be considerably greater. Russia and Brazil have also both faced uneven growth rates over the past two decades. But unlike Brazil, Russia's energy profile is strongly dependent on fossil fuels, making its carbon emissions profile more similar to that of the North.

Although forests cover a similar proportion of both countries, Russia has experienced a net increase in forest cover over recent years, while Brazil faces rampant deforestation.

Starting in 1989, the gross domestic product (GDP) of the Russian Soviet Federative Socialist Republic (RSFSR), and successor Russian Federation, declined continuously until 1997. The drop in output by century-end was about 42%—a far steeper fall than was recorded during the Great Depression in the United States in the early 1930s. Paradoxically, poverty in Russia was halved from 1999 to 2003 yet adult mortality is the highest of all countries in the European Region, and has increased dramatically over the past decade [7]. At least some of this mortality is probably due to a high rate of suicide and even higher rates of alcoholism.

The major exports of Russia are its natural resources – particularly hydrocarbons. Fish production and exports are also significant. In 2005 Russia was the world's 15th largest exporter with a little more than 2% of total merchandise trade, nearly half of which to the European Union [9], but is among the top 10 fish exporters. Russia is also the world's third largest energy consumer. In terms of CO_2 emissions intensity in relation to GDP, Russia far outstrips all other BRICS countries (see Table 1).

In summary, the changes that took place in Russia over the course of the past 15 years include first decline, and then growth in GDP, dramatically falling life expectancy, increased income differentiation, first reduced and then increased CO_2 emissions. These types of changes are related but require a multidimensional perspective for their comprehension and management.

India

On the Asian scene, India and China have reassumed their historical global dominance in generation of wealth, yet growth and prosperity have been differentiated within each country, primarily along an urban-rural divide, and along the coastal zones. At 1.05 billion, India is second only to China in population, but its per-capita GDP is only about one-third that of China (Table 1). With a considerably smaller landmass, population density is also high (475 persons/km² of arable land, and since much of the population resides in rural areas (72%), pressure on arable land is evident. Degradation of arable lands continues to constitute one of India's most serious environmental problems, while fertilizer consumption has increased by 20% in less than a decade [see Table 1].

Sectoral growth in India is concentrated in industry in services, while agriculture has stagnated. The opening of the national economy has flooded the domestic market with imports, increasing 20% over the last five years; exports are growing but at a slower pace. Investment is around 27% of GDP, although the country's latest development plan seeks to boost this rate to 35%.

India's continued dependence on coal for a high proportion of electricity generation remains a source of concern, although this share (68%) is still lower than that of China and South Africa. Investment in renewable or lower CO_2 emitting energy sources is the primary focus of India's engagement in the Clean Development Mechanism, in which several hundred projects have been approved, accounting for nearly 15% of Certified Emissions Reductions registered by the UNFCCC [10].

Due to Government's persistent efforts to preserve the natural resources, an assessment in 2001 estimated that total land area covered under different forests had been maintained at 20.6% [11]. Reserved and protected forests together account for 19% of the total land area, as a measure to maintain biological diversity.

India also seems to be on course in reducing population growth. For the first time, India has reached a stage where despite the growing base of population less people are added than the previous year, both in rural and urban areas [12].

At the same time, the population below the poverty line has been reduced. The Government of India estimates that poverty fell from 36% of the population in 1993/94 to 26% by the end of the decade [12]. The pace of decrease in poverty has been higher after the introduction of new economic policies in the 1990s.

Since independence in 1947, life expectancy has more than doubled, reaching 67 years in 2006 and literacy has more than quadrupled and reached about 65.6% in 2006 [13]. Over these years, economic growth has gradually accelerated, with per capita income rising at 1.5% annually until 1975, at 3% until 1993, and at 8% in the last three years [14]. These growth rates were achieved as part of a national economic planning process, in which growth targets are set. Infrastructure such as power, road, water, and sewerage, irrigation and railways are bottlenecks to attaining the Government set growth target.

Due to increased energy pricing, technology change and conservation efforts, energy use per $ GDP has declined consistently from about 36 kg oil equivalent in 1991-92 to about 32 kg oil equivalent in 2003-04 [14]

Urban systems are already under severe stress from extreme climate events due to unexpected extremes of precipitation, causing floods and ensuing environmental destruction. The traditional systems of urban drainage are unable to absorb severe downpours.

China

Similar to Brazil and Russia in the size and variability of its land area and biomes, China is an immense subcontinent of over 9.3 million km², whose population of nearly 1.3 billion is still primarily rural (62% in 2002), placing serious pressures on arable land (554 rural inhabitants/km²). Fertilizer use is substantially higher than other parts of Asia, but still on average far less than that of the other BRICS excluding South Africa. Rural-urban migration is often cited as a particularly troubling aspect of China's rapid growth trajectory: somewhere around 60 million people joined the ranks of the urban population in the 1995-2002 period. Rigorous population control has had a negligible effect on these migrations.

But probably the most troubling aspect of China's accelerated growth phenomenon is the composition of its energy production and the profile of its consumption patterns [15]. Most of the nation's electricity generation is reliant on coal-fired thermoelectric facilities. Hydroelectric potential is rapidly diminishing; where additional potential has been harnessed the loss of arable land and incremental pressures on rural population are controversial (e.g., the Three Gorges dam will displace 1.9 million people from the Yangtze River banks). Although technology permitted a decline in CO_2 emissions per capita from 1995-2000, the index returned to its 1995 level by 2005. The share of coal-fired electrical generation actually grew to over 79%. And while China still has a smaller number of cars per household than east Asia overall, vehicle demand is growing rapidly, compounding per capita greenhouse emissions.

China's voracious demand for raw materials has a far larger footprint than the country itself. Recent forays into Africa and Latin America to guarantee resource flows, and joint ventures in steel and cement manufacture multiply the impacts of the phenomenon. For this reason, China has become the primary focus of global CDM and related emissions reduction investment.

Even in the country's most energy-efficient area of Shanghai, energy consumption is far higher than that in the United States or Japan, for example. Urban sprawl in major population centers has taken on crisis proportions; investment demands for those in the suburbs are sapping resources available for the urban core. In consequence, China is facing water shortages as per capita water resources of 2,200 cubic meters, are only 31 percent of the world's average. Currently, about 400 out of the 660 Chinese cities lack water and 136 have reported severe water shortages [16].

South Africa

South Africa is a middle-income, emerging economy with an abundant supply of natural resources. Tourism and the extractive resources sectors combined contribute a third of South Africa's national income [17]. Well-developed financial, legal, communications, energy, and transport sectors; a stock exchange that ranks among the 10 largest in the world; and a modern infrastructure supporting an efficient distribution of goods to major urban centers throughout the region. However, growth has not been strong enough to lower South Africa's high unemployment rate, and daunting economic problems remain from the apartheid era - especially poverty and lack of economic empowerment among the disadvantaged groups.

South Africa has been referred to as a country of two economies, or, alternatively, a double-decker economy [18]. Thus, the country is in many ways a microcosm of the global human economy today. Depending on the poverty measure used, in 2003 between 45% and 55% of all South Africans lived under the poverty line of approximately US$2/day, and 82% of the population earned less than 67% of the average national income per capita [19].

About 70% of the poor live in rural areas and most of them depend on government remittances and grants for survival [20]. The country faces severe and pressing water scarcity: nearly all water available for human use (98.6%) is already appropriated [21]. Within this context of poverty being predominantly a rural phenomenon, access to water becomes an important livelihood concern. Only 24% of people in rural areas have access to piped water and only 15% have access to sanitation.

Common themes

The negative growth experience of Brazil and Russia suggests the need to be attentive not only to the possible effects of accelerated growth, but also to the pressures on natural resources occasioned by insufficient growth, as persistent poverty forces communities to reproduce production patterns that are unsustainable.

Furthermore, it is necessary to consider that many of the issues associated with sustainability cannot be resolved solely by national governments acting alone. Multilateral cooperation is essential. However, such cooperation should not imply that states be obliged to adopt institutional and regulatory models prevalent in advanced economies. Models cannot be simply transplanted without regard to local specificities. Key concepts for successful sustainable development policies are those of <u>ownership</u> (appropriation and protagonism in policy choice) and <u>empowerment</u> (the "agent" as central to the development process, as Sen [22] emphasizes).

The wealthier nations' contribution to this process should focus on technical and financial assistance, above all to facilitate environmental technology transfer to emerging nations. However, transfer alone is insufficient: "Georgescu-Roegen was unequivocal in asserting that residents of 'developed' nations must accept a lower standard of living if 'underdeveloped' countries are ever to escape poverty" [23].

Finally, growth in income alone is not a sufficient condition to promote sustainable development. Although increased income certainly augments economic opportunities for all, despite distributive imbalances. Martinez-Alier emphasizes that we must focus on the composition and qualitative aspects of the cake and not only on its size [24].

There is also an underlying need to de-link growth from resource depletion by focusing on unnecessary conversion of natural capital and the need for ecosystem restoration [25]. The longer term land requirements associated with increased demand for biofuels, and their potential impacts on settlement expansion at the Amazon frontier is an important example of the paradox between substitution of nonrenewable fuels and the land hungry character of biomass alternatives.

Institutional innovation by the BRICS

A number of questions emerge from criticism of the EKC hypothesis, regarding the potential for institutional innovation toward sustainability. The idea that exacerbation in material and energy demand may be avoided by borrowing from experience in the North is attractive, but those adaptations came in response to cultural change as well as shifts in relative factor prices. Innovations may very well be pushed along by increasing petroleum prices, but a thoroughgoing change will require that the comfort and status associated with personal vehicle autonomy be downplayed by society.

The BRICS have in some cases been proving ground for bold experiments in alternative development styles and governance approaches. The following sections describe some of these experiments, concluding with observations on their generalization and uptake by other nations.

Integrated development policies

Rather than segregating environmental concerns into specialized ministries whose role is primarily to license and monitor enterprises whose actions may harm the human or physical environment, some BRICS nations have begun to search for ways to better integrate these concerns into line agency responsibilities or overall development planning. At the same time, dialogue processes that engage economic actors and civil society representatives in debate and conflict resolution over regional development alternatives have been institutionalized as standard practice rather than an exception. China, India, Brazil and South Africa offer particular examples in this realm.

"New Development Strategy" in China

Institutional capacity building has led to recent changes in environmental governance structures in China, under this rubric. The new strategy has been promoted by the central government in a top-down approach, calling for a whole scale, coordinated sustainable development and humanity-centered approach. A circular-economy based industrialization process is also called for. The new strategy emphasizes innovation in approaches and modes of development, quality of growth, coordination of all sectors, and sustainability.

Narrowing the gap between rural and urban areas is another priority on the agenda of many local governments in 2006. Energy efficiency has begun to concern local governments in their new blueprints. In southwest China's Sichuan Province, the government's 2006 program calls for reducing the energy consumption per unit GDP by 4 percent.

China aims to reduce water usage by 69 billion cubic meters by 2010, according to the country's water conservation plan for the 2006-2010 period. According to the plan, mapped out by the National Development and Reform Commission, and the Ministries of Water Resources and Construction, China hopes to cut water consumption per unit GDP by 20 percent compared with 2005. The plan said that China would try to improve efficiency of water conservation by popularizing the use of water-saving facilities and technologies in agriculture, industry and everyday life. Instead of exploring water resources, China has begun to switch its focus to conservation, protection and proper distribution of water to ease water shortages and a possible water crisis amid its soaring economic growth. In Beijing, a water conservation campaign has helped the city save 100 million cubic meters of water per year, enough for 10,000 three-member families for four years, but well below the amount required for long-term sustainability [26].

Better natural resources governance in India

Better environment, recycling and waste management are now actively becoming issues at the planning stage. Government has engaged itself in the task of managing environmental issues by focusing on the development of important administrative tools and techniques, impact assessment, research and collection and dissemination of environmental information. Although it is perceived that economic progress along with adoption of social and environmental goals can lead to sustainable societies, it is equally clear that a mere increase in government expenditure will not be sufficient. Civil society and local communities will have to play a larger role. Massive capacity building not only at primary education level but spread of Information, Communication and Technology (ICT) empowers poor to take control of their livelihoods and markets for their products.

Mainstreaming environmental policy in Brazil

Cross-cutting policy making approaches undertaken through "transversal" planning engage the full spectrum of responsible sectors in building a response to regional development and environmental problems. Transversal approaches involve societal control and stakeholder participation as key to yielding sustainable solutions.

The planning processes adopted to reach transversal solutions involve firstly a broad-brush diagnosis of the problem at hand, from a multi-sectoral perspective. Agency constituents and stakeholder representatives form working groups to inform an officially designated interagency working group to identify possible responses and budgetary requirements. An immediate action plan is set in motion, and then closely monitored as it unfolds, leading to regular evaluation and adjustments as initial assumptions are tested in practice.

The most important aspects of this approach for policy effectiveness include: i) high-level government commitment; ii) flexibility to reallocate existing resources where necessary to meet incremental demands; and iii) capacity to quickly leverage partnerships to stimulate the flow of private sector and international resources, as well as technical support.

To date, transversal approaches have been adopted most notably in the structuring of integrated regional sustainable development plans for paving a road through a pristine corridor in the central Amazon region, for multistate river basin planning along the San Francisco River in the semi-arid Northeast, and in an interministerial plan to combat the continuing high rates of deforestation in the Brazilian Amazon. At an international level, the process has also been applied to biodiversity protection in the context of river basin management in the Amazon basin.

Accelerated and Shared Growth Initiative in South Africa

In its overarching goal to reduce poverty, South Africa has adopted a quest for accelerated economic growth. A specific national level growth initiative, called the Accelerated and Shared Growth Initiative of South Africa (ASGISA), aims to halve poverty by 2014, to attain and maintain an economic growth rate of 6%, to launch various major infrastructure projects (also motivated by the upcoming 2010 Soccer World Cup event), and to mainstream broad-based black economic empowerment (the official policy of government to involve more black people in the formal economy) [27].

Contradictory to stated government policies and objectives, however, over half of ASGISA's 11 provincial turnkey projects are extremely resource intensive. These projects include large-scale plantation forestry using exotic species, water intensive mining projects (especially platinum), a biofuel (biodiesel and bio-ethanol) project, and commercial irrigation farming and livestock schemes. These agricultural, livestock, and mining projects are all water and energy intensive, and require large areas of land, all of which compromise biodiversity and environmental conservation. They also have a limited poverty alleviation impact since they are all focussed on existing establishments with little access to new greenfields companies. A sustainable and workable solution has to be sought, through broader discussion of these projects among South African society.

Public-private partnerships

In recent years, specific user taxes, earmarked funds, retained earnings; tolls and private sector participation have played an important role in infrastructure development in India as well as other BRICS nations. Increasingly public-private partnerships (PPP) are developing in infrastructure, which was earlier limited primarily to the public sector. While PPP initiatives are multiplying among the BRICS, environmental and social safeguards are often not clearly established in the conditions for private sector involvement in such undertakings. This represents a challenge for which institutional oversight is clearly needed, while offering flexibility to avoid repelling investors.

In India's case, while stepping up public investment in infrastructure, the Government is actively engaged in setting an appropriate policy framework, which gives private sector adequate confidence and incentives to invest on a massive scale, but simultaneously keeps adequate checks and balances through transparency, competition and regulation.

In the 1990s Brazil engaged in a number of privatizations, notably of most state-owned public banks, major mining industries, energy and telecommunications services, although the pace of privatization slowed nearly to a standstill under the Lula administration. The order of the day is also now public-private partnership, but here as well the rules need to be clearly set out. The lack of explicit norms on the participation and guarantees of government toward such investments have led to continuing uncertainties and delay in implementation.

Despite a call for small-scale biofuel technologies so that small farmers can benefit, much fear exists that new demands for liquid fuels will reinforce the highly concentrated agribusiness model that has been followed in the 30 years in which Brazil has been engaged in fuel ethanol production. An innovative measure to counter this tendency is the adoption by government of a "social fuel label" provided to companies that refine biofuels from feedstocks purchased from small farmers under contract. Those who agree to do so receive tax breaks and credit subsidies.

Contrary to common knowledge, privatization is also well underway in many facets of China's economy. The growth of rural industry in China since 1978 was explosive, grounded in a system of Township-Village Enterprises (TVEs). By means of a combination of privatization, liberalization and fiscal decentralization, rural industrialization took off. Much of the groundwork for this explosive rural industrialization was laid during the Maoist era, but it has indeed blossomed since China embraced the market economy [28]. The privatization process begun in the mid-1990s was deep and fundamental. More than 50% of local government-owned firms have transferred their shares to the private sector, partially or completely [29].

Multicriteria sustainability assessment for Russia

Russia's fifty-year experiment with central planning was vanquished by its entry into global financial markets, leaving a far more chaotic and vulnerable system in its place. Yet some efforts are being made to resuscitate national capacity to plan for the future, with a more explicit incorporation of environmental quality and human well-being. The current economic revival offers new opportunities and presents new challenges for Russia's sustainable development.

Application of the UN Sustainable Development framework of indicators and sustainability assessment to Russia has begun, using multi-criteria evaluation methods [30]. The potential of several MCE methods for the sustainability analysis was evaluated. Incommensurability [31] and strong sustainability determined the choice of methods for the multi-criteria dynamic assessment of sustainability at the macro level. Incomparability of values – environmental, economic, and social goods cannot be substituted for each other in the condition of relative scarcity – suggest the need to analyze the trajectory of development from a multidimensional and dynamic perspective to be able to understand the system and processes involved.

The analysis shows that the choice of policy priorities explicitly affects the assessment results and determines the changes that are desired by the society.

More emphasis should be drawn to the elicitation of social preferences and democratic articulation of different interests within a society.

China: New Indices for Measurement of Sustainable Development

As part of its "New Development Strategy" (see 3.1.1, above), a significant change in institutions for environmental governance is underway in China. It is hoped through this process that GDP will be gradually excluded as a primary indicator of development by government. Natural resource and environmental costs will be taken into account in the green GDP system and in the performance assessment of governmental officials. This will shed light on government decision on the process of how decisions are made and who participates in these decisions. However, this change is still in the process and local environmental governance and institutional innovation is still very weak.

In the meantime, some development indices familiar to the general public are fading out from the local governments' development schemes. The industry added value, tertiary industry added value, retail sales volume, fixed assets investment, export trade volume, the value of used foreign investment, and the average life expectancy are all removed from the development program of Shanghai municipal government [26].

India and the Millennium Development Goals

The Millennium Development Goals (MDG) will contribute to streamlining and strengthening monitoring and enhancing accountability for sectoral agencies and ministries in relation to specific targets and indicators. Local government needs to proactively ensure the both women and men are fairly represented in the development and implementation of the MDG-linked local development strategy. If gender equality considerations are successfully incorporated into efforts to achieve the Goals, the MDG process will help serve to mainstream gender in a broader range of national programmes and policies than may previously have been possible.

Institutional innovations to restore natural capital

Although Brazil has by far the world's worst record on containing deforestation, it is refreshing to note the turnaround toward forest restoration underway in other BRICS countries. Whether forced to do so due to overwhelming indications that upland watersheds had lost their ability to regulate stormwater, or in response to growth in demand for wood, afforestation or reforestation is now fairly common. Successful tree planting may not however restore environmental services.

In South Africa, an extended public works program currently underway to restore critical natural capital is the "Working for Water" program. Unemployed people are provided with training and the opportunity to remove invasive alien vegetation. The concept has been expanded upon into areas such as the active restoration of indigenous vegetation areas and wetlands, although as yet it is on a very small scale. Such restoration activities provide direct employment and education opportunities and it leaves a lasting legacy.

In Gawula, for example, a remote rural and impoverished village in South Africa the only affordable form of energy is that of fuelwood. The unsustainable harvest of fuelwood has lead to widespread and serious environmental degradation to the point that the increasing lack of the resource has increased the community's vulnerability to adverse climatic conditions and a reduced ability to prepare food. This has given rise to an ecological restoration programme, called ARISE [32]. Restoration has increased the stock of natural capital and it provides much needed employment opportunities (approximately 250 direct jobs in total) in an area where the unemployment figure is as high as 90%.

In India, common property wastelands that were previously subject to unsustainable harvest have been gradually allowed to regenerate through natural succession, where management responsibility and the goods and services that flow from forests has been vested in local communities. Such approaches toward collaborative public-community wasteland regeneration and management have now become widespread [33].

Although considerable efforts are underway to restore degraded forests, burgeoning populations continue to place pressure on these resources for agricultural expansion, fuel and timber. International cooperation has been modest, complicated by concern for sovereignty. The Kyoto Protocol holds out the prospect that forest restoration in lands already deforested or never forested may be compensated by carbon markets, but as yet is silent on how to protect standing forests from destruction. Brazil, whose deforestation and burning contributes 75% of the greenhouse gases it emits, has now proposed that its good faith efforts to reduce deforestation in standing forests such as the Amazon be rewarded by voluntary contributions [34].

Conclusions

Innovation and governance offer avenues for emerging nations to face the challenges of sustainability within the context of rapid economic change, but do not counter the underlying paradox that makes growth fundamentally unsustainable. Political will to face the difficult choices associated with resource conserving restraint is seldom available, except perhaps in the face of major natural disaster or looming man-induced catastrophe. Even when environmental problems assume a global dimension, however, innovative attempts are often stymied by hidden agendas that impede progress to reach common goals.

The experience of the BRICS countries suggests that imaginative solutions may be promoted as a means to avoid "overshoot" in resource consumption. For this to occur, opportunities for South-South interchange are needed to find pathways to "tunnel under" the EKC. This will require, in turn, the help of propitious international terms of trade and institutional arrangements, costless and smooth technology transfers and above all, societies willing to forego current consumption for future social benefit and environmental quality.

Acknowledgments

The author acknowledges substantive contributions from each of the BRICS panelists at the December 2006 biennial conference of the International Society for Ecological Economics in Delhi, India, including James Blignaut (University of Pretoria, South Africa), Zhu Dajain (Tongji University, Shanghai, China), Jyoti Parikh, (Integrated Research and Action for Development, Delhi, India), Ademar Romeiro (University of Campinas, São Paulo, Brazil), Stanislav Shmelev (Open University, UK, and RSEE, Russia), and Luciana Togeiro de Almeida (State University of São Paulo, Brazil). A version of the paper was also presented at the 2007 biennial conference of the United States Society for Ecological Economics (USSEE) in New York City.

References

Aronson, J., Milton, S. and Blignaut, J. (Eds.). *Restoring natural capital: Science, business and practice.* Island Press, Washington D.C., 2007.

Bramall, C. *The Industrialization of Rural China*, Oxford University Press, 2007.

Brasil. Ministry of Science and Technology. *Carbon dioxide emissions and removals from forest conversion and abandonment of managed lands.* Brasília, 2004.

China. Changes in blueprints reflect new development strategy in China. *Peoples Daily Online.* January 18, 2006.

China. Ministry of Land and Resources. Report on groundwater resources, 2003.

Chomitz, K. At Loggerheads? Agricultural expansion, poverty reduction, and environment in the tropical forests. The World Bank, Washington, D.C., 2007

CIA. *The World Factbook*, 2006.

Clewell A.F. and Aronson J. Motivations for the restoration of ecosystems. *Conservation Biology* 20(2), 2006, 420-428.

Department of Water Affairs and Forestry (DWAF). *National Water Resource Strategy.* DWAF, Pretoria, 2004.

Government of India. *Census of India*, 2001.

Government of India. *Economic Survey*, 2006-2007.

Gowdy, J. and Mesner, S. The evolution of Georgescu-Roegen's bioeconomics *Review of Social Economy* 61 (2), 1998, 136-156.

Grumbine, E. China's emergence and the prospects for global sustainability. *Bioscience,* 57 (3) March 2007, 249-255.

Hassan, R. and Blignaut, J.N. Policies and practices for financing sustainable development and environmental management in South Africa. University of Pretoria: CEEPA Discussion Paper No. 6, 2002.

Hongbin, L and Rozelle, S. Saving or stripping rural industry: an analysis of privatization and efficiency in China, *Agricultural Economics* 23 (3), 2000, 241-252.

India, Planning Commission. *10th Five-year Plan: 2002-2007*, 2002.

Martinez-Alier, J. Opening remarks, 9th Biennial Conference of the International Society for Ecological Economics, Delhi, India, December, 2006.

Martinez-Alier, J. Munda, G. and O'Neill, J. Weak comparability of values as a foundation of ecological economics, *Ecological Economics* 26, 1998, 277-286.

Munasinghe, M. Is environmental degradation an inevitable consequence of economic growth: tunneling through the environmental Kuznets curve. *Ecological Economics*, 29, 1999, 89-109.

National Remote Sensing Agency (NRSA). 2001 forest inventory.

Poffenberger, M. and McGean, B. *Village Voices Forest Choices Joint Forest Management in India*. Oxford University Press, Oxford, UK, 1998.

Romeiro, A. Biofuels in Brazil: a prospective option against deforestation, income concentration and regional disparities. Research report to Netherlands Environmental Assessment Agency, 2006.

Schmelev, S. Environmental, economic and social aspects of the development of modern Russia: a multidimensional analysis of sustainability. *Proceedings*, 9th Biennial Conference of the International Society for Ecological Economics, Delhi, India, December 2006.

Schreiner, B. and Van Koppen, B. Catchment management agencies for poverty eradication in South Africa. *Physics and Chemistry of the Earth* 27, 2002, 969–76.

Sen, A. *Development as Freedom*. Oxford University Press, Oxford, UK, 1999.

South Africa. Accelerated and Shared Growth and Initiative of South Africa. The Presidency, Pretoria, 2006.

Southern Africa Regional Poverty Network (SARPN). 2003. Poverty indicators.

Sparks, A. Beyond the Miracle. *Inside the New South Africa*. Jonathan Ball, Cape Town, 2003.

Special issue on the Environmental Kuznets Curve. *Environment and Development Economics* 2 (4), 1997, 357-515.

UNDP. *Human Development Report,* 2006.

UNFCCC. Amount of annual average certified emissions reductions registered by host party. Accessed July 31, 2007.

Wilson, D.; Purushothaman, R. Dreaming with BRICs: the path to 2050. *Goldman Sachs Global Economics Paper* No. 99, October, 2003.

World Bank, *Little Green Data Book*, 2006.

WTO. Trade statistics country profiles. Russia. 2005.

14 Structural Challenges to Preventing Transmission of HIV/AIDS in the Niger Delta of Nigeria

Isidore A. Udoh, Joanne E. Mantell, and Theo Sandfort

ABSTRACT

The high prevalence HIV/AIDS in Nigeria has exacerbated the crisis of health care management and public health administration in the country. Ironically, the Niger Delta region, Nigeria's poorest region, which produces its oil wealth, is the most affected by the epidemic. Analysts and commentators have attributed the high vulnerability to HIV in the region to a number of social determinants of health inequalities, including high-risk sexual relationships and practices, multiple sexual partnerships, lack of a normative condom use culture, and gender inequality. They reiterate that these health determinants constitute acute and ambient stressors that weaken the nervous and immune systems and expose people to the risk of HIV infection in the region. This paper argues that key structural factors, including national and regional instability and negative effects of oil production, and poverty, exacerbate HIV/AIDS transmission and complicate its prevention and treatment in the Niger Delta. The goal of this paper is to briefly examine how the confluence of these structural factors creates a pattern of injustice and makes the region vulnerable to the HIV epidemic.

Keywords: HIV and Nigeria; Niger Delta; Oil and HIV/AIDS; HIV Prevention; Structural Factors and AIDS; Health inequalities/disparities and HIV/AIDS

Introduction

With its vast endowment of natural resources, including petroleum, Nigeria has enormous potential for economic growth and development (EIA, 2007). In spite of this economic potential, UNDP has classified Nigeria as one of the twenty poorest countries of the world (UNDP, 2006). Nigeria has a GDP per capita of 1,154, a human development value of 0.448, a human poverty index of 40.6, and Nigerians have an estimated life expectancy of 43.4 years at birth. The probability of Nigerians surviving past 40 years of age is 54%, while 52% lack access to clean water sources (UNDP, 2006a). This bleak human development assessment has been attributed to a chronic crisis of leadership and endemic corruption issues (Vaughan, 1995; Ukiwo, 2003). The successive impositions of military regimes since the country's independence in 1960 has led to a chaotic and shifting policy culture, which has burdened Nigeria with an unhealthy economy and social infrastructures that inadequately meet the needs of its estimated 131 million population (Nwagwu, 1997).

Within the last decade, the HIV/AIDS epidemic and the crisis of health care management have added to the myriad of problems, creating a major public health concern in the country. The World Health Organization (2007), UNODC (2007), and UNAIDS (2006) reports suggest that after South Africa, Nigeria currently has the second largest absolute number of people (nearly three million adults) living with HIV/AIDS in the world today; and almost two million children have been orphaned as a result of the epidemic (UNODC, 2007; WHO, 2007; FHI, 2005). Estimates of HIV/AIDS prevalence in Nigeria increased from 1.8% in 1991 to 5.8% in 2001 and leveled off at 3.9% among all adults (aged 15 to 49) and 4.4% among adult women aged 15–49 years at the end of 2005 (UNAIDS, 2006; NASCP, 2006; NASCP, 2005).

As alarming as this situation may sound, the severity of the burden of HIV/AIDS is not equally shared across all six geopolitical zones in Nigeria. Ironically, the Niger Delta region, known as the South-South zone, the source of Nigeria's oil wealth, bears the greatest burden of the epidemic. This region is also noted to be the poorest in Nigeria, lacking even the most basic social infrastructures that could provide education and skills for prevention against viral infections such as HIV (UNDP, 2006; Jike, 2004).

The crisis of the HIV/AIDS epidemic in the Niger Delta is a critical public health issue that requires urgent intervention. Indeed, it is in the interest of Nigeria's economic viability and world energy security to ensure that this region is supported to combat an epidemic which threatens communities from which migrant oil and gas workers are drawn (UNDP, 2006). This paper argues that to combat HIV/AIDS in the Niger Delta, key structural factors, including the intersection of national and regional instability, negative effects of oil exploration, and poverty, which create multiple vulnerabilities and exacerbate the epidemic in the region need to be addressed. Here, we examine how these structural factors exacerbate the transmission and complicate the prevention and treatment of HIV/AIDS in the Niger Delta.

Structural Factors in the Niger Delta

National and regional instability. Nigeria is a tenuous mosaic of more than 250 ethnic groups. Being one of the most diverse societies in Africa, in the last four decades since independence, Nigeria has been searching for a formula for unifying its diverse ethno-cultural groups around a stable and enduring political entity. The search for this elusive formula has resulted in the creation of 36 states and 774 local government areas from formerly powerful provincial blocks and the strengthening of the central government (NASCP, 2005). Yet

Nigeria remains essentially unstable and embroiled in ethno-religious conflicts that threaten its fragile national cohesiveness (Nwagwu, 1997).

In a recent report, for example, Foreign Policy (2007), published by the Washington DC-based Carnegie Endowment for International Peace, ranked Nigeria as seventeenth among 60 most unstable countries in the world, with it registering high scores on key instability indicators, including group grievance, delegitimization of state, heavy-handed security apparatus, factionalized elites, and uneven development. The search for national unity and stability is not made any easier by Nigeria's reputation as a corrupt and wasteful country where the vast majority of the citizens live below the poverty line (UNDP, 2006a; 2006b) The perception of government by the citizens as uncaring, neglectful, and corrupt, and the grievance over perceived regional exclusion from oil wealth fuel the current socio-economic disruptions in the Niger Delta. Omeje (2005) and Akpan (2006) also attribute the conflict and instability to what they describe as oil companies' indiscriminate and cavalier system of land expropriation from local communities for exploration purposes without adequate consultation and compensation; this land expropriation has been backed by the Land Use Act through the absolute power of eminent domain, which cannot be challenged in any court in Nigeria. In the absence of meaningful channels of recourse, community frustration is expressed in protest activities. The tendency of the Nigerian government and oil companies to use force or bribery to repress dissent or silence critics rather than through negotiation has forced some in the region to resort to armed struggle.

Oil exploration. Since oil was first discovered in the Niger Delta in 1956, Nigeria has developed its production capacity from 5,100 barrels per day in 1958 to an average of 2.45 million barrels per day in 2006. As the largest producer of oil and natural gas in Africa, Nigeria is believed to have had about 36.2 billion barrels of proven oil reserves as of January 2007 and plans to expand to 40 billion barrels by 2010. In January 2007, its proven holding of natural gas reserves was estimated at 182 trillion cubic feet, making Nigeria the sixth largest natural gas reserve holder in the world. Currently, oil accounts for 95% of Nigeria's export earnings, 80% of federal revenue, and 40% of GDP (EIA, 2007; UNDP, 2006b; Ile & Akukwe, 2001; Okonmah, 1997; Ajomo, 1987).

Since the majority of Nigeria's oil and gas is extracted from the Niger Delta, this region is therefore strategic and critical to the economic viability and political stability of the country. One may be ask: how does this wealth in oil and gas improve the economic and social well-being of the Niger Delta people? Does it help or impede the development of social infrastructures in the region? Does it promote or hinder the health of the citizens? Researchers and analysts generally conclude that although it has created monumental wealth for multinational oil companies and the elites who rule in Nigeria, oil exploration in the Niger Delta has more negative than positive socio-economic and health outcomes for the Niger Delta people (UNDP, 2006b; Akpan, 2006; Aaron, 2005; Frynas, 2005; Ite,

2005; Watts, 2005; Omeje, 2005; Human Rights Watch, 2002; Ikelegbe, 2001; Human Rights Watch, 1999; Ile & Akukwe, 2001; Okonmah, 1997).

Pollution has been indicted as the most potent direct outcome of oil exploration which has the direst impact on the environment and health of the people who live in the oil-producing areas. Although some argue that pollution may not be totally avoided in this context (Etikerentse, 1985), others believe that the frequency and volume of oil spills in the Niger Delta may be enabled and exacerbated by the Nigerian government's policies and enforcement mechanisms with respect to regulating oil industry business practices (Aprioku, 1999; Okonmah, 1997). Oil spill fires and gas flaring have been noted to produce high levels of carbon dioxide, which in turn, are believed to cause respiratory problems, rashes, and cancers (Aprioku, 1999; Okonmah, 1997). Toxic waste dumping in water and on land in the region has been associated with killing fish, crabs, and birds, affecting agriculture, and triggering widespread economic insolvency in the region. These factors lead to unemployment, food scarcity, hunger and malnourishment, and deepening health disparities (Chokor, 2004; USAID-Nigeria, 2003).

Poverty. The Niger Delta covers an area of about 12, 428 square miles, 3, 728.4 of which is mangrove forest (Human Rights Watch, 1999; Ofonagoro, 1979). This delta is the largest wetland in Africa, with a high biodiversity of unique species of plants and animals. It is also home to more than 20 million people. Nearly 80% of working-age and able adults, comprising almost two-thirds females, are employed in the largely subsistent agricultural and commercial fishing sectors (CWIQ, 2003; Udonwa et al., 2004). Turner (2001) argues that the pollution of the Delta and damage to agriculture and fishing hurt women the most by destroying their main source of economic capital, diminishing their personal agency, as well as aggravating gender inequalities in the Niger Delta (Omorodion, 2000).

What constitutes poverty in Nigeria? According to the National Bureau of Statistics (NBS) (2006), incidence of poverty is assessed based on key indicators, such as inadequate access to government utilities and services, poor infrastructure due to surging population growth and rural-urban migration, effects of the environment on development, illiteracy and ignorance, insecurity, social and political exclusion, and poor health. The NBS claims that poverty has indeed declined in many parts of southern Nigeria, including the Niger Delta. The NBS suggests that reductions in poverty can be achieved by implementing the government's National Economic Empowerment and Development Strategy (NEEDS) as the medium-term framework for creating wealth and employment, re-orienting the value, and rolling back government's role at the local, state, and federal levels in favor of market forces.

Interestingly, not everyone shares the upbeat assessment made by the NBS. For example, the UNDP Niger Delta report (2006) questions the accuracy of the NBS poverty estimates in the Niger Delta and argues that the assessment of poverty in this region must consider unique local characteristics, such as higher price regimes for goods and services due to oil production, which diminishes local citizens' purchasing power. Similarly, Geo-Jaja and Azaiki (2007) reject the NEEDS framework for alleviating poverty in the Niger Delta because the region is disadvantaged relative to the rest of Nigeria due to the damage to its ecosystem by oil production. Rather, they suggest a broader and stronger state involvement in mobilizing resources for economic empowerment and sustainable development in the region. We argue that there are pros and cons to broader and greater Nigerian government involvement which may not necessarily help the economic development of the Niger Delta. The important question is how specific structural factors – national and regional instability, oil exploration, and poverty – contribute to health inequalities in the Niger Delta and increase citizens' risk of transmitting and acquiring HIV.

The Nexus of Structural Factors and Vulnerability to HIV/AIDS

The association of socioeconomic status, environmental and cultural variables with morbidity and mortality has been widely researched and established in parts of the industrialized world. A number of studies, for example, have found strong associations between increases in income with increases in life expectancy (Marmot, 2006; Wilkinson, 1992), between income inequality and poverty with mortality (Fiscella & Franks, 1997), and between social class and morbidity (Marmot et al., 1991). Similarly, changes in the social environment and relationships have been associated with changes in the causation and rates of diseases (Marmot, 2006). Wallace and Wallace (1997) found that vulnerability to infectious diseases in key United States cities was driven by economic marginalization, which breeds community disintegration and fragmentation of social networks. House (1987:136) reiterates that social structures, networks and support "can reduce morbidity and mortality, lessen exposure to psychosocial stress and perhaps other health hazards, and buffer the impact of stress on health."

Link and colleagues (1998) offer two explanations for understanding the relationship of socioeconomic status to disease outcomes. The first of these, the hierarchy-stress explanation, assumes that where one resides in the socioeconomic hierarchy affects the nervous and immune systems, which control vulnerability to disease. How does this happen? Geronimus and Thompson (2004) further elucidate that a population exposed to 'weathering', or more frequent experiences with social and economic adversities, such as conflicts, hunger, poverty, environmental pollution, or infection, cope with such acute stressors by temporarily activating an allostatic response which ejects stress hormones into the body to deal with the threat. However, when the stressors are either chronic or ambient, the body stays permanently alerted and the allostatic system remains constantly activated, resulting in overexposure and, possibly, damage to the cardiovascular, metabolic, and immune systems. This may result in accelerated aging as well as susceptibility to infection (McEwen, 1998).

The "fundamental cause" explanation proposed by Link and colleagues (1998) states that socioeconomic "patterns in exposure to risks and protective factors and SES patterns in morbidity and mortality will change when there are historical shifts in the profile of diseases, treatment, risk factors, and knowledge thereof." (p. 377). Thus, as knowledge and technology become available, people of higher SES are better equipped to procure protection against diseases. Whereas the hierarchy-stress explanation provides a context for understanding the patterns of HIV transmission, the fundamental cause explanation provides a comparable context and theoretical underpinning for understanding the economy of HIV prevention and AIDS treatment in resource-limited environments such as the Niger Delta.

Effects of Structural Factors on HIV/AIDS Transmission

National and regional instability. The conflicts raging in communities in the Niger Delta are intricately tied to the region's status as a sociopolitical minority in the Nigerian state. Consequently, it is often excluded from critical policy formulation and decision-making systems and processes that directly impact the region's environment, health and well-being. The approach to resource management in Nigeria, mired in secrecy and tribal networking, assures that the wealth extracted from the region is not applied toward creating social infrastructures or developing healthy coping interventions to lessen exposure to psychosocial stress, immune deficiencies, and vulnerability to HIV (Aaron, 2005). This dynamic constitutes the sociopolitical context for understanding the particular susceptibility of the Niger Delta region to HIV transmission in Nigeria.

Oil exploration. Oil spills, gas flaring, acid rains and exposure to sulphur-saturated hydrocarbon and carcinogenic chemicals, and other forms of pollution (Okonmah, 1997) have an enormous corrosive impact on the human habitat. This environmental situation generates chronic and ambient stressors that overexpose the citizens of the Niger Delta to stress hormones and "allostatic load" that cause weathering and a progressive depreciation of the nervous and immune systems, resulting in vulnerability to a variety of stress-related diseases and viral infections, including HIV/AIDS (McEwen, 1998; Geronimus & Thompson, 2004). As the effects of population growth and pollution on the agriculture and fishing-based rural economy limit opportunities for gainful employment in the rural areas, men and boys migrate to urban centers where they seek employment in the oil or service sector. Away from their wives and families, these men patronize commercial sex workers, become infected with HIV, and return to their villages where they may transmit HIV to their wives and other sexual partners (Alubo et al., 2002; Odulana & Olomajeye, 1999).

Poverty. The decline of agriculture and fishing is partly attributed to population growth and environmental degradation (Aaron, 2005). The shock to community cohesiveness and the disruption of the extended family and lineage support systems resulting from the loss of livelihood create conditions of high poverty. In this context, resources are concentrated in very few hands, often with the privileged who work for the oil industry or government. The demand by migrant oil workers, separated from spouses and family support, for sexual partners supports a thriving sex industry in the region (Omorodion, 2004). Unemployed youth and impoverished women, driven primarily by survival needs, resort to desperate measures, including commercial sex work, multiple sexual partnerships, and other high-risk sexual practices (Omorodion, 2006; 2000). They provide unprotected heterosexual and homosexual sex to migrant male oil workers, who have the money to pay for the services of multiple sexual partners (Nwauche & Akani, 2006a; 2006b). In addition, the less than enthusiastic condom promotion policy as well as lack of regulation of commercial sex work and sexual and reproductive health education in spite of the changing sexual culture, ensure that the acquisition of HIV is a predictable outcome for many people in the region.

Effects of Structural Factors on HIV/AIDS Prevention and Treatment

The cumulative effects of the structural factors discussed in the paper present serious challenges to preventing HIV/AIDS transmission as well as treating those living with HIV/AIDS in the Niger Delta. These factors affect the allocation and management of resources, creation of healthy environmental conditions for effective prevention, treatment, and care, and access to sexual and reproductive services.

National and regional instability. Conflicts complicate HIV/AIDS prevention and treatment efforts in the Niger Delta. When resources such as HIV education and treatment centers are allocated based on tribal interests, and not on fairness and need, sections of the country, such as the Niger Delta region, are deprived of health infrastructures and programs that they need for HIV education, testing. and treatment. Corruption and mismanagement divert scarce dedicated resources to uses other than the promotion of sexual and reproductive health education, HIV prevention, treatment and care. When funds are misused, health care workers may go for months without pay. This situation forces them to embark on strike actions, which often disrupts the treatment of HIV+ people on antiretroviral medications, posing a risk of non-adherence and viral drug resistance (Nwauche et al., 2006).

Oil exploration. The most obvious results of the damage to farming and fishing by oil-related pollution is reduced food yield and nutritional sources, scarcity, hunger, and malnourishment. This trend weakens immunity, complicates the management of AIDS-related opportunistic infections, and places a tremendous strain on the already under-resourced health care system. The high-risk sexual behavior of migrant oil workers can potentially lead to re-infection for people living with HIV/AIDS (Nwauche & Akani, 2006a; 2006b; Omorodion, 2004). This may create a society of many chronically ill people needing constant care and result in a huge death toll and the ballooning of the number of AIDS-related orphans, burdening the extended family and lineage systems and government.

Poverty. In the Niger Delta, material lack affects mobility. Often, individuals who are screened in remote rural clinics and referred to urban-based hospitals for HIV testing and treatment are unable to afford the cost of transportation. This results in unnecessary suffering and preventable loss of lives. Limited or inadequate knowledge of HIV transmission routes or protection methods and the inability to translate high HIV awareness into sexual risk-reduction behavior pose serious HIV prevention challenges in the region (Akani & Akani, 2006; Aisien & Shobowale, 2005). Unprotected sex resulting from lack of access to sexual and reproductive information or condoms creates the risk of co-infection with other sexually transmitted diseases, such as hepatitis B or C, and complicates the management of AIDS (Ejele et al., 2004; Ejele et al., 2005). This is an illustration of the fundamental cause explanation provided by Link et al (1998) regarding the association of socioeconomic status with morbidity and mortality, even in the context of HIV/AIDS management.

Conclusions

This paper has argued that national and regional instability, negative oil production effects, and poverty create health inequalities that are likely to exacerbate HIV transmission and complicate its prevention and treatment in the Niger Delta. Reduction in health inequalities and HIV incidence in this region is an ethical and moral imperative -- vulnerability to HIV/AIDS in the Niger Delta is itself a result of an unjust distribution of the burden of economic production that is supposedly beneficial to the entire country (Woodward & Kawachi, 2000). In addition, legal analysts insist that health is a requirement of justice because it is enshrined in most countries' constitutions, including Nigeria's body of law, as a right (Okonmah, 1997).

John Rawls (1971) argues that justice demands that primary goods be more equitably distributed based on a "fair equality of opportunity." Variations of applications of the Rawls' theory to the social determinants of public health have suggested the flattening of socio-economic gradient in a more egalitarian manner to assure that life opportunities, such as education, housing, income, and other key social security indices, are more equitably distributed. Daniels and colleagues (2000) reiterate that the way to eliminate the most critical injustices in health outcomes, in accordance with the basic tenets of the Rawlsian theory, is by "establishing equal liberties, robustly equal opportunity, a fair distribution of resources, and support for our self-respect." (http://bostonreview.net/BR25.1/daniels.html).

While (2004) applauds some aspects of John Rawls' theory, she concurs with critics that a Rawlsian analysis of the social determinants of health is too far-reaching and advocates policy positions that are not evidence-based in public health. She believes that the theory of justice proposed by Amartya Sen is more suited for public health as it shifts emphasis from merely leveling of socioeconomic status to expanding human capabilities through increasing personal agency and freedoms beyond a limited focus on resources as propounded by Rawls.

These two ethical philosophical positions represent varied perspectives for addressing the crisis of HIV/AIDS in the Niger Delta. Both are important for mapping the path to justice for victims of environmental pollution in the region and all who are vulnerable to diseases and infections, including HIV/AIDS, due to the structural factors examined in this paper. In so far as their lives and social environment are impacted by oil production, poverty, national and regional instability, and other stress-generating activities in the region, the rights of those who become infected by HIV/AIDS in the region are being unjustly violated.

In this case, who has responsibility to remedy this injustice? Is it the Nigerian government, oil companies, or both? Or is it the individuals and communities whose rights have been unjustly violated? The structural factors identified earlier appear to have severely deprived individuals and communities of resources and diminished their personal or collective agency to the extent that they are not in a position to remedy their vulnerabilities without external support. Yet, neither the Nigerian government nor the oil companies appear to have the credibility to address these problems independently or jointly. As the UNDP (2006) observes, from 1946, prior to Nigeria's independence, to 1998, successive governments have set up commissions to address poverty and development challenges in the Niger Delta, but none of them have ever succeeded. This is due in part to the association of these efforts with "an income-centered development paradigm. Short-term and based on official convictions, they lacked essential civil society and grass-roots inputs or participation. They failed to be sufficiently far-reaching, longitudinal or symmetrical in scope and coverage to pursue the inclusive goals of human development. In most cases, traditional planning efforts amounted to ends in themselves and were either not implemented or, at best, largely unimplemented" (UNDP 2006: 11).

Similar intentions by oil companies to address development problems in the region have turned out to be largely public relations campaigns without any evidence of substantially accomplished development initiatives (Akpan, 2006; Ite, 2005; Frynas, 2005). An approach that may have some chance of success would be one based on sincere partnership among the government, oil companies, civil society, educational institutions, and other grassroots stakeholders in the region. The current initiative by oil companies to address HIV prevention and treatment in Bonny Island could prove to be an important baseline effort which potentially could be replicated in other parts of the region (Macilwain, 2007). To ensure that the successes made by such interventions are sustained, the social determinants of HIV transmission in the region, including measures of socioeconomic status and skills development, must be addressed concurrently and beyond any interventions.

References

Aaron, K. K. (2005). Perspective: Big oil, rural poverty, and environmental degradation in the Niger Delta of Nigeria. *Journal of Agricultural Safety and Health*, 11(2), 127–134.

Aisien, A. O., Shobowale, M. O. (2005). Health care workers' knowledge on HIV and AIDS: Universal precautions and attitude towards PLWHA in Benin-City, Nigeria. *Nigerian Journal of Clinical Practice, 8*(2), 74–82.

Ajomo, M. A. (1987). Law and changing policy in Nigeria's oil industry, in J. A. Omotola (ed.), "Law and Development", Lagos, 86.

Akani, C., & Akani, N. (2006). HIV awareness and traditional birth practice in the Niger Delta of Nigeria. *Tropical Doctor, 36*(4), 208–210.

Akpan, W. (2006). Between responsibility and rhetoric: some consequences of CSR practice in Nigeria's oil province. *Development South Africa*, 23(2), 223–240(8).

Alubo, O., Zwandor, A., Jolayemi, T., & Omudu, E. (2002). Acceptance and stigmatization of PLWA in Nigeria. *AIDS Care, 14*(1), 117–126.

Aprioku, I. M. (1999). Collective response to oil spill hazards in the eastern Niger Delta of Nigeria. *Journal of Environmental Planning and Management*, 42(3), 389–408.

Chokor, B. A. (2004). Perception and response to the challenge of poverty and environmental resource degradation in rural Nigeria: Case study from the Niger Delta. *Journal of Environmental Psychology, 24,* 305–318.

Core Welfare Indicators Questionnaire Survey CWIQ. (2003). Cross River state main report. Abuja, Nigeria: Federal Office of Statistics.

Daniels, N., Kennedy, B., & Kawachi, I. Justice is good for our health: How greater economic equality would promote public health. Retrieved September 16, 2007 from http://bostonreview.net/BR25.1/daniels.html

Doyal, L., & Pennell, I. (1981). The political economy of health. Boston: South End Press.

Ejele, O. A., Nwauche, C. A., Erhabor, O. (2004). The prevalence of hepatitis B surface antigenaemia in HIV positive patients in the Niger Delta, Nigeria. *Nigerian Journal of Medicine, 13*(2), 175–179.

Ejele, E., Osaro, E., & Chijioke, A. N. (2005). The prevalence of hepatitis C antibodies in patients with HIV infection in the Niger Delta of Nigeria. *Highland Medical Research Journal, 3*(1), 11–17.

Etikerentse, G. (1985). Nigerian petroleum law. London: Macmillian Publishers.

Family Health International (FHI) (2005). Country profile, Nigeria-GHAIN: Major challenges to combat HIV/AIDS. Retrieved September 19, 2007 from http://www.fhi.org/NR/rdonlyres/exxw7n5mrql4bf3rfd5wonkwwvx6w

uir2vj3ear2p4ufv4jngpuc3j6vr4qcx7msg7bthgelq2147p/Nigeria GHAINProfileWithShell.pdf

Fiscella, K., & Franks, P. (1997). Poverty or income inequality as predictor of mortality: Longitudinal cohort study. *British Medical Journal*, 314(1724), 1724–1727.

Foreign Policy. (2007). The failed states index 2007: The rankings. Retrieved on September 10, 2007 from http://www.foreignpolicy.com/story/cms.php?story_id=3865&page=7

Frynas, J. G. (2005). The false developmental promise of corporate social responsibility: Evidence from multinational companies. *International Affairs*, 81(3), 581–598.

Geo-Jaja, M. A., & Azaiki S. (2007). Poverty and inequality in the Niger Delta: Is national economic empowerment and development strategy (NEEDS) the answer? *Education Canadienne et Internationale*, 36(1), 75–92.

Geronimus, A. T., & Thompson, J. P. (2004). To denigrate, ignore, or disrupt: Racial inequality in health and the impact of a policy-induced breakdown of African American communities. *Du Bois Review*, 1(2), 247–279.

House, J. S. (1987). Social support and social structure. *Sociological Forum*, 2(1), 135–146.

Human Rights Watch. (1999). The price of oil: Corporate responsibility and human rights violations in Nigeria's oil producing communities. Retrieved June 4, 2007, from http://www.hrw.org/reports/1999/nigeria/Nigew991-01.htm

Human Rights Watch. (2002). The Niger Delta: No democratic dividend, summary. Retrieved June 4, 2007, from htttp://www.hrw.org/reports/2002/nigeria3/Nigeria1002.htm

Ikelegbe, A. (2001). Civil society, oil and conflict in the Niger Delta region of Nigeria: Rmifications of civil society for a regional resource struggle. *The Journal of Modern African Studies*, 39(3), 437–469.

Ile, & Akukwe, C. (2001). Niger Delta, Nigeria: Issues, challenges and opportunities for equitable development. Nigeria World Feature. Retrieved April 17, 2005, from http://nigeriaworld.com/articles/2000-2001/niger-delta.html

Ite, U. E. (2005). Poverty reduction in resource-rich developing countries: What have multinational corporations got to do with it? *Journal of International Development*, 17, 913–929.

Jike, V. T. (2004). Environmental degradation, social disequilibrium, and the dilemma of sustainable development in the Niger-Delta of Nigeria. *Journal of Black Studies*, 34(5), 686–701.

Link, B. G., Northridge, M. E., Phelan, J. C., & Ganz, M. L. (1998). Social epidemiology and the fundamental cause concept: On the structuring of effective cancer screens by socioeconomic status. *The Milbank Quarterly*, 76(3), 375–402.

Macilwain, C. (2007). On the brink. *Nature*, 445, 140–143.

Marmot, M. (2006). Harveian oration: Health in an unequal world. *The Lancet*, 368(9552), 2081–2094.

Marmot, M. G., Smith, G. D., Standsfeld, S., Patel, C., North, F., Head, J., White,

I., Brunner, E., & Feeney, A. (1991). Health inequalities among British civil servants: the Whitehall II study. *The Lancet*, 337(8754), 1387–1393.

McEwen, B. S. (1998). Protective and damaging effects of stress mediators. *New England Journal of Medicine*, 338, 171–179.

National AIDS Control Programme (NASCP) (2006). 2005 national HIV seroprevalence sentinel survey: Process findings. Abuja: Federal Ministry of Health. Retrieved September 19, 2007 from http://www.nigeria-aids.org/pdf/2005SentinelSurvey.pdf.

National AIDS Control Programme (NASCP) (2005). National health sector strategic plan for HIV & AIDS. Abuja: Federal Ministry of Health.

National Bureau of Statistics (NBS). (2006). Nigeria living standard survey. Retrieved September 15, 2007 from http://www.nigerianstat.gov.ng/nlss/2006/index.html

Nwagwu, C. C. (1997). The environment of crisis in the Nigerian education system. *Comparative Education*, 33(1), 87–95.

Nwauche, C. A., & Akani, C. I. (2006a). An assessment of high risk sexual behaviour and HIV transmission among migrant oil workers in the Niger Delta area of Nigeria. *Nigeria Journal of Clinical Practice, 9*(1), 48–51.

Nwauche, C. A., & Akani, C. I. (2006b). Homosexuality amongst migrant oil workers in the Niger Delta region of Nigeria. *Highland Medical Research Journal, 4*(1), 53–59.

Nwauche, C. A., Erhabor, O., Ejele, O. A., & Akani, C. I. (2006). Adherence to antiretroviral therapy among HIV-infected subjects in a resource-limited setting in the Niger Delta of Nigeria. *African Journal of Health Sciences, 13*(3-4), 13–17.

Odulana, J. A., & Olomajeye, J. A. (1999). The impact of government's alleviation of poverty program on the urban poor in Nigeria. *Journal of Black Studies, 29*(5), 695–705).

Ofonagoro, W. I. (1979). From traditional to British currency in southern Nigeria: Analysis of a currency revolution, 1880–1948. *The Journal of Economic History*, 39(3), 623–654.

Okonmah, P. D. (1997). Right to a clean environment: The case for the people of oil-producing communities in the Nigerian Delta. *Journal of African Law*, 41(1), 43–67.

Omeje, K. (2005). The rentier state: oil-related legislation and conflict in the Niger Delta, Nigeria analysis. *Conflict, Security and Development*, 6(2), 211–230.

Omorodion, F. I. (2006). Sexuality, lifestyles, and the lures of modernity: participatory rural appraisal (PRA) of female adolescents in the Niger Delta region of Nigeria. *Sexuality and Culture*, 10(2), 96–113.

Omorodion, F. I. (2004). The impact of petroleum refinery on the economic livelihoods of women in the Niger Delta region of Nigeria. *JENDA: A Journal of Culture and African Women Studies.* 6, 1–15.

Omorodion, F. I. (2000). Sexual and health behavior of commercial sex workers in Benin City, Edo state, Nigeria. *Health Care for Women International*, 21, 335–345.

Rawls, J. (1971). *A theory of justice.* Cambridge, MA: Harvard University Press.

Ruger, J. P. (2004). Ethics of the social determinants of health. *The Lancet,* 364(9439), 1092–1097.

Turner, T. E. (2001). The land is dead, women's rights as human rights: The case of the Ogbodo Shell petroleum spill in Rivers state, Nigeria, Retrieved June 4, 2005, from http://www.waado.org/Environment/OilCompanies/ States/Rivers/OgbuduSpill/TerisaTurner.html

Udonwa, N., Ekpo, M., Ekanem, I., Inem, V., & Etokidem, A. (2004). Oil doom and AIDS boom in the Niger Delta region of Nigeria. *Rural and Remote Health Journal,* 4, 273.

Ukiwo, U. (2003). Politics, ethno-religious conflicts and democratic consolidation in Nigeria. *Journal of Modern African Studies,* 41(1), 115–138.

UNAIDS. (2006). Report on the Global AIDS Epidemic. Geneva: UNAIDS.

UNDP. (2006a). Human development report 2006: Human development indicators, country fact sheet. Retrieved September 13, 2007 from http://hdr.undp. org/hdr2006/statistics/countries/country_fact_sheets/cty_fs_NGA.html

UNDP. (2006b). Niger Delta human development report. Abuja, Nigeria.

UNODC. (2007). Press release: 2.5 million people in India living with HIH, according to new estimates. Retrieved September 4, 2007 from http://www. unodc.org/india/article_unaids.html

U.S. Energy Information Administration. EIA. (2007). Country analysis briefs: Nigeria. Retrieved September 14 from http://www.eia.doe.gov/emeu/ cabs/Nigeria/pdf.pdf

USAID-Nigeria. (2003). Nigeria Food Security Assessment. RAISE IQC, Contract No. PCE-1-819-99-00003-00, Task No. 819, 2. Washington, DC: Chemonics International, Inc.

Vaughan, O. (1995). Assessing grassroots politics and community development in Nigeria. *African Affairs,* 94, 501–518.

Wallace, R., & Wallace, D. (1997). Socioeconomic determinants of health: Community marginalization and the diffusion of disease and disorder in the United States. *British Medical Journal,* 314(1341), 1341–5.

Watts, M. J. (2005). Righteous oil? Human rights, the oil complex, and corporate social responsibility. *Annual Review of Environment and Resources,* 30, 373–407.

WHO. (2007). 2.5 million people in India living with HIV, according to new estimates.Retrieved September 4, 2007 from http://www.who.int/media-centre/news/releases/2007/pr37/en/index.html

Wilkinson, R. G. (1992). Income distribution and life expectancy. *British Medical Journal,* 304,165–168.

Woodward, A., & Kawachi, I. (2000). Why reduce health inequalities? *Journal of Epidemiology and Community Health,* 54(12), 923–929.

15 Conceptualizing the Value of Ecosystem Services in Deserts

Robert B. Richardson

ABSTRACT

Most studies of the economic value of ecosystem services have overlooked the services provided by deserts. However, deserts perform important functions such as erosion control, and they provide ecosystem services such as biodiversity protection and recreation, which are particularly important in areas such as the southwestern United States where the scale of population growth, urban expansion, and motorized recreation threaten many desert species and intensify emissions of particulate matter. This paper considers the Mojave, Sonoran, and Great Basin Deserts of southeastern California, and presents a conceptual framework for the valuation of ecosystem services provided by these deserts. Unpaved roads are used heavily for motorized recreation, military base operations, and industrial activities such as mining. Increasing emissions of particulate matter have exacerbated already poor air quality and have led to increases in asthma, chronic lung disease, and infant mortality. Motorized recreation in this desert region is rapidly increasing in popularity, and most use occurs on federal lands; the scale of activity suggests important implications for efficiency in policy decisions such as recreation management and wilderness designation. Roads on federal lands account for half the unpaved road dust emitted in California, and the human health effects are much worse in counties with high population density, which implies that common resources of desert ecosystems may be unable to sustain rising levels of economic activity. The marginal benefits of erosion control alone are estimated at over $70 million per year for the California desert region.

Keywords: Ecosystem services; deserts; erosion control; wilderness.

Introduction

Ecosystem services are the conditions and processes through which natural ecosystems sustain and fulfill human life (Daily, 1997). Examples of ecosystem services include clean air and water (for both human health and economic security), essential support in producing renewable resources (such as agriculture and forest products), sequestration of carbon, and the absorption and treatment of waste matter. Clean air and water are vital in their support of human life. Also, one in four medicines and pharmaceuticals owes its origin to vital products of plant species, and another one in four to animals and microorganisms (Joyce, 1992). Wilderness and other natural areas play an important role in sustaining natural resources and providing ecosystem services that support human life (Odum, 1997). These areas provide high-quality undisturbed soil, water, and air, all of which are crucial to ecosystem health (Dombeck, 2002).

Deserts are frequently overlooked in studies of the economic value of ecosystem services, Research on the global values of ecosystem services has not identified any valuation studies for desert biomes (Sutton and Costanza, 2002; Costanza *et al.*, 1997). Still, desert environments provide numerous functions that "sustain and fulfill human life" and have measurable economic values. Important ecosystem services in deserts include erosion control, climate regulation, waste treatment, refugia, pollination, recreation, and cultural benefits (Jasoni *et al.*, 2005; Hastings *et al.*, 2005; Rosenstock *et al.*, 2005; Stabler *et al.*, 2005; Pellmyr and Segraves, 2003; Grijalva *et al.*, 2002; Shaw and Jakus, 1996; Simpson and Neff, 1987). A conceptual framework for the valuation of ecosystem services in deserts is presented here, followed by a discussion of several desert ecosystem services using protected areas in California as a case study for demonstration. A theoretical model for the valuation of erosion control in deserts is presented, along with a discussion of the public health and recreation dimensions. Other ecosystem services described in this analysis include recreation and habitat/refugia.

Deserts of the southwestern USA in particular are threatened by pressures of urban expansion, population growth, and increasing popularity of motorized recreation. Population growth in desert-proximate counties of the Southwest has exceeded that of the USA (U.S. Census Bureau, 2006), which has led to increases in construction, transportation, and recreation activities. The accompanying demands on soils, hydrological systems, air quality, flora, and fauna highlight the importance of understanding the importance of ecosystem functions in deserts. The valuation of ecosystem services in deserts has implications for natural resource management and land use policy, and is motivated by the importance of incorporating non-market values in land and resource allocation decisions. The importance for valuation of ecosystem services—particularly erosion control, nutrient cycling, stormwater control, recreation, and aesthetic value—is particularly relevant near urban areas where large human populations are proximate and environmental alteration has rendered natural capital scarce.

Deserts are mentioned in the ecosystem services literature primarily in the context of desertification and the loss or interruption of the flows of ecosystem services on degraded landscapes (Curtis, 2004; Limburg *et al.*, 2002). Deforestation and overgrazing have been associated with disturbances in hydrological cycles that lead to encroaching deserts, increased salinity, and erosion. Such degraded deserts are considered to provide the lowest levels of ecosystem services (Curtis, 2004). However, natural vegetation and soil crusts in deserts protect the important function of erosion control. Deserts serve as habitat for a diverse array of flora and fauna, including species of commercial importance such as the endangered desert pupfish and several varieties of cactus (Alary *et al.*, 2007; Hernández *et al.*, 2004). Desert bats, hummingbirds, and bees provide important pollination services for plants, including some commercial crops such as dates, almonds, alfalfa, olives, and sunflowers (Kremen *et al.*, 2007). Deserts also provide abundant recreation opportunities for wilderness visitors, rock climbers, and motorized recreation enthusiasts. Desert vegetation and soils provide climate regulation services by sequestering carbon that would otherwise contribute to climate change (Luo *et al.*, 2007; Housman *et al.*, 2006; Jasoni *et al.*, 2005), and by mitigating heat island effects through shading and evapotranspiration (Stabler *et al.*, 2005; McPherson, 2001; Grimmond *et al.*, 1996). Ants in deserts have been found to provide waste treatment and nutrient cycling services, particularly in areas where grazing occurs (Wagner and Jones, 2006). Some of these services are discussed below, following a description of a conceptual framework for valuation.

Conceptual Framework for the Value of Ecosystem Services in Deserts

The values of specific ecosystem services and the various methods for valuation are well-documented (Zhongmin *et al.*, 2003; Costanza *et al.*, 1997; Bockstael *et al.*, 1995; Aylward and Barbier, 1992). The economic value of ecosystem services may be conceptualized in a number of ways. Some services are associated with market goods that carry a price (*e.g.*, revealed preference), such as the value of habitat for fish in coral reefs or the value of climate regulation for agricultural production. Alternatively, people who benefit from ecosystem services can be directly asked what they would pay for these services using contingent valuation (*e.g.*, stated preference). Loomis *et al.* (2000) used this method to measure the economic value of restoring ecosystem services in an impaired river basin (2000). Indirect valuations may be used to measure society's willingness to pay for other services for which there is no market.

A more common approach to valuing ecological services is to calculate the cost savings (or costs avoided) from protecting the ecosystem's ability to continue providing the services (de Groot *et al.*, 2002; Farber *et al.*, 2002). Purer source water requires less treatment costs in the form of settling basins, sediment precipitators, etc. to municipal water treatment agencies and aquaculture producers (Moore and McCarl, 1987). The benefits of ecosystem service restoration may reflect the avoided costs of environmental damages from invasive species (Zavaleta, 2000). The value of controlling the invasive woody shrub Tamarisk in the arid western United States was calculated by considering the costs of flood damages and sedimentation; annual costs were estimated at nearly $7,500 per hectare. The cost savings approach also can be applied to the nutrient cycling and carbon storage properties of wilderness forests. Desert shrubs and woody plant species have been found to play an important role in climate modulation and regulation through the net CO2 exchange in arid and semi-arid ecosystems (Luo *et al.*, 2007; Jasoni *et al.*, 2005; Hastings *et al.*, 2005). In the case of carbon sequestration, marginal benefits can be understood as either the cost savings over the next cheapest storage option or the economic value of the emission generating activity if the emissions limitations become binding on a particular emitter.

Farber *et al.* (2002) describe six techniques for valuing ecosystem services, where no market value exists or where market values do not capture the total social benefit. These are avoided costs (where ecosystem services allow for the avoidance of costs that would have been incurred in the absence of the services), replacement costs (cost of replacement of service by restoration or manufactured capital), factor income (where services increase income), travel cost (where costs of travel can be used to elicit a demand curve for the service), hedonic pricing (where the service enhances the price of associated goods), and contingent valuation (where service value is obtained through stated-preference questions about hypothetical scenarios).

Ecosystem services have economic value since they are relatively scarce (Batabyal *et al.*, 2003) and can be shown to increase human well being (Farber *et al.*, 2002; Howarth and Farber, 2002; Costanza *et al.*, 1997). The services of ecological life-support systems could be considered as having infinite economic value, since the human economy is dependent upon their provision, but given their relative magnitude with variable human population density, economic production intensity, and other factors, estimates of *marginal* values of ecosystem services can be useful in order to better inform economic decisions and public policy (Balmford *et al.*, 2002, Farber *et al.*, 2006).

Table 1 describes eleven ecosystem services identified with desert environments, along with the valuation methods most appropriate for the services.

California desert region

The desert region of southeastern California includes parts of the Mojave, Sonoran, and Great Basin Deserts, which occur in the four-county region of Inyo, San Bernardino, Riverside, and Imperial Counties (see Figure 1). The California desert region is comprised of the Mojave, Great Basin, and Sonoran Desert ecosystems, and is one of the largest wild and undeveloped areas in the conterminous United States. The Mojave Desert is the smallest of the four North American deserts, but it is dominant in southeastern California. Its arid mountains and basins are surrounded by large urban centers with populations in the millions (Mettermeier *et al.*, 2002). Annual precipitation is highly variable—ranging from less than ten inches over most of the area to as high as around 65 inches—and the landscape is characterized by rough, unsettled terrain. The predominant vegetation is creosote shrub habitat, which supports a great diversity of plants and animals (Bury *et al.*, 1977).

Table 1 Conceptual framework for valuation of ecosystem services in deserts

Ecosystem Service	Description	Valuation Method
Climate regulation	Carbon sequestration in vegetation and soils; urban microclimate/heat island mitigation	Avoided costs; replacement costs; contingent valuation
Freshwater regulation and supply	Provision of fresh water by slowing evaporative loss, maintaining riparian aquifers	Avoided costs; replacement costs; travel costs; hedonic pricing; market values
Waste treatment	Decomposition of waste, *e.g.*, cow manure by ants where grazing occurs	Avoided costs; replacement costs; contingent valuation
Nutrient regulation	Provision of nutrients by perennial and ephemeral plants to otherwise low nutrient systems	Avoided costs; contingent valuation
Habitat/refugia	Value of commercially important species, existence value	Avoided costs; replacement costs; market values
Soil retention and formation	Slow soil formation; high value for erosion control, air quality, human health impacts	Avoided costs; replacement costs; contingent valuation; hedonic pricing; market values
Disturbance prevention	Reduction in flood peaks by desert areas	Avoided costs
Pollination	Pollination of commercially valuable crops by native pollinators	Replacement costs
Recreation	Use of desert for passive or active recreation	Travel costs; contingent valuation
Aesthetic	Increased value of real property near natural or scenic areas	Hedonic pricing; travel costs; contingent valuation;
Spiritual and historic	Natural and cultural heritage preservation, religious uses; likely to differ by culture and traditional uses of specific areas	Contingent valuation

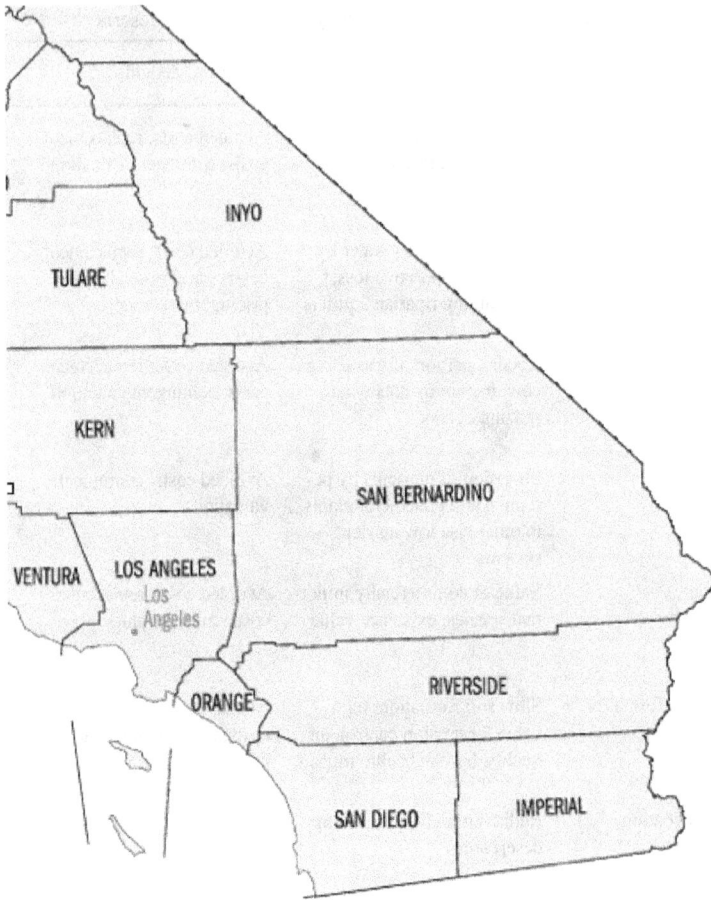

Figure 1 Map of Southern California

The region covers approximately 41,637 square miles (U.S. Census Bureau, 2006), and is dominated by several vast areas managed by the federal government. A few large military bases and weapons-testing sites in the area are managed by the Department of Defense. The Bureau of Land Management (BLM) manages over 10.7 million acres of desert and steppe lands in the region, of which more than three million acres is managed as wilderness (see Table 2).

Death Valley National Park, Mojave National Preserve, and Joshua Tree National Park are managed by the National Park Service (NPS), and are among the largest protected areas in the area (see Table 3). The National Park Service manages 5.5 million acres in the California desert, of which 4.4 million acres has been designated as wilderness.

Table 2 California desert BLM land by county

County	Total BLM Acres	BLM Wilderness Acres
Imperial	1,260,050	204,082
Inyo	1,789,326	764,004
Riverside	1,549,655	563,343
San Bernardino	6,174,135	1,651,990
TOTAL	10,773,166	3,030,712

Source: Bureau of Land Management

Wilderness areas are primarily roadless and are managed for non-motorized recreational uses. Many of the values of these areas were recognized by the California Desert Protection Act of 1994, which designated several national parks and wilderness areas in the California desert area for "the people of this and future generations" (CDPA, 1994). The Act stated that "these desert wildlands display scenic, historical, archaeological, environmental, ecological, wildlife, cultural, scientific, educational, and recreational values used and enjoyed by millions of Americans" (CDPA, 1994). The parks and wilderness areas in the region are interspersed among other federal lands, some of which are used for mining, cattle grazing, and agricultural uses while others are popular for off-road vehicle recreation.

Exclusive of urban centers, the population of the region is about 490,000, which translates to a density of about 6.1 people per square mile. Total population of the four-county region that includes Inyo, San Bernardino, Riverside, and Imperial Counties is approximately 4.2 million (U.S. Census, 2006). The metropolitan areas of Los Angeles and Las Vegas are within a short drive of most of the area, and urban and suburban sprawl from these areas have increased development pressures both within desert cities and on surrounding public lands.

Table 3 California desert NPS land by county

National Park	Total NPS Acres	NPS Wilderness Acres
Death Valley National Park	3,323,772	3,128,000
Joshua Tree National Park	768,886	557,802
Mojave National Preserve	1,460,304	695,200
TOTAL	5,552,962	4,381,002

Source: National Park Service

Table 4 California desert population by county

County	2006 population	1990-2000 growth	2000-2006 growth
Imperial	160,301	30.2%	12.6%
Inyo	17,980	-1.9%	0.2%
Riverside	2,026,803	32.0%	31.2%
San Bernardino	1,999,332	20.5%	17.0%
California desert region	4,204,416	23.1%	25.7%
California	36,457,549	7.6%	13.8%

Source: U.S. Census Bureau

Population growth in the region has outpaced the state average. Population growth for the four-county region is presented above in Table 4.

Population growth and urban expansion have strained natural resources and ecosystem services in this region and in desert communities across the southwestern United States; some of the fastest growing counties in the USA are located in or near desert environments. As population expands, the accompanying pressures on air quality, water quality, waste generation, and recreation carrying capacity exemplify the importance of considering the values of ecosystem services in land use policy decisions.

Erosion control in deserts

Natural vegetation and soil aeration protects desert soil from wind and water erosion. Soil stability and productivity often depend upon surface cryptogamic crusts that develop slowly over many dozens of years. These crusts are easily destroyed, and soil recovery is a slow process. In a study of soil recovery in the Mojave Desert region, Webb and Wilshire (1980) found that in an arid desert environment, soils disturbed by vehicle use may take centuries to recover. Road construction first strips away the surface layer; the use of roads then grinds desert soil into a fine dust powder that is extremely vulnerable to wind erosion. When such discrete particles become suspended in the air, they are known as particulate matter, a major source of air pollution associated with poor visibility and severe risks to human health. These tiny particles penetrate deep into human lungs and increase the risk of asthma and other health problems. Federal studies have found that high levels of particulate matter are associated with premature death, aggravated asthma, childhood respiratory problems, chronic bronchitis, haze, and visibility in national parks and wilderness areas (EPA, 1999). Woodruff *et al.* (1997) found a statistically significant relationship between particulate

Table 5 Particulate matter data for California desert air basins, 2003

PM_{10} Measurements	State Standard	Great Basin Valleys	Mojave Desert	Salton Sea	South Coast
Maximum 24-hour concentration ($\mu g/m^3$)	50	15,641	169	848	164
Maximum annual average ($\mu g/m^3$)	30	130.4	27.9	79.7	56.9
Calculated days above state 24-hour standard	n.a.	71	69	315	252

Source: California Air Resources Board

air pollution in the United States and post-neonatal infant mortality. A study of the effects of air pollution on children in southern California found that particulate matter can also retard the growth of children's lungs (Gauderman *et al.*, 2000). According to a report by the Natural Resources Defense Council, particulate pollution claims the lives of over 64,000 Americans every year (NRDC, 1996).

Federal and state air quality management agencies measure the levels of particulate matter with an aerodynamic diameter of 10 microns[1] or smaller (PM_{10}) and of 2.5 microns or smaller ($PM_{2.5}$). Air quality levels are measured in micrograms of particulate matter per cubic meter of air ($\mu g/m^3$). National standards indicate that levels of PM_{10} should not exceed 150 $\mu g/m^3$ more than once per year, or 50 $\mu g/m^3$ as annual arithmetic mean averaged over 3 years. State standards in California for PM_{10} are set at a maximum of 50 $\mu g/m^3$ in 24 hours, or 30 $\mu g/m^3$ as annual geometric mean. Even with its stricter measurement standards, the state of California ranks high among US states in terms of emissions of PM_{10} particulate matter (EWG, 1997). Air quality data for California desert air basins are presented below in Table 5. Air quality levels in the desert region are particularly poor—the Great Basin Valleys Air Basin (which includes parts of Inyo County) annual average PM_{10} concentration in 2003 was 130.4 $\mu g/m^3$; the Salton Sea Air Basin (which includes parts of Imperial and Riverside Counties) average was 79.7 $\mu g/m^3$; and the South Coast Air Basin (which includes parts of both Riverside and San Bernardino Counties) average is 56.9 $\mu g/m^3$. These three air basins have the highest annual values of PM_{10} concentration in the State, and the highest 24-hour concentrations occur where the problem of windblown dust is widespread. PM_{10} levels in the Salton Sea Air Basin exceeded the state 24-hour standard 315 days in 2003, and the South Coast Air Basin exceeded the state standard 252 days (Alexis and Cox, 2005).

There are many sources of PM_{10} emissions. Automobile emissions, cement production, military bases, and road dust all contribute to excessive PM_{10} levels

1   A micron is one-millionth of a meter

Table 6 Sources of directly-emitted PM_{10} emissions, 2004

Sources of PM_{10} emissions	Statewide		South Coast Air Basin	
	Tons per day	Percentage	Tons per day	Percentage
Area-wide sources	1,835	88.0%	239	80.7%
Stationary sources	131	6.3%	17	5.7%
On-road mobile sources	49	2.3%	19	6.4%
Other mobile sources	70	3.4%	21	7.2%
Total, all sources	2,086	100.0%	296	100.0%

Source: California Air Resources Board

in the area. However, area-wide sources account for 88% of PM_{10} emissions in California, and the dominant area-wide source is fugitive dust from roads (Alexis and Cox, 2005). Gravel and unpaved roads, in particular, are sources of long-term soil loss and erosion, even in the absence of vehicular use (Havlick, 2002). Road use exacerbates surface erosion, particularly on unpaved road surfaces. Compacted soils of unpaved roadbeds discourage revegetation and are more prone to erosion than vegetated, undisturbed sites. Construction, particularly in rapidly-growing urban and suburban areas, contributes to emissions of particulate matter through physical site disturbance and repeated use of machinery. Sources of PM_{10} emissions in California (statewide) and in one desert air basin are presented in Table 6.

Dust from unpaved roads is the highest source of PM_{10} emissions in San Bernardino County (ARB, 2007). Fugitive windblown dust and unpaved road dust combined account for 87% of PM_{10} emissions in Imperial County. Total emission data for each of the four desert counties is presented below in Table 7.

Table 7 County-level PM_{10} emissions data for California desert air basins, 2005

County (tons per day, annual average)	Great Basin Valleys	Mojave Desert	Salton Sea	South Coast	Total Desert Region
Imperial	--	--	237	--	237
Inyo	150	--	--	--	150
Riverside	--	7	24	52	103
San Bernardino	--	95	--	48	143

Source: California Air Resources Board

Over 9,000 deaths in the State can be attributed to particulate pollution each year (more than motor vehicle accidents, accidental poisonings, and homicides combined) (Sharp and Walker, 2002). More than 1,200 deaths due to particulate pollution (15.3%) occur in the Riverside/San Bernardino area alone (the second highest in the state) (Sharp and Walker, 2002; EWG, 1997; NRDC, 1996). A study of the effects of PM emissions on hospital admissions in the San Joaquin Valley found that higher levels of PM were associated with increased chronic and acute respiratory hospitalizations and emergency room visits (Hall *et al.*, 2006). Visibility throughout the southern region of the State is frequently obscured by the effects of particle emissions, smog, and dust from wind erosion. Currently, over 99% of Californians breathe air that violates State PM_{10} standards at least part of the year (Alexis and Cox, 2005; ARB/OEHHA, 2000). Although the Environmental Protection Agency (EPA) has mandated that air quality around national parks be subject to the most stringent level of protection, Joshua Tree National Park consistently exceeds the ozone and particulate matter concentration levels set by the EPA for human health (JTNP, 2002).

In addition to the public health risks of particulate matter, emissions from vehicles and industrial activities cause pollution that can worsen visibility in parks and desert wildlands, harm vegetation, and increase the risk of wildfires. The Los Angeles Basin, with a population of over 12 million, is the major contributor of ozone and other pollutants that impact air quality in the California desert. Visibility at Joshua Tree National Park is often obscured by haze caused by high concentrations of particulate matter (Sullivan *et al.*, 2001)., and cumulative concentrations of ozone in the Park exceed levels known to cause injury to vegetation. Nitrogen pollution from vehicle exhaust, industrial emissions, and agricultural sources promote the growth of non-native species, which have been shown to increase the risk of wildfires (Harrod and Reichard, 2001). The sparse vegetation that is endemic at Joshua Tree protects against lightning-sparked fires; non-native plants provide fuel for fires and can quickly consume thousands of acres of slow-growing Joshua trees, juniper, and pinyon pines (JTNP, 2002).

Wilderness designation is the highest level of protection for federal lands in the United States. In order to protect the ecological values specified in the Wilderness Act, wilderness areas are primarily roadless and are managed for non-motorized recreational uses. Industrial, mechanical, or motorized uses of any kind are prohibited. Therefore, wilderness and other designated roadless areas are ideal as ecological reference points for the measurement of ecosystem services such as erosion control. Clearly, wilderness areas do not contribute to emissions of particulate matter, and they protect against other types of pollution as well—over 17,000 tons of carbon monoxide and over 3,000 tons of nitrogen dioxide are emitted each day in California (28% of which is emitted from off-road recreation vehicles alone); both of these pollutants have been associated with increased risk of congestive heart failure, respiratory illnesses, birth defects, and in some cases, death (Alexis and Cox, 2005; Sharp and Walker, 2002).

Theoretical model for valuing erosion control

The value of erosion control in deserts can be understood as either the willingness to pay (WTP) for better air quality (through reductions in emissions of
particulate matter), or as the costs avoided by greater protection of the flows of
the erosion control service. Empirically, these two frameworks may be thought
of inversely; that is, the ecosystem service value is either the WTP for greater
erosion control services, or willingness to accept (WTA) compensation for
damages due to lower levels of erosion control. Theoretically, these two values
may be equivalent; empirically, they have been found to differ due to potential
bias (Freeman, 1993).

   Freeman (1993) adapted the Harrington and Portney (1987) model of deriv-
ing the value of reduced morbidity by estimating a health production function
which relates exogenous (environmental) variables such as air pollution and endogenous (choice) variables such as preventive activities and treatment costs.
Health is measured as the number of sick days, s, and is assumed to be a function of exposure to an environmental pollutant. Let exposure be measured by
the dose of a contaminant such as particulate matter; it is represented by a sca-
lar variable, d, which is a function of pollution concentration, c, and the degree
of any preventive or averting activities, a. Mitigating activities (such as medical treatments) are represented by b. An individual's health production function
can be written as

$$s = s(d,b) \tag{1}$$

$$d = d(c,a) \tag{2}$$

An individual's utility u is derived from consumption (represented by a numer-
aire good, X) and leisure, f; the utility function is represented as

$$u = u(X, f, s) \tag{3}$$

Assume that utility increases with consumption and leisure, and decreases with
illness, as follows:

$$\delta u/\delta X, \delta u/\delta f > 0$$
$$\delta u/\delta s < 0 \tag{4}$$

Utility is maximized with individual choices of X, f, a, and b, subject to a budget constraint, which are used to derive an observable measure of marginal
willingness to pay to reduce ambient pollution. Since pollution enters the utility
function through health, the value of the reduction to an individual can be interpreted as the maximum amount she would pay to reduce the number of sick
days without reducing utility. Marginal willingness to pay (*WTP*) is understood
as the reduction in sick days times the marginal cost of achieving the reduction

(either the cost of mitigating activities or the cost of averting activities divided by their respective effects on reduced sick time). Prices of averting (a) and mitigating (b) activities are represented by p_a and p_b, respectively. By solving for first-order conditions for utility maximization, we obtain

$$\begin{aligned} WTP \quad & = -p_a \times \delta s/\delta c/\delta s/\delta a = p_a \times \delta a/\delta c \\ & = -p_b \times \delta s/\delta c/\delta s/\delta b = p_b \times \delta b/\delta c \end{aligned} \quad (5)$$

The two presentations are theoretically the same, based on the assumption that expenditures on mitigating activities would be equal to the costs of pollution reduction. So-called "impure" models (Freeman, 1993) may take into account unobservable (or indirect) effects of pollution on utility, outside of the health effects (such as the impact of emissions on visibility for recreation at national parks and other protected areas).

Demand for non-substitutable environmental benefits (such as air quality) escalates as supply diminishes (Balmford et al., 2002), causing the value (as shadow price) to increase. In the absence of market prices, scarcity does not trigger the development of substitutes (Batabyal et al., 2003). With increasing industrial activity, pressures from motorized recreation, and an expanding human population, the economic costs of particulate pollution increase rapidly, implying an upward-sloping marginal cost curve. Since wilderness areas do not permit motorized uses of any kind, they provide greater protection of the ecosystem service of erosion control, thereby lowering the costs associated with particulate pollution. The avoided costs provide the basis for the valuation of the ecosystem service of erosion control.

The value of erosion control can then be understood as two specific benefits. First, there is the public health benefit, the marginal value of which is estimated as the avoided marginal costs of health care and lost work productivity directly associated with particulate pollution. Second, there is the value of air quality for recreation, which is estimated as the economic benefits (or net willingness to pay) (Loomis and Walsh, 1997) of preserving visibility in national parks.

Firstly, the marginal value of the public health benefit can be estimated by applying costs per acre of area-wide particulate emissions to the federal acres where motorized and industrial activities occur. The avoided public health costs per acre can be used as an estimate for the valuation of erosion control in wilderness areas, which prohibit motorized and industrial activities. Using data from the California Air Resources Board and the Office of Environmental Health Hazard Assessment, Sharp and Walker (2002) estimated that PM_{10} pollution is responsible for more than 16,000 hospital or emergency room admissions, at a cost of $132 million; nearly five million lost work days per year amounts to a loss to the state's economy of more than $880 million. Thus, the estimate of the total cost associated with PM-related illnesses in California is over $1 billion per year—not including the costs of thousands of less severe illnesses that result from excessive PM_{10} levels. The costs associated with asthma hospital admissions, emergency room visits, and work loss days from PM_{10} exposure in the four-county region amount to approximately $115 million per year, and these estimates do not include the costs associated with chronic bronchitis, pneumonia, cardiovascular disease, and other ailments. Cost estimates were much higher for the more densely-populated counties of Riverside and San Bernardino (Sharp and Walker, 2002).

The economic value of the public health benefits of erosion control in desert counties can be estimated by applying the marginal cost of mitigation to the number of wilderness acres, accounting for the contribution of area-wide particulate pollution sources only (*i.e.*, road dust). The estimate of this benefit is $23.9 million per year for the California desert region, based on the assumption that the intensity of motorized recreation uses (*e.g.*, miles driven per acre) does not vary with changes in area designated for non-motorized uses.

The second component of the value of air quality is measured as the economic benefits (or net willingness to pay) of preserving visibility for recreation. Schulze *et al.* (1983) measured the economic benefits of preserving visibility in national parks in the southwestern United States (Arizona, California, and Colorado). In a contingent valuation study, average household willingness to pay ranged from $12.45 to $18.15 (2004 dollars) per month for the preservation of air quality and visibility in three national parks in the Southwest. Extending the average value per household from this study ($17.06) to the nearly three million visitors to Death Valley National Park, Mojave National Preserve, and Joshua Tree National Park yields a total estimate of $47.6 million per year for the economic benefits of preserving visibility. However, the value of clean air likely extends beyond national parks to the other wilderness and related recreation areas throughout the desert region, which would magnify this estimate.

The combined estimate of the economic benefits of erosion control (public health and visibility) is over $71.4 million per year, or $9.63 per acre based on total acres of designated wilderness areas. It should be noted that the value estimate for erosion control is limited by the availability of cost data for particulate-related diseases and therefore does not include many other benefits.

Other ecosystem services in deserts

Ecosystem services of deserts include on-site recreation and the enjoyment of cultural and heritage sites, and the economic value of these uses are measured as the benefit to the users. Wilderness and other natural areas provide opportunities for non-motorized recreation, including hiking, horseback riding, backpacking, camping, wildlife viewing, fishing, and hunting. Recreation is significant throughout the California desert region; data collected for this study indicates that California desert wildlands attract more than three million visitors annually. The preservation of desert wildlands for recreation use is important to visitors. In a 1997 visitor study at Mojave National Preserve, roughly 80% of respondents indicated that scenic views and their desert recreation experience were either "extremely important" or "very important." Interestingly, 87% of respondents indicated that the preservation of wilderness and open space was "extremely" or "very" important, and 86% rated the importance of solitude and quiet at the same level. When asked about the importance of clean air, nearly 85% responded with ratings of "extremely" or "very" important. About 70% of respondents rated viewing wildlife and wildflowers at the same degree of importance (MNP, 1997).

Economists treat recreation use as a consumer good—that is, the number of recreation trips taken (or consumed) is assumed to vary depending on the associated costs, or prices. Costs of travel (*e.g.*, gasoline prices, lodging) and recreation (*e.g.*, park fees) are among the factors that influence consumer decisions about the number of trips taken. The economic benefit of recreation use is defined as net willingness to pay (or consumer surplus) and should be understood as the benefits accrued to the recreation user. It is a measure of the total demand for recreation, after subtracting travel and recreation costs (Loomis and Walsh, 1997). The recreation benefit per visitor day can be interpreted as the amount that the average visitor would be willing to pay rather than forego one day of recreation. There are two methods used by economists to measure the economic benefits to recreation users. The travel cost method uses variations in visitation and travel costs to statistically estimate the net benefits of recreation for a particular site (Loomis and Walsh, 1997). This method assumes that visitors who travel longer distances (and incur greater travel costs) for recreation receive greater net economic benefit from the experience, as revealed by their willingness to pay higher costs. The contingent valuation method is a survey technique that creates a hypothetical market for recreation to calculate visitors' willingness to pay for goods for which there is no market. Both of these methods have been approved by two federal agencies as recommended approaches for estimating non-market values such as the economic benefits of recreation and costs of natural resource damages (U.S. Water Resources Council, 1983; U.S. Department of Interior, 1986, 1994). The recreation use values cited in this report were developed using these two methods and were published in peer-reviewed academic journals. Visitation data for the national parks reviewed in this study are collected annually and are publicly available and accessible. However, recreation use data for BLM wilderness areas are only collected for certain areas in Inyo County. The BLM does not collect or even estimate recreation use data for dozens of wilderness areas and wilderness study areas throughout the California desert. The agency maintains a national database called Recreation Management Information System (RMIS) which is intended to be the storehouse for recreation use on BLM lands, but there are no historical data for thousands of wilderness acres in several BLM districts throughout California. In fact, Loomis (1999) noted that wilderness visitation data are reported for less than half of the designated wilderness acreage in the state. The low priority of wilderness recreation management within the BLM provides little incentive for agency staff to measure recreation use or utilize the RMIS database. Recreation management is integral to an agency's wilderness management program

(Loomis, 1999); with no record of current use levels, it is nearly impossible to assess trends, monitor impacts, and evaluate management alternatives.

There have been more than twenty empirical studies of the economic value of recreation in wilderness areas (and other primitive areas in the U.S.); these were originally compiled by Sorg and Loomis (1984) and updated by Loomis *et al* (1998). These studies valued recreation benefits at wilderness areas throughout the U.S., including California, and revealed an average value of wilderness recreation per day of $47.38 (adjusted for inflation to 2004 dollars). This is the amount that the average wilderness visitor would be willing to pay in additional costs rather than forego one day of recreation. When this value is applied to the estimate of over three million recreation visitor days in California desert wildlands, the aggregate value of recreation benefits is $159 million per year.

Biological diversity and refugia represent another important ecosystem service in deserts. Under Bailey's (1995) system of ecosystem classification, most of the area considered in this study is classified as the American semi-desert and desert province. As previously mentioned, three desert ecosystems are present in the California desert region—the Mojave, the Sonoran, and the Great Basin. The Mojave Desert represents a distinct transition zone between the hot Sonoran Desert of the southwestern United States and the colder, shrub steppes of the higher elevations to the north (Ricketts *et al.*, 1999). Most waterways drain into closed basins. The Mojave River is the main water system to the west and is an unpredictable source of water, and it is a mostly dry streambed for much of the year (Mettermeier *et al.*, 2003). Still the area sustains a surprising number and diversity of plant and animal species. Certain areas within the region support more endemic plants per square meter than other similarly-sized areas in the U.S. (Ricketts *et al.*, 1999). Even the sparse riparian vegetation significantly contributes to biodiversity in the region.

Major threats to the biological diversity of the California desert include the construction and use of roads. Roads slice up lands to create fragments of habitat that can no longer support the population or diversity of species found in large, unroaded areas. This fragmentation has been associated with reductions in wildlife populations and a loss of biological diversity; for example, bald eagle production has been found to diminish with proximity to roads (Havlick, 2002; Anthony and Isaacs, 1989). In addition, roads—especially dirt and gravel roads—generate and disperse dust that can lead to reductions in plant photosynthesis, respiration, and transpiration, all of which threaten species viability (Havlick, 2002). Biological diversity in fragile desert ecosystems can be seriously damaged by a single passage of a motor vehicle (Heydendael, 2002).

Furthermore, road use has been shown to act as a vector for biological invasion. In a study of public desert lands, research determined that roadsides are more substantially invaded by exotic species and contained fewer native species than adjacent interior habitat. Roads acted as conduits for biological invasions, especially when they passed through areas of multiple use common to BLM lands (Havlick, 2002).

Table 8 Special Status Plants and Animals in the California Desert Region

Species Class	Federal Status		California Status	
	Endangered	Threatened	Endangered	Threatened
Plants	25	11	19	2
Fish	6	2	5	1
Amphibians	3	2	2	0
Birds	3	4	9	4
Mammals	5	0	2	4
Reptiles	0	2	1	3
Invertebrates	3	1	0	0

Source: California Department of Fish and Game, Natural Diversity Data Base, 2003.

Several vegetation communities occur in the region. The Joshua tree (*Yucca brevifolia*) is the most visibly dominant species in the region. Creosote bush (*Larea tridentata*) reaches its northern limit in the Mojave Desert. Desert salt-brush (*Atriplex spp.*) and several cactus species occur in the area. The region also supports numerous species of bryophytes, mosses, and liverworts (Metter-meier *et al.*, 2003). The desert supports an unusually large number of endemic ephemeral plants, and many are winter annuals; 80% to 90% of the 250 taxa with this characteristic are endemic in the area (Ricketts *et al.*, 1999).

The region provides habitat for roughly 360 non-fish vertebrate species, which places it among the three richest ecoregions in the U.S. in terms of terrestrial vertebrate diversity. There are 230 bird species, 71 mammals (16 of which are bats), 45 reptiles, and 14 amphibian species (Mouat *et al.*, 1998). There are 131 known fish taxa from the region, but of these, 10 (8%) are extinct, and 75 (62%) are either listed or under consideration for protection under the Endangered Species Act (Davis *et al.*, 1998).

There are an unusually large number of threatened and endangered species in the region, which highlights both the biodiversity of the desert as well as the increasing threats in the region. Federally-listed endangered species in California increased by more than 210% between 1990 and 2005, from 95 to 298. California has more listed species than all of its bordering states combined; about half of the State's federally-listed species' habitat is on public lands (BLM, 2003). A summary of special status plants and animals in the California desert region is provided in Table 8.

By managing for non-motorized recreation uses, California desert wilderness areas protect the diversity of plant and animal species that are assumed to suffer under other management objectives. The effects of motorized recreation in this region are well-documented (Bury *et al.*, 1977; Carter, 1974). In a U.S. Fish and Wildlife Service study of the effects of off-road vehicles on vertebrates in 16 desert test sites in San Bernardino County, Bury *et al.* (1977) found that the diversity of reptiles and mammals are inversely related to levels of off-road vehicle (ORV) usage. Census tracking at three of the study sites showed decreased diversity of breeding birds in areas used for motorized recreation. Studies have shown that ORV noise can cause bleeding from the ears and frantic behavior in endangered kangaroo rats, and hearing loss in lizards such as the Mojave fringe-toed and desert iguana (Brattstrom and Bondello, 1983). ORV usage was found to have a direct impact on wildlife populations by either killing or maiming ground-dwelling animals, and also an indirect effect by crushing ground nests and breaking bushes containing nests. The authors extrapolated their findings to estimate that ORV use on a square kilometer of creosote shrub habitat is associated with 12.5% to 45.1% fewer terrestrial vertebrates than a comparable area of the same size without motorized recreation.

Research on the economic benefits of protecting biodiversity has been of a limited extent.[2] The contingent valuation method (CVM) has the potential to estimate the value of biodiversity, but such an analysis would be quite complex and expensive. It has been well documented that biological diversity in the California desert is vulnerable to a range of threats, including rapid urbanization, air pollution, and motorized recreation. For purposes of this study, the benefits of biodiversity are merely noted, along with the limitations of economic research to estimate their values. The uniqueness and fragility of desert environments underscore the high values of the biological diversity that is protected there.

Conclusion

Values of ecosystem services inform policy making by demonstrating the degree and extent of benefits and costs of alternative policy decisions. Values of ecosystem services in deserts have received little attention in research or policy arenas. Erosion control is one example of an ecosystem service that supports and sustains human life in and near deserts. Erosion control is valuable in terms of both its public health and recreational benefits; these benefits can be measured by various methods, including the costs avoided for public health damages as well as the willingness to pay for visibility in recreational uses. Habitat/refugia is an important ecosystem service in deserts, and can be measured in terms of species diversity and by the number of threatened and endangered species. In addition to erosion control and refugia, there are numerous other ecosystem services provided by desert environments for which very little research has been conducted. Carbon sequestration properties of soils and vegetation help to regulate climate, yet little is known about the value of carbon in desert

---

2   Montgomery et al. (1999) attempted to estimate what they called "management prices" for biodiversity. That study's implicit values are specific to a localized case study and cannot be generalized. Still, their approach illustrates a potential method to calculate dollar values of biodiversity.

soils (Lal, 2004). The benefits of waste treatment and nutrient cycling in deserts have not been valued, and may be significant, particularly in areas where human population growth and industrial activities are increasing. Non-motorized recreational uses, including hiking, mountain biking, and rock climbing, have gained popularity in desert regions. However, present scientific understanding of ecosystem services is substantial and extremely policy-relevant; failure to ensure the continued delivery of ecosystem services in desert environments undermines economic prosperity, diminishes other aspects of human well-being, and threatens the very persistence of human communities in the California desert, as well as other ecosystems (Daily, 1997).

Acknowledgements

This study was supported by funding from The Wilderness Society. Dr. Jay Arnone of the Desert Research Institute provided useful input on the discussion of carbon sequestration in deserts. Kenneth Bagstad of the University of Vermont made significant contributions to the conceptual framework and literature review. The manuscript benefitted from the comments of an anonymous reviewer. The methods and conclusions presented herein solely represent the work and opinions of the author.

References

ARB (Air Resources Board), 2007. California Emission Inventory Data. 2006 Emission Inventory. Sacramento, CA: California Air Resources Board. Retrieved September 21, 2007, from www.arb.ca.gov.

ARB/OEHHA (Air Resources Board and Office of Environmental Health Hazard Assessment). 2000. Adequacy of California's Ambient Air Quality Standards: Children's Environmental Health Protection Act. Staff Report. Sacramento, CA: California Air Resources Board and Office of Environmental Health Hazard Assessment. Retrieved February 17, 2006, from www.oehha.ca.gov.

Alary, V., A. Nefzaoui, and M. Ben Jemaa. 2007. Promoting the adoption of natural resource management technology in arid and semi-arid areas: modeling the impact of spineless cactus in alley cropping in Central Tunisia. *Agricultural Systems 94*(2): 573-585.

Alexis, A. and P. Cox. 2005. The California Almanac of Emissions and Air Quality – 2005 Edition. Sacramento, CA: California Air Resources Board. Retrieved February 17, 2006, from www.arb.ca.gov.

Anthony, R. G. and F. B. Isaacs. 1989. Characteristics of bald eagle nest sites in Oregon. *Journal of Wildlife Management 53*(1): 148-159.

Aylward, B. A., Barbier, E. B., 1992. Valuing environmental functions in developing countries. *Biodiversity and Conservation 1*(1): 34-50.

Bailey, R., 1995. Description of ecoregions of the United States, 2nd edition. Miscellaneous Publication 1391. USDA Forest Service, Washington, DC.

Balmford, A., et al. 2002. Economic reasons for conserving wild nature. *Science* 297(5583): 950-953.

Batabyal, A. A., Kahn, J. R., O'Neill, R. V., 2003. On the scarcity value of ecosystem services. J*ournal of Environmental Economics and Management 46*(2): 334-352.

Bockstael, N., Costanza, R., Strand, I., Boynton, W., Bell, K., Wainger, L., 1995. Ecological economic modeling and valuation of ecosystems. *Ecological Economics 14*: 143-159.

Brattstrom, B. H., M. C. Bondello, 1983. Effects of off-road vehicle noise on desert vertebrates. In Webb, R. and H. Hilshire (eds.). *The Environmental Effects of Off-Road Vehicles: Impacts and Management in Arid Regions*, pp. 167-206. New York: Springer-Verlag.

BLM (Bureau of Land Management), 2003. California Public Lands. BLM/CA/ GI-2003/009. U.S. Department of Interior, Bureau of Land Management, Sacramento, CA.

Bury, R. B., Luckenbach, R. A., Busack, S. D., 1977. Effects of off-road vehicles on vertebrates in the California desert. U.S. Department of the Interior, Fish and Wildlife Service, Washington, D.C. Wildlife Research Report, 8. I49.47/4:8.

Carter, L., 1974. Off-road vehicles: a compromise plan for the California desert. *Science 183*: 396-398.

CDPA (California Desert Protection Act), 1994. California Desert Protection Act of 1994, S. 21. Federal Register 59: PL 103-433.

Costanza, R., et al. 1997. The value of the world's ecosystem services and natural capital. *Nature 387*: 253-260.

Curtis, I., 2004. Valuing ecosystem goods and services: a new approach using a surrogate market and the combination of a multiple criteria analysis and a Delphi panel to assign weights to the attributes. *Ecological Economics 50*: 163-194.

Daily, G. C., 1997. Introduction: what are ecosystem services? In: G. C. Daily, ed. Nature's Services. Washington, DC: Island Press.

Davis, F. W., et al. 1998. *The California GAP Analysis Project, Final Report.* Santa Barbara, CA: University of California, Santa Barbara.

de Groot, R. S., Wilson, M. A., Boumans, R. M. J., 2002. A typology for the classification, description and valuation of ecosystem functions, goods and services. *Ecological Economics 41*: 393-408.

Dombeck, M., 2002. Foreword. In D. G. Havlick, *No Place Distant.* Washington, DC: Island Press.

EPA (U.S. Environmental Protection Agency), 1999. The benefits and costs of the Clean Air Act: 1990-2010: EPA report to Congress, November 1999. EPA 410-R-99-001. Office of Air and Radiation, Office of Policy, Washington, DC.

EWG (Environmental Working Group), 1997. Particulate Air Pollution. Washington, DC: Environmental Working Group. Retrieved September 21, 2007 from www.ewg.org.

Farber, S., et al. 2006. Linking ecology and economics for ecosystem management. *Bioscience 56*: 121-133.

Farber, S. C., Costanza, R., Wilson, M. A., 2002. Economic and ecological concepts for valuing ecosystem services. *Ecological Economics 41*: 375-392.

Freeman, A. Myrick. 1993. *The Measurement of Environmental and Resource Values: Theory and Methods.* Washington, DC: Resources for the Future.

Gauderman, W. J., et al. 2000. Association between air pollution and lung function growth in southern California children. *American Journal of Respiratory and Critical Care Medicine, 162* (4 Pt 1): 1383-90.

Grijalva, T. C., R. P. Berrens, A. K. Bohara, P. M. Jakus, and W. D. Shaw. 2002. Valuing the loss of rock climbing access in wilderness areas: a national-level, random-utility model. *Land Economics, 78* (1): 103-20.

Grimmond, C. S., C. Souch, M. Hubble. 1996. Influence of tree cover on summertime surface energy balance fluxes, San Gabriel Valley, Los Angeles. *Climate Research 6,* 45–57.

Hall, J. V., V. Brajer, and F. W. Lurmann. 2006. The health and related economic benefits of attaining healthful air in the San Joaquin Valley. Working paper. Fullerton, CA: California State University, Institute for Economic and Environmental Studies. Retrieved February 21, 2007 from http://cbeweb-1.fullerton.edu/Centers/iees.

Harrington, W. and P. R. Portney. 1987. Valuing the benefits of health and safety regulations. *Journal of Urban Economics 22*(1): 101-112.

Harrod, R. J., and S. Reichard. 2001. Fire and invasive species within the temperate and boreal coniferous forests of western North America. Pages 95–101 in K.E.M. Galley and T.P. Wilson (eds.). Proceedings of the Invasive Species Workshop: the Role of Fire in the Control and Spread of Invasive Species. Fire Conference 2000: the First National Congress on Fire Ecology, Prevention, and Management. Miscellaneous Publication No. 11, Tall Timbers Research Station, Tallahassee, FL.

Hastings, S. J., W. C. Oechel, and A. Muhlia-Melo. 2005. Diurnal, seasona and annual variation in the net ecosystem CO_2 exchange of a desert shrub community (Sarcocaulescent) in Baja California, Mexico. *Global Change Biology 11*:927-939.

Havlick, D. G. 2002. *No Place Distant.* Washington, DC: Island Press.

Hernández, H. M., C. Gómez-Hinostrosa, and B. Goettsch. 2004. Checklist of Chihuahuan Desert Cactaceae. *Harvard Papers in Botany 9*(1): 51-68.

Heydendael, A. 2002. Sustainable tourism within the context of the ecosystem approach. In F. di Castri and V. Balaji (eds.). *Tourism, Biodiversity and Information.* Leiden, The Netherlands: Backhuys Publishers.

Housman, D. C., H. H. Powers, A. D. Collins, J. Belnap. 2006. Carbon and nitrogen fixation differ between successional stages of biological soil crusts in the Colorado Plateau and Chihuahuan Desert. *Journal of Arid Environments 66*: 620-634.

JTNP (Joshua Tree National Park). 2002. Air quality. ParkNet: Nature & Science – Environmental Factors. Washington, DC: U.S. Department of the Interior. Retrieved February 17, 2006, from www.nps.gov.

Jasoni, R. L., S. D. Smith, and J. A. Arnone III. 2005. Net ecosystem CO_2 exchange in Mojave Desert shrublands during the eighth year of exposure to elevated CO2. *Global Change Biology 11*:749-756

Joyce, C., 1992. Western medicine men return to the field. *BioScience 42*: 399-493.

Kremen, C., et al.2007. Pollination and other ecosystem services produced by mobile organisms: a conceptual framework for the effects of land-use change. *Ecology Letters 10*(4): 299-314.

Lal, R. 2004. Carbon sequestration in dryland ecosystems. *Environmental Management 33*(4): 528-544.

Limburg, K. E., O'Neill, R. V., Costanza, R., Farber, S., 2002. Complex systems and valuation. *Ecological Economics 41*:409-420.

Loomis, J., P., Kent, L. Strange, K. Fausch, A. Covich. 2000. Measuring the total economic value of restoring ecosystem services in an impaired river basin: results from a contingent valuation survey. *Ecological Economics 33*: 103-117.

Loomis, J. B., Walsh, R. G., 1997. *Recreation Economic Decisions: Comparing Benefits and Costs*, 2ⁿᵈ edition. State College, PA: Venture Publishing.

Luo, H., W. C. Oechel, S. J. Hastings, R. Zulueta, Y. Qian, and H. Kwon. 2007. Mature semiarid chaparral ecosystems can be a significant sink for atmospheric carbon dioxide. *Global Change Biology 13*:386-396.

McPherson, E. G. 2001. Sacramento's parking lot shading ordinance: environmental and economic costs of compliance. *Landscape and Urban Planning 57*: 105-123.

Mettermeier, C. G., W. R. Konstant, R. E. Lovich, and J. E. Lovich. 2003. The Mojave Desert. In R. A. Mittermeier, et al. (eds.), *Wilderness: Earth's Last Wild Places.* Chicago: University of Chicago Press.

Montgomery, C., R. Pollak, K. Freemark, and D. White. 1999. Pricing biodiversity. *Journal of Environmental Economics and Management 38*(1): 1-19.

Moore, W., McCarl, B., 1987. Off-site costs of soil erosion: a case study of the Willamette valley. *Western Journal of Agricultural Economics 12*(1), 42-49.

Mouat, D. A., A. L. Kiester, R. Fisher, M. Meyers, and J. S. Heaton. 1998. *Analysis and Assessment of Impacts on Biodiversity: A Framework for Environmental management on DoD Lands within the California Mojave Desert: A Research Plan.* Corvallis, OR: U.S. Environmental Protection Agency.

NRDC (Natural Resources Defense Council), 1996. Breath-Taking: Premature Mortality Due to Particulate Air Pollution in 239 American Cities. New York, NY: Natural Resources Defense Council, 154 pp. Retrieved February 17, 2006, from http://www.nrdc.org/air/pollution/bt/btinx.asp.

Odum, Eugene P. 1997. *Ecology: A Bridge Between Science and Society.* Sunderland, MA: Sinauer Associates.

Pellmyr, O. and K. A. Segraves. 2003. Pollinator Divergence within an Obligate Mutualism: Two Yucca Moth Species (Lepidoptera; Prodoxidae: Tegeticula) on the Joshua Tree (Yucca brevifolia; Agavaceae). *Annals of the Entomological Society of America 96*(6): 716-22.

Ricketts, T. H., E. Dinerstein, D. M. Olson, C. J. Loucks, W. Eichbaum, D. Dellsaia, K. Kavanagh, P. Hedao, P. T. Hurley, K. M. Carney, R. Abell, and S. Walters.

1999. *Terrestrial Ecoregions of North America: A Conservation Assessment.* Washington, D.C.: Island Press.

Rosenstock, S. S., V. C. Bleich, M. J. Rabe, and C. Reggiardo. 2005. Water quality at wildlife water sources in the Sonoran Desert, United States. *Rangeland Ecology and Management* 58(6): 623-627.

Sharp, R. and B. Walker. 2002. Particle Civics. Washington, DC: Environmental Working Group. Retrieved September 21, 2007, from www.ewg.org.

Shaw, W. D. and P. M. Jakus. 1996. Travel cost models of the demand for rock climbing. *Agricultural and Resource Economics Review* 25: 133-42.

Simpson, B. B. and J. L. Neff. 2003. Pollination ecology in the arid southwest. *Aliso* 11(4): 417-440.

Stabler, L. B., C. A. Martin, and A. J. Brazel. 2005. Microclimates in a desert city were related to land use and vegetation index. *Urban Forestry and Urban Greening,* 3:137-147.

Sutton, P. C. and R. Costanza. 2002. Global estimates of market and non-market values derived from nighttime satellite imagery, land cover, and ecosystem service valuation. *Ecological Economics* 41: 509-527.

U.S. Census Bureau, 2006. State & County Quick Facts. Washington, DC. Retrieved February 17, 2006, from www.census.gov.

Wagner, D. and J. B. Jones. 2006. The impact of harvester ants on decomposition, N mineralization, litter quality, and the availability of N to plants in the Mojave Desert. *Soil Biology and Biochemistry* 38: 2593-2601.

Webb, R.H. and H. G. Wilshire. 1980. Recovery of soils and vegetation in a Mojave desert ghost town, Nevada, U.S.A. *Journal of Arid Environments,* 3: 291-303.

Woodruff, T. J., J. Grillo, and K. C. Schoendorf. 1997. The relationship between selected causes of post-neonatal infant mortality and particulate air pollution in the United States. *Environmental Health Perspectives,* 105(6), June 1997.

Zavaleta, E., 2000. The economic value of controlling an invasive shrub. *A Journal of the Human Environment,* 29(8): 462-467.

Zhongmin, X., Guodong, C., Zhiqiang, Z., Zhiyong, S., Loomis, J., 2003. Applying contingent valuation in China to measure the total economic value of restoring ecosystem services in Ejina region. *Ecological Economics* 44(2-3): 345-358.

16 Valuation of Mangrove Ecosystems

A case of the Bhitarkanika Mangrove Ecosystem, India

Ruchi Badola and Syed Ainul Hussain

ABSTRACT

South Asia is home to nearly half of the world's poor where poverty is inextricably linked to environmental degradation, as majority of the people depend on natural resources for their sustenance and well being. This in turn is the cause for multiple environmental hazards that jeopardize the economic condition of the people. The local economies lack resilience in the face of natural disasters such as storms, cyclones and tsunamis. The condition and management of ecosystem services is a dominant factor influencing the resilience of local communities. This paper outlines the role of mangrove forests in sustaining the livelihoods of local people as well as in securing their lives and properties from storms and cyclones. It highlights these with the help of an empirical study conducted in the east coast of India that valued the key ecological services provided by the mangrove forests. We concluded that while villages protected by mangrove forests suffered least damage from cyclones, property damaged was highest in the areas shielded by manmade structures. Mangrove forests contributed $c15\%$ of the local income besides enhancing the productivity of local agro-ecosystems as well as fishery resources. Studies that link functions performed by natural ecosystem to human well being can help put conservation on the 'livelihoods' agenda of the local communities and resolve the classic battle of conservation *vs* development.

Keywords: mangroves, ecological services, valuation, local people, livelihoods

Introduction

Mangroves are the characteristic littoral plant formations of tropical and sub-tropical sheltered coastline that grow in the inter-tidal areas and estuary mouths between land and sea. Mangrove forests are one of the most productive and bio-diverse wetlands on earth since they provide critical habitat for a diverse marine and terrestrial flora and fauna. The ecological functions or processes ascribed to mangroves are found at the global, ecosystem, and population levels. Ecosystem functions include hydrologic transfers and storage of water (Richardson and McCarthy, 1994), biological productivity (Mitsch and Gosselink, 2000) and biogeochemical transformation (Walbridge and Lockaby, 1994). At the population level, mangroves function as wildlife habitats, maintaining unique species and biological diversity. The mangrove ecosystems are widely recognized as the providers of a wide variety of goods and services to people including provision of a variety of plant and animal products (MacNae, 1974; Spaninks and van Beukering, 1997; Rasolofo, 1997), sediment trapping and nutrient uptake and transformation and protection from floods and storms (Semesi, 1998) and stabilization of coastal land (Carlton, 1974; Wolanski, 1985). Ecosystem services like protection against floods and hurricanes, reduction of shoreline and riverbank erosion sustain economic activities in coastal areas throughout the tropics (Moberg and Ronnback, 2003). The mangroves can be considered as a natural barrier protecting the lives and property of coastal communities from storms and cyclones, flooding, and coastal soil erosion (Sathirathai and Barbier 2001). The above ground root systems retard water flow that not only encourages the sediment to settle but also inhibits their re-suspension. Stabilization of sediments provides protection to shorelines and associated shore based activities, and can lead to land gains. Further the resistance, which mangroves offer to water flow, is particularly important during extreme weather events such as cyclones, typhoons and hurricanes (MacNae, 1974). Mangrove ecosystems mitigate against flooding and flood damage by dissipating the energy of floodwaters. Mangrove ecosystems also function as a sink. Sedimentary processes as well as uptake by organisms filter through-flowing waters, incorporating extracted substances in the sediments and/or in the ecosystems biomass (Gilbert and Jansen, 1997).

Despite of centuries of biological research on mangrove structure, productivity and ecosystem dynamics (Rollet, 1981), and in spite of an understanding and recognition of mangrove benefits by scientists, governments and local population (Saenger *et al*, 1983), destruction of these ecosystems continues. Mangrove forests rank among the most threatened of coastal habitats, particularly for developing countries (Field *et al.,* 1998; Saenger *et al.,* 1983). The total mangrove area of the world has been estimated to be approximately 15 m ha, declining at the rate of 1.1% per annum (Wilkie et. al., 2003). The highest loss of mangroves has occurred in Asia, and Americas due to aquaculture and tourism infrastructure.

The highest cost of mangrove loss is borne by the coastal communities who depend on these for their day to day needs and for their survival. The protection provided by the mangroves to coastal areas from storms and floods is well documented (Badola & Hussain 2005; Kathiresan & Rajendran 2005; Carlton 1974; Maltby 1986; Semesi 1998). Observations of the Asian tsunami of 2004 further highlight this protective role and provide a stark reminder that environmental sustainability and human security are inseparable (Walters 2005). The ecosystem services provided by mangroves are often ignored in the ongoing process of mangrove conversion (Barbier 1993; Ruitenbeek 1994; Swallow 1994).

This is so because the values of mangrove forests are not created in isolation but rather are subjective, relative (reflecting scarcity) and institutionally embedded through property rights. The economic value of direct products from mangrove forests proves more important in decision making for their management as these usually accrue locally (Adger *et al.* 1997). Hence, the exploitation of mangroves usually focuses only on single uses based on narrow economic valuations. For mangrove conservation and exploitation to occur simultaneously, economic analyses that focus on multiple-use aspects of mangroves are needed (Ruitenbeek 1994). Appropriate values for ecosystem services once derived may be inserted into the decision-making process in order to correct the market signals (Costanza *et al.* 1989). The following section presents the results of a study that attempted to value some of the benefits provided by mangrove forests to the local communities living in their vicinity.

Study Area

Bhitarkanika mangrove ecosystem

The study was conducted in the Bhitarkanika Conservation Area (BCA) located between 86^0 45'E to 87^0 50' E longitude and 20^0 40' to 20^0 48' N latitude (Patnaik et al. 1995) in the east coast of Orissa, India (Figure 1). It is formed by the estuary of Brahmani, Baitarani and Dhamra rivers. The delta is a large estuarine system with depositional and porgrading environment with fluvial, aeolian and coastal landforms (Mahapatra 2000). The main feature of the Orissa coast is micro-mesotidal, monsoonal wave dominated to mixed energy wave-tide dominated (Davis 1987). The gross littoral drift is 1.5–2.0 million m^3/year (Mohanty 1990). The terrain is formed by the alluvial filling up of the littoral zone of the Bay of Bengal. It is composed of sandy and muddy beach along the coast and networks of creeks and channels (Choudhury et al. 1999). The general elevation of the area above mean tide level is between 1.5 and 2 m (Dani and Kar 1999). Most of the area gets submerged during fair monsoons. Surface soils close to the rivers vary from 2 m to 4 m in depth that decreases gradually from shore to the mainland (Patnaik et al. 1995).

This mangrove ecosystem and the associated coast, harbor the highest diversity of Indian mangrove flora (Naskar and Mandal 1999) and its obligate faunal species. The mangrove forests of Bhitarkanika differ considerably from other Indian mangroves because of their dominant tree species *Sonneratia apetala, Heritiera fomes, H. littoralis* and several *Avicennia* species. Badola and Hussain (2003) reported a total of 64 species of plants from Bhitarkanika Conservation Area, which include 28 true mangroves, 4 mangrove associates and 32 other species. The mangrove formations in the BCA once wide spread are now restricted to 145 km^2 of the National Park, where as the Sanctuary has few degraded mangroves and palm swamps. Considering its ecological and social value the area has been identified as a Ramsar site.

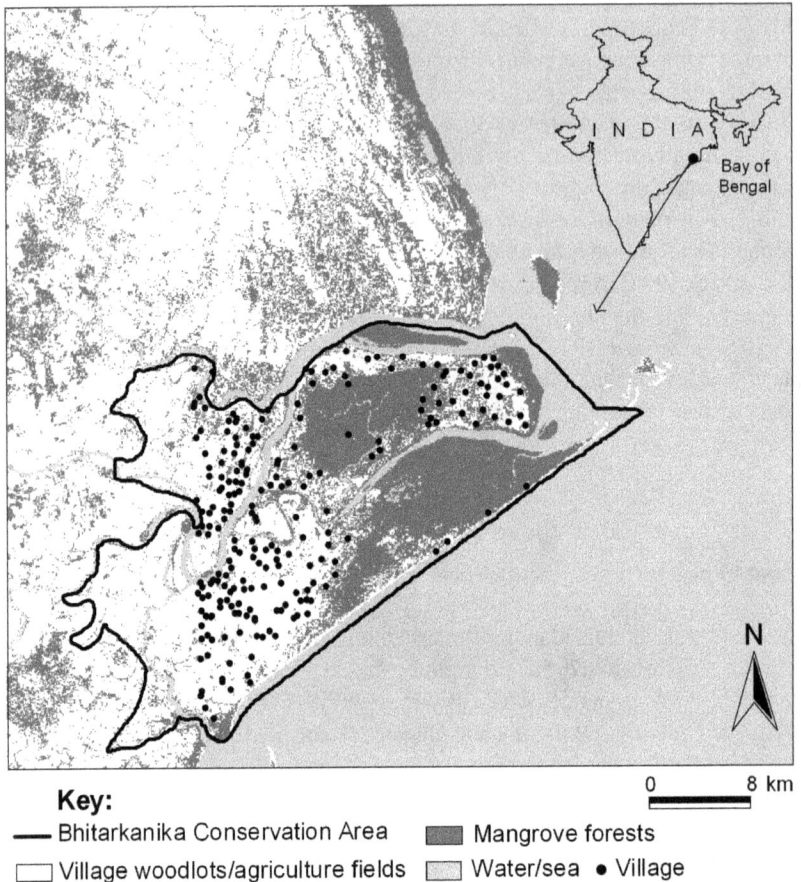

Figure 1 Location of Bhitarkanika Conservation Area, India, land use pattern and
distribution of villages in the region

The agro ecosystem of Bhitarkanika Conservation Area

Table 1 provides information about the agro ecosystem of BCA. This agro ecosystem consists of 247.9 km² of human habitation in 336 villages, village wood-
lots and agricultural fields. Subsistence based, non-mechanized agriculture is
the main occupation of the people, characterized by small land holdings and dependent on the monsoon. In addition to a single crop of paddy, small quantities
of vegetables, coconut and fish are the only output of the agro ecosystem. The
local people have low per capita income as few opportunities for small-scale
industries exist due to the lack of infrastructure facilities. c 13.5% of the people
in the working age category of 20-60 years are unemployed. Many people are
working as skilled and unskilled laborers in other states. The average family
income is US$ 488.9 per annum (Table 1).

Table 1 Characteristics of the agroecosystem of Bhitarkanika Conservation Area, India

Parameters	Total
Average village size (ha)	113.27 $\pm$3.98
% cultivated area irrigated	8.7
Mean family size (number)	7.59 $\pm$ 0.11
Average size of paddy fields (ha)	1.32 $\pm$0.12
Overall paddy yield (kg/ha)	948.83 $\pm$0.56
No. of coconut trees/household	9.44 $\pm$1.05
No. of months of employment	6.25 $\pm$0.22
% People engaged in agricultura	60.30
% People engaged in fishing, animal husbandry and allied activities	1.96
% People engaged in labor	25.47
Income of the family (US$/annum)	488.86 $\pm$10.40
% People unemployed	13.58 $\pm$0.61
% People literate	48 $\pm$0.01

Methods

Though mangrove perform host of ecological services, during the present study five major services were valued (Table 2).

Nutrient retention and recycling

To assess the nutrient retention function of the Bhitarkanika mangrove forest and its contribution to local agro ecosystem, sixty soil samples collected from the mangrove and non-mangrove areas of the Bhitarkanika Conservation Area

Table 2 Selected functions and values of Bhitarkanika estimated and method used for each parameter

Parameters assessed	Methods used
Nutrient retention	Replacement cost approach
Fish and shellfish production	Market value
Storm abatement	Damage costs avoided
Land accretion	Market value
Direct use (forestry and fishery products)	Market value

were analyzed following Allen (1989) and Jackson (1967). Subsequently, physical and chemical parameters of soil samples were analyzed, including nutrient values. The replacement cost method (Bockstael et al. 2000; Freeman 2003; Sundberg 2004) was used to measure the comprehensive value and the benefits accruing from mangroves on account of nutrient retention process. The cost of increasing the soil nutrients in the non-mangrove areas to the level of mangrove areas was calculated by estimating the cost of fertilizers that if added to the soil in non-mangrove areas would bring their nutrient level to that of mangrove areas (Badola & Hussain 2003).

Storm protection

The Bhitarkanika Conservation Area is situated in one of the most cyclone prone areas of coastal India. We used the damage-cost avoided approach (Bann 1998) to value the storm protection function of the Bhitarkanika mangrove ecosystem. The actual damages avoided due to mangrove forest were estimated after a cyclone hit the area in October 1999. Socio-economic data pertaining to local demography and economic conditions were collected from 35 villages located in and around the BCA. Data on demography, land use and occupational patterns, resource use, and perceptions and attitudes were gathered through a questionnaire survey from 10% of the households. We collected preliminary information randomly by asking people about the losses they incurred because of the 1999 cyclone. On this basis, we tried to compare the impact of the cyclone in villages that had mangrove cover with those unprotected by mangrove forests, but since coastal embankments have been constructed in Orissa to prevent seawater intrusion into reclaimed paddy fields, it was imperative that the effects of embankments and mangroves be separated. Hence, the following three situations were identified: (1) a village in the shadow of mangrove (2) a village not in the shadow of mangrove and having no embankment, and (3) a village not in the shadow of mangrove, but with an embankment on the seaward side. Based on a land-use cover map prepared in a geographical information system domain (Fig. 1), three study villages were identified, representing the three situations. Care taken to avoid variations in damage attributable to wind, water logging and distance of villages from the coast and mangrove forests limited the sample size to three villages. Bankual village was in the shadow of mangrove forest, Singidi village was neither in the shadow of mangroves nor protected by embankment from storm surge, and Bandhamal village was not in the shadow of mangroves, but had seaward side embankment. The intensity of the impact of the 1999 cyclone on these villages should have been fairly uniform, as all the three selected villages were equidistant from the seashore and had similar aspects. The two villages outside mangrove cover were located close to each other, but both were far from the mangrove forest in order to eliminate any effect of mangrove forest presence. We conducted a door-to-door survey and sampled 100% of the selected households to assess the socio-economic status of the villages, the actual damage to houses, livestock, fisheries, trees and other assets owned by the people and the rate, level and duration of flooding. To assess the type of damage caused to houses, we developed a composite score or damage rating (DR) for each of the households surveyed in the three villages. The scores were in the range of 0–19 depending on the intensity of damage to the house, 19 representing total collapse. We used Statistical Package for the Social Sciences (SPSS) software for data processing (SPSS, 1999) and one-way ANOVA tests (Zar, 1984) to compare the means of various variables for the three villages.

Land acreation

Wetland ecosystems frequently contribute to ecological, geomorphological or geological systems or processes. Geomorphologic processes lead to the development of landforms such as flood plains and coastal mudflats. Mangroves trap sediments and accelerate land formation in the coast initially as islands or mudflats. Subsequently, due to succession these newly created land forms develop into tidal swamps with mangrove species. The Bhitarkanika mangrove ecosystem has contributed significantly in the formation of mudflats and islands along the coast and in the associated riverine ecosystems. Time series maps of Bhitarkanika area for the years 1887–1889, 1939–1941, 1975–1976 and satellite imageries for the year 2000 were used for comparison of land formation in the area. Since land is a traded commodity in the area, the current price of land prevailing in the area was used to value this function of the Bhitarkanika mangroves.

Fish and shell fish production

The contribution of Bhitarkanika mangrove ecosystem to fish productivity was evaluated from three aspects- offshore fishery, inshore fishery and its suitability as nursery ground for fish and shellfish.

To estimate the fish capture in offshore areas with or without mangroves, the data of fish catch from the following two zones along the Orissa coast was considered (Gopi *et al.,* 2002).

Zone I: The Gahirmatha coast (zone with mangroves). The length of this zone is 35 km; it forms the eastern boundary of the Bhitarkanika Wildlife Sanctuary. In this zone 12 experimental trawling were carried out.
Zone II: The Paradip coast (zone without mangroves) stretches for 55 km. In this zone, 29 experimental trawls were carried out.

On the basis of the market prices of the fish, the catch was classified in to three classes, A-class, B-class and C-class and the economic value of fish catch for each class was calculated by the formula:

Contribution to fishery benefits (cbf) = value of fish catch/hour in mangrove areas (x) – value of fish catch/hour in areas where no mangrove is present (y)

Fish and shellfish production in six creeks of the Bhitarkanika National Park were sampled to estimate the species composition and catch/hour (Badola and Hussain, 2003). This method was also used to estimate the role of Bhitarkanika mangrove ecosystem as a nursery ground for fish and shellfish, in five creeks in the National Park The value of the catch was estimated by comparing the price of various fish species in local market following Bann (1998) - *Total Value of the catch = Unit market price X Quantity*

Provision of biomass resources to local communities

The dependency of local people on mangrove forests in 36 villages situated in the Bhitarkanika Conservation Area was examined. These villages were selected from 336 villages on the basis of 35 parameters through a hierarchical cluster analysis and subsequently villages were randomly selected from each of the clusters proportionately. For each selected village 10% of the housing units were picked up randomly for the household and attitude survey. A structured questionnaire was used for intensive household surveys. A point was made to evenly distribute the households over the total area of the villages in order to get a full representation of all communities and economic groups.

Results

Nutrient retention

It was found that nutrients such as organic carbon, total nitrogen, available phosphorus and available potassium were present in higher quantity in mangrove areas as compared to the non-mangrove areas. Most of the chemical properties including nutrient contents of soil such as PH, organic carbon, total nitrogen, available phosphorus and available potassium of mangrove soils were significantly different from soil of non-mangrove areas ($p = 0.000$; $df = 59$; $t = 0.05$). The value in US$ of nitrogen, phosphorus and potassium in one hectare of mangrove soil was found to be 618.51, 9.23 and 1222.46 respectively, while it was 437.80 6.59 and 184.41 respectively (Table 3) in one hectare of non-mangrove soil. The area under mangrove forest is 145 km^2 or 14,500 ha. The monetary value of nutrients (N+P+K) provided by total area under mangrove forest was estimated at US$ 3'406,787 for the total mangrove forest of Bhitarkanika Conservation Area (Table 3) and US$ 863.75/ha of mangrove forests. From the study it was concluded that as the soils of mangrove areas act as nutrient sink and help in nutrient retention, they have significantly high amount of nutrient.

Storm protection

The high-speed winds and storm surge generally damaged the mud and thatch houses, with not many cases of damage to roof frames being reported, the

Table 3 Value of available nutrient in the soil collected from the Bhitarkanika Conservation Area, India

Nutrients	Nutrient in mangrove (kg/ha)	Nutrient in non-mangrove (kg/ha)	Market value (US$/kg)	Estimated value for a ha of mangrove (US $/kg)	Estimated value for a ha of non-mangrove (US$/kg)	Estimated value in total mangrove area (US$)	Estimated value for extra nutrients in total mangrove area (US$)
	(1)	(2)	(3)	(4) = (1 x 3)	(5) = (2 x 3)	(6) = (3 x 4)	(7)
Available N	2,907.00	2,057.67	0.21	618.51	437.80	8'968,404.30	2'620,295.00
Available P2O5	28.11	20.08	0.33	9.23	6.59	133,812.57	38,225.36
Available K2O	1,564.55	1,222.46	0.15	236.01	184.41	3'422,203.46	748,267.30
Total value of N+P+K				863.75	628.80	12'524,420.30	3'406,787

Source: Fertilizer Association of India, Statistics 2000

Table 4 Basic description and mean values of the variables (per household) examined for comparing the damage due to cyclone in three study villages in the Bhitarkanika Conservation Area, India. (US\$ 1 = INR 45, August 2004)

Variables	Description	Villages			n	df	F	p value
		Singdi	Bankual	Bandhamal				
DR	Damage to houses (0–19 scale)	9.40	5.34	10.44	107	1	14.633	0.000
PTD	Tree damage (%)	21.0	3.3	15.5	93	1	9.891	0.000
DPP	Damage to other personal property (INR)	108.11	0.00	2375.00	107	1	6.814	0.002
DL	Damage to livestock in money terms (INR)	54.05	127.63	1044.37	107	1	5.398	0.006
FP	Flooding in premises (m)	0.34	0.29	0.58	103	1	7.670	0.001
FF	Flooding in fields (m)	1.99	1.09	1.39	100	1	35.102	0.000
WLF	Water logging in fields (days)	9.46	5.63	12.87	102	1	18.654	0.000
CR	Cost of repair and reconstruction (INR)	996.97 US\$ 24.92	682.86 US\$ 17.77	973.21 US\$ 24.33	96	1	1.270	0.286
Y99	Yield for the year 1999(kg ha⁻¹)	531	1479.5	335.9	59	1	99.029	0.000
LFS	Loss of fish seedlings (fingerlings) released prior to cyclone (INR)	310.81 US\$ 7.77	69.74 US\$ 1.76	260.94 US\$ 6.92	107	1	1.506	0.227
TML	Total quantifiable variables (INR)	1983.36 US\$ 49.58	1454.13 US\$ 36.35	6918.62 US\$ 172.96	98	1	17.936	0.000

maximum mean DR being 9.4 ± 0.7 for Singdi village and the minimum mean DR being 5.3 ± 0.5 for Bankual village (Table 4). The percentage of trees dying (PTD) attributed to the cyclone was highest in Singdi (21.0%), while only 3.3% of trees were damaged in Bankual (Table 4), which had the highest number of trees. Costs for reconstruction work per household (CR) did not differ between villages (Table 4). Loss to private property such as boats, nets (DPP) and livestock casualties (DL) were highest in Bandhamal (Table 4), the village far from the mangrove forests but protected by the embankment.

Saline water intrusion into houses (FP) was highest in Bandhamal (0.6 m ± 0.05 m) and lowest for Bankual (0.3 m ± 0.04 m) (Table 4). The highest level of saline water intrusion in the crop fields (FF) was for Singdi, followed by Bandhamal and Bankual. Flood water remained in fields (WLF) for longest duration in Bandhamal, flood retreat for Singdi and Bankual being faster (Table 4). The standing crops of paddy were severely affected by the cyclone. Crop production differed among the three villages (Table 4), Bankual having the greatest paddy yield for 1999 (Y99) of 1,479.5 kg ha^{-1}, while in Singdi the yield was 531 kg ha^{-1} and in Bandhamal it was 335.9 kg ha^{-1}. The mean paddy yield differed for all three villages between the years 1999 and 2001 ($F = 99.029$, $df = 1$, $p = 0.000$); in 1999 it was 568 kg ha^{-1} while in 2001 it was 1,012.7 kg ha^{-1}. The greatest damage to fish seedlings per household (LFS) was in Singdi, where INR 310.8 ± 144.97 (US$ 7.77) of seedlings released were washed away, and the least damage was in Bankual (INR 69.7 ± 32.20, US$ 1.76; Table 4). The loss incurred per household (TML) was highest in Bandhamal (US$ 172.96) followed by Singdi (US$ 44.58) and Bankual (US$ 36.35) (Table 4).

Land accretion

In last one hundred eleven years a total of 4.68 km^2 of land formation has oc-curred within the Bhitarkanika Conservation Area. Most of this land is being used for agricultural purposes or has been planted with mangrove species.

Fishery

Offshore fishery   Significant difference in total catch/hr between zone I and II was found. Zone I (with mangrove) had considerably high fish yield (123.34 kg/hr) than the zone II (without mangrove) (17.89 kg/hr) resulting in the differ-ence of Rs 1679.77/hour of trawling (Table 5).

Inshore fishery   The value for inshore fishery catch per hour was Rs 89.91 for 3.77 kg of fish. The values of Shannon Index, I_{sh} varied considerably between sites (between 0.599-0.745, mean=0.673). For example, sites with dense man-groves had higher value (Badola and Hussain 2003).

Nursery ground for fish and shellfish   During the study a total of fifteen spe-cies were caught from the sampling sites. The catch per hour was found to be

Table 5 Comparison of off shore fishery production at Gahirmatha and Paradip coasts, India

Fish class	Gahirmatha coast (Zone 1)			Paradip coast (Zone 2)		
	Rate (Rs/kg)	Catch (kg/hr)	Earning (Rs/hr)	Rate (Rs/kg)	Catch (kg/hr)	Earning (Rs/hr)
A-Class	51.17	15.78	807.50	55.92	0.24	13.27
B-Class	15.00	43.93	658.94	15.48	0.31	4.83
C-Class	5.00	63.63	318.16	5.00	17.35	86.73
Total		123.34	1784.60		17.89	104.83

highest for *Penaeus indicus*, other commercially important shellfish caught were *Scylla serata* and *Penaeus monodon*. Shannon's index was calculated to examine the diversity of fish and shellfish seedlings in the five sampling stations. The values of the Index, I_{sh} for each sampling site varied considerably 0.637-0.743 (mean 0.688). Of the fifteen species of fish and shellfish seedlings caught only three species were commercially exploited. These were *Penaeus indicus*, *Scylla serata* and *Penaeus monodon*. The price of these species varied- for *Penaeus indicus* Rs 0.10 to 0.50 per seedling, for *Scylla serata* Rs 0.20 to 0.40 per seedling and for *Penaeus monodon* Rs 0.40 to 0.60 per seedling. From these prices earning per hour was calculated which varied between 2.36-32.65 Rs/hour (Badola and Hussain 2003).

Provision of biomass resources to local communities

The use of the mangrove forests by the local people range from timber, poles and posts to firewood and fibre. Non-wood forest products include thatch, honey, wildlife, fish, fodder and medicine. Though the area has protected status and legally no extraction is allowed, the villagers living in mangrove areas use mangrove trees mainly for fuel wood, construction of houses and agricultural implements. Table 6, enumerates the various use values derived from Bhitarkanika mangrove forest by the local people. The study of socio-demographic characteristics, economic situation, and other aspects of life in the mangrove villages in Bhitarkanika Conservation Area reveal a high degree of resource use despite the protected status of the Bhitarkanika mangroves. Conservatively

Table 6 Dependency of local people on various resources from the Bhitarkanika mangrove forests (n = 324)

Uses	Quantity (Kg/household/annum)	Mean	SEM	Monetary value (Rs)
Fuel	Total consumption of fuel	2205.0	104.2	
	National Park firewood	312.0	32.2	249.6
	Other firewood	21.0	23.5	
	Cow dung, farm refuse, others	1949.0	375.0	1949
Fish	Fish caught from sanctuary and roadside creeks and from the National Park	98.0	28.3	2730
Timber	Used as rafters	343.0	36.9	617.4
	As roof supports	27.0	4.3	185.49
Non Wood Forest Produce	Honey	525.0	239.7	3.64
	For thatching (*Phoenix paludosa*)	49.0	8.7	98

estimated, the resources extracted from the mangrove forests contribute more than 14.5% to the total income of the households on an average. This proportion is approximately 30% for the poor and marginalized households residing in the immediate vicinity of the mangrove forests.

Attitudes and awareness of the people

About 90% people in the area were aware that the Bhitarkanika mangrove forests have protected status. A high percentage (84%) of people felt responsible for the conservation of flora and fauna, while 93% were in favour of an integrated conservation and development programme (ICDP). Approximately 43% of people were willing to cooperate with the forest department in mangrove restoration. Only 18% people felt the park's declaration violated rights, the main reason being the access denied to firewood (Table 7).

Table 7 Attitudes of local people towards Bhitarkanika Wildlife Sanctuary, India and conservation initiatives taken by Forest Department of Government of Orissa (n = 268)

Questions	Responses (%)		
	Yes	No	Indifferent
Are you aware that Bhitarkanika is declared national park and sanctuary?	89.6	10.4	0
Do you feel any sense of responsibility for the protection of diverse flora and fauna?	84.3	13.4	2.2
Do you think your rights have been violated after declaration of park?	18.3	72.8	9
Do you face any problems because of park?	5.6	84.7	9
Are you in favour of integrated conservation and development projects for the area?	92.9	2.2	4.9
Would you like to cooperate with forest department for mangrove restoration?	43.3	23.1	36.6

Discussion

Mangroves have been extensively studied for decades by botanists, ecologists and marine scientists (Macnae, 1968; Chapman, 1976; Saenger et al., 1983; Tomlinson, 1986; Kathiresan and Bingham, 2001; Lacerda, 2002). Yet, it was not until the 1980s and early 1990s that significant research attention was brought to bear on the human dimensions of these unique forested wetlands (FAO, 1985; Hamilton et al., 1989; FAO, 1994; Cormier-Salem, 1999). Population pressure is typically greatest along the coast, so it is little surprise that human influences on the world's mangrove forests are significant and growing. Mangroves have been cleared and degraded on an alarming scale during the past four decades (Valiela et al., 2001; Wilkie and Fortuna, 2003), yet they remain an important source of renewable marketed and non-marketed goods and services. However, their most significant contribution is the ecological services provided to the coastal agro ecosystems, thereby increasing the resilience and sustainability of the local economy.

Ecological functions such as storm protection may be very important components in the total economic value of a wetland and may constitute almost 80% of the estimated value (Costanza *et al.* 1989). This is a major indirect benefit and the principal reason for restoring mangrove forests along much of the low-lying deltaic coasts. It is also probably always cheaper to aim at preserving ecosystem functioning that trying to restore or substitute them when they have been degraded or lost (Moberg and Ronnback 2003). Recognition of this is important in the present scenario when large-scale removal and degradation of mangroves has already taken place.

The main cause of global mangrove loss has been coastal economic development, especially aquaculture expansion (Barbier, 2003). Yet ecologists maintain that global mangrove loss is contributing to the decline of marine fisheries, leaving many coastal areas vulnerable to natural disasters. Fisheries production constitutes the major value of marketed natural resources from mangrove ecosystems. Mangrove support to commercial, recreational and subsistence fisheries is well documented ((Pauly, 1985; Staples et al., 1985; Yanez-Arancibia et al., 1985; Pauly and Ingles, 1986; Sasekumar et al., 1992; Chong et al., 1994; Kathiresan et al., 1994; Chong et al., 1996; Twilley et al., 1996; Vance et al., 1996 a, b; De Graaf and Xuan, 1997; Baran and Hambrey, 1998; Kathiresan and Bingham, 2001; see review in Rönnbäck, 1999). For instance, 80% of all marine species of commercial or recreational value in Florida, USA, have been estimated to depend upon mangrove estuarine areas for at least some stage in their life cycles (Hamilton and Snedaker, 1984). The relative contribution of mangrove-related species to total fisheries catch can also be significant, constituting 67% of the entire commercial catch in eastern Australia (Hamilton and Snedaker, 1984), 49% of the demersal fish resources in the southern Malacca Strait (Macintosh, 1982), 30% of the fish catch and almost 100% of shrimp catch in ASEAN countries (Singh et al., 1994). Non-marketed catch is never included in fishery statistics, although coastal subsistence economies in many developing countries harvest substantial amounts of fish and shellfish from mangroves. The annual subsistence harvest per household has been valued at US $610 in Fiji (Lal, 1990) and $900 in Irian Jaya, Indonesia (Ruitenbeek, 1994). The mangrove crab was collected and sold by 42% of households and forms main source of income for 38% in North Brazil (Glaser, 2003). For the poorest rural families, mangrove fisheries have an emergency food provision function and constitute the main source of protein in their diet (Magalhes et al., 2007). The failure to take this non-commercial direct use value into account is often a major factor behind policy decisions that lead to overexploitation of mangroves (Barbier, 1994).

During monsoons a large area at the Brahmani-Baitarani-Dhamra estuary gets inundated. This flooding of the entire area by rain water is the principal vehicle for transportation of nutrients in the estuary and the surrounding areas. This contribution of mangroves in enriching the surrounding agricultural areas is well recognized by the local people. In addition the local people also other NTFP such as vegetables, honey medicinal plants etc. from the mangroves. This allows them to live on lower amount of cash that if they had to buy all these from the market (Delang, 2006).

Ecosystem services are supplied to the economic system at a range of spatial and temporal scales, varying from the short-term, site level (e.g., amenity services) to the long-term, global level (e.g., carbon sequestration) (Turner et al., 2000; Limburg et al., 2002). In order to apply ecosystem services valuation to

Table 8 Summary of value of ecosystem services provided by Bhitarkanika mangrove forests and the distribution of the benefits

Mangrove ervices		Method used	Estimated value (US$)	Distribution of value
Nutrient retention		Replacement cost	863.75 /ha	Local, regional
Land accretion		Market value	983795.7	National
Fish & Shell Fish Production	Offshore fishery	Market value	37.97/hr	Regional
	Inshore fishery	Market value	1.9/hr	Local ? Regional
	Fish Seedling	Market value	0.2/hr	Local ? regional
Storm abatement		Damage Cost Avoided	120.34/ household	Local, regional
Direct use (forestry and fishery products) (cost)		Market value	82.64/ household/ annum	Local ?

? Since it is a PA local people are not allowed access to these services

support decision making on ecosystem management, it is necessary to explicitly consider the scales at which ecosystem services accrue to the different stakeholders (Millennium Ecosystem Assessment, 2005). In case of the Bhitarkanika mangroves it is clear that most of the direct benefits of the ecosystem services do not go to the local stakeholders, since the Bhitarkanika Mangroves are protected as a National Park (Table 8). As a result the use of mangrove resources by the local people is De *facto* and indiscriminate and they have no stake in the conservation of these forests. In fact the opportunity cost of conservation of this ecosystem is high for them while the benefits are going at higher spatial levels. The tenure insecurity over use of mangroves as well as the imbalance in benefit costs distribution is a major factor in the lack of investment and interest in improving productivity of the system by the local people.

It has been increasingly recognized by economists and ecologists that the greatest 'challenge' they face is in valuing the ecosystem services provided by a certain class of key ecosystem functions – regulatory and habitat functions. Because these services are 'non-marketed', their benefits are not considered in commercial development decisions. The excessive mangrove deforestation is clearly related to the failure to measure explicitly the values of habitat and storm protection services of mangroves. Consequently, these benefits have been largely ignored in national land use policy decisions (Barbier, 2007). Unless the value to local coastal communities of the ecosystem services provided by protected mangroves is estimated, it is difficult to convince policymakers to consider alternative land use policies.

Although a better understanding of the economic value of the natural resources does not necessarily favor their conservation and sustainable use, it at least permits them to be considered as economically productive systems alongside other land uses (IUCN, 2003). The south Asian region being one of the most disadvantaged in the world, about 30% of its 1.4 billion people live on less than one dollar a day, making it home to nearly half of the world's poor (United Nations, 2005). In a situation such as in the BCA, where the family income is US$/488.9 per annum, the contribution of mangrove forests becomes important for sustaining the livelihoods of the local people, although this may not have the same significance in developed countries with high incomes (Millennium Ecosystem Assessment, 2005). Conducting studies to value such functions and thereby influencing the awareness and perception of the local people as well as the policy makers would go a long way in eliciting support for the conservation of mangrove ecosystems as well as put conservation on the 'livelihoods' agenda of the local communities and help in resolving the classic battle of conservation *vs* development.

Studies such as the present provide information about the contribution of such ecosystems as well as about local people's opinions that might be useful in targeting education and public awareness programs and in shaping policy (e.g. Streever et al., 1998). It provides an opportunity to highlight the importance of these ecosystems to the livelihoods of the local people and the urgent need to sustain this through diversification and strengthening the resource base and through proper policy and market interventions. It is also important to consideration of scales and stakeholders to enhance the applicability of ecosystem services valuation to support decision making (Hein et. al., 2006). Stakeholders at different scales often attach a different value to ecosystem services, depending upon their cultural background and upon the impact of the service on their income and/or living conditions. These different interests often result in different visions on the management of the area. The formulation of management plans that are acceptable to all stakeholders requires the balancing of these different interests (Hein et. al. 2006). Given the reliance of the poor on environmental services for their livelihoods, a central element in the adaptation approach should be ecosystem management and restoration activities. By protecting and enhancing the natural services that support livelihoods, vulnerable communities can maintain safety nets and expand the range of options for coping with disruptive shocks and trends (IUCN, 2003). This combination of institutional change, socio-economic realization and public education can form foundation for wise stewardship of one of the most productive and sensitive ecosystem.

Acknowledgments

We would like to convey our gratitude to Mr. P. R. Sinha, Director, Wildlife Institute of India and Dr. V. B. Mathur, Dean for providing guidance and support in executing this work. We express our sincere gratitude to Mr. S. Singsit, IFS, former Director, WII and Dr. A. J. T. Johnsingh, former Dean, WII for allowing us to carry out this work. We would like to thank the Field Director and the Deputy Director, Corbett Tiger Reserve for providing information on Reserve budget and tourism management. We gratefully acknowledge the field support extended to us by Mr. Gyan Sarin, Director, Corbett Foundation without which this work would not have been possible. We would like to thank Prof. Karen E Limburg, President, United States Society for Ecological Economics (USSEE), and Marsha Kopan, International, Society for Ecological Economics (ISSEE) Secretariat for funding support.

References

Adger, W. N., Kelly, P. M., and Tri, N. H. (1997). Valuing the products and services of mangrove restoration. *Commonwealth Forestry Review 76*(3): 198–202.

Allen, S. E. (1989). *Chemical Analysis of Ecological Materials.* Oxford: Blackwell Scientific Publications.

Badola, R., and Hussain, S. A. (2003). Valuation of Bhitarknika mangrove ecosystem for ecological security and sustainable resource use. Study report. Wildlife Institute of India, Dehra Dun. 101 pp.

Badola, R., and Hussain, S. A. (2005). Valuing the storm protection function of the Bhitarkanika mangrove ecosystem, India. *Environmental Conservation 32*(1).

Badola, R. (1998). Attitudes of local people towards conservation and alternatives to forest resources: A case study from the lower Himalayas. *Biodiversity and Conservation 7*: 1245–1259.

Bann, C. (1998). The economic value of mangroves: a manual for researchers. Economy and Environment Program for Southeast Asia, Singapore.

Baran, E., and Hambrey, J. (1998). Mangrove conservation and coastal management in Southeast Asia: What impact on fishery resources? *Mar. Poll. Bull. 37*(8-12): 431–440.

Barbier, E. B. (2007) Valuing ecosystem services as productive inputs. *Economic Policy* (Jan 2007): 177–229.

Barbier, E. B. (1993). Sustainable use of wetlands valuing tropical wetland benefits: Economic margin methodologies and applications. *Geographical Journal 159*: 22–32.

Barbier, E. B. (1994). Valuing Environmental Functions: Tropical Wetlands *Land Economics 70*(2): 155-173.

Bockstael, N. E., et al. (2000). On measuring economic value for nature. *Environmental Science and Technology* 34: 1384-1389.

Carlton, J. M. (1974). Land building and stabilization by mangroves. *Environmental Conservation 1*: 285–294

Chapman, V. J. (1976). *Mangrove Vegetation*. Leutershausen, Germany: Strauss & Cramer.

Chong, V. C., Sasekumar, A., and Wolanski, E. (1996). The role of mangroves in retaining penaeid prawn larvae in Klang Strait, Malaysia. *Mang. Salt Marsh. 1*: 11–22.

Chong, V. C., Sasekumar, A., and Lim, K. H. (1994). Distribution and abundance of prawn in a Malaysian mangrove system. In Sudara, S., Wilkinson, C. R., and Chou, I. M. (Eds.), *Proceedings of Third ASEAN—Australian Symposium on Living Coastal Resources, Vol. 2*. Bangkok: Ihula Long Korn University, 437–444.

Choudhury, B. P., Subudhi, H. N., and Biswal, A. K. (1999). *The Mangrove Forest of Bhitarkanika National Park* (Proposed). Report. Nature and Wildlife Conservation Society of Orissa. India.

Cormier-Salem, M. C. (1999). The mangrove: An area to be cleared . . . for social scientists. *Hydrobiologia 413*(0): 135–142.

Costanza, R., Faber, C., and Maxwell, J. (1989). The valuation and management of wetland ecosystems. *Ecological Economics 1*: 335–361

Dani, C. S., and Kar, S. K. (1999). *Bhitarkanika-A unique mangrove ecosystem*. Nature and Wildlife Conservation Society of Orissa. 30–42 pp.

Davis R. A. (1987). Coastal geology. In *Encyclopedia of Physical Science and Technology, Vol 3*. Orlando: Academic Press.

Graaf, G. J., and Xuan, T. T. (1997). Shrimp farming and natural sherries in the southern provinces of Vietnam. Coastal Wetlands Protection and Development Project. Ho Chi Minh City, Vietnam.

FAO (1985). Mangrove management in Thailand, Malaysia and Indonesia. FAO Environment Paper 4. Food and Agriculture Organization of the United Nations, Rome.

FAO (1994). Mangrove forest management guidelines. FAO Forestry Paper 117. Food and Agriculture Organization of the United Nations, Rome.

Field, C. B., et al. (1998). Mangrove biodiversity and ecosystem function. *Global Ecology and Biogeography Letter 7*(1): 3–14.

Freeman A. M. (2003). *The Measurement of Environmental and Resource Values: Theory and Methods*. Second Edition. Washington, D.C.: Resources for the Future.

Gilbert, A. J., and Jansen, R. (1997). The use of environmental functions to evaluate management strategies for the Pagbilao Mangrove Forest. CREED Working Paper No. 15.

Glaser, M. (2003). Interrelations between mangrove ecosystem, local economy and social sustainability in Caete Estuary, North Brazil. *Wet. Ecol. Manage. 11*: 265–272.

Gopi, G. V., Pandav, B., and Chaudhury, B. C. (2002). Experimental trawling along the Orrisa coast to estimate the mortality of sea turtles. Wildlife Institute of India.

Hamilton, L. S., and Snedaker, S. C. (Eds.) (1984). Handbook for Mangrove Area Management. IUCN/Unesco/UNEP. East-West Centre. Honolulu, Hawaii.

Hamilton, L. S., Dixon, J. A., and Miller, G. O. (1989). Mangrove forests: An undervalued resource of the land and of the sea. In Borgese, E. M., Ginsburg, N., Morgan, J. R. (Eds.), *Ocean Yearbook 8*. Chicago: University of Chicago Press, 254-288.

Hein, L., K. van Koppenb, R.S. de Groot & E.C. van Ierland (2006). Spatial scales, stakeholders and the valuation of ecosystem services. *Ecological Economics* 57: 209–228.

IUCN (2003). Valuing Wetlands in Decision Making: Where are we Now? Integrating Wetland Economic Values into River Basin Management. Wetland Valuation Issues Paper 1. IUCN-The World Conservation Union. Gland, Switzerland.

Kathiresan, K. and Bingham, B. L. (2001). Biology of mangroves and mangrove ecosystems. *Adv. Mar. Biol. 40*: 81–251.

Kathiresan, K., and Rajendran, N. (2005). Coastal mangrove forests mitigated tsunami. *Estuar. Coast. Shelf Sci. 67*(3): 539–541.

Kathiresan, K., Ramesh, M. X., and Venkatesan, V. (1994). Forest structure and prawn seed in Pichavaram mangroves. *Environ. Ecol. 12* (465-468): 1–41.

Lacerda, L. D. (Ed.) (2002). *Mangrove Ecosystems: Function and Management*. New York: Springer.

Lal, P. N. (1990). *Conservation or Conversion of Mangroves in Fiji*. East-West Environment and Policy Institute. Honolulu Occasional Paper No. 11, 108 pp.

Limburg, K. E., O'Neill, R.V., Costanza, R., and Faber, S. (2002). Complex systems and valuation. *Ecological Economics 41*: 409–420.

MacNae, W. (1974). Mangrove forest and fisheries. FAO/UNDP Indian Ocean Fishery Program. Indian Ocean Fishery Commission. Publication IOFC-Dev/74/, pp 34-35.

Macnae, W. (1968). A general account of the fauna and flora of mangrove swamps and forests in the Indo-West-Pacific region. *Adv. Mar. Biol. 6*: 73–270.

Magalhaes, A., et al. (2007). The role of women in the mangrove crab (*Ucides cordatus*, Ocypodidae) production process in North Brazil (Amazon region, Pará) *Ecological Economics*. (In Press)

Mahapatra, K. (2000). The coastal Zone of Orissa, Bay of Bengal: Status and framework for sustainable management. In *Subtle issues in Coastal Management*, R. Sudarashana (Ed.). Delhi: Daya Publishing House.

Maltby, E. (1986). *Waterlogged Wealth*. London, UK: Earthscan.

Maltby, E., and van Ierland, E. C. (2000). Ecological-economic analysis of wetlands: Scientific integration for management and policy. *Ecological Economics 35*: 7–23.

Millennium Ecosystem Assessment (2005). Ecosystems and Human Well Being: Biodiversity Synthesis. Washington, D.C.: World Resources Institute.

Mitsch,W. J., and Gosselink, J.G. (2000). *Wetlands*. 3rd Ed. New York: Van Nostrand Reinhold.

Moberg, F., and Ronnback, P. (2003). Ecosystem services of the tropical seascape: interactions, substitutions and restoration. *Ocean and Coastal Management 46* (1-2): 27–46.

Mohanty, M. (1990). Sea level rise: Background, global concern and implications for Orissa coast, India. In *Sea level variations and its impact on Coastal Environments*, G. V. Rajamanicken (Ed). Tamilnadu University Publication, No.131. Chennai, India.

Naskar, K. R., and Mandal, R. N. (1999). Ecology and biodiversity of Indian mangroves. Delhi: Daya Publishing House.

Patnaik, M. R., Purohit, K. L., and Patra, A. K. (1995). Mangrove swamps of Bhitarkanika Orissa, India—A great eco habitat for wildlife. *Cheetal* 34(1): 1–9.

Pauly, D., and Ingles, J. (1986). The relationship between shrimp yields and intertidal (mangrove) areas: A reassessment. In IOC/FAO Workshop on Recruitment in Tropical Coastal Demersal Communities. IOC, UNESCO, Paris, pp. 227–284.

Pauly, D. (1985) Ecology of coastal and estuarine fishes in southeast Asia: a Philippine case study. In Yañez-Arancibia, A. (Ed.), *Fish Community Ecology in Estuaries and Coastal Lagoons, Towards an Ecosystem Integration.* Mexico: UNAM Press, 499–535.

Rasolofo, M. V. (1997). Use of mangroves by traditional fishermen in Madagascar. *Journal of Mangrove Salt Marshes*: 243–253.

Richardson, C. J., and McCarthy, E. J. (1994). Effect of land development and forest management on hidrologic response in southeastern coastal wetlands: a review. *Wetlands 14*(1): 56–71.

Rollet, B. (1981). *Bibliography on mangrove research, 1600–1975.* UNESCO, Paris.

Ruitenbeek, H. J. (1994). Modeling economy-ecology linkages in mangroves: Economic evidence for promoting conservation in Bintuni Bay, Indonesia. *Ecological Economics 10*(3): 233–247.

Saenger, P., Hegerl, E. J., and Davie, J. D. S. (1983). Global status of mangrove ecosystems. *The Environmentalist: Supplement 3*: 49.

Sasekumar, A., Chong, V. C., Leh, M. U., and D'Cruz, R. (1992). Mangroves as a habitat for fish and prawns. *Hydrobiologia 247*: 195–207.

Sathirathai, S. & E.B. Barbier (2001). Valuing mangrove conservation in southern Thailand. *Contemporary Economic Policy* 19 (2): 109-122.

Semesi, A.K. (1998). Mangrove management and utilization in Eastern Africa. *Ambio* 27 (8): 620-626.

Singh, H. R., et al. (1994). Value of mangroves as nursery and feeding grounds. In: Wilkinson, C. R., Suraphol, S., Chou, L. M., (Eds.), Proceedings of the Third ASEAN-Australia Symposium on Living Coastal Resources, Vol. 1: Status Reviews.

Spaninks, F., and Beukering, P. V. (1997). *Economic valuation of mangrove ecosystems: Potential and limitations.* CREED Working Paper No. 14.

SPSS Inc. (1999). SPSS Base 10.0 User's Guide. Chicago.

Staples, D. J., Vance, D. J., and Heales D. S. (1985). Habitat requirements of juvenile penaeid prawns and their relationship to offshore sherries. In

Rothlisberg, P. C., Hill, B. J., and Staples, D. J. (Eds.), Second Australian National Prawn Seminar. CSIRO. Cleveland, pp. 47–54.

Streever, W. J., et al. (1998). Public Attitudes and Values for Wetland Conservation in New South Wales, Australia. *Journal of Environmental Management 54*: 1–14.

Swallow, S. K. (1994). Renewable and non-renewable resource theory applied to coastal agriculture, forest, wetland and fishery linkages. *Marine Resource Economics 9*: 291–310.

Sundberg, S. (2004). Replacement costs as economic values of environmental change: A review and an application to Swedish trout habitats. Beijer Discussion Papers Series. 184. The Beijer International Institute of Ecological Economics. The Royal Swedish Academy of Sciences. Stockholm, Sweden.

Tomlinson, P. B. (1986). *The Botany of Mangroves*. Cambridge: Cambridge University Press.

Turner, R. K., et al. (2000). Ecological-economic analysis of wetlands: scientific integration for management and policy. *Ecological Economics 35*: 7–23.

Twilley, R.R., et al. (1996). Biodiversity and ecosystem processes in tropical estuaries: perspective of mangrove ecosystems. In: Mooney, H. A., et al, *Functional Roles of Biodiversity: A Global Perspective*. New York: Wiley, 327–370.

Valiela, I., Bowen, J. L., and York, J. K. (2001). Mangrove forests: one of the world's threatened major tropical environments. *Biosci 51*: 807–815.

Vance, D. J., et al.(1996). How far do prawns and fish move into mangroves? Distribution of juvenile banana prawns *Penaeus merguiensis* and fish in a tropical mangrove forest in northern Australia. *Mar. Ecol. Prog. Ser. 131*: 115–24.

Walbridge, M. R., and Lockaby, B. G. (1994). Effects of forest management on biogeochemical functions in southern forested wetlands. *Wetlands 14*(1): 10–17.

Wilkie, M .L., and Fortuna, S. (2003). Status and trends in mangrove area extent worldwide. Working Paper FRA 63. Forest Resources Division, Forestry Department, UN Food and Agriculture Organization. 292 pp.

Wilkie, M. L., Fortuna, S., and Souksavat, O. (2003). Changes in world mangrove area. In Proceedings XII World Forestry Congress B-Forests for the Planet, pp. 165–175. Quebec city, Canada, Sep. 21–28, 2003.

Wolanski, E. (1985). Numerical modeling of flows in the tidal creek-mangrove swamp system. Proceedings 21ˢᵗ, Congress International Association for Hydraulic Research. Melbourne, Victoria, 3: 80–85.

Yañez-Arancibia, A., Soberon-Chavez, G., and Sanchez-Gil, P. (1985). Ecology of control mechanisms of natural fish production in the coastal zone. In Yanez-Arancibia, A. (ed.), *Fish Community Ecology in Estuaries and Coastal Lagoons, Towards an Ecosystem Integration*. Mexico: UNAM Press, 571–595.

Zar, J. H. (1984) *Biostatistical Analysis*. Englewood Cliffs, NJ: Prentice-Hall.

17 Insights from Europe

Women at the Crossroads with Transportation, the Environment and the Economy

Meike Spitzner [1]

It started with Women's "Initiatives" (ed: citizens petitions) in Germany. "Women in Motion" was the name of a national network of women involved in transportation "initiatives," transportation policy, planning, research, administration, related organizations, and businesses. The network was founded in 1989. It grew out of protests against transport policies all over the country, which ignored every day-needs and mobility patterns of all but able-bodied, employed men. The "rail-free inner city" program, in the 1980's, was such a case. The government wanted to get rid of streetcars in Frankfurt, as it had done in so many other cities. Based on intensive and meticulous research, the women confronted the male-centred transportation research community with the conditions they had been living under. Until then, the special needs of men prevailed in transportation research and contributed to present gender relations. After that national politics in Germany were, for the first time, faced with the reality of "women in motion."

It finally dawned on those responsible for traffic conditions, laws and regulations in our communities that in a country with a high level of population density, urbanization and public transport and railways networks, "emancipation from the car" could be a thinkable prospect. "Emancipation from the car" was also the title of the first petition to parliament, in 1990. The petition addressed the gendered realities in the field of transportation. Men especially should take the prospect of "emancipation from the car" serious. The car based urban regions and their "suburbanizing" rural periphery pose a tremendous environmental problems. Until now, shaping the politics and policies of German socio/economic reality, was not in women's hands; neither was running the economy, transportation or the protection of the environment. This article focuses therefore on how gender, environment, economy and transportation intersect.

1   This contribution was translated by Regula Modlich from the original published in *Women & Environments*, Spring/Summer 2006: 31–34.

Gendered Transportation Reality and Rationality

Until now transportation science, planning and politics have always assumed responsibility for planning, financing and improving mobility for all. Yet, in the past, transportation professionals prioritized needs for the movement of both of people and goods, based on their personal experiences and perspectives. Traditionally, transportation enjoyed large shares of public budgets, financing and bureaucracies at all levels of government to manage road construction, especially for long distance expressways, which would "boost the economy." Gradually however, this has proven to be at the expense of public transportation, especially non-motorized movement. The trend of the European Union to privatize public services jeopardizes the longstanding responsibility of the public transportation sector for long-term transportation needs of the whole society. Changing sections of the German constitution to allow for the privatization of the German rail roads without ensuring basic levels of social or environmental services is a case in point. The first step of this transition was the division of the old non-transparent public transport planning into a public "ordering" and a commercial "selling" section of public transportation services. The mandate for public decision making, offered a great opportunity for developing strict procedures for "ordering" which would ensure public transparency, participation and allow women's and gender initiatives including "zero-ordering." Thus the selling off of the longstanding public service railway maintenance, especially in the critical short-distance sector to ad hoc, for-profit and competitive contracts failed to ensure public services at environmentally and socially sustainable and gender equitable levels. European, national and local privatization policies only com pound these infrastructure problems.

Transportation professionals have a mindset, which reduces human existence and actions to that of "clients" or "consumers," which are linguistically subsumed under the male gender. Humans are considered neutral, without gender, age or ability constraints, without domestic or community context and without feelings. This reduces humans to a-social and a-sexual beings, that can then be selectively fitted to suit assumed social constructs and imagined gender roles. This is how in the industrial age, the notion of the stereotypical middle class household developed. It consisted of a bread-winning husband, full time housewife and children. Today, such households are no longer prevalent, nor socially desirable.

The ongoing fight of the women's movement, feminist research and policies to advance the status of women have lent 30 valuable credibility and strength 25 to women's efforts for change. The women's representations 20 revealed that the entire transportation system including its management had turned a blind eye to 10—and glossed over the reality and pervasiveness of structural oppression of women. While this can be attributed to "being different," or 0 the prevailing acceptance of male domination or to trivializing and rendering women invisible, it is a reality, with which women are all too familiar. How else can one explain the alienating subway stations? They stink of male urine, are built with coarse materials and painted in ugly colours. How else can one explain aligning walkways and bike lanes under highways ramps?

Women know that the "general" trend to fuel-based transportation is solely male, catering to middle-aged men, who do not share responsibility for care giving work. People have very different transportation needs in regard to transportation mode, origin, destination, schedule, trip purpose, distance, speed etc. Instead of accepting this diversity of transportation requirements and ensuring democratic access to mobility for all groups, a marginal group of professional transportation experts reigns over the field. The risk is obvious and evaluations prove that these experts serve and identify their own interests as those of their 'clients' and that they have simply not bothered to correct their subjective outlook to become more objective.

In a democracy, it should be the responsibility of transportation professionals to safeguard the public interest. To start with, this could include: an end to the androcentric irrational affair with transportation technology; a minor symbolic surtax on "mobility" with cars which would allow drivers to compensate for their mobility advantages; re-establish the priority of the "forgot ten body and nature" over the scale, functions and design of the built environment, especially a return to walking, a scientific database of transportation decisions, which are not male-centred, but rooted in social and natural sciences ; this would be an interdisciplinary database which would replace the cur rent ones which are devoid of social references or objectives, yet are still used to determine road construction; a balanced representation of woman power and of gender competence on transportation related committees.

No more women-only night taxis! We need a totally different concept of transportation infrastructure and policies. Such a concept would aim at minimizing traffic, respond to social needs, be fully accessible and effectively meet the requirements of caregivers. Such a transportation system would also make up for the socio-economic problems caused by past development and planning mistakes. Women are aware how urban planning has increased distances and encouraged ever more remote destinations, even for getting every day necessities. Transportation planning has caused a jump in the number of "mobility disadvantaged" people who need to be chauffeured. Flexibility for individual travelers and the transportation needs of private enterprise have received priority. These policies have been at the expense of social interaction. Fewer people mingle in public places and on transit. Speeding cars, narrow walkways, worries about the safety of children in their care, pedestrian bridges or underpasses built without consideration for women's safety or structural male violence, all affect women while they walk or look after dependents. No wonder that women want to adopt male patterns of mobility and travel by car. In this way the androcentrism of transport planning and politics is causing an enormous rise of—environmentally, economically and socially unsustainable car traffic.

Gendered Economic Reality and Rationality

At the root of this male oriented mind- set is the denial of the existence of a whole sector of the economy, which until now has been sustained solely by women. The traditional gender hierarchy and the lack of men's participation, has kept the "domestic" economy from being validated socially or politically. The transportation system therefore considers the "domestic" economy with its social, bodily and natural elements and qualities as "non-economy" or "consumption" of the products of the "real economy." The whole complex and structural reality of women's lives as well as their issues are attributed to the "private," non-public or politically un-accountable sphere. The privatization of the old public enterprises—even if they were run with a patriarchal mindset—threatens to destroy the crucial concept of public interest which today should embody the interests of women i.e. the needs of the caring giving economy.

Practically all women have to deal with issues ranging from care giving, domestic chores, employment, community involvement to the risk of harassment even male violence. Still, established wisdom considers social and care giving activities as "individual" choices and as "non-structural" and "non infrastructural" questions. Undervaluing the caring, domestic and public not-for-profit economies strengthens gender hierarchy and weakens environmental sustainability. The tension between freedom/abandon and linkages/bonds, between independence and contextualized existence is mostly "solved" in a gender hierarchic way. The first values are socially masculine, the second set of values are attributed to the socially feminine. Androcentrisms within the transport sector give priority to the first values, to "independence," a longing to get away, be alone, free of social constraints, excited by change and conquest of nature's limitations. Women's values are often considered "nature" or a "natural resource." They can sustain them selves at no or little economic cost: stability and security of social relations, feeding the body's needs, sustaining a good environment.

By following this androcentric vision and longing, the so-called "productive" sector of our economy encourages consumption and waste of renewable and non renewable natural, human and social energy and strength. At the same time, this "productive" sector is jeopardizing the integrity of nature and physis, devaluating the social and natural integrity and destroying history as well as future opportunities. Transportation related to the "real economy" comes at the expense of the "non-production" or domestic economy. Public transportation ends up in crisis, because this narrow understanding of "domestic" economy and the under valuing of caring within public economy. One can expect, therefore, that women, and the spheres for which they have been—and amazingly still are—responsible, and in which they still provide a quality safety net for society, will again suffer most, be that in private or public service sector of the economy.

The commitment to reorient transportation research, planning and policies to become more sensitive to the environment, have not reduced androcentrism nor led to the integration of gender considerations because the same thinking reigned also here. Bureaucrats and officials selectively accept ed and institutionalized some demands of the environmental movement and of citizens transportation "initiatives" in terms of two strategies: the so called "efficiency" and the so called "sufficiency" strategies.

Transportation officials define "efficiency" as striving to increase the effectiveness of applied energy/power, while they define "sufficiency" as reducing demands on social and natural resources. They keep these two components separate and attribute each through their gender hierarchy coloured lens and gender ranked economies, along the line of production and consumption. Efforts for efficiency are made for the production sector, while sufficiency and moderation is assigned to the so called consumption, which is subsumed under the sphere of "domestic" economy.

Yet, there is no thought given how more moderation, more sufficiency could be integrated in production. There is no consideration given to how the care givers' and consumers' power could be more efficient in getting environmentally and socially more sustainable products.The production sector harvests unripe fruit, to better survive a lengthy transport; they then ripen it quickly with chemicals, totally disregarding the serious risks to health and the environment. Until now politics have turned a blind eye to the question of how to research, discuss and apply gains in science, awareness and efficiency within in this conflicting context. In most economies the Gross Domestic Product, counts the repair efforts of an environmental disaster such as an oil spill as "production," yet all unpaid domestic and nurturing work such as caring for a good environment, for partners, elderly, the ill or children—done until now almost completely by women—is excluded.

Moving Forward

Gender Mainstreaming can therefore be a meaningful tool for looking at transportation from a sustainability perspective. However, it has to be understood as a double strategy of "push and pull" or mainstreaming in the sense of reorienting sufficiency in terms of social masculinity and an efficiency revolution in terms of empowerment of women. It should, how ever, not be the kind of strategy, which experts from women's NGO's recently endured when the EU head office for the environments invited them on behalf of its male mid-management level. That was "gendermalestreaming" simply to co-opt women's "closeness to the grass roots," and let them "have their say," but not to bring about change and to adjust their mindset. "Closeness to the grass roots" seems to be an adaptation of the classic motherhood statement "closeness to life" or "closeness to nature."

Come on already! Even in the socially, financially and for the future of society so important field of transportation, there is finally some motion in the encrusted thinking along male social categories! This advance is happening thanks to national obligation flowing from international agreements. At the European level,

Scandinavian states strengthened these agreements. At the global level, women of the South and East raised the level of negotiations of gender issues.

In Germany the federal government has finally taken the initiative. It was the result of years of stubborn efforts by a few women experts in gendered transportation research, of the commitment of the nation al Network of Women Inc., of the Taskforce on Environment and Development and of the specialized feminist expertise in the Office of the Secretary of State. The UN Commission's decisive preparations for the world summit on Environment and Development, "Rio+l0" in 2002 in Capetown, S.A. reflected this progress. It included women delegates from the North and South who brought their first studies conducted by them selves, face to face exchanges amongst experts and researched position papers on "Gender Perspectives on the Earth Summit 2002: Transport, Energy and Information for Decision Making." The German government had commissioned and submitted this document to the Commission on Sustainable Development and UN.

The German government also instituted a regular national exchange between the Ministry for the Environment, representatives from environmental and women's organizations and experts on gender environment and sustainability questions. Through "WAVE" (Women as the Voice for Environment), UNEP, at the UN's Global Conference on Women and the Environment in 2004 in Nairobi, enabled for the first time ever, a global focus on connections between problems with transportation policies and gender relations. This realization happened in the context of climate policy, the link between climate change and the transport sector of the North and the need for gender equity. Europe too, is making baby steps. In 2006, the European Parliament commissioned east and west European gender experts to cooperate on a first, though limited, investigation of "Women and Transport."

What however, is still missing today, on practically every level and in practically all countries, is the serious commitment and appropriate funding of gender focused reorientation in transportation research. This needs to include professionals in related departments such as ministries, commissions, public offices etc. and in the professional institutions and their branches throughout the country. It also needs the institutionalizing and anchoring of legal, procedural and professional practice of these responsibilities before unilateralism and injustice in gender relations can be eliminated, especially in the area of transportation. The demand for reorientation of the malestream on the one hand and for strengthening of centres for the development of structural analysis, strategies, methods and measurements for gender-sustainability can be interwoven. Yet this direction is still not covered by the appropriate commitment of resources. Such preconditions are necessary, to advance a care giving, community orient ed economy, and a forward looking society which is committed to far reaching and long term socio/environmental harmony. These would truly advance the public interest.

Further Reading

Brouns, Bernd, and Spitzner, Meike. (2004). Gender: The Forgotten Pillar of International Climate Policy. *Sustainable Energy News,* Dec. 2004 (*47*): 6–7. http://www.inforse.org/europe/pdfs/SEN47.pdf

Spitzner, Meike, Weiler, Frank. Andi, Rahmah, and Turner, Jeff. (2007). *Urban Mobility and Gender: Promoting the regional public transport system in the greater Jakarta area.* Focus on Development Policy, KfW Entwick-lungsbank Position Paper. http://www.kfw-entwicklungsbank.de/DE_Ho me/Service_und_Dokumentation/Online_Bibliothek/PDF-Dokumente_ Fokus_Entwicklungspolitik/FE_Transport-Gender_Jabotabek_ 2007-08_englisch.pdf

Spitzner, Meike, and Beik, Ute. (1999). *Reproduktionsarbeitsmobilität.* Theoretische und empirische Erfassung, Dynamik ihrer Entwicklung und Analyse ökolo-gischer Dimensionen und Handlungsstrategien. (*Caring Mobility. Theoretical and empirical recognitions, analysis of their dynamic, of sustainable dimen-sions and strategies of action.*) In Hesse Markus, Holzapfel Helmut, Spitzner Meike (Eds.), Entwicklung der Arbeits- und Freizeitmobilität - Rahmenbedingungen von Mobilität in Stadtregionen. Forschungsberichte des vom Bundesministeriums für Bildung, Wissenschaft, Forschung und Technologie geförderten Verbundforschungprojekts Bd. 5. Wuppertal: Forschungsverbund Ökologisch verträgliche Mobilität, 40–140.

Spitzner, Meike, and Zauke, Gabriele. (2003). *Evaluation of the Involvement of Women in Transport Science, Traffic Planning and Mobility Politics in the Past and in the Present.* City & Shelter, Brussels. http://www.cityshelter. org/13_mobil/4.%20bilanz-meike-spitzner.doc

Spitzner, Meike. (2008). *The need for gendered approaches in Transport policy: Results from case studies in industrialised and developing countries.* Presentation at the United Nations Framework Convention on Climate Change, Side Event "Women for Climate Justice" in June 2008 at Bonn. http://regserver.unfccc.int/seors/file_storage/snkd13p2hkrn2dd.pdf

Spitzner, Meike. *Netzgebundene Infrastruktursysteme unter Veränderungsdruck Genderanalyse am Beispiel Öffentlicher Personennahverkehr.* netWORKS-Papers,Nr.13.Berlin:DeutschesInstitutfürUrbanistik,2004.(*Transformation and Privatisation of Infrastructures and Gender. Concept for Gender Ana-lysis,* developed by an evaluation of the results within the public transport sector. Study commissioned by the Federal Ministry of Research). http:// www.networks-group.de/veroeffentlichungen/DF9369.pdf

Turner, Jeff, Spitzner, Meike, Hamilton, Kerry, Seserko, Leo, and Krizkova, Alena. (2006). *Women and Transport in Europe.* Ed. European Parliament, Brux-elles. http://www.europarl.europa.eu/meetdocs/2004_2009/documents/dv/ tran20060912_womentransportstudy/tran20060912_womentransport study.pdf

Turner, Jeff, and Spitzner, Meike. (2007). Reality check: How effective have efforts been to integrate gender into donor agency transport interventions? In the

18 Responsibility and the Bordering of Sustainable Development

Experimenting with Regional Sustainability Strategies in Western Australia

Natalie McGrath and Peter Newman

ABSTRACT

The clear and equitable distribution of responsibility for sustainable development is critical to the success of sustainable development strategies. However, the cause of many of the issues that concern sustainable development is complex and is found across institutional sectors, geographical boundaries and also importantly must be considered to run across sectoral interests. Thus the responsibility for solving these issues is also diffuse and is complicated by the forces of globalization. This paper will discuss the importance of the concept of regionalism for sustainable development as this provides an opportunity to draw boundaries which relate to geographical areas and to better clarify and coordinate the responsibilities for sustainable development. This necessary task will not be easy, and will require a participatory process approach based upon learning to better coordinate across sectors in one geographical location and ultimately across geographical locations towards a process of global sustainable development. The paper outlines the Pilbara Regional Sustainability Strategy in Western Australia which will be employed as a case study to demonstrate how this analysis can be enacted. This regional strategy was a methodological experiment in formulating and understanding sustainable development at the regional level and followed from the recommendations of the Western Australian State Sustainability Strategy. A discussion reflects upon the lessons learnt from the strategy relates these to earlier sections of this article.

Introduction

There are many different interests that meet in a framework based upon sustainable development. For the purposes of analysis these are often simply categorized as environmental, socio-political and economic. More recently culture and spirituality have been included as a fourth 'pillar' though we prefer these to be seen as underlying each of the other three pillars and in essence cultural and spiritual values are driving the process that integrates the three pillars, hence creating the synergies which are at the heart of sustainable development. Within sustainable development literature the interests of each pillar are seen to be expressed and managed by organizational sectors that include non-governmental organizations, government and business. Reality however is complex and the meeting of these interests (or pillars) across organizational sectors and space not only creates many opportunities for collaboration to advance sustainable development but also creates diverse tensions and significant conflict. In particular the clarification of responsibility for particular interests is complex and this is in part the focus of the article.

The clear and equitable distribution of responsibility for sustainable development is critical to the success of sustainable development strategies. However, responsibility has become an increasingly complex issue in a world that is continually transformed by the forces of globalization. When thinking about issues such as climate change, biodiversity or global poverty, it is impossible to trace the cause of these issues to a single institutional point, for example the nation state or a particular trans-national corporation, in a particular geographical location. Instead the cause of many of the issues that concern sustainable development at a global level can be found across institutional sectors, such as government, corporations or civil society, across geographical boundaries and also importantly must be considered to run across environmental, socio-political and economic interests, as well as cultural and spiritual interests. Thus the responsibility for solving these issues is also diffuse.

The above complexity is discussed in the early sections of this paper. This paper will then discuss the importance of the concept of regionalism for sustainable development. The concept of a region is heavily contested by the different interests that exist. This however provides the opportunity in which to draw boundaries which relate to geographical areas and to better clarify and coordinate the responsibilities for sustainable development in accordance with the actions of institutions and individuals within that particular geography. This necessary task will not be easy, and will require new governance with a process approach based upon learning to better coordinate across sectors in one geographical location and ultimately across geographical locations. A participatory approach to decision making will enable the different perspectives on sustainable development issues to be brought to bear in analysing policy for the future and will help to enable ownership of responsibility for sustainable development strategies.

The last section in this article focuses upon the Pilbara Regional Sustainability Strategy which will be employed as a case study to demonstrate how this analysis can be enacted. This regional strategy was a methodological experiment in formulating and understanding sustainable development at the regional level and followed from the recommendations of the State Sustainability Strategy. Conclusions reflect upon the lessons learnt from the strategy and relate these to earlier sections of this article.

The many borders of sustainable development

Sustainable development has over the last few decades become institionalized across geographical space, organizations and cultures (Frazier 1997; Pezzoli 1997; Mebratu 1998; Castro 2004). Definitions and frameworks of sustainable development vary widely which is perceived as both a strength (Davison 2001) and a weakness (Scott and Gough 2003). The contested nature of sustainable development is seen in this chapter to be a strength as it allows for dominant cultural values to be challenged. This is articulately argued by Kinnane who writes that Indigenous involvement with sustainable development discourse provides for diversity and leads to a necessary rethinking of other movements within this discourse and subverts the unity of interests model (Kinnane 2005).

Fundamental to all the definitions is the need for long term solutions to the environmental problems we face and how these intersect with social and economic factors. Particularly contested within a sustainable development framework is the possibility of sustaining economic development whilst improving social and environmental health. Contested concepts invariably direct us to deeper values as a means of finding ways forward. Reconciling local and global values remains problematic particularly in regards to the distribution of wealth and how this intersects with cultures. Thus the integrative framework that the concept of sustainable development creates helps to surface these and other tensions. This framework ideally creates space for not only collaboration which is strongly emphasized in sustainable development discourse; it also involves conflict and compromise.

Sustainable development can thus be seen as a moving concept through space and time, which is being constantly negotiated in the human world through the meeting of different values and worldviews, some of which place high value on a close and respectful relationship with the non-human world. A well known Indigenous academic Mick Dodson captures this negotiation process by writing that sustainable development is "a direction more than a place: it is about innovation and opportunity and involves value judgments about the direction and speed of change" (Dodson and Smith 2003 p 3-4).

Within any particular geographical area there are countless narratives (or interests), including the environment, that can be seen as threads that compose the tapestry of a sustainable development framework. It is important to consider how these interact across space and time, which is inevitably complex and will only ever be partly understood by any particular human narrative. In the case of Australia it can be observed that some of these narratives are less easily visible than others and thus are not well considered in policy formulation or implementation. Indigenous cultural narratives are certainly an obvious case of this and also help to highlight the differing types of borders that a sustainable development framework helps to compare and contrast.

The landscape of Australian Indigenous culture is both diverse and dynamic. This landscape is seen to have been traditionally composed of distinct language groups that were internally related through responsibilities to each other and to the country. The relationships that run between these groups are now called

Songlines and these continue to define Indigenous responsibilities across Australia today. The reality of Indigenous regions has not met well with the multitude of Federal, State or local government boundaries that have been developed since the time of settlement. Although, Indigenous cultural geography is itself today a complicated terrain and is layered by tradition and also by contemporary changes, the point here is that Indigenous borders were not considered within the construction of government borders in Australia. The discourse around the concept of shared sovereignty continues to be a priority for Indigenous political leaders and this will require a number of different borders to be drawn for a nation to nation's relationship. This tension requires negotiation not only for issues relating to social justice for Indigenous people but also because of the lessons Indigenous cultural relationships of responsibility have to offer the sustainable development agenda more generally. The reality is that land management today needs an ecological and regional approach and the boundaries established over 30,000 years probably had a lot to do with these matters. The chances of such lessons being transferred into mainstream Australian policy are likely to be greater if this policy recognizes and negotiates with Indigenous political boundaries.

Thus negotiating the borders of Indigenous regions in Australia is a complex issue and will require considerable effort to negotiate. This however is just one of the narratives within the sustainable development agenda that requires ongoing attention to the drawing of borders. The consideration of these bordering processes together emphasizes the complexity of negotiating sustainable development but is a necessary task. To make this point clearer it is useful to name just a few of the diverse range of narratives that need to be considered within Australia which also have a regional boundary as part of their frame. Table 1 utilizes the categories of environment, culture, economic and political, that are sometimes used to analyse sustainable development. They are listed with the kinds of regional boundaries that are typically at the base of any of their narratives within an Australian context. They are generally closely guarded boundaries by the 'gatekeepers' of these sectors who ensure that their perspective must be prioritized in any debates.

Table 1: Regions based on the different silos of sectors in Australia

- **Environment:** Natural Resource Management regions, bioregions based on water catchments or on key biota or on key landscape features; water supply areas . . .
- **Culture:** regions related to sense of place, identity, social capital and community . . .
- **Economic:** regions based on mining, farming/pastoralism, tourism and local or regional services such as shopping, communications, electricity supply, banking . . .
- **Political:** regions based on local government, State and Territory government regions or even Federal Government regions, also incorporated bodies including Native Title Prescribed Body Corporates covering regions . . .

Because the regional boundaries that frame particular approaches to issues are so embedded the complexity of finding overall sustainable development solutions is overwhelmingly and can disenable coordination. This is why cultural and spiritual values are sought to try and find some deeper base for finding solutions that can be common to all. These values may have a regional basis also although in our discussion we have sought to try and use those values that are more universal rather than regional which we tend to describe as social values.

The discussion in this section has endeavoured to demonstrate that the analysis of how different narratives co-exist and complement and conflict is a necessary task for the coordination of sustainable development. The following section will provide a discussion about globalization and responsibility. These two sections taken together provide a necessary prelude to the subsequent discussion about regionalism and the clarification of responsibility for sustainable development that is necessary for global sustainable development.

Globalization and the complexity of responsibility

Globalization is resulting in increased complexity with the appearance of new actors, different interactions, different relationships from the local to the global (Nederveen Pieterse 2004). The theory of reflexive modernity is of great relevance to sustainable development in part because it points to the need for further clarity about the roles and responsibilities of government, business and communities across space. Reflexive modernity is traced by Beck and others to a number of processes relating to globalization including regionalization up and down from the nation state and the increasing flexibility of employment practices. Reflexive modernity is a risk society, in which the unintended side effects (reflexive changes) are unavoidable and intractable. Reflexive modernity requires a focus upon: the globalized, complex and non-linear side-effects of modernity; the unintended, uncontrollable and circular consequences of these side-effects; and the new asymmetries of risk and also conflicts over responsibility. Control and linearity can no longer be justified and a different approach is necessary (Latour 1993; Beck 1994; Beck 1995; Sachs 1999; Beck et al. 2003).

Globalization is resulting in the reconfiguration of institutional frameworks which may be making global issues like greenhouse easier to solve but further complicates issues relating to risk and responsibility in nations and probably regions. Beck (2000 p11) describes globalization as "the processes through which sovereign national states are criss-crossed and undermined by trans-national actors with varying prospects of power, orientations, identities and networks" (Beck 2000). Globalization is crossing organizational, ideological and geographical boundaries and is resulting in simultaneous widening of cooperation and inequity (Nederveen Pieterse 2004). The power of resource industries is no longer that of colonization, but instead the threat of not investing. Industries however still rely heavily upon public trust and legitimacy (Beck 2001) and may in some ways help in the enabling of regional sustainable development.

Large multinational mining companies for example seeking to exercise corporate responsibility will invariably find that the regional scale where they operate to be the most appropriate scale for their focus and operation of their sustainable development legacies (Newman, Stanton Hicks, and Hammond, 2006).

The literature on reflexive modernity also points to the individualization of responsibility. Bauman uses an alternative term, a 'liquid modernity' which is described as a "'light', or 'liquefied' modernity—as distinct from 'heavy', and better still 'hard' and 'solid' modernity of yore: ours is not the 'constructed', administered and managed, but a diffuse, all-permeating, all-penetrating, all-saturating kind of modernity" (cited in Beilharz 2001 p 339).

This discussion points to a critical need to better understand how institutional sectors and individuals within and across these sectors negotiate risk and responsibilities across a variety of contexts. Complexity and non-linearity result in the need for a participatory approach in which the negotiation of the sharing of risks, responsibilities and thus also benefits is transparent and equitable. Sustainable development provides a useful framework for such negotiations and to nurture cooperative, creative and innovative communities. However, the complexity that arises from the meeting of the many narratives within a sustainable development framework requires attention to the process of bordering within each narrative and between the narratives. The concept of regionalism has much to offer for this task and is the focus of the following section.

Constructing borders for sustainable development through participatory regionalism

Sustainable development has traditionally been a globally driven process. Local Agenda 21, developed out of the Rio Earth Summit of 1992, highlighted the importance of connecting local areas to this regional agenda. The connection between these two levels of analysis is important for the coordination of responsibility across space and time for sustainable development. The complexity of this task however is expressed by the concept of glocalization. This term was first used by Robertson to indicate global-local dialectics, and thus the diverse local intersections with globalizing processes (Robertson 1992). Consideration of situational context is necessary for the process of sustainable development, and in particular for defining the distribution of responsibility within and across these diverse and changing glocal spaces.

The concept of regional sustainable development provides a conceptual bridge between global and local sustainable development and enables iterative understanding of the diverse processes in a globalizing world across institutional and geographical spaces. The creation of a geographical boundary is important as it provides context and definition in which to clarify and coordinate responsibility across institutional sectors. This could appear to be contrary to much of the sustainable development discourse which is typically seen to be about border crossing or the deconstruction of borders. This article argues that sustainable development in fact requires both the deconstruction and the reconstruction of borders in order to solve the deeper problems of our day, but this will require a participatory, dialogical and learning based process approach around the most appropriate borders for achieving this.

To understand the concept of regional sustainable development it is useful to firstly define the concept of regionalism as "regional communities having greater influence over and participating more directly in the decision making that impacts their regions and their futures; . . . increased attention to the regional scale and consequent regional initiatives, and the general trend towards greater stakeholder participation, often resulting in partnerships between the community, industry and governments" (Dore & Woodhill 1999, p. vi).

There is certainly no doubt that the creation of a geographical regional border to coordinate the multitude of narratives (and their diverse bordering processes) within sustainable development will require a participatory approach and will require ongoing evaluation of the effectiveness of this boundary. The very essence of sustainable development is often expressed through overarching principles which require participation, empowerment, ownership and a process that can account for difference in order to implement sustainable development at the local and regional levels. Pretty supports this view and stating that sustainable development is time and place specific and therefore requires a participatory approach (Pretty 1995). The 'politics of inclusion' has certainly had enormous influence over the affairs of public policy across the globe in recent years. Direct participation in the decision-making process is now considered necessary (Owen 1994).

The Western Australian State Sustainability coordinated by one of the authors of this paper, Peter Newman, recognizes the importance of the region for achieving sustainable development goals. The creation of regional strategies is proposed by the State Sustainability Strategy and in particular the strategy emphasized the need to focus upon methodological aspects of such regional strategies. The following section outlines a case study which involved both authors of this paper in experimenting with a regional strategy in the Pilbara of Western Australia.

A Case Study: The Pilbara Regional Sustainability Strategy

This section will outline the development of the Pilbara Regional Sustainability Strategy. It will firstly however provide a brief discussion about regional Western Australia. Regional here is used as a descriptor of the spaces outside of the capital city Perth. This is a distinctly different use of this term than what is being developed in this article, and helps to disentangle some of the unnecessary confusion that the term region invokes.

Regional Western Australia

The landmass of Western Australia can roughly be equated to the size of Western Europe. The area outside of Perth, the capital city of Western Australia, commonly referred to as regional Western Australia is approximately 90% of the land mass of the State yet only 27% of the population live outside Perth. Across this vast landmass there is a dispersed population that lives in a vastly varied environment and also faces quite different types of economic and social conditions. However, this is a set of generalized problems which are shared by regional Western Australia which a sustainable development framework would be required to address. These include social breakdown (suicide, feeling of isolation, depression, youth leaving), varying degrees of environmental degradation, declining levels of fiscal resources, remoteness from service delivery and decision making, low levels of employment and often monopoly industry (usually mining or petroleum) (McGrath, Armstrong and Marinova 2004).

A diversity of narratives representing different interests including the environment (although this can only be partially understood by human perspectives) are layered across the State and do not easily fit together into a regional boundary that has operational responsibility for the purpose of coordinating sustainable development.

The Pilbara

The Pilbara is a vast and geologically ancient region in the North West of the State consisting of 500,000 square kms and a population of approximately 40,000. It is responsible for the generation of a large proportion of State and Federal wealth as it is a major source of minerals and oil/gas. It is also a largely untouched wilderness with extraordinary attractions for tourists and it remains the home of Indigenous people who trace their origins back 30,000 years. This region has a series of local Indigenous areas that are progressively being recognized with native title as well as having a regional Indigenous character that is different to the other regions of Western Australia. Indeed one of the major mining companies, Rio Tinto is creating a 'Pan Pilbara Indigenous Partnership' based on the many overlapping interests between the different Indigenous groups. Socially the Pilbara shares many of the characteristics that are found in other 'regional' areas of the State as outlined in the above discussion with a much higher income variation between the mining community and the Indigenous community who have life expectancies 20 years less than the Australian average.

There is no regional government in the Pilbara. Most decisions about the Pilbara are made in Perth. Four local councils (Shires of Ashburton, Roebourne, East Pilbara and the town of Port Hedland) are each responsible for large tracts of land which together define one understanding of a regional boundary that defines the Pilbara region. Each Shire has insufficient resources to adequately service their locality, due mainly to the remoteness and large size of the Shires themselves. These councils came together to form a Pilbara Regional Council which was established in 2002 to better coordinate local government responsibilities across this larger shared boundary. This body acts as an agent of change on longer term issues when the local councils see they need to act together. However, the powers of this regional council are limited to those of the Local Government Act. Funding for projects comes from the Local Government Association as a contribution to the Pilbara Regional Council as a part of the Establishment Agreement. The limitations in financial resources and of regulative authority of each council and also of the Pilbara Regional Council result in these layers of government experiencing limited local or regional power relative to that of either the State or Commonwealth governments.

The boundary of the Pilbara Regional Council coincides with that of the Pilbara Development Commission, whose board is elected by the Minister and who coordinate economic development within this boundary. This however is one of the few boundaries that do coincide across this large tract of land. Government service provision rarely coincides and this acts as a significant barrier towards coordinating responsibility between departments and is an impediment to actualizing emerging Australian governmental discourse about a whole of government approach. Additionally the geographical responsibilities for each government department are large due to the dispersed population across this landscape. O'Donoghue (1999) writes that the tyranny of distance in regional Australia results in minimal services in remote regions (O'Donoghue 1999). Government employees are thinly spread and are being required to spend significant portions of time travelling between settlements (McGrath 2007). These issues are exacerbated by the lack of a mechanism to bring even a small proportion of the wealth generated in the area back to the region. The issue of boundaries particularly is further complicated by the differing borders of the growing number of mining companies and other supporting industries operating in the region.

The mining industry in the Pilbara is situated in a unique period of its history and is characterized by what is commonly referred to as a 'resource boom'. This is a necessary point of consideration in any discussion about sustainable development of this particular regional area. There has been a growing perception by Pilbara governments and long term concerned residents that little of the revenue generated from the mining activities is invested back into the region. Internationally it is noted that globalization is resulting in resources and knowledge being channelled away from regional areas where resource industries operate resulting in negligible longer term benefits within these communities (International Institute for Environment and Development 2002). Resource extraction is also dominated by a fly in fly out workforce which results in minimal local and regional training and very little to no local/regional economic development opportunities towards a healthy diversified economy (Armstrong 2004). To be fair, resource industries often operate in regional and remote environments where there is generally minimal government infrastructure and support. Solomon argues that mining supports the development of infrastructure and economic growth in comparison to other institutional sectors (Solomon 2000). As a result infrastructure and economic development tend to mainly revolve around mining activities.

The coordination of responsibility for sustainable development, including investment into regional infrastructure and community livelihoods lies between the geographical and institutional borders of the multitude of government departments and the numerous mining associated industries. Prior to the development of the strategy there had been no attempt to bring together these different groups to determine the visions and actions required for sustainable development within the Pilbara. This was the aim of the Pilbara Regional Sustainability Strategy. The following section outlines the development of this strategy.

Developing the Pilbara Regional Sustainability Strategy

The Pilbara Regional Sustainability Strategy was initiated in May 2004. It was based upon a partnership project between the Institute for Sustainability and Technology Policy (ISTP) where both authors are members of staff, the Western Australian Sustainability Roundtable of the Premier and Cabinet, the Western Australian Planning Commission, the local governments through the Pilbara Regional Council, the Pilbara Development Commission and major mining companies. The overarching border of the Strategy was created by the Pilbara Development Commission who was the body primarily responsible for creating the central funding for the development of the strategy. The project team was composed of Murdoch staff and postgraduate students from ISTP. Undergraduate students also were involved through their coursework project.

The strategy represented an opportunity to methodologically experiment with addressing issues relating to coordination across the borders of institutional sectors and narratives or interests and across the large geographical space of the Pilbara regional area. It also provided a timely opportunity to address some of the emerging concerns that had been surfaced by the resource boom, relating to the long term sustainable development of the economy and community health across the region.

An overview of the methodology of the strategy is provided in Figure 1. The following discussion details individually the methodological components included in this figure.

Baseline Information
The background data gathering took place in 2003 as a prelude to the formal initiation of the strategy. The aim of this exercise was to determine the most appropriate approach of the strategy and thus how to best frame the proposal to seek supportive partners. The data was categorized into social, economic and environmental aspects. Links were established between these categories and was published in the form of an interactive CD.

Snapshot and Gap Analysis
A summarized version of the CD was put together to provide a snapshot of the Pilbara. This snapshot was combined with a gap analysis to help with the early formulation of a Pilbara Regional Sustainability Strategy in mid 2004. The gap

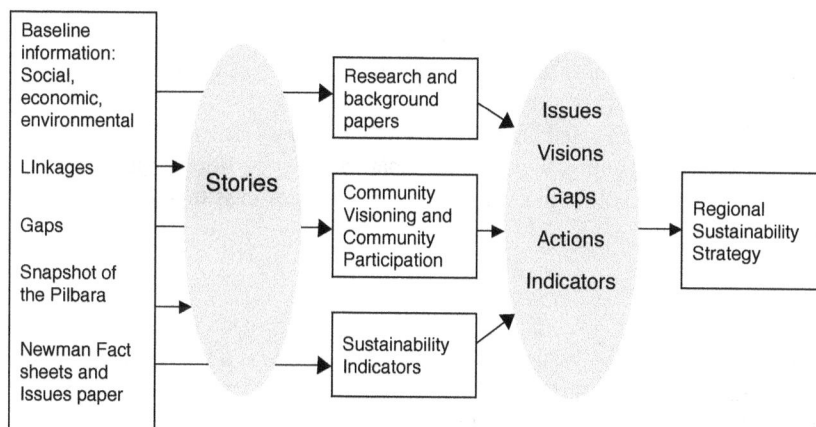

Figure 1 Overview of the methodology of the Strategy

analysis found that there was significant information available with regards to the social, economic and ecological makeup of, and issues in, the Pilbara. Additionally, it found that although there was general information available, such as the likely impacts of global economic trends, local economic development and diversification strategies, sustainable rangelands management, health promotion and so on, there was significant gaps in the availability of Pilbara specific data in relation to these issues. The gap analysis thus found that applying the Pilbara data and other relevant information through integrated regional and local participatory processes is the next step. It also found that to support this, a community vision for a sustainable future is required and this is a central gap in the current Pilbara information.

Stories
Stories are a tool to negotiate values which is necessary for ongoing process of sustainable development. A major recommendation of the State Sustainability Strategy was the need to incorporate place stories into policy and planning frameworks. This recommendation was taken up by the Pilbara Regional Sustainability Strategy, and a story approach became a central method of relaying a sense of place of the Pilbara that is rarely captured by typical consultancy reports. A number of narratives were written based upon a wide literature review. These narratives included Indigenous, pastoralists, mining, government, other minorities and youth. Each narrative included a number of short excerpts or stories reflecting the visions and concerns that had been expressed in the literature. The choice of stories in each narrative reflected consideration of age and gender. A DVD was produced in which a number of different actors were employed to vocalize on film the excerpts that had been written. This DVD became a useful instrument to stimulate discussion about the diverse perspectives that cross the population in the Pilbara and was used in the major participatory event in the development of the strategy.

Community Visioning and Community Participation
The community visioning and community participation of the Pilbara Regional
Sustainability Strategy was based primarily upon two approaches, the first was
a participatory forum titled Dialogue with the Pilbara: Newman Tomorrow and
the second was a youth visioning participatory exercise titled: Pilbara 2020 –
The Kind of Place I Want to Live In. The following discussion outlines each of
these respectively.

The Dialogue with the Pilbara: Newman Tomorrow

The Dialogue with the Pilbara: Newman Tomorrow was a participatory forum
in Newman hosted by the Minister for Planning and Infrastructure and helped
to surface community concerns and visions for the town of Newman and surrounds. This became a case study for participatory input into Pilbara Regional
Sustainability Strategy. It was agreed that the outcomes of the Dialogue would
become State Government priorities over the next two decades.

In particular regards to Newman, a major objective of the Dialogue was to
address particularly the issue of the long term sustainable development of Newman, a mining town in the State's far north. Rich in resources, Newman's mining economy is booming. Such growth offers both challenges and opportunities. By engaging the Newman community, it was hoped to develop a sustainability strategy 'owned' by the people of Newman, for the town's growth
beyond the iron ore industry. The broad community, industry, and all levels of
government needed to be engaged. In Newman's case, it also needed to include
the voice of the Indigenous Martu who had lived in the area for perhaps more
than 30,000 years and were likely to be there after mining.

A steering team (comprising local organization representatives, branches of
government, and industry within the Newman area) guided the process in partnership with the Department for Planning and Infrastructure. A number of methods were employed in which to advertise for the day: articles were placed in local newspapers; one thousand invitations were sent to a random sample of residents; participants were recruited in the local shopping centre; and invitations
were sent to local organizations. Confirmed participants were sent case studies,
fact sheets and a paper canvassing current issues confronting Newman.

Participation of the Martu people in the Western Desert region including the
Newman community began in June-July. A Dialogue with the Martu, who are
a significant majority of Newman and of the Western Desert, required a quite
different participatory approach than one that is suited to the non-Indigenous
population in Newman. A Dialogue with the Western Desert required an equal
recognition of the regional level in which the Martu relate in addition to the local differences that exist between the communities. A strategy arising from the
Dialogue, outlining government service provision would necessarily need to
account for both of these levels.

With this in mind, a process approach that was inclusive of all the Martu communities within the Western Desert was initiated in late June 2004, over 3 months

prior to the one day Dialogue event. The meetings were held on July 8th –19th July 2004. Organization of the meetings required approximately 2 weeks prior to the first meeting. The communities were chosen based on consultation with government agencies, who service the Western Desert, and with key Martu in Newman with the aim of covering the most important communities to the Martu population. A number of questions were posed, based on the proposed one day forum's agenda, which include:

- What do you really want for the future for yourselves, your children and your grand children?
- What's happening now - what is good and what is not so good?'
- What are some of the important things we need to start doing now if we want to get to where you want to be?

A focus on the future of the communities' children and grandchildren helped to cross the different perspectives on time that might arise through cultural differences.

Contact was maintained regularly with the communities primarily through the community coordinator, including with the Martu community in Newman, between the meetings and the Dialogue one day event.

The Dialogue was held on the 30th September 2004 and was met with participation from approximately 150 members of Newman. This was by far the largest public meeting in the town's history. Dialogue participants were seated at 20 tables of approximately 6 to 8 people with a scribe and a facilitator. There was considerable Martu participation, all from the Newman community. Three separate tables were assigned to the Martu, which was their stated preference. Computers at every table were networked, feeding the ideas of each group to a theme team who worked collaboratively to find the common threads emerging in the room. Facilitators were primarily local and regional government agencies and also from Murdoch University. Common themes were collated by the theme team and were projected on a large screen.

The tables were given a series of questions relating to the visioning of Newman's future, and the necessary implementation. The questions required participants to think in terms of sustainable development—long term integration of economic, social and environmental elements. A series of four discussion sessions were held asking:

- What are your key hopes for the future of Newman and its surrounds?
- Remembering your key hopes for Newman:
    - What do we need to keep?
    - What changes do we need to make?
- You have been transported to 2020. Describe how you would like Newman to be socially, economically, and environmentally.
- You are now in charge of this town. Your job is to head Newman in the direction of the 2020 vision. What are you going to do socially, economically and environmentally to ensure Newman thrives?

Table 2 Vision priorities from the Dialogue with the Pilbara process in Newman 2004

- Respectful treatment and celebration of Indigenous culture; and an Indigenous focus on education, training, and employment
- Developing the community to become less reliant on the mining economy
- More activities and opportunities for the community, particularly young people (traineeships, apprenticeships)
- Developing tourism with the promotion of inland Pilbara attractions and a focus on Newman
- Revamping the town area and town approaches and more variety in shopping areas
- Improved housing development, especially for low-income earners
- Greater social responsibility by industry to community issues – listening, respect for ideas, closer participation
- Improved modern services – medical, educational, recreational, and an improved air service
- Local government status for the Martu people in the area east of Newman

To the great surprise of all the organizers and community leaders the number one priority for the future was to improve relationships and opportunities for Indigenous people. The second set of priorities was to send a strong message back to Perth that the benefits from development needed to be returned more to the region in terms of local services. The list of priorities for the future is provided in Table 2.

The research team for the Pilbara Regional Sustainability Strategy analysed the data and produced the final report.

Pilbara 2020: The Kind of Place I Want to Live In

The Postcards from the Pilbara competition aimed to engage the youth of the Pilbara in a participatory exercise to gain an understanding of their desired future scenarios. Youth input does not typically feature as a major priority within most formal planning processes. Youth participation however is a significant component of sustainable development for a number of reasons. The very long term and inter-generational aspects of sustainable development requires that planning for the future include the voices of the young people today. Young people have the greatest stake in the future, as they will live the longest and will face the consequences of decisions that are made today. Young people generally bring fresh new ideas to the planning arena. Youth participation for sustainable development also serves an educative function and helps to build youth capacity to participate more generally in decision making processes.

The theme of the entry was titled "Pilbara 2020 – The Kind of Place I Want to Live In". The competition was based upon the creation of a postcard and prizes were presented to the winning entries. Cultural complexities including language in particular regards to Indigenous communities were an important consideration. A poster was designed using three languages and English which was sent to the Indigenous communities.

It is no surprise to report that the lack of fast food and retail outlets was a strong theme within all of entries. Population expansion was mentioned in a number of entries. Many of the entries included a vision for the further development of infrastructure including, health, education, transport, recreation and entertainment, some of which focused upon renewable energy. The upgrading of services within the hospital, doctors surgery and education facilities were included. Improved regional and international accessibility also featured. A local bus service improves local transport considerably. Housing is improved in both quantity and quality. Environmental and social concerns also feature. In one entry Greenpeace has created a nature resort for the rare and endangered Karner Blue Butterfly. An aged care facility exists, as does a rehabilitation centre and a drop in place. One entry discussed the role of improved leadership towards a sustainable future. The importance of local economy was highlighted in one entry where all of the money stays in the town.

Research and Background Papers
A number of research and background papers were produced on particular key issues that were identified by the gap analysis. These included education and training, governance, Indigenous agreements, Indigenous governance, economic diversification and indicators of sustainable development in the Pilbara. These were researched by students at ISTP and helped towards providing the necessary information to focus the development of the strategy.

Discussion

The Pilbara Regional Sustainability was finally brought together under the frame of 'enduring regional value'. This concept is used by Newman, Stanton Hicks and Hammond (2006) to demonstrate how mining companies in Western Australia can contribute to the long term legacy of the regions where they are extracting so much wealth. However this cannot occur properly until the appropriate governance structures and support are in place that can enable money to be channelled into the issues that matter locally and that can lead to long term value. Responsibility for 'enduring value' cannot be attributed to any one sector. It does in fact belong across sectors and the critical first priority is that of coordination and priority setting.

The key policy conclusions from the Pilbara Regional Sustainability Strategy are listed below. They show in particular that the crossing of sectoral borders, institutional borders and regional borders was achieved and a new model for regional governance emerged.

1 Pilbara Pact

The Strategy recommended that a Pilbara Pact be initiated through a participatory process between State Government, the Pilbara Regional Council (local governments), resource companies, the Pilbara Chamber of Commerce, Pilbara Indigenous representatives, the Rangelands NRM group, Pilbara tourism representatives and major communities.

2 Pilbara Sustainability Fund

The Strategy recommended that the Pilbara Fund (established in 2004 by the State Government) be extended into a Pilbara Sustainability Fund and include contributions of resource companies and the State and Federal governments. The aim of this fund would be to create long term regional value with a particular focus upon improving the life expectancy of Indigenous people.

3 New Governance arrangements, including a Pilbara 'Parliament' or Assembly

The new governance arrangements recommended by the Strategy are shown in Figure 2. A major focus of this model is to enable the priorities of the region to be better amplified within Australian politics through devolution of power to this regional scale. The establishment of a Pilbara 'Parliament' or Assembly would allow for the integration of a regional budget from all State government sources, the Pilbara Sustainability Fund and from each local government. Investigation into how the governmental bureaucracies could better align to regional priorities under the direction of the Assembly may present opportunities for improved coordination for the provision of regional and local services. It was suggested in the Strategy that a new local government be formed in the Western Desert around the boundaries of the Martu people, recently recognized through the Native Title Tribunal agreement. This model integrates the major aspects of the Strategy recommendations. Governance is cross-institutional and allows for the clarification of responsibility around regional and local boundaries.

4 Pilbara Eco Efficiency Strategy

The Strategy recommended that the growth phase in the Pilbara presented an ideal time for innovation towards the region becoming a global leader of eco-efficiency. A number of areas for investigation are suggested by the Strategy ranging from solar, resource efficiency, recycling and research towards the possibility of a diesel free region.

5 Pilbara Regional Sustainable Tourism Strategy

The Strategy suggested that tourism provided an opportunity to enable Indigenous employment and environmental stewardship.

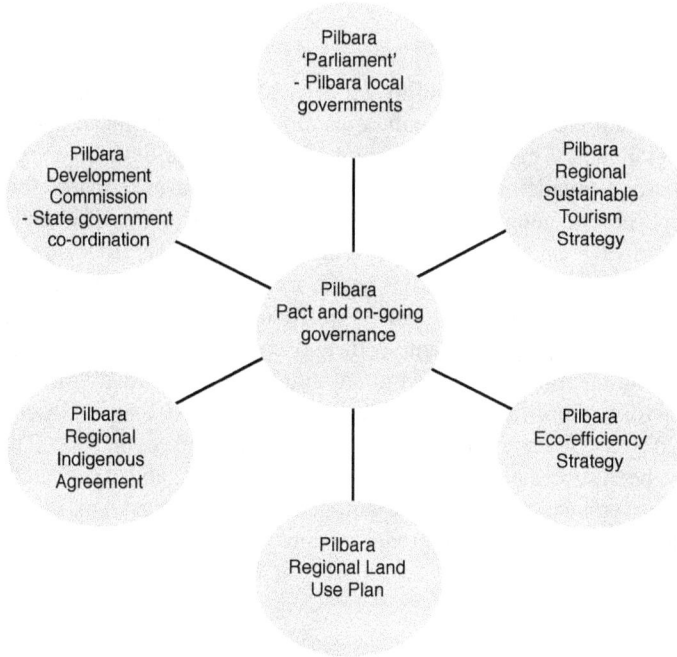

Figure 2 New Governance Model for the Pilbara

6 *Pilbara Regional Land Use Plan*

A number of issues were outlined in the Strategy relating to the need to review land use planning in the Pilbara.

The clearest issue that arose from the strategy was the need for a stronger regional political border that encapsulates all four local councils and which is responsible for a **Pilbara Fund** which is negotiated through a **Pilbara Pact** and a **Pilbara 'Parliament'** which has substantially more autonomy in the governance system. The complexities of Indigenous governance would be better recognised by this boundary. The conclusions remain in political limbo but for the first time a new regional governance model has been placed on the table.

The process of the strategy was important as it allowed other narratives to rise to the surface. The community were able to outline their deeper issues and were free to assert their cherished and unrecognized values. This helped to shape the Strategy.

Howitt (1995 p 390) writes that "social, economic, political and cultural life in resource localities are silenced as everything is subsumed into the story of the mine...(d)iverse voices are replaced and displaced by a generalized and homogenized interpretation in which diversity is devalued in favour of a the common currency of jobs, revenue and trade as measures of success". A dialogue process that recognizes the different narratives of the area was necessary to break through this boundary on how the Pilbara is seen and sees itself.

Conclusion

The Pilbara Regional Sustainability Strategy has been an exercise in crossing boundaries and creating new boundaries more relevant to managing sustainable development. This process is critical to sustainable development both in terms of conceptualizing sustainable development and in terms of focussing on the appropriate geographical boundaries. The refocussing of boundaries is at the heart of breaking through on long term issues that are not being addressed by the present system and is necessary for a process approach to global sustainable development. The process of dialogue in a participatory spirit is essential to developing the framework and community values necessary for breaking and creating boundaries in an ongoing manner. Ideally this process should involve the different narratives (especially those that are rarely heard such as Indigenous narratives) in analysis to better enable ownership. The work will have been successful when governance is institutionalized around the new regional governance boundaries as outlined in the Strategy. This remains incomplete but the reality of the model remains waiting its political opportunity to be implemented.

References

Armstrong, R. (2004). *Sustainability and Mining: Towards Economic diversification and resolution of the issue of Fly in Fly out mining in the Pilbara.* Background Paper for the Pilbara Regional Sustainability Strategy.

Beck, U. (1994). Self-Dissolution and Self-Endangerment of Industrial Society: What Does This Mean? In *Reflexive Modernization: Politics, Tradition and Aesthetics in the Modern Social Order*, U. Beck, A. Giddens, and S. Lash. Stanford: Stanford University Press, 174–183.

Beck, U. (1995). *Ecological Enlightenment: Essays on the politics of the risk society.* Atlantic Highlands: Humanities Press.

Beck, U. (2000). *What is Globalisation.* Cambridge: Polity Press.

Beck, U. (2001). "Redefining power in the global age: Eight theses." *Dissent* 48(4): 83–89.

Beck, U., W. Bonss, and C. Lau (2003). "The Theory of Reflexive Modernisation Problematic, Hypotheses and Research Programme." *Theory, Culture and Society 20*(2): 1–33.

Beilharz, P. (2001). *The Bauman Reader.* Oxford: Blackwell.

Castro, C. J. (2004). "Sustainable Development: Mainstream and Critical Perspectives." *Organisation and Environment 17*(2): 195–225.

Davison, A. (2001). *Technology and the Contested Meanings of Sustainable Development.* New York: State University of New York Press.

Dodson, M., and D. E. Smith (2003). Governance for sustainable development: Strategic issues and principles for Indigenous Australian communities. Discussion Paper 250 Centre for Aboriginal Economic Policy Research.

Dore, J., and Woodhill, J. (1999). *Sustainable Regional Development: Executive Summary of the Final Report*. Canberra, Greening Australia.

Frazier, J. G. (1997). "Sustainable development: modern elixir or sack dress?" *Environmental Conservation 24*(2): 182–193.

Howitt, R. (1995). SIA, Sustainability, and Developmentalist Narratives of Resource Regions. *Impact Assessment 13*: 387–402.

International Institute for Environment and Development (2002). "Breaking New Ground: Mining, Minerals and Sustainable Development."

International Institute for Environment and Development (2002). Local communities and mines. *Breaking New Ground: Mining, Minerals and Sustainable Development*.

Kinnane, S. (2005). Indigenous Sustainability: Rights, Obligations, and a Collective Commitment to Country. *International Law and Indigenous Peoples*. J. Castellino and N. Walsh. Leidon/Boston: Martinus Nijhoff Publishers, 159–193.

Latour, B. (1993). *We Have Never Been Modern*. London: Longman.

Mebratu, D. (1998). "Sustainability and Sustainable Development." *Environmental Impact Assessment Review 18*: 493–520.

McGrath, N., Armstrong R., and Marinova D. (2004). Participatory development for regional sustainability in Western Australia: An enabling State? *Local Environment 9*(6): 561.

McGrath ,N. (2007). Dialoguing in the Desert: Ambivalence, Hybridity and Representations of Indigenous People. Unpublished PhD thesis.

Nederveen Pieterse, J. (2004). *Globalisation and Culture Global Melange*. New York: Rowan and Littlefield Publishers.

Newman, P., Stanton-Hicks, E., et al. (2006). Pursuing Sustainability Through Enduring Value Creation. In *Management Models for Corporate Social Responsibility*, J. Jonker, and M. de Witte (Eds.). Nijmegan, Germany: Springer-Verlag: 306–313.

O'Donoghue, L. (1999). "Towards a culture of improving indigenous health in Australia." *Australian Journal of Rural Health 7*: 64–69.

Pezzoli, K. (1997). "Sustainable development: a transdisciplinary overview of the literature." *Journal of Environmental Planning and Management* 40(5): 549–574.

Robertson, R. (1992). *Globalization: Social Theory and Global Culture*. London: Sage.

Sachs, W. (1999). Sustainable Development and the Crisis of Nature: On the Political Anatomy of an Oxymoron. *Living with Nature Environmental Politics as Cultural Discourse*. F. Fischer and M. Hajer. New York: Oxford University Press, 23–41.

Scott, W. and S. Gough (2003). *Sustainable Development and Learning Framing the Issues*. London: RoutledgeFalmer.

Solomon, M. H. (2000). *Growth and Diversification in Mineral Economies*. United Nations Conference on Trade and Development. The Mineral Corporation.

www.ingramcontent.com/pod-product-compliance
Lightning Source LLC
Chambersburg PA
CBHW060148280326
41932CB00012B/1681